Multiple Secularities Beyond the West

Religion and Its Others

Studies in Religion, Nonreligion, and Secularity

Edited by
Stacey Gutkowski, Lois Lee, and Johannes Quack

Volume 1

Multiple Secularities Beyond the West

Religion and Modernity in the Global Age

Edited by
Marian Burchardt, Monika Wohlrab-Sahr, and
Matthias Middell

DE GRUYTER

ISBN 978-1-61451-574-6
e-ISBN (PDF) 978-1-61451-405-3
e-ISBN (EPUB) 978-1-61451-978-2
ISSN 2330-6262

Library of Congress Cataloging-in-Publication Data
A CIP catalog record for this book has been applied for at the Library of Congress.

Bibliographic Information published by the Deutsche Nationalbibliothek
The Deutsche Nationalbibliothek lists this publication in the Deutsche Nationalbibliografie; detailed bibliographic data are available on the Internet at http://dnb.dnb.de.

© 2015 Walter de Gruyter Inc., Boston/Berlin/Munich
Printing and binding: CPI books GmbH, Leck
♾ Printed on acid-free paper
Printed in Germany

www.degruyter.com

Table of Contents

Marian Burchardt, Monika Wohlrab-Sahr and Matthias Middell
Multiple Secularities beyond the West: An Introduction —— 1

Part I: **Religious Communities and the State: Fault-Lines of Religion and Secularity in South Asia**

Rina Verma Williams and Laura Dudley Jenkins
Secular Anxieties and Transnational Engagements in India —— 19

Anandita Bajpai
"Speaking" the Nation Secular: (E)merging Faces of India —— 39

Beatrice Renzi
Anti-caste Radicalism, Dalit Movements and the Many Critiques of Secular Nationalism in India —— 63

Part II: **Nationalism, Islam and Democratization: Secular Dynamics in the Arab World**

Daniel Kinitz
Deviance as a Phenomenon of Secularity: Islam and Deviants in Twentieth-century Egypt—A Search for Sociological Explanations —— 97

Gudrun Krämer
Secularity Contested: Religion, Identity and the Public Order in the Arab Middle East —— 121

Part III: **Secularities in East Asia**

Mark R. Mullins
Japanese Responses to Imperialist Secularization: The Postwar Movement to Restore Shinto in the Public Sphere —— 141

Elisabetta Porcu
The Religious-Secular Divide at the Community Level in Contemporary Japan —— 169

Part IV: African Scenarios: (Post-)Colonial Secularity vs. African Religiosity?

Paul S. Landau
Moments of Insurgency: Christianity in South African Politics, from the 18th Century to Today —— 189

Rijk van Dijk
After Pentecostalism? Exploring Intellectualism, Secularization and Guiding Sentiments in Africa —— 215

Part V: The Sacred Secular: Secularities in post-Communist Central and Eastern Europe

Alexander Agadjanian
Vulnerable Post-Soviet Secularities: Patterns and Dynamics in Russia and Beyond —— 241

Klaus Buchenau
Socialist Secularities: The Diversity of a Universalist Model —— 261

Conclusions

Matthias Koenig
Between World Society and Multiple Modernities: Comparing Cultural Constructions of Secularity and Institutional Varieties of Secularism —— 285

List of Contributors —— 305

Index —— 311

Marian Burchardt, Monika Wohlrab-Sahr and Matthias Middell
Multiple Secularities beyond the West: An Introduction

For more than two decades, theorists of modernity have grappled with the new visibility of religion in many parts of the world. Scholars have made efforts to accommodate phenomena such as religious resurgences, new forms of public religion and new religious movements within conceptualizations of modernity in order to move beyond the linear and deterministic narratives of modernization that dominated the social sciences in their formative period in the twentieth century (Casanova 1994; Hervieu-Léger 2000). In response to the same observations, and in a sometimes very general way, theories of secularization have become subject to intense criticism and have given way to notions of 'de-secularization' (Berger 1999). Very recently, yet another set of studies, in many ways inspired by Charles Taylor's path-breaking book *A Secular Age* (Taylor 2007), began to interrogate and question monolithic understandings of secularism, broadly construed in terms of the institutional arrangements specifying the relationships between, and often the separation of, religion and the state. The majority of these studies, however, were either focused on a relatively narrow set of questions related to challenges to secularism posed by migration-driven religious diversity in Europe and North America, or explored the trajectories of a few cases of secularity imposed by modernist state projects in the context of existing religious pluralism, as in India and Turkey (Cady and Shakman Hurd 2010; Kuru 2009).

   This book moves beyond these limitations and breaks new ground by exclusively exploring formations of secularity beyond the West. Analysing scenarios of secularity in East Asia, the post-Communist world, the Arab Middle East, Africa and India, it takes into consideration a set of regions that have largely been ignored in sociological and anthropological debates on the relationships between religion and the secular in modernity thus far. Importantly, while in virtually all of the existing literature religion is readily construed as a marker of cultural difference and identity (of countries, regions, communities), the secular is still peculiarly seen as homogenizing, as something outside culture.

   With this interdisciplinary volume we propose to move beyond such conceptualizations and explore the social constructions of the religious-secular divide, including their institutionalized practices, in five different world regions. With a strong conceptual focus on comparative research, we examine how shared but also contested forms and practices of distinguishing religious and secular spheres of society acquire cultural meaning, and how they shape and define the meaning of religious identities, membership, practices and modes of incorporation. In this introduction, our goal is to chart the terrain of scholarship on secularity, point to some of its shortcomings and explicate our own ambitions. We suggest that secularities beyond the West are most productively addressed by an approach that combines attention to the specificities of cultural-historical pathways with an emphasis on power relations and places them in the contexts of both the *longue durée* of global interconnectedness and transnational exchanges of values and ideas.

1 The Secular in Question

Our main interest in this book lies in the multiple ways in which religious-secular dynamics unfold and are interpreted and acted upon by religious and secular communities, as well as by governments, courts, religious bodies or other actors exerting political and epistemic authority in this regard. Such dynamics may imply the cultural construction and institutionalization of what is called 'the religious-secular divide' (e. g. Beyer 2013), although we do not take this as a given.

We thus draw on the notion of the 'secular' while being fully aware that as a signifier it comes with multiple semantic valences and connotations anchored in Western history. In most of the literature it is used with regard to secularization and secularism. Secularization, chiefly the domain of sociologists, is usually taken to mean the process whereby religion gradually lost its grip on other spheres of social life and was constituted as a discreet domain with its own ontology and epistemology (Casanova 1994). In addition, it referred to the diminishing of religious participation, membership and belief on the part of the population and the privatization of religion (Luckmann 1980; Dobbelaere 1984; Tschannen 1991); in other words, its gradual removal from the public sphere, variously conceptualized as an abstract sphere of political will formation or the sphere between civil society and the state where states interact with citizens organized as 'publics' (Habermas 2006; Warner 2002).

Secularism, on the other hand, is often understood in terms of the regimes, ideologies, and practices of separating religion from politics, and states from religious bodies, that is, a modern principle of governance and statecraft. In addition, as Casanova (2009: 1051) has argued, 'Secularism refers more broadly to a whole range of modern secular worldviews and ideologies that may be consciously held and explicitly elaborated into philosophies of history and normative-ideological state projects, into projects of modernity and cultural programs. Or alternatively, it may be viewed as an epistemic knowledge regime'.

The effects of secularism as an epistemic knowledge regime are visible wherever the secular is assumed to stand in for, or embody, the 'real', as in much of modern science. They are especially powerful in what Taylor (2007) called the subtraction theories of secularization that often rely on some notion of demystification (see also Koenig 2011). Criticism of these orthodox sociological secularization theories is by now well established. Universalistic and deterministic in their approach, some of these theories depended on essentializing, uniform notions of modernity, as well as of religion and the secular as its conceptual cognates. Accordingly, they saw secularization as a product of modernization and assumed that modernity in the long run would have the same consequences *anywhere*.

These assumptions were accompanied by the idea that modernization and secularization would be homogenizing forces grinding down religious and cultural traditions and producing a standard version of 'modern society', replete with standard forms of religiosity measurable in terms of membership, ritual participation, religious belief and knowledge. But how would one measure 'levels of religiosity' with regard to traditions such as Japanese Shinto, which – as a cult of the state – has no meaningful notion of membership at all? The methodological commitments of quantitative social research, especially in sociology and political science, to standardized indicators of 'religious behaviour' and secularization proved to be almost insurmountable barriers against contextualized and meaningful understandings of religion and secularity outside the West.

Significantly, the problem here is not the use of numbers per se but the use of indicators drawn from Western Christian historical experiences with religion and its relationship to modernity and the ways which these have been assembled and packaged in scholarly genealogies.[1] We must take into account the deep Christian historicity of the notion of the secular (Asad 2003) and the global historical implications of its transformation in the wake of the Protestant Reformation and the emergence of modern scientific knowledge regimes. In this context, as Asad (1993: 207) remarked, we see the 'construction of religion as a new historical object: anchored in personal experience, expressible as belief-statements, dependent on private institutions, and practiced in one's spare time.'

Universalist theories of secularization are singularly ill-suited for exploring secularities beyond the West. For them, cultural particularities are only relevant if they defer or accelerate secularization processes. More dramatically still, as they register all sorts of religious phenomena through the same categories within

---

[1] For a culturally sensitive quantitative analysis of secularization in Japan, see, for instance, Reader (2012).

the same Western archives, they are unable to grasp religious-secular dynamics on societies' own terms. Against orthodox and neo-orthodox secularization theories, we emphasize that the cultural meanings of religious/secular distinctions differ across cultures and political spaces. Instead of simply registering the ebbs and flows of religious passion we ask: How exactly are these different meanings of secularity linked to specific histories of religious and ethnic diversity, of processes of state-formation and nation-building? How do they document the social conflicts that occurred in these processes? What are the cultural and conceptual proxies through which secularity is addressed in different societies, and what are the sacralized values attached to it?

Secularization theories severely restrained the study of secularities beyond the West, as they equated high religiosity with a lack of modernization. At the same time – and paradoxically – the emphasis on the Christian origins of the idea of the secular and on the cultural distinctiveness of non-Western societies, found in some strands of anthropology, postcolonial studies and area studies, had the same effect. Addressing secularism exclusively in terms of *Western* secularism and its impact *on non-Western societies*, postcolonial approaches were bound to interpret the vocabulary of secularity as culturally inauthentic, homogenizing and oppressive (for example, Madan 2007; Nandy 2007). Inadvertently, they thereby contributed to foreclosing explorations of the multiple flows, exchanges and appropriations of meanings of secularity that are at the centre of this book. In addition, religion has turned in anthropological imaginaries to some extent into a new site of resistance against Western imperialism and the hegemonic power of domestic states, inheriting this place from 'indigenous communities' and their 'traditional cultures' after these gradually disappeared through their enlistment into state-sponsored modernization. As a result, while religious expressions in the public sphere are celebrated as emancipatory, the conditions of secularity associated with them are sometimes ignored.

While the concept of secularism conflates the ideological 'secularist' program with the empirical institutional differentiations between religion and the state, the notion of secularization is still closely tied to the evolutionist underpinning of the social-science study of religion. We therefore propose to reserve the term 'secularism' for the ideological-philosophical program of separation, and – by contrast – use the concept of secularity as an analytical term for the culturally, symbolically, and institutionally anchored forms of distinction between religious and non-religious spheres and material spaces (Wohlrab-Sahr and Burchardt 2012).

We thus suggest studying expressions of the secular in terms of *cultures of secularities*. While much of the secularism debate is focussed on the state and its institution, we deem it useful to construe the remit in much wider terms and to differentiate it into three tendencies. First, researchers must examine religious-secular distinctions across the whole range of institutional fields, including law, fine arts, education and so on. Secondly, secularity becomes manifest not only in terms of institutionalized rules, but also in public discourse, media practices and importantly, in the sphere of everyday life, that is, people's life-worlds, with their multiple forms of embodying religious and secular ways of being, knowing and sensing.[2] And thirdly, although secularity is not 'neutral', it is a cultural program with strong values, ethical investments and political stakes.

We have elaborated the diversity of these stakes in the concept of 'multiple secularities' (Wohlrab-Sahr and Burchardt 2012). Similar to how Eisenstadt's concept of *multiple modernities* (2000) offered a way out of the crisis in modernization theories, so the concept of multiple secularities can stimulate new ways of thinking about the relationships between religion and secularity in modernity that go beyond secularization theories. We assume that secularities 'respond' to specific societal problems as their reference problems and offer 'solutions' to them. Obviously, these problems arise with different degrees of urgency and at different points in time.

Based on both theoretical and empirical considerations, we identify four such reference problems: (1) the problem of individual freedom vis-à-vis dominant social units, be they groups or the state; (2) the problem of religious heterogeneity and the resulting potential or actual conflictuality; (3) the problem of social or national integration and development; and (4) the problem of the independent development of institutional domains. These four problems constitute motives and provide motifs for institutionalizing distinctions between religious and non-religious social spheres. As latent motives and practices they can certainly coexist; as overt motives and motifs they may compete with each other. It seems, however, that under specific circumstances one of them can become dominant by being associated with a guiding idea, thereby pushing other motifs, at least temporarily, to the background. Undoubtedly these motifs are often highly contested.

We use the formula 'secularity for the sake of ...' to designate such basic types. Articulating the societal problems, we distinguish between the following forms: (1) secularity for the sake of individual rights and liberties; (2) secularity for the sake of balancing religious diversity; (3) secularity for the sake of societal integration and national development; and (4) secularity for the sake of the independence of institutional domains. The distinction between basic types of sec-

---

[2] Nilüfer Göle (2010) distinguishes between self, state and the public sphere as sites for the manifestation of the religious-secular divide.

ularity is an ideal-typical construction in the Weberian sense. This implies that in empirical cases we will often find more than one of these motifs intermingling with or contesting one another. Only under very specific circumstances will one of them become dominant.

Significantly, cultures of secularity are by no means identical or coextensive with atheist or irreligious worldviews, subjectivities and sensibilities. Secular sensibilities may imply moral or aesthetic aversions to religion, but in most parts of the world, and much more commonly, they are embodied states mobilized in response to perceived infringements of settled rules about the 'proper place' of religion without rejecting religion as such. At the same time, there is considerable debate in some parts of the world on whether secularity inevitably leads into secularism and whether it rests in fact on unrecognized ontological assumptions about irreligion or atheism that it smuggles in through the backdoor (Lee 2012).

Moreover, while often being historically tied to the histories of religious traditions that are dominant in specific parts of the world, secularities are not determined by those histories. There are overarching motifs that guide religious-secular distinctions, and motives that unite their proponents. This is most clearly demonstrated with regard to the communist and post-communist worlds. Communist regimes emerged in areas with very different religious traditions, ranging from Protestantism in East Germany and Orthodoxy in Russia to Catholicism and Santería in Cuba, Confucianism in China and Buddhism in Vietnam. In almost all of the countries with communist regimes, state-sponsored, top-down secularism was part of the political program, and notions of social progress and national unity as strong values often legitimized the secular–religious divide. As Agadjanian and Buchenau make clear in their chapters in this book, none of the societies with communist regimes remain(ed) unaffected by that; what is more, although the consequences and historical legacies of state-sponsored secularism differ dramatically, they cannot be explained in terms of a return to preceding, religiously defined civilizational pathways.

We do not suggest that cultures of secularity exist everywhere in the world; in fact, their emergence hinges on a whole range of social and political conditions. But we do suggest it is important to make conceptual space for their analysis, even in societies that are strongly religious. Nor do we assume, contrary to studies exclusively centred on state-sponsored secularism, that religious and secular spheres are neatly separated. If in the current moment of the decentring, questioning and redefinition of the modern project 'secularism stands exposed', as Cady and Shakman Hurd (2010: 5) cogently observed, the task is to examine the inextricable entanglements of religion and the secular and the ways in which practices shaping their contact zones are reordered and recomposed. Some authors suggest that this decentring of modernity amounts to a 'postsecular' constellation in which the normative tenability of secularism as a premise of the management of religious diversity is increasingly questioned (Habermas 2006; Rosati and Stoeckl 2013). Remaining agnostic on the value of this argument for empirical research,[3] we do not see this concept as meaningful for our purposes, as it suggests an unrealistic appreciation of the 'power of the secular modern' beyond the West to begin with (Casanova 2006).

Four conceptual dimensions are central to the approach taken in this book and distinguish it from most other contributions in the field, as follows.

2 Global Interconnectedness and Transnational Flows

While different notions and institutionalizations of secularity emerge from different histories, it is clear that they are also critically shaped through civilizational encounters and processes of globalization. Historically, this has happened through military and colonial conquest and missionary movements (van der Veer 1996). Currently, the entanglements of different secularities are often associated with transnational migration, new regimes of religious pluralism, emerging patterns of postnational citizenship and the changing place of religion in international politics (e.g. Bramadat and Koenig 2009; Levitt 2007). At the same time, the definition of secular spheres is associated with international human rights regimes and the expansion of a world polity made up of NGOs and other transnational organizations (Koenig 2008). Under which conditions and with which consequences do such mutual entanglements between different territorially grounded notions of secularity or between local cultures and transnational secular arenas unfold? Why do some societies or groups develop indigenized notions of secularity, while others reject it as alien? In response to which influences are understandings of secularity reinterpreted? What is the empirical relationship between standardized programs of secularism in world polity institutions on the one hand and culturally embedded notions of religious–secular distinctions on the other?

As Anandita Bajpai shows for India, secularity is promoted through international politics and economies and is interpreted as a marker of democracy. But it seems that this is not a homogenized version of secularity, but one that is con-

---

[3] But see the critical view taken by Beckford (2012).

nected to the respective context; in India secularity is seen as the necessary basis for a religiously pluralist state (see also Burchardt and Wohlrab-Sahr 2013).

The analysis of secularities beyond the West must thus reckon with multifarious local appropriations and redefinitions, indigenizations and contestations (Cady and Shakman Hurd 2010: 20) occurring throughout the history of global interactions. Interestingly, however, while the critical analysis of the academic construction of a unified and universalistic concept of religion measuring religious phenomena against the yardstick of 'world religions' is very advanced,[4] similar endeavours regarding secularity are still in an embryonic stage. Crucial is the fact that, however fallacious and factually incorrect such projections may be, religions are increasingly modelled on one another, not least through the globalization of the concept of religion as it occurs through constitutional protections of religious freedom and international legal treaties. Furthermore, 'under conditions of globalization', Casanova (2008: 119) observed, 'all the world religions do not only draw upon their own traditions but also increasingly upon one another':

> Intercivilizational encounters, cultural imitations and borrowings, diasporic diffusions, hybridity, creolization, and transcultural hyphenations are as much part and parcel of the global present as Western hegemony, cosmopolitan homogenization, religious fundamentalism or the clash of civilizations. (Ibid.)

3 The Politics and Practices of Secular Translations

Significantly, as with the concept of religion, a fundamental aspect of global interconnectedness and transcultural diffusions of secular concepts is their translation into local languages, and the result is almost by definition semantic hybridity. In fact, while the initial impulse in some world regions to engage with secularity may have happened through colonial or imperial encounters, more important was the question of what kinds of ideas and practices were eventually registered within the vernacular categories that were created. In Japan, as Mark Mullins and Elisabetta Porcu show in their chapters, religious-secular distinctions are in some way indebted to the import from the West in the late nineteenth century of the term *shūkyō* for religion, and conversely *mushūkyō* for non-religion. While the latter term is sometimes seen, according to Mullins, as an

---

[4] See the important studies by Masuzawa (2005) and Fitzgerald (1990).

artificial construct, it now widely circulates in Japanese discourse connoting people's distance from religion (see Porcu's chapter) and is even used by governments for legal and administrative purposes. Once developed, the term *sezoku* (used to denote 'secularism') became central for navigating the government's involvement in Shinto rituals, whose meanings – shifting between religion and secular traditional folkways – had been a matter of conflict and court contestation ever since the end of the Second World War (see Nelson 2012). In a similar and highly lucid effort to understand the politics of secular translation, Agadjanian charts the ways in which meanings of secularity are found in Russian spheres of influence in a whole host of notions ranging from *svetskii* for worldly high society in pre-Revolutionary Russia to *dünyevi* (for 'secular') in post-Soviet Azerbaijan.

The changes in the concepts and translations of secularity have internal points of reference expressing changing evaluations of history and religious authority. However, such changes also reflect the shifting geopolitics of collective identities. After the fall of the Soviet empire, the former Soviet and newly independent states had to redefine their relationship to the former foreign rulers, and they did so, among other things, by negotiating the meaning of secularity.

The articulations of the geopolitics of collective identities with debates over secularity are much more prominent today in the Arab Middle East. There is an overwhelming consensus in the majority Muslim societies of the Arab Middle East that Islam needs to play a central role in the public domain and that it, particularly also through references to the Shar'iah, constitutes the *ordre public*. According to Krämer's analysis, this positive connotation creates a situation in which, 'in spite of the demonstrable effects of secularization [...] a secular approach continues to be widely seen in negative terms as a loss of integrity rather than positively, as a means to liberate creative energies and to enhance social and national integration.' In addition, in public and scholarly Islamic discourses in Egypt, as Kinitz shows in his chapter, throughout twentieth-century history secularists have been, and are, conceptually and politically associated with deviants (*almānīyūn*) by established Islamic scholars. As such, they are immediately perceived as competitors over cultural authority, and socially marginalized as promoters of *al-ālmānīya*, coined by their critics as 'anti-Islamic secularism'. The upshot of this, as Krämer perceptively argues, is that religion is resolutely public while secularity is forced into private niches; note the inversion here of the Western liberal formula of privatized religion and the secular public sphere.

The crucial question in this context seem to be whether the politics and practices of translating secular concepts had positive cultural resonances which would afford them a socially integrative spin and render them acceptable by diverse social and political groups. Highly problematic as this was and is in the Arab Middle East, it has worked much better in India. Here secularism, often equated with tolerance and equal respect for all religion, was generally understood as closely associated with the concept of *Sarva Dharma Sambhava*, meaning 'all Dharmas are equal to or harmonious with each other'. While there is no consensus on the precise origins of this phrase (see Burchardt, Wohlrab-Sahr, and Wegert 2013: 619), it created a common point of reference in which an indigenous (or indigenized) idea of the secular could be fixed.

What remains as a residual question is how one is to approach secularity sociologically in areas where, for all practical purposes, translations of secularity never happened or remained marginal to historical and cultural dynamics and political life. Would that imply the need to assume that secularity is fundamentally alien here? Not necessarily. One needs to be extremely cautious not to impose secular vocabularies on the analysis of any kind of cultural practice with no link to religion. Chieftaincy, for instance, may not have religious dimensions in all African societies, but that does not make it secular in any meaningful way. However, one must be open to the possibility of *indigenous* and *vernacular secularities* if their forms and conditions of emergence offer good reasons to analyse them as such. To this end, we propose a methodology of creatively shifting between on the one hand *analytical uses* of the term secularity – to register, for instance, religious disestablishments which might not be called as such – and on the other hand *semantic analysis* that remains faithful to a narrower set of clearly defined concepts. In this spirit, Porcu (in this volume) also cautions us not to rely too closely on the emic use of religious and secular vocabularies, as such uses may also conceal (parts of) the cultural dynamics one wants to uncover.

4 Secularity in Colonial and Missionary Encounters

Thus, global connections clearly can have a powerful impact on religious–secular dynamics almost anywhere in the world. As mentioned above, this can especially be gleaned from the histories of colonialism, imperialist military expansion and the world religions' missionary movements that occurred in their wake or preceded them. One way in which global interconnectedness can play out is through coercive top-down action by foreign powers, termed by Demerath (2007: 72–76) 'imperialist secularization'. As Mark Mullins shows in his chapter, the American occupation of post-World War II Japan came along with the strict separation of state and religion and the forced removal of Shinto from the public sphere since it was associated with the aggressive nationalism of the war and pre-war periods. All Shinto symbols had to be removed from schools, public offices and so on. Similarly, we find instances of Western colonial expansion leading to the partial or total loss of public power on the part of religious authorities in the majority Muslim countries of the Middle East and North Africa.

It is indeed often assumed that Western colonialism came with the promotion of a secularist regime of some sort and by implication religious disestablishment. Much less acknowledged is the inverse impact, namely that the secular political ethics of non-intervention in religious matters by colonial states may increase the power of local religious authorities. Beatrice Renzi shows in her chapter how in British India the colonial government's abdication of responsibility for adjudicating issues of ritual status among the local population helped to shape the emergent Hinduism as a Brahmanical religion with nationalist pretensions in decisive ways.

Historically, once political and ecclesiastical powers were differentiated in Christian Europe in terms of their attendant secular and religious spheres and prerogatives, such differentiations turned into the premises on the basis of which Christian missions would engage with political rulers in faraway foreign lands. In their historical ethnography of Christian nonconformist missions in South Africa, Comaroff and Comaroff (1997: 63) argued that in their negotiations with local chiefs, missionaries used the separationist argument to convince their counterparts that they had no intention of undermining the chiefs' worldly authority – and were thus granted access to establish their Kingdom of God. Yet within the authority structures of African chieftaincy such distinctions made no sense, as the chieftaincy was at the centre of the entire local cosmology (see also Burchardt, Wohlrab-Sahr, and Wegert 2013: 621). Paul S. Landau's chapter demonstrates just how fundamentally these readings of the situation changed over time in concert with the changes in the conceptual apparatus of colonial ethnography and administration, and later apartheid, and its notions of Africans' presumed religiosity. In the course of the nineteenth century 'Africans' politics' were marked as religious in contradistinction to the rule of black Africans by whites which proliferated a field of secularity, bureaucratic memory, and "expertise" (see Landau, in this volume). The criminalization of indigenous/black African political life by the apartheid authorities implied that the only legal way for Africans to meet was for religious purposes. In his contribution, Landau scrutinizes the complex historical circumstances leading to this situation and its conceptual implications for the analysis of secularity in South Africa.

The concept of 'multiple secularities' (Wohlrab-Sahr and Burchardt 2012) suggests, among other things, that secularity can be mobilized in the name of different collective projects and goals. Secularity can be promoted and institutionalized in projects of radicalized enlightenment 'for the sake of national development' under the guiding ideas of progress and modernity (Wohlrab-Sahr and Burchardt 2012: 890). As Buchenau's and Agadjanian's chapters demonstrate in this book, this was a unifying feature in the communist world, while, as especially Buchenau points out, this universal model had a number of variations.

5 Secularities and the Question of Diversity

While in societies the notion of secularity for the sake of national development dominates the nation and 'the national' figure predominantly in terms of temporality and imagined collective destinies, they point to a different problematic in countries such as India, which have from the outset defined the nation and secularity less in relation to historical teleology than to cultural diversity. Within the concept of 'multiple secularities', we have called this understanding 'secularity for the sake of balancing diversity' (Wohlrab-Sahr and Burchardt 2012; Burchardt, Wohlrab-Sahr, and Wegert 2013). In their chapter, Rina Verma Williams and Laura Dudley Jenkins point out that Indian secularism cannot be understood outside the transnational context. But even as it took shape historically as a response over and against other conceptions, they argue that secularism became a proactive and unique conception for a new Indian nation. In line with that, Anandita Bajpai shows in her chapter that Indian diversity and the notion of secularism were employed as ideals with identifiable roots in an Indian past by several prime ministers, although the emphasis gradually shifted to ideological conformity with the language of the United Nations, where democracy, liberalism, secularism and pluralism are celebrated themes.

While putting major analytical stress on such cultural and political constructions of secularity, we also note the ongoing, and in fact, renewed significance in many parts of the world of Weberian concerns with religious rationalization, cultural change and individuality. In his chapter on the changes in African Pentecostalism over the last thirty years, Rijk van Dijk shows how educated economic elites in Botswana are beginning to reject the religious and material burdens placed on their shoulders by their congregations. In his lucid analysis, van Dijk traces the transformations of the religious aspirations of an upwardly mobile and socially powerful class of people whose inchoate religious location is tentatively described with the notion of 'post-Pentecostalism'. Swidler (2013: 691) succinctly recaptured the role of Pentecostalism for modern secularity as follows:

It is here that the differentiation of the sacred, and its containment within a sphere that individuals can struggle to control, fundamentally changes the nature of religion, from a property of collective life, embedded in institutions like clan, lineage, and chieftaincy, or in communities like those of church, nation, or state, to a property of individuals, attached to their own aspirations and their own destinies. In this understanding, modern secularities are primarily a matter of the recession of religion from public authority [rather than] but of the shifting locus of the sacred, as the sacred becomes increasingly invested in individual destinies while collective institutions are relegated to the realm of the profane.

With this volume, we demonstrate the internal diversity and complexity of concepts of secularities as they take shape through processes of social change in the non-Western world. We suggest that chief among them are colonial and missionary encounters, increasing transnational connectedness in the contemporary period, the globalization of cultural vocabularies through practices of translation, new regimes of religious diversity and shifting locations of the sacred. While scholars, such those present in this volume, have taken the first steps in exploring the importance of secularity for understanding the relationships between religion and modernity, much of the work in fact still lies ahead of us.

Acknowledgments

This edited volume is based on the proceedings of a conference on 'Multiple Secularities and Global Interconnectedness' jointly organized at the University of Leipzig in October 2011 by the editors and the Centre of Area Studies. The concept of 'multiple secularities' was developed in a research project headed by Monika Wohlrab-Sahr. We wish to thank Roman Vido, Ute Wegert, Cora Schuh, Susanne Lemke and Susanne Schenk for their collaboration and contributions to the project. The project was funded by the Saxon Ministry of Science and the Fine Arts, while the conference was generously supported by the Federal Ministry of Education and Research. We wish to thank all participants for their intellectual contributions. For critical and stimulating comments on earlier versions of this chapter, we thank Matthias Koenig and Zeynep Yanasmayan. Special thanks go to the anonymous reader who gave stimulating comments on behalf of de Gruyter. Last, but not least, we wish to thank Lois Lee for her great and tireless support during the preparation of this volume.

References

Asad, Talal. 1993. Genealogies of Religion: Discipline and Reasons of Power in Christianity and Islam. Baltimore: Johns Hopkins University Press.
—. 2003. Formations of the Secular: Christianity, Islam, Modernity. Stanford: Stanford University Press.
Beckford, James A. 2012. "SSSR presidential address on public religions and the postsecular: critical reflections." Journal for the Scientific Study of Religion, 51(1): 1–19.
Berger, Peter L., ed., 1999. The De-Secularization of the World. Washington D.C.: Ethics and Public Policy Center.
Beyer, Peter. 2013. "Questioning the secular/religious divide in a post-Westphalian world." International Sociology, 28(6), 663–679.
Bramadat, Paul, and Matthias Koenig, eds., 2009. International Migration and the Governance of Religious Diversity. Montreal and Kingston: McGill-Queen's University Press.
Burchardt, Marian, and Monika Wohlrab-Sahr. 2013. Von Multiple Modernities zu Multiple Secularities: kulturelle Diversität, Säkularismus und Toleranz als Leitidee in Indien. Österreichische Zeitschrift für Soziologie, 38(4): 355–374.
Burchardt, Marian, Monika Wohlrab-Sahr, and U. Wegert. 2013. "'Multiple secularities': postcolonial variations and guiding ideas in India and South Africa." International Sociology, 28(6): 612–628.
Cady, Linell E., and Elizabeth Shakman Hurd. 2010. "Comparative secularisms and the politics of modernity: an introduction," in Comparative Secularisms in a Global Age, ed. Linell E. Cady, and Elizabeth Shakman Hurd, 3–24. New York: Palgrave Macmillan.
Casanova, José. 1994. Public Religions in the Modern World. Chicago: The University of Chicago Press.
—. 2006. "Secularization revisited: a reply to Talal Asad," in Powers of the Secular Modern: Talal Asad and His Interlocutors, ed. David Scott, and Charles Hirschkind, 12–30. Stanford: Stanford University Press.
—. 2008. "Public religions revisited," in Religion: Beyond a Concept, ed. Hent de Vries, 101–19. New York: Fordham University Press.
—. 2009. "The secular and secularisms," Social Research 76(4): 1049–66.
Comaroff, Jean, and John Comaroff. 1997. Of Revelation and Revolution: the Dialectics of Modernity on a South African Frontier, Vol. II. Chicago: The University of Chicago Press.
Demerath, Nicolas Jay III. 2007. "Secularization and sacralization deconstructed and reconstructed," in Sage Handbook of the Sociology of Religion, ed. James Beckford, and Nicolas Jay III Demerath, 57–80. London: Sage.
Dobbelaere, Karel. 1984. "Secularization theories and sociological paradigms: convergences and divergences." Social Compass, 31(2–3): 199–219.
Eisenstadt, Shmuel N. 2000. "Multiple modernities." Daedalus 129: 1–29.
Fitzgerald, Tim. 1990. "Hinduism and the 'world religion' fallacy." Religion, 20(2): 101–118.
Göle, Nilüfer. 2010. "Manifestations of the religious-secular divide: self, state, and the public sphere," in Comparative Secularisms in a Global Age, ed. Linell E. Cady, and Elizabeth Shakman Hurd, 41–53. New York: Palgrave Macmillan.
Habermas, Jürgen. 2006. "Religion in the public sphere." European Journal of Philosophy, 14 (1): 1–25.

Hervieu-Léger, Daniele. 2000. Religion as a Chain of Memory. New Brunswick: Rutgers University Press.
Koenig, Matthias. 2008. "Institutional change in the world polity international human rights and the construction of collective identities." International Sociology, 23(1): 95–114.
—. 2011. "Jenseits des Säkularisierungsparadigmas?" KZfSS Kölner Zeitschrift für Soziologie und Sozialpsychologie 63(4): 649–73.
Kuru, Ahmed. 2009. Secularism and State Policies toward Religion: The United States, France, and Turkey. Cambridge: Cambridge University Press.
Lee, Lois (2012). Research note: Talking about a revolution: Terminology for the new field of non-religion studies. Journal of Contemporary Religion, 27(1), 129–139.
Levitt, P. 2007. God Needs no Passport: Immigrants and the Changing Religious Landscape. The New Press: New York and London.
Luckmann, Thomas. 1980. "Säkularisierung – ein moderner Mythos," in Lebenswelt und Gesellschaft: Grundstrukturen und geschichtliche Wandlungen, ed. Thomas Luckmann, 161–71. Paderborn: Schöningh.
Madan, T.N. 2007. "Secularism in its place," in Secularism and Its Critics, ed. R. Bhargava, 297–344. New Delhi: Oxford University Press.
Masuzawa, Tomoko. 2005. The Invention of World Religion, Or, How European Universalism was Preserved in the Language of Pluralism. Chicago: The University of Chicago Press.
Nandy, A. 2007. "The politics of secularism and the recovery of religious tolerance," in Secularism and Its Critics, ed. R. Bhargava, 321–379. New Delhi: Oxford University Press.
Nelson, John K. 2012. "Japanese secularities and the decline of temple Buddhism." Journal of Religion in Japan, 1(1): 37–60.
Reader, Ian. 2012. "Secularisation, RIP? Nonsense! The rush hour away from the gods and the decline of religion in contemporary Japan." Journal of Religion in Japan, 1(1): 7–36.
Rosati, Massimo, and Kristina Stoeckl, eds. 2013. Multiple Modernities and Postsecular Societies. Farnham: Ashgate Publishing.
Taylor, Charles. 2007. A Secular Age. Boston: Harvard University Press.
Tschannen, Olivier. 1991. "The secularization paradigm: a systematization." Journal for the Scientific Study of Religion, 30(4): 395–415.
Warner, Michael. 2002. "Publics and counterpublics." Public Culture, 14(1): 49–90.
Van der Veer, Peter. 1996. "Introduction," in Conversion to Modernities: the Globalization of Christianity, ed. Peter Van der Veer, 1–21. New York: Routledge.
Wohlrab-Sahr, Monika, and Marian Burchardt. 2012. "Multiple secularities: toward a cultural sociology of secular modernities." Comparative Sociology, 11(6): 875–909.

Part I: Religious Communities and the State: Fault-Lines of Religion and Secularity in South Asia

Rina Verma Williams and Laura Dudley Jenkins
Secular Anxieties and Transnational Engagements in India

India's unique approach to secularism has been shaped in crucial ways, in both a legal/legislative and a philosophical sense, by transnational entanglements. In this chapter we focus on two such entanglements, illustrating them in two case studies. In the first instance, Indian secularism was forged in the crucible of British colonial rule. Indians long suspected the British of employing "divide and conquer" tactics based most obviously on deploying and entrenching religious differences while maintaining a rhetorical policy of "non-interference" in native religious affairs and building (on) discourses of minority and majority religions in India.

These contexts fed in turn into the second major source of transnational engagements that have had profoundly constitutive effects on Indian secularism: these are the role and status of what we term "global religions" in India. Hinduism occupies a unique status as a major world religion: it is the world's third largest religion after Christianity and Islam, with almost 1 billion adherents worldwide. Yet, despite the presence of Hindus in every region of the world, it is also the world's most concentrated religion. The vast majority of its adherents are largely concentrated in one geographical location: South Asia. Ninety seven percent of all Hindus live in countries in which they are in the religious majority, namely India, Mauritius and Nepal (Pew Forum on Religion and Public Life 2012).[1] At the same time, India is home to all of the world's major religions, with Muslims constituting the largest minority at about 13% of the population, and Christians constituting the second largest minority at about 2% of the total population. Globally, Christians and Muslims are both more numerous and their populations are more geographically dispersed than Hindus.

It is contestation and anxiety over India's colonial legacies and the status of these "global religions" that we argue have had formative effects on Indian approaches to secularism. This anxiety is not primarily unease over secularization, but, rather, plays out as ongoing struggles over the religious rights and freedoms

---

[1] According to data from the Pew Forum on Religion and Public Life, "the percentage of each religious group that lives in countries where its adherents are a majority" are: Hindus 97 percent, Christians 87 percent, Muslims 73 percent, Unaffiliated 71 percent, Jews 41 percent, Buddhists 28 percent, Folk religionists 1 percent, other religions 0 percent (http://www.pewforum.org/global-religious-landscape-exec.aspx#living. Accessed 22 May 2013.)

that constitute the Indian version of secularism. Indian secularism has long grappled with the conception of Islam and Christianity as religions with "external ties"—that is, as religions with fewer adherents in number within India, but with far-reaching global footprints in terms of connections beyond South Asia. In political terms, anxiety about the transnational connections of these global religions has been most explicitly expressed by conservative Hindu groups, and those anxieties have been deployed by such groups to foment intolerance toward adherents of these global religions. We explicitly separate ourselves from such approaches and also argue that they represent only one view on Indian secularism. At the same time, we will seek to demonstrate through two case studies of secular policies in action—religious family laws, or "personal laws," and laws related to conversions—that similar anxieties have underpinned Indian approaches to secularism more broadly, even if the anxieties have manifested differently.

On the political right, anxieties about secularism include a sense that it undermines the Hindus by offering special privileges to religious minorities, leading to what some term "pseudo-secularism." On the left, secular anxieties include a preoccupation with bolstering India's international credibility as a modern state that protects the rights of minorities. Where some political conservatives have reacted to religious minorities with intolerance and persecution, including violence against Muslims or Christians, left-leaning and mainstream political figures have been more likely to react with policies of protection and multicultural accommodation (which some conservative groups read as "appeasement"). Even as these responses diverge radically, we suggest their root source is a similar set of anxieties about the role of global religions in India: the left worries whether secularism is enough to protect minority religions, while the right worries whether secularism will undermine the status of the Hindu majority.

The nationalist movement for independence was led by the Indian National Congress, which claimed to represent all Indians, but whose claim was challenged—and never truly accepted—by religious minority Muslim as well as lower-caste Hindu groups. In this context, India's moment of independence was simultaneously the moment of partition of the territory on the basis of religion, with the creation of Pakistan as a homeland for South Asian Muslims. Just as the role of Islam in the Constitution(s) of the Pakistani state has always been contested, Indian independence and partition left the country with an unresolved question of the extent to which India was, or was meant to be, a "Hindu" country for the majority religious population (75% before partition; 80% throughout the period of independence) of Hindus.

Growing from these roots, Indian secularism has in some ways been defined as much in terms of standing "against" some things as in terms of standing positively for something. The ruling Congress Party and the first Prime Minister, Jawaharlal Nehru, committed India to secularism. Nehru himself was a western-educated lawyer with strong socialist inclinations who had little (personal) patience for what he saw as the superstitions and silliness of religion. Yet he subscribed to a British construction of India as a deeply religious people and place, and hence believed that antagonizing vested religious interests or the religious sentiments of the people was an unproductive path.

In the crucible of partition and the consequent bloodletting between religious communities, Nehru could not, and would not, conceive of a theocratic Hindu Indian state in any sense of the words. He staunchly believed in secularism, perhaps defined broadly in a sense of confining religion to the private sphere of personal, individual practice and belief. But he could see that a "western" conception of secularism—defined in terms of separation of state and religion—was inappropriate for the Indian context. Hence under his governance a uniquely Indian conception of secularism evolved in which the state would maintain some contact with, rather than separation from, all the different religious traditions of the subcontinent: Hinduism, Islam, Christianity, Buddhism, Jainism, Sikhism, and Zoroastrianism.

There is no one agreed upon definition of what Indian secularism actually constitutes, in either a legal/legislative or philosophical sense. Indeed, there are as many definitions of Indian secularism as there are scholars and politicians who deploy them. There has been debate over what to call India's approach to secularism, or indeed whether "secularism" is even the right term in this context. Nehru himself pondered these questions:

> The word "secular" is not a happy one. And yet for want of a beeter [sic] word we have used it. What exactly does it mean? It does not obviously mean a state where religion is discouraged. It means freedom of religions and conscience, including freedom for those who have no religion...The word "secular" [conveys...to me] the idea of social and political equality. (Bhatt 1992: 263)

One term used to describe India's approach to secularism has been "equidistance," suggesting that the Indian state should maintain an equal distance from all religions—not pulling closer to one over another, but involved with all and treating each one equally. The term is widely attributed to Dr. S. Radhakrishnan, a philosopher and the first Vice President and second President of India from 1962–67 (see: Mishra 2000: 191). Thus the Indian state does provide funding for private religious educational institutions (for example, Aligarh Muslim University and Benares Hindu University) but does so "equally." Of course, this formulation leaves dangling the question of what constitutes equal treatment: proportional to population? Absolute equality? Based on need? Defined how? Another difficulty with the concept of "equidistance" has been the variation over time in the extent to which it has meant the Indian state has remained equally distant from matters of religion, as opposed to becoming increasingly entangled with—or proximate to—matters of religion.[2]

Another strand of secularist theorizing in India has been called "equal respect" for all religions, which "entailed not that the state stay away from all religions equally but that it respect all religions alike" (Jha 2002: 3176). It is notable that there is no word in Hindi (or, to our knowledge, in other major South Asian languages) that corresponds to the word "secularism." For a conception of secularism that corresponds to the sense of separation, the Hindi phrase "*dharma nirpekshata*" is often used. It can be translated roughly as "disinterest" in religion. Trying to capture a more engaged Indian formulation of secularism, the Hindi phrase "*sarva dharma sambhava*" is often used, which translates roughly to "equal respect" (or "equal feeling") for all religions (Chiriyankandath 2000: 10).

More recently, Amartya Sen argued that the dominant approach to Indian secularism is "a basic symmetry of treatment" of all the different religious communities, as opposed to the idea that "the state must stay clear of any association with any religious matter whatsoever" (Sen 2005: 296). Yet critics from both the right and the left argue precisely that secularism in practice has been *asymmetrical* in India—a point that is borne out in both the cases of religious laws and conversion laws examined below. This criticism has also been made with particular force by right-wing Hindu conservatives, who have argued that Congress-style secularism is really a "pseudo-secularism" that is interested primarily in cynical appeasement and courting the votes of minority communities. More progressive voices also argue that the implementation of policies related to secularism in the areas of personal law and conversion law have uneven and unfair implications for certain religious groups, women or lower castes. These will be a focus of our case studies below.

The debates over the best terminology and definition for Indian secularism have periodically intensified into an underlying debate over whether secularism —however defined—is the best approach for India at all. In the 1990s, a partic-

---

[2] This was a common argument in the 1980 s, under the Congress Party government of Prime Minister Rajiv Gandhi (Nehru's grandson). Gandhi was seen as (mis)interpreting equidistance by balancing concessions to Muslim conservatives with concessions to Hindu conservatives—thus drawing the Indian state closer into religious matters rather than keeping the state at a distance from them.

ularly troubled juncture in Indian political history for inter-religious (or communal) conflict, some even suggested that secularism was actually causing or making such conflict worse.[3]

The twisting and turning negotiations over secularism in India and its transnational roots and entanglements are manifested in concrete policy areas. In this chapter, we first examine the constitutional underpinnings of Indian secularism, and then consider its application in two legal areas, personal laws and laws regulating religious conversions. Our discussion of personal laws will focus mostly on Muslim law and our discussion of conversions will focus mostly on Christian conversions because these religions are central in political debates on these particular issues. Indeed these issues demonstrate how anxieties about the status of global religions manifest in policy debates about secularism.

1 Constituting Secularism

It is worth noting that the word "secular" was not originally included anywhere in the text of the Indian Constitution. The inclusion or exclusion of the term was hotly debated in the Constituent Assembly between 1948–50.[4] In the end the Assembly decided not to include the term, so the very first words of the Constitution, the Preamble, originally read "We, the people of India, having solemnly resolved to constitute India into a Sovereign, Democratic Republic..." Then in 1976, during the height of Emergency Rule under then-Prime Minister Indira Gandhi (Nehru's daughter)—India's only interlude with authoritarian rule—the words "Secular Socialist" were added to the Preamble, which now reads "We, the people of India, having solemnly resolved to constitute India into a Sovereign Secular Socialist Democratic Republic..." The initial exclusion of the word "secular" is not generally understood as indicating any flagging of Nehru's commitment to the principle; indeed it could be argued that he was more committed to the principle than his daughter was, thus her need to buttress her secular credibility with the inscription of the word into the Preamble.

India's Constituent Assembly worked during a period of transnational legal developments in the area of human rights, when the Atlantic Charter (issued in 1941) and the United Nations Charter (signed in 1945) emerged. Members of the

---

[3] For broad contours of this debate see: Nandy 1995; Madan 1987; Bilgrami 1994.
[4] The Constituent Assembly was elected from provincial legislatures and convened in December 1946, charged with the task of drafting the Constitution of independent India. It met and debated for four full years after independence; the Constitution came into effect on 26 January 1950, which is annually celebrated as 'Republic Day' in India.

Assembly were well aware of these developments and "sensitive to these currents" (Austin 1966: 59). Their recent experience with British colonialism made them leery of the British constitutional model, especially its lack of an explicit, written bill of rights. The desire for specific constitutional protections related to religion also emerged due to the concerns of the many religious minority communities, who "believed that their safety depended upon the inclusion in the Constitution of measures protecting their group rights and character" (Austin 1966: 58–9). Protecting these rights meant the state had to take a more active role in religion than in many other "secular" contexts. Ultimately, Indian secularism allows various religious communities some legal pluralism and autonomy, rather than uniform legal codes, and a substantial amount of state support for various religious institutions.

India's leaders looked to the rest of the world in designing its democracy but did so in order to come up with something better rather than simply to adopt someone else's pre-existing model. In his speech to the Constituent Assembly Nehru said, "We are not just going to copy, I hope, a certain democratic procedure or an institution of a so-called democratic country. We may improve upon it" (Nehru December 13, 1946, quoted in Keating 2011: 59). The authors of the Indian Constitution examined international constitutions and ideas in order to develop their own notions of the relationship between the many religious communities of India and the newly independent nation state (Chiriyankandath 2000: 6). K.M. Munshi, for example, looked to the US but found its secularism unsuitable, arguing that the US Constitution's nonestablishment clause was "inappropriate to Indian conditions" and that India needed a "characteristically Indian secularism" (quoted in Jha 2002: 3176). Arguing that Indians have "deeply religious moorings" and a "tradition of religious tolerance" due to the "broad outlook of Hinduism," Munshi said India "could not possibly have a state religion, nor could a rigid line be drawn between the state and the church as in the US" and ultimately advocated a secularism based on "equal respect" (Jha 2002: 3176).[5]

In addition to western examples, Pakistan became a point of reference in Indian conceptualizations of secularism. The partition of British India into two independent states, India and Pakistan, was the "backdrop" to the Constituent Assembly's discussions (Keating 2011: 66). Partition impacted discussions of secularism in India in two important ways. It created worries about separatism and further divisions of India if the proper relationship between religion and pol-

---

5 For a parallel but more critical argument about the moorings of Indian secularism in Hindu self-conceptions of tolerance, see Rao 2006. See also Adcock 2014.

itics was not achieved, and it created a new, neighboring state that was both a benchmark and a counterpoint in discussions of Indian secularism.

Participants in the debates expressed varied ideas about secularism, and disagreements over the nature of Indian secularism permeate most arguments about religion and politics in India to this day. We agree with Wohlrab-Sahr and Burchardt (2012), drawing on Bajpai (2002), that the Constituent Assembly voiced competing notions of secularity (including arguments based on individual freedom, national unity, and other emphases) but that India has increasingly shifted toward a predominant emphasis on *secularity for the sake of accommodating religious diversity* (24, emphasis in original). To some extent this shift was already underway during the course of the debates. In the end, the Constituent Assembly emphasized the accommodation of religious diversity in the constitutional provisions for Muslims and other religious minorities, including policies of religious freedom and legal pluralism; in contrast, low castes received guaranteed political representation in the form of reserved legislative seats and a system of affirmative action to offset their social and economic disadvantages (Keating 2011: 74; Tejani 2008: 252).

The Constituent Assembly ultimately decided to end the colonial policy of reserved legislative seats for religious minorities after independence (after initially including limited reservations for Muslims and Christians in earlier drafts). Transnational concerns permeated the arguments made by the advocates of this change, as they criticized the British colonial model, voiced concerns about partition and Pakistan, and emphasized the need to demonstrate Indian secularism to the world. Nehru, for example, commented in 1949 that "doing away with this reservation business" was "a very good move for the nation and the world. It shows that we are really sincere about this business of having a secular democracy" (quoted in Jha 2002: 3178). Sardar Patel argued that the "reservation of seats for religious communities" contributed to "separatism" and was "contrary to the conception of a secular democratic state" (quoted in Jha 2002: 3178). Alladi Krishnaswami Ayyar's speech in support of the Constitution later that same year, on November 23, 1949, included both transnational comparisons and references to secularism. He criticized the "communal electorate" as a "device adopted by the British imperialists to prevent the free growth of democracy" and noted the external audience for India's Constitution: "we have to demonstrate to the world, to the class of people who have flourished and who have been nurtured on communal claims, our genuine faith in the fundamental principles of democracy and in the establishment of a secular state" (Lok Sabha Secretariat 1990: 163).

Ayyar proudly noted the non-discrimination clause in the Constitution, which outlaws discrimination on several grounds, including religion, saying, "we may well claim that our Constitution is much more democratic, much more rooted in the principles of democracy than even the advanced constitution of America" (Lok Sabha Secretariat 1990: 163). Indeed, the list of groups protected from discrimination in the Indian Constitution was much more comprehensive than in many of its contemporaries, including religion, sex, caste, race, and more, and the rights of religious freedom were very far reaching, including the right to profess, practice and propagate religion (Article 25). In other ways, however, various marginalized groups in India faced newly differentiated sets of rights under the new Constitution.

Whereas late colonial policies treated religious minorities and lower castes more similarly, with each getting some reserved legislative seats, the Constitution of independent India bifurcated these groups (Keating 2011: 74; Hasan 2009: 8; Tejani 2008: 253). Religious minorities retained policies that emphasized cultural and legal autonomy (such as community-based personal laws) but, as noted above, were denied reserved seats in the name of secularism and national unity. In contrast, lower castes secured policies that emphasized political and socioeconomic empowerment via reservations in legislative seats, government jobs and educational institutions reservations for lower castes in legislative (Jenkins 2003). Downsides of this bifurcation include perennial blindness to the socioeconomic plight of the Muslim minority in India due to the "cultural diversity" lens, and difficulties achieving political unity among the various nondominant minorities in India, due to some being conceived of as culturally diverse and others being viewed as socioeconomically disadvantaged. The cultural and legal autonomy given on the basis of religion also perpetuated gender inequalities in the name of religious freedom. As Keating compellingly argues, the "postcolonial social contract" in India both promoted and constrained religious minority and gender struggles for justice (2011: 59–76).

The question of secularism was contested throughout the constitutional process and certainly not settled with the adoption of independent India's Constitution, which has been in place since 1950. Although certain voices, many of which we quote above, had more influence than others on the constitutional underpinning of Indian secularism (Chiriyankandath 2000: 6–7), so many different ideologies of secularism appeared in the Constituent Assembly debates that scholars have grouped them into three or even five types (Jha 2002: 3176; Chiriyankandath 2000: 9). Wohlrab-Sahr and Burchardt (2012) advocate more research on the "social mechanisms and power relations through which particular understandings of secularity become dominant while others become marginalized or remain insignificant" (31). The following case studies examine the way particular understandings of secularism played out through two of the most contentious religious issues in India: personal laws and conversion laws.

2 Hindu and Muslim Religious Laws

Both of the defining transnational entanglements of Indian secularism that we have outlined above—colonial legacies and global religions—can be traced through the political contestations over India's religious legal system of personal laws, established in the late nineteenth century under British colonial rule. Rather than imposing a uniform, secular code of laws (as was done for criminal and civil codes by the 1860s), Warren Hastings, then the Governor-General of India, decreed in 1772 that on the topics of "inheritance, marriage, cast [sic] and other religious usages, or institutions, the laws of the Koran with respect to the [Muslims], and those of the [Shastras] with respect to the [Hindus], shall be invariably adhered to" (quoted in Griffiths 1986: 6).[6] These family laws included laws on marriage, divorce, maintenance, inheritance, succession, adoption and guardianship.

The family laws so preserved came to be known as the personal laws. Most personal laws today are an amalgamation of three types of laws: (a) customary laws, often unwritten, based on the traditions and practices of different regions or communities; (b) some imported western laws and accumulated case-law; and (c) religious laws, associated with the religions that evolved their own self-contained, self-regulating social systems, including a legal system. The last category includes Islamic, Hindu, and Judeo-Christian laws. In India and parts of the Muslim world, personal laws are applied primarily on the basis of religion. In other parts of Asia, Africa and the Caribbean, they are applied on the basis of tribe, custom and ethnicity as well as religion.

The British originally preserved these indigenous family laws for at least two reasons. First, they saw family laws as intimately tied to religion; therefore, preserving them accorded with the British colonial policy of neutrality in native religious affairs.[7] Second, they considered it too potentially dangerous to tamper with religion-based family laws, due to the fear of ethnic or communal protest. Thus personal laws came to serve two critical purposes for British colonial rule:

---

6 Notably, the very process of "preserving" these family laws effected a fundamental transformation in them. Substantively, the colonists' interpretation of the content of the laws was partial or incomplete at best, and flawed at worst. Procedurally, western administration and institutionalization also altered the laws, not least because they were administered by western judges who inevitably imported their own legal training and conceptions of jurisprudence into their decisions. See Derrett 1961; Anderson 1991.
7 It is unclear why the British considered these particular topics to be especially or intimately connected to religion; the reason may have stemmed from their understanding of the division of jurisdiction between English secular and ecclesiastical courts at that time. See Mansfield 1993.

to preserve and demonstrate their claims to religious neutrality, and avert ethnic unrest. It is perhaps not coincidental that the personal laws have continued to serve much these same functions for the post-colonial Indian state as well.

The personal laws clearly demonstrate the multi- (and not uni-, or even bi-) directionality of transnational colonial entanglements. The influence of Indian personal laws spread via British colonialism far beyond the subcontinent. After their institutionalization in 1772, India's personal laws served as a model for British colonies in Africa and elsewhere.[8] When these colonies attained independence, a few of them eliminated the personal laws and established uniform family law to achieve goals such as modernization and development. Most countries, however, retained the personal laws, and contestation over them continues to shape the politics of many former British colonies (see Charrad 2001 for one example). As discussed above, India retained the personal laws as a form of multiculturalism: a way to protect cultural and religious diversity and guarantee cultural autonomy, especially for minority religious communities.

Personal laws have become a proxy for community identity in Indian politics, for both majority Hindu and minority Muslim communities. The system of personal laws worked (in tandem with other aspects of British colonial rule, such as the censuses) to entrench a conception of religious communities as internally homogeneous, clearly bounded, and shaped primarily by religious legal texts—and also constitutive of Indian society as a whole. In this way, Indian society became a collection of religious communities so defined. The personal laws as a form of multiculturalism and a manifestation of secularism, in turn, became a primary way to "manage" this particular form of "religious diversity"—which colonial rule had arguably shaped if not created.

The retention of the personal laws falls broadly under Article 25 of the Constitution, which deals with the right to freedom of religion. Section 1 states that "Subject to public order, morality and health and to the other provisions of this Part, all persons are equally entitled to freedom of conscience and the right freely to profess, practise and propagate religion." In general terms, the provision for religious personal laws is seen to conflict with the impulse in the Indian Constitution towards gender equity. This can be seen in the tension between Article 25 and Article 15, which prohibits discrimination on the basis of sex (among other things). Based as they are in religion and custom, the personal laws are widely seen as discriminating against women, conferring unequal legal rights on them.

---

[8] Mamdani (2012) makes this argument about the strategy of indirect rule: that it was an approach the British used in India that they 'transplanted' to their African colonies.

There was some debate in the Constituent Assembly over whether to retain the personal laws, or establish a uniform code of family law for all Indians regardless of religion (Williams 2006). The first draft of the Constitution included an article that called on the state to "endeavor to secure for the citizens a uniform civil code throughout the territory of India" (Article 35; Article 44 in the final draft of the Constitution). The Article is a directive principle rather than a fundamental right, meaning it cannot be enforced in a court of law. It provides neither any timetable for establishing a uniform civil code, nor any guidelines for how it could be done, nor what the content of the laws might be. Instead, it merely lays out a desired goal of state policy. Despite opposition from Muslims and many Hindus as well, many in the Congress Party, including Nehru, felt it was important to include the principle of a uniform civil code in the Constitution for the sake of national unity. Dr. B. R. Ambedkar (the country's first Minister of Law and the main author of the Constitution) assured minorities that the government would not forcibly impose a uniform civil code. In the end, Article 44 was included in the Constitution, and the personal laws were also retained (though without explicit Constitutional protection).

The politics of contestation of the personal laws in post-independence India demonstrate the insecurities around majority/minority and global religions in especially stark ways. Recognized personal laws in India include Christian, Jewish, and Parsi laws; but the most politically salient axis of disputation has arisen around Muslim and Hindu personal laws in particular. Under Nehru's purview, Hindu personal laws were codified and (ostensibly) reformed in the early- to mid-1950s, in one of independent India's first major legislative undertakings: the Hindu Code Bills (HCB). Yet because of the sensitivities and immediate wounds of partition, Nehru was loath to undertake similar reforms and codification of Muslim (or any other minority) personal law.[9]

This initial bifurcation between Hindu and Muslim personal laws served, over time, to perpetuate the idea that significant reform of Hindu personal law had been accomplished, when in fact by many standards (and certainly by standards of women's rights and gender equity), the HCB fell short of achieving significantly meaningful change. A series of concessions and compromises with the opposition diluted the substantive reforms proposed in early versions of the bills, especially with regard to property rights for women (Williams 2006: 113; Agnes 1995: 144–146). Such concessions together with a lack of almost any im-

---

9 This was likely also partly attributable to the sense that only the members of a given community should take the lead in matters related to their own personal laws; and as Nehru himself and the majority of Congress leaders of the time were themselves Hindu, they were more likely to view the reform and codification of Hindu law as "their own" law. See Parekh 1991.

plementation led to a widespread understanding of the legislation as being "more symbolic than substantive in character" (Som 1994: 171) At the same time, the rhetorical marginalization of conservative Hindu views—which staunchly opposed any codification or reform of Hindu personal law—contributed to the myth of a "progressive" Hindu community and a "reformed" Hindu personal law. This myth has been perpetuated and used over time by the Hindu nationalist right to validate their rhetoric that the Hindu community has moved forward and reformed its personal law, while the Muslim community lags behind, clinging to an outmoded, oppressive personal law and refusing to integrate into the "national mainstream" (Williams 2006, Ch. 6).

Whereas their general discourse is to accuse Indian Muslims of divided loyalties (to their national homeland of India versus to their religious homeland outside of South Asia)—and thus express their anxieties about the global connections of Islam—in this case Hindu nationalists called on Indian Muslims to take a lesson from Pakistan and reform Muslim personal law as it relates to the rights of women in particular. Despite subsequent, extremely retrograde legislation (especially the Hudood Ordinances of 1979) Pakistan passed a fairly comprehensive reform and codification of Islamic family laws with the Family Laws Ordinance of 1961. This legislation, though poorly if-at-all enforced (like most legislation pertaining to personal laws in the subcontinent) did restrict or eliminate, even if only in name, several of the provisions of Muslim personal law that were most egregious in terms of women's rights. For example, it placed restrictions on polygamy as well as on a husband's unfettered rights of immediate divorce (*talaq*).[10] Yet these have been practices that conservative Muslim leaders in India have insisted on retaining as integral to the protection of Muslim religious identity in India. Scholars understood this difference to be attributable to the difficulties of being a minority community (as Muslims are in India) as opposed to being the dominant, majority community (as they are in Pakistan). But Hindu nationalist political elements constructed the difference instead as intransigent anti-nationalism (refusal to integrate into the progressive, national mainstream) and retrograde oppression of women by the Indian Muslim community. This tendency is exacerbated, in the Hindu nationalist narrative, by Nehruvian secularism.

Finally, in a positive light, transnational connections have provided a path for Muslim women in India seeking models to advocate for internal reforms of the Muslim personal laws. One example in which outside views filter into

---

10 *Muslim Family Laws Ordinance* [Pakistan], VIII OF 1961, available at: http://www.refworld.org/docid/4c3f1e1c2.html. Accessed 6 May 2013.

India is the international NGO Women Living Under Muslim Laws (WLUML). This organization works to put Muslim women living in different countries in communication with each other in order to learn how Islamic laws are being reformed in more gender-just ways. WLUML operates in over 70 countries, including "secular states where political groups are demanding religious laws" (http://www.wluml.org/node/5408; accessed 21 May 2013). Another example in which an Indian organization reaches out beyond national borders is the All India Muslim Women Personal Law Board, formed in 2005 to affirm and assert the rights given to Muslim women under Islam and Islamic law. Although largely drawing on homegrown expertise, the All India Muslim Women Personal Law Board's website also cites various transnational examples of reforms or interpretations of Muslim laws that are favorable to women.[11]

3 Laws against "Forcible" Religious Conversion

Like personal laws, the issue of religious conversions highlights how transnational entanglements shaped and continue to shape discourses on Indian secularism. Secularism in India has always been about managing religious freedoms in a context of religious diversity, and Article 25 of the Indian Constitution, on freedom of religion, is central to Indian secularism. Colonial legacies and the perceived encroachment of global religions on the Hindu heartland each play a role in contemporary legal efforts to control conversions. Hindu nationalist activists and politicians periodically emphasize the perceived transnational threat from missionaries or others involved in conversions to non-Hindu religions (especially Christianity, but also Islam). As noted above, adherents of these reli-

---

[11] "Many Islamic countries like Egypt, Sudan, Jordan, Iran, Syria, Lebanon, Morocco and Iraq are updating Shariat laws relating to marriage and have imposed a court injunction against the husband pronouncing talaaq. In Turkey and Cyprus, unilateral divorce has been disapproved and needs court intervention. Turkey is trying to reinterpret and radicalise Hadis, the second-most sacred text based on the sayings of the Prophet. The Iranian Family Protection Law 1967 does not grant a man the right to divorce his wife without judicial intervention. But the mullahs and clerics in India are creating their own rules, forcing men and women to either follow them or be condemned through fatwas." *News and Events*, http://muslimwomenpersonallaw.com/news.html. Accessed 13 May 2013.
The All India Muslim *Women* Personal Law Board was formed as an alternate voice to the All India Muslim Personal Law Board—consisting entirely of men—founded in 1972 as an organization of Islamic scholars (*ulama*) seeking to protect the status of Muslim personal law in India. See their websites at http://muslimwomenpersonallaw.com. Accessed 7 May 2013; and http://aimplboard.in/index.php. Accessed 7 May 2013.

gions constitute a small percentage of the Indian population but outnumber Hindus and have a larger global "footprint" worldwide. This global demographic situation can be used to spark anxiety at any sign of "inroads" by these global religions into India. A spate of state-level legislation against "forcible" conversions, and other legal and administrative limitations on conversions, has accompanied persistent rhetoric about threats to the Hindus' status as the majority religious community from "foreign" interference. This legislation, in turn, sparks anxieties among religious minorities about the durability of their religious freedoms.

Although not yet national in scope, state-level laws regulating religious conversions demonstrate the difficulties of achieving secularism as equal respect or equal distance in practice. The five states with active laws restricting religious conversion as of this writing are Madhya Pradesh, Chhattisgarh, Odisha (formerly Orissa), Gujarat and Himachal Pradesh. Various state-level laws against conversion via "force" or "allurement" purport to protect religious freedom yet reinforce the idea that certain groups (such as women or lower castes) are inherently vulnerable and in need of protection from nefarious outside influences. These laws also perpetuate the notion that certain groups (particularly religious minorities) are illicitly converting people. Although such laws are one possible way to implement secularism and arguably fit the dominant emphasis of contemporary Indian secularism, namely the accommodation of religious diversity (Wohlrab-Sahr and Burchardt 2012: 24), legal limits on conversions circumscribe the religious agency of particular populations within India.

Laws limiting conversion extend back to the colonial era in India, when over a dozen princely states (indirectly ruled by the British through local royalty) had such laws, inspired by concerns about public order and about increasing foreign influences within these princely states. Colonial-era limitations on conversion can be found in various laws about conversion, apostasy or public safety. Even British administrators in directly ruled areas had public order concerns associated with conversion and, although by and large Christians themselves, did not necessarily support Christian missionary activity. Legal challenges to Christian conversions in Bombay included accusations of "undue, improper, and fraudulent means to convert and seduce" a young convert "from the religious faith of his ancestors and family," foreshadowing similar language in contemporary laws targeting conversions via force, fraud or allurement (quoted in Palsetia 2006: 615, 622). Colonial legacies impacted the subsequent debates over conversions in two ways. One, as in the case of personal laws, colonial rule created legal precedents (in this case for laws limiting conversions) that re-emerged in independent India. Two, the largely Christian colonizers left behind a religious minority population that has the taint of association with a period of foreign domination.

Like personal laws, conversion rights fall under Article 25 of the Constitution on freedom of religion, which, as noted above, states in section 1: "Subject to public order, morality and health and to the other provisions of this Part, all persons are equally entitled to freedom of conscience and the right freely to profess, practise and propagate religion." This clause provoked debates in the Constituent Assembly over the verb "propagate," as some members wanted to drop this word altogether and others advocated for a clause disallowing the conversion of minors, but ultimately such restrictions were dropped from the final draft and the word "propagate" remained (Jha 2002: 3178). Whether Indian secularism entails the right to maintain one's religion (justifying legal protections from converters), the right to change one's religion (justifying legal protection of the right to convert oneself), or both is an ongoing dilemma. Many of the contemporary conversion laws are entitled "freedom of religion" laws, but advocates and opponents can each invoke "freedom of religion." Advocates say these laws protect the religious freedom of groups that are vulnerable to missionary inducements; opponents argue that they restrict the rights of citizens to propagate their religion to others or to change their own religious identities (Jenkins 2008: 111).

The idea of ominous, foreign funded conversions as a threat to the Hindu majority is an example of what Arjun Appadurai has called the "fear of small numbers": In other words, "majorities can always be mobilized to think that they are in danger of becoming *minor* (culturally and numerically) and to fear that minorities, conversely, can easily become *major*....In a variety of ways globalization intensifies the possibility of this volatile morphing" (Appadurai 2006: 83). This anxiety gave energy to Hindu *re*conversion campaigns in the 1980s "especially among poorer rural and tribal populations, alleged to have been duped into conversion by the forces of global Islam;" additional targets for reconversions to Hinduism were Indian Christian communities (Appadurai 2006: 70).

In 2006, Bharatiya Janata Party senior leader L.K. Advani called for national and state legislation to control conversions with a typical argument for these laws:

> We strongly condemn the campaign of proselytisation which poses a grave threat to Hindu society and to the national integration as well. We demand stern action against those who indulge in such activities.... It is bad enough that religious conversions are conducted in a systematic manner through inducements and coercions. But such activities acquire an extra edge of ominousness when they are facilitated by foreign funded organisations ostensibly under the garb of social service for poor and under-privileged families (*Hindustan Times*, April 17, 2006).

Although some states already had legislation restricting conversions, including Madhya Pradesh (1967), Chhattisgarh (1968), Orissa (1977), and Arunachal Pradesh (law passed in 1978 but not implemented due to rules never being framed by state government), the last decade has seen new legislation in Tamil Nadu (enacted in 2002 and repealed in 2004),[12] Gujarat (act passed in 2003, rules framed in 2008), Rajasthan in 2006 (act passed in 2006 but never signed into law by state governor, reintroduced in 2008) and Himachal Pradesh (act passed in 2006, governor signed into law in 2007). Politicians' calls for new laws in Jharkhand and Uttarakhand have not materialized. The rise and fall of these laws has much to do with the rise and fall of the Hindu nationalist Bharatiya Janata Party in state politics either as a ruling party or coalition partner, but the laws have also faced legal challenges. Certain provisions in Himachal Pradesh's law were struck down in 2012 by the state's High Court, which upheld banning conversions by force, inducement or fraudulent means but struck down the rule that that those planning to convert needed to give one month's notice to the District Magistrate. Gujarat's law, which similarly requires advance notification, in effect, permission, from the government for conversion, is currently facing a legal challenge. These cases revolve around opposing arguments each based on a key element of India's secularism, namely, religious freedom.

Assumptions that certain people or groups are more easily lured or forced into conversion, or that any group conversion is suspect, are embedded in several of these laws. For example, some laws, such as those in Odisha, Himachal Pradesh, Gujarat, and (briefly) Tamil Nadu, impose higher fines or prison terms on those found to be converting lower castes, tribes or women. Some required that people register their change of faith with a local official (in some states, prior to conversion), in order to track or possibly prevent group conversions. The impact of these laws on religious minorities is not just due to prosecutions (by one estimate, less than a dozen in all states, and even fewer convictions) but also due to the anxiety they provoke among minority communities—as well as the Hindu majority (Dayal 2012). Indeed the existence of such laws gives official validation to fears or suspicions about conversion (particularly to "global religions") that become a common pretext for violent attacks on minority religious institutions, leaders or adherents. Secularism has been at the root of contestations over religious propagation and conversion from the time of the Constituent Assembly debates. Some advocate a secular framework that protects all religions

---

12 The Tamil Nadu government headed by Chief Minister Jayalalitha repealed this on 18 May 2004. The Tamil Nadu Prohibition of Forcible Conversion of Religion (Repeal) Act, 2006, (Act No. 10 of 2006) further formalized the demise of the law and was "deemed to have come into force on the 18th day of May 2004."

through comprehensive and robust religious rights and freedoms, whereas others are concerned that too many religious freedoms, particularly for members of proselytizing religions, will threaten Hindu society and even secularism itself.

4 Conclusion

In conclusion, we hope to have demonstrated that Indian secularism—legally or philosophically—cannot be understood outside its transnational contexts, both before and after independence. States and constitutions never stand alone but always "speak to" other political actors and operate in a broader global milieu. In very real senses, they constitute themselves for external as well as internal consumption. In the case of India, the leaders of the postcolonial state sought to project India's image transnationally as a newly modernizing, industrializing, and secularizing nation still rooted deeply and firmly in an ancient and glorious history and civilization.

In the context of partition, how independent India "managed" the relation of religion and politics and how it treated religious minorities became an issue of defining importance. Indian leaders reacted by simultaneously adopting and rejecting other models and conceptions of secularism. Fundamental tenets of Indian secularism can, in certain critical ways, be traced back to British colonial policies: of "non-interference" and of an attempted stance of neutrality or non-preferentialism between different Indian religions.

Other aspects of Indian secularism were intentionally distinct from western, British colonial or American approaches, or from what were taken as Pakistani entanglements of religion and politics. But even as Indian secularism began as a reaction against other conceptions, it became a proactive and unique conception for a new Indian nation. Whether that model can easily be defined is an entirely different matter. Notions of secularism associated with "equal respect" can encompass some variations over time. At times, under certain leaders, it meant equidistance between the state and religion, while at other times, under other leaders, it devolved into periods of state-religion entanglements. While equal respect captures one of the foremost (among the many) ideologies associated with Indian secularism, secularism in practice has been fraught with inequalities. Our case studies of personal laws and conversion laws reveal some of the ways laws rooted in or justified by secular ideologies can contribute to social inequalities for nondominant groups, including women and lower castes.

Challenging such inequalities, however, is difficult due to the anxieties associated with Indian secularism, some of which stem from transnational sources. The legacies of colonial rule mean postcolonial Indian leaders have criticized but in some spheres adopted or reactivated some colonial legal approaches, such as distinct religious civil laws or limits on conversion in the name of order. The very idea of minorities, a legacy of colonial rule and postcolonial nation building, is complicated by a global view of religions. Religious minorities in India are uneasy about legal reforms to existing policies (such as personal laws), and even the Hindu majority can become apprehensive about the religious minorities in India, resulting in legislation (such as laws limiting conversions) inspired more by global religious demographics or transnational conspiracy theories than significant national or local threats. Indian secularism remains complex, contested and difficult to capture. What can be done is to trace the manifestations, negotiations and anxieties of Indian secularism in concrete and critical issue areas, which is what we have sought to do here.

Works cited

Adcock, C. S. 2014. The Limits of Tolerance. New York: Oxford University Press.
Agnes, Flavia. 1995. "Redefining the agenda of the women's movement within a secular framework," in *Women and Right-Wing Movements: Indian Experiences*, eds. Tanika Sarkar and Urvashi Butalia, 136–57. New Jersey: Zed Books.
Anderson, Michael. 1991. "Islamic law and the British colonial encounter," in *Islamic Family Law*, eds. Chibli Mallat and Jane Connor, 205–24. London: Graham & Trotman.
Appadurai, Arjun. 2006. *Fear of Small Numbers*. Durham and London: Duke University Press.
Austin, Granville. 1966. *The Indian Constitution: Cornerstone of a Nation*. Delhi: Oxford University Press.
Bajpai, Rochana. 2002. "The conceptual vocabularies of secularism and minority rights in India." *Journal of Political Ideologies* 7, no. 2: 179–197.
Bhatt, S.R. 1992. "Secularism and pluralism," in *Secularism in India: Dilemmas and Challenges*, ch. 17, ed. M.M. Sankhdher, 261–71. New Delhi: Deep & Deep.
Bilgrami, Akeel. 1994. "Two concepts of secularism." *Economic and Political Weekly* (July 9, 1994): 1749–61.
Charrad, Mounira. 2001. *States and Women's Rights: the Making of Postcolonial Tunisia, Algeria, and Morocco*. Berkeley: University of California Press.
Chiriyankandath, James. 2000. "'Creating a secular state in a religious country': the debate in the Indian Constituent Assembly." *Commonwealth and Comparative Politics* 38, no. 2: 1–24.
Dayal, John. 2012. "Court upholds anti-conversion law, knocks out major clause." *UCAN India* August 31, 2012. Available at: http://www.ucanindia.in/news/court-upholds-anti-conversion-law-knocks-out-major-clause/18945/daily. Accessed 25 May 2013.
Derrett, J. D. M. 1961. "The administration of Hindu law under the British." *Comparative Studies in Society and History* 4, no. 1 (November): 10–52.
Ghose, Sanjoy. 2001. "Unsustainable Laws." The Lawyers Collective. Available at: http://lawyerscollective.org/lc_mag/freedownloads/magazine2001/January%202001/unsus_stein_able_laws.htm. Accessed 18 February 2006.

Griffiths, John. 1986. "What is legal pluralism?" *Journal of Legal Pluralism and Unofficial Law* 24, no. 1: 1–56.
Hasan, Zoya. 2009. *Politics of Inclusion: Castes, Minorities and Affirmative Action.* New Delhi: Oxford University Press.
Jenkins, Laura Dudley. 2003. *Identity and identification in India: Defining the disadvantaged.* London and New York: Routledge.
—. 2008. "Legal limits on religious conversion in India." *Law and Contemporary Problems* 71, no. 2: 109–127.
—. 2009. "Diversity and the constitution in India: what is religious freedom?" *Drake Law Review* 57, no. 4: 913–947.
Jha, Shefali. 2002. "Secularism in the constituent assembly debates, 1946–1950." *Economic and Political Weekly* 37, no. 30: 3175–80.
Keating, Christine. 2011. *Decolonizing Democracy: Transforming the Social Contract in India.* University Park: Pennsylvania State University Press.
Lok Sabha Secretariat. 1990. *The Constitution and the Constituent Assembly: Some Select Speeches.* New Delhi: Lok Sabha Secretariat.
Madan, T.N. 1987. "Secularism in its place." *Journal of Asian Studies* 46:4 (Nov. 1987): 747–759.
Mamdani, Mahmood. 2012. *Define and Rule: Native as Political Identity.* Cambridge MA: Harvard University Press.
Mansfield, John. 1993. "The personal laws or a uniform civil code?" in *Religion and Law in Independent India*, ed. Robert D. Baird, 139–78. New Delhi: Manohar.
Mishra, Shree Govind. 2000. *Democracy in India.* New Delhi: Sanbun Publishers.
Nandy, Ashis. 1995. "An anti-secularist manifesto." *India International Centre Quarterly* 22:1 (Spring): 35–64.
Palsetia, Jesse L. 2006. "Parsi and Hindu traditional and nontraditional responses to Christian conversion in Bombay, 1839–45." *Journal of the American Academy of Religion* 74:3 (September): 615–45.
Parekh, Bhikhu. 1991. "Nehru and the national philosophy of India." *Economic and Political Weekly* 26, no. 1–2 (5 January): 35–48.
Pew Forum on Religion and Public Life. 2012. *The Global Religious Landscape.* http://www.pewforum.org/global-religious-landscape-exec.aspx#living. Accessed 22 May 2013).
Rao, Badrinath. 2006. "The variant meanings of secularism in India: notes toward conceptual clarifications." *Journal of Church and State* 48, no. 1 (Winter): 47–81.
Sen, Amartya. 2005. *The Argumentative Indian: Writings on Indian History, Culture and Identity.* New York: Allen Lane.
Som, Reba. 1994. "Jawaharlal Nehru and the Hindu code: A victory of symbol over substance?" *Modern Asian Studies* 28, no. 1: 165–94.
South Asia Human Rights Documentation Center. 2008. "Anti-conversion laws: challenges to secularism and fundamental rights." *Economic and Political Weekly* 43, no. 2: 63–73.
Tejani, Shabnum. 2008. *Indian Secularism: a Social and Intellectual History, 1890–1950.* Bloomington and Indianapolis: Indiana University Press.
Williams, Rina Verma. 2006. *Postcolonial Politics and Personal Laws: Colonial Legal Legacies and the Indian State.* New Delhi: Oxford University Press.
Wohlrab-Sahr, Monika and Marian Burchardt 2012. "Multiple secularities: toward a cultural sociology of secular modernities." *Comparative Sociology* 11, no. 6: 875–909.

Anandita Bajpai
"Speaking" the Nation Secular: (E)merging Faces of India

This contribution aims to unveil how the prime ministers of India project the imagination(s) of a 'secular emerging' India through the medium of their public speeches. It will be elucidated how the discursive production of Indian secularity converges with the staging of an 'emerging' India, both for what the prime ministers conceive as the outside world as also for 'Indians' (in and outside India). The temporal focus of the chapter is post 1991, when the Indian economy witnessed the formal institutionalization of the neo-liberal economic reforms, which were discursively framed and backed by political rhetoric, formulating the very starting point in the projections of India as the 'Emerging Giant. 'Two concrete events acquire prominence: Firstly, the demolition of a sixteenth century Mosque (*Babri Masjid*) in the city of Ayodhya in 1992, which was instrumentalized by the Hindu Right Wing and was followed by communal riots in the state of Uttar Pradesh and numerous other parts of the country. Secondly, the religious riots in Gujarat in 2002, a continuation of the ongoing *Mandir-Masjid* (temple-mosque) controversy between the Hindu and Muslim communities. These two events have been India's very own critical ruptures, which have made secularism an important discursive stake in the forefront of active debates. In the face of such conflicts, which intensified the urgency to re-weave the national imagination, the prime ministers' public speeches have tried to rescue the ideal of India's proclaimed secular democracy. Secularism here is projected as a necessary basis for a religiously pluralist India. Thus, India's secularity becomes a pre-condition for its emergence, a means to concretize its ideological cohesion with the world as a secular, and therefore a trustworthy democracy, ready to 'emerge.'

This contribution presents how the paradigm of secularism is translated for 'Indians' as well as how the Indian state positions itself through it in and for the world, by analyzing the public speeches of three Indian prime ministers–Pamulaparti Venkata Narasimha Rao, Atal Behari Vajpayee and Manmohan Singh, all of whom have served complete five year terms as the prime ministers of India after 1991 (1991–96, 1999–04 and 2004–14 respectively). It thus utilizes *the most official* and *the most public* state narrative and how the same weaves the profile of a secular emerging India. Though the underpinning objective to project India's secularism lies at the heart of the rhetoric of all three prime ministers, the inherent subtle differences which permeate in *how* they do so, will illustrate the ambivalences which the paradigm comes to connote.

1 Secularism as the Interface

My primary argument is that secularism, as a paradigm, formulates an interface, 'a common shared boundary,' a zone of contact between the *perceived* 'Internal' and 'External,'[1] as sketched by the prime ministers through their addresses, to profile a *secular emerging* India. It will be shown how the prime ministers use the term as a dual-faced mirror: Each side of this two-way mirror reflects understandings of the term which are derived from the particular context (internal and external). In internal settings, it acquires different ambivalent understandings which draw their resources from the Indian context of religious pluralism. In the external settings, the term is used as such to concretize the image of India being in ideological cohesion with the world as an 'emerging' *yet* 'secular' democracy. The ambivalences produced by the different understandings to the paradigm are never demarcated clearly in their contours within the prime ministers' addresses. The term 'secularism' thus becomes a terminological common ground on the basis of which the prime ministers produce parallel semantic zones, which allow for multiple comprehensions of the paradigm to co-exist. Through their speeches, all three prime ministers, revoke and even *creatively re-interpret* it to fit the dual purpose at stake. Besides these spatially located demarcations, it is also utilized as a temporal interface between India's projected past and its projected future. It helps construct the image of India's new promising future as also becoming a bridge to its selectively remembered past. It is used for generating, to borrow François Hartog's conceptualization, a Regime of Historicity. This refers to "methods of relating to time: forms of experiencing time, here and elsewhere, today and yesterday, ways of being in time" (Hartog 2005) whereby the "Present is the focal point of the representation of time; the past and the future are represented, thought of, and felt as departing from and returning to the present. In other words, in this order of time, the categories of past and future are instrumentalized to determine what the present is or is not" (Hannoum 2008: 458). The prime ministers feed into the imagination of an India of the future, to inform the world, as also 'India,' of an India which is emerging and secular. Simultaneously, the past is also utilized as a reservoir for projecting an abstract, homogenized 'national' heritage.

---

[1] The terms 'internal' and 'external' (Inside and Outside) are not products of assumptions made by the author, rather emic categories derived from the analysis of the material i.e. they refer to the distinctions which are drawn within the addresses *by* the three Indian prime ministers. Thus, the demarcation exists from the perspective of the prime ministers and how they draw the categories of the intended audiences within the speeches.

When looking at the political speeches which were delivered before and after the demolition of the *Babri Masjid* in Ayodhya, and in the face of riots across the country (1991–95), the underlying assumption is that in the face of such conflicts, the discursive attempts to 'rescue' the paradigm of secularism, as also the idea of national solidarity, are at the pinnacle of their intensity, resonating with the desperation to re-weave a national imagery. However, during the same phase, the attempts to paint a 'secular' India also overlap remarkably with the 'emerging' India discourse(s), in that after 1991, and the formal institutionalization of the neo-liberal economic reforms, there was a new vigour with which the narration of a rising India was also undertaken. Speeches delivered to audiences on the commemorational anniversary of Indian independence (August 15, 1991–2008) are used to reflect how the special occasion of 'remembering' independence is used to revisit ideas of secularism and national unity. The material also incorporates addresses delivered in the face of the immediate outbreak of violence in India, when the prime ministers delivered 'Messages to the Nation' on the national television channel (*Doordarshan*) (1992–93 after Ayodhya and 2002 after Godhra), and those delivered before audiences at the UN General Assembly, at the prime ministers' visits abroad or visits of foreign ministers, diplomats to India etc. and other international platforms. Finally, those which were delivered by the current prime minister (2004–2009) to instigate the memory of the events and on topical issues of national integration and religious/communal harmony also formulate a part of the material under consideration.

2 Self-Portrayals for the Inside – Fixating the 'secular India' at the home turf

In an address to the Upper House of the Indian Legislature in 1993, a few months after the events of Ayodhya, P.V. Narasimha Rao, stated with regard to the Constitution of India:

> The word secular was used in the forty-second amendment (of the Constitution)...The forty-second amendment makes it very clear that the kind of democracy, the brand of democracy in this country is going to be secular democracy. It could be any other democracy, non-secular also, if the nation wants it. But this nation in particular wants secular democracy.[2]

---

[2] Rao, P.V. Narasimha, *Agenda Before the Nation*, Address at the Indian Upper House of Legislature, The Rajya Sabha (New Delhi: March 11, 1993).

References such as the above are obvious instances of profiling India as a secular democracy. The Constitution of India, which establishes India's secularity, is revoked repetitively to stress that India is and *has to be* secular. However, such references do not elaborate explicitly upon what it is that the term means. They serve, at best, as an opening window to legitimize India's claim to secularism, validate it by emphasizing its constitutional career.

In order to explain the ingredients of the term to perceived 'internal' audiences, *all three* prime ministers have at different stages of their respective political careers, resorted to numerous Indian neo-logisms to the term. Thus, terms and phrases like *Tolerance, Sarva Dharma Sambhav* (all religions are true), *Dharma-nirpekshta, Unity in Diversity, communal non-bias*, etc. are employed by all three, but not without variances in the meanings implied or the frequency of usage. Each of these terms and phrases has a particular career in India and is used as a mechanism to legitimize and re-assert its image as a 'secular' nation.

One such derivative is *tolerance*. The term is employed repetitively in co-occurrence with the term secularism in addresses which were delivered to Indian audiences, especially in the aftermath of the Ayodhya conflict.[3] During this phase, the objective was to inform the 'inside' that secularism in India ought not to be viewed merely as a constitutional embellishment but as a lively philosophical idea, embedded in India's long tryst with the value of tolerance.[4] However, it has persisted as a referral point to secularism even in the case of the prime ministers to follow. In the following lines, Manmohan Singh, India's prime minister after 2004, touches upon numerous parallel themes while explaining the term, in his address to the National Integration Council

> For centuries our society has been characterized by a spirit of tolerance. This has been a value which has been at the core of our civilization, at the core of our very concept of a nation. Ours is a society which has rejoiced in its diversity; in its ability to shelter an incredible range of thoughts, ideas and beliefs (...) It is this wonderful open-mindedness which has enabled all religions of the world to find a place under the Indian sun. As we have

---

[3] Within the context of a sample of 13 addresses made by P.V. Narasimha Rao, the term is used 63 times while the term secular or secularism occurs 62 times. In most cases, the two terms have a co-occurrence in the addresses.

[4] Rao, in a speech delivered at the UNESCO symposium, states, "To me, tolerance means the intensely creative interplay between different religious and philosophical systems, or between differing secular ideologies and worldviews within a society. Such creative interplay transforms the notion of tolerance from a passive to an active agency, through which an individual or the community enriches the material and spiritual life." (Rao, PV Narasimha, *Tolerance for a Better World Order*,Speech delivered at the UNESCO sponsored symposium on Tolerance (New Delhi: May 1, 1995)).

grown as a nation, this value which has been enshrined in our constitution has become one of the defining features of our nation.[5]

Here the 'our' and 'we' celebrate an Indian-ness evoked while simultaneously establishing that the 'spirit of tolerance' is *not new* to India, that it has a distinct history in India's civilizational past ('for centuries'). The notion of *tolerance* and diversity inhabit parallel semantic zones within the speech and become the co-equivalents of secularism. The phrase 'at the core of our very concept of a nation,' shows clearly that secularism (here equivalent to tolerance) is a 'defining feature,' rather a pre-condition, for the very existence of the Indian nation.

The remembrance of a staged civilizational memory serves to establish a unified 'national' self, one with a "wonderful" past embedded in the ideal of secularism. Tolerance thus becomes a derivative of secularism which provides the common space for both 'traditional' values of a homogenized, abstract, Indian past and the ideals of a 'modern' Nation-State (as constitutional values) to be projected. In fact, a natural continuity between the two is sketched to underline how one has provided room for the other. For example in the following address Singh states

> I do sincerely believe that our civilization has made it possible for diversity to thrive and flourish. Every great religion of the world has found a home in this great and blessed land of ours. We Indians are intrinsically a tolerant people. Intolerance is an aberration. Our democracy is built on our civilizational commitment to pluralism. Religious intolerance is alien to both our culture and constitutional values.[6]

Tolerance thus becomes a common meeting ground, a confluence, for the civilizational past as well as the present. As emerges from the above two examples, when explaining the paradigm to internal audiences there is no hesitation in employing references to religion. In fact, a persistent emphasis laid by *all three* prime ministers is that secularism does not imply irreligiousness. On the contrary, religious diversity is celebrated. There is an underlying comprehension that in order to appeal to the sensibilities of the listeners, religion cannot be relegated. It is in this regard also that numerous ambivalences arise when it comes to personal religious codes. Here a note on the language in which the speeches were delivered also deserves mention. Whereas for those speeches delivered in English all three prime ministers occasionally use the term tolerance, for those delivered

---

[5] Singh, Manmohan, *Sustaining our Diversity and Pluralism: Challenges Ahead*, Address to the National Integration Council (New Delhi: August 31, 2005).
[6] Singh, Manmohan, Address at the Indira Gandhi Peace Prize for National Integration (New Delhi: October 31, 2006).

in Hindi, the term shifts from *sahisnutā* (forbearance, sufferance), *sabr* (moderation, patience), *sahanaśīlatā* (endurance, passiveness, longanimity), *udāratā* (magnanimity, generosity, charity, liberality, openness) to *dhairya* (adherence, patience) (Mishra and Satyaprakaśa 1971). Though each of these Hindi terms carries *tolerance* as *one* of the meanings when translated into English, they are nonetheless accompanied by a plethora of other meanings in Hindi which make it vague, open, abstract and ambiguous in interpretation. That tolerance as an equivalent of secularism can stand for patience, charity, endurance and even passiveness, all at the same time, thus opens a new space where the term secularism is creatively left ambivalent in its meaning. This, in fact, is the most prominent strategy- that of showing state secularism as a *fact* making a claim to a normative understanding to the term as something available, known, and fixed, when actually leaving the meaning open.

The theme of religious diversity extends further into another prominent Indian derivative of secularism, a phrase which has been the bone of contention throughout the history of the secularism debate in India. Often projected as a philosophy with a specific career in the Indian context, the dictum of *Sarva Dharma Sambhava*, is the most commonly referred to understanding of secularism by the prime ministers. The phrase literally may be translated as 'All religions are true,' or 'All religions are possible.'

In an address commemorating Swami Vivekananda's (the Indian socio-religious reformer) participation in the World Parliament of Religions, Chicago 1893, Rao elucidates the phrase

> Sarva Dharma Sambhava which we call secularism today, equal respect for all religions, is a unique contribution of our country to the world. It is amazing how people cannot understand secularism. They may be having different religions in their countries but still, from their point of view it is not an aggregate-one plus one-it is not like that; it is something much above the aggregate, and this is what we consider secularism is. Our secularism is neither atheistic, nor irreligious. It is not even indifferent to religion. It accepts religion as a vital element in the life of an individual for so it is in India and among the vast majority of people of the world. It then goes a step further and recognizes the spirit of the long held Indian tradition, that there can be more than one true religion and all of them should be shown due deference.[7]

As evident, the phrase is sometimes even utilized as a direct translation of the term secularism. In a twist of formulations, the English term is thus domesticat-

---

[7] Rao, P.V. Narasimha, *Swami Vivekananda-A true Liberal*, Inaugural Address at the Centenary celebrations of Swami Vivekananda's participation at the World Parliament of Religions in Chicago, (October 9, 1993).

ed, added the Indian flavor, and used to inform Indians, and the world, that in fact secularism as an ideal is not an externally induced paradigm for India-its roots may be traced in Indian *sanskriti*[8]. In the above lines '[...] is a unique contribution of our country to the world,' and 'It is amazing how people cannot understand secularism,' quantify that India not only has a long tradition of secularism but is rather even a trend-setter, a contributor to the paradigm (see also Bhargava 2006). Thus, two objectives are simultaneously attained here: First the nation is imagined through a re-projection of history, through shifting references to the past and this re-projection is embedded with an inherent understanding that secularism in India can neither be 'atheistic nor irreligious,' and second, informing Indians *and* the world that not only has India always been secular but that it is even distinct, unique in the world for having a model that is worthy of emulation. Noteworthy is the semantic shift in that the emphasis is not on drawing the boundaries between the state and the 'religious' sphere, in coherence with the strict 'wall of separation,' but rather on propagating an equal respect for all religions. What is propagated is the celebration of Indian pluralism as a basis of its secularism and exceptionalism. However, what is not made public is the nuanced meaning of what is entailed within the public and private spheres and how this secularism envisions that "religion and culture were elevated to an ostensibly apolitical level, above the profanities of the political" (Blom Hansen 1999: 11).

In the following lines, A.B. Vajpayee, who would later assumeprime ministership in 1999, states

> Secularism is in the veins of this country. This country never saw a theocracy. It has never seen conflicts between the Church and the state as the West has. Here the king ruled and the priest, at the very most, gave instructions and speeches about discipline. The priests never attempted to amass power from the king and the state. This is a multi-religious country. Even if Christianity and Islam wouldn't have entered, even then this nation would have advanced with the paradigm of Sarva Dharma Sambhava, that is, all religions are true and possible.[9]

As emerges, a clear distinction is established between India and the 'West' here. The Indian audiences are *informed* and *reminded* of how India's secularism has always been a functional dictum,a premise for the definition of nation-hood. A 'we' is thus staged vis-à-vis the 'other,' the lose category of 'the West.' Simulta-

---

[8] *Sanskriti*may be translated as culture. The usage of the word has also become commonplace in colloquial Hindi.
[9] Vajpayee, Atal Behari, Reaction to the No-Confidence Motion of the then prime minister H.D. Devegowda, (June 12, 1996).

neously, an internal otherization is seen at work here. Christianity and Islam are projected as 'outsiders.'[10] However, what is maintained is that in spite of such heterogeneity, a sense of homogeneity has prevailed in India *historically*, owing to the ideal of secularism.[11] Thus, once again, secularism becomes the pre-condition for the very existence, the imagination of the nation.

It is important here to zoom into the specificity of these words delivered by Vajpayee in terms of the internal subtle shifts which may be located in the rhetoric of the three prime ministers. The only of the three who headed a Bharatiya Janata Party (BJP) led coalition government,[12] Vajpayee's referential archive to explain the term secularism, especially to internal audiences, is primarily informed by a *Hindu* and a *Hindi* vocabulary. Here India always stands for Hindu traditions and secularism is primarily a Hindu achievement (essentially conceived as tolerance exercised by Hindus). This is a notable difference compared to the rhetoric of Rao and Singh, both of whom are Congress leaders and who, even though not shying away from using Hindu resources to make sense of the term secularism, are seen as emphasizing more on Indian pluralism

---

10 This is also reflective of a more general rhetoric which may be attached to numerous voices who lay claims to a Hindu 'indigenous' population and historically trace the entry of the 'outsider.' Many also have stressed how Muslims in India have a Hindu ancestry. One such recent speaker of the same is Subramanian Swamy, President of the Janata Party (People's Party) (see article *How to Wipe Out Islamic Terror*, (July 16, 2011) http://bharatabharati.wordpress.com/2011/10/04/how-to-wipe-out-islamic-terror-subramanian-swamy/ (accessed on March 17, 2012).

11 This greatness of the Indian tryst with Secularism is also celebrated in other speeches by the prime minister. Some examples: "India's great contribution to human kind is the idea of Sarva Dharma Sambhava." (Singh, Manmohan, *Remembering Netaji S.C. Bose- A Great Life dedicated to Nation Building*, Address at the Birth Anniversary Celebrations of S.C. Bose, New Delhi, (January 23, 2007)); "Secularism in the Indian context can only be explained through Sarva Dharma Sambhava. From the Vedic age until the modern age it is this dictum that has kept us alive." (Vajpayee, Atal Behari, Speech in honour of the India's first President, Rajendra Prasad, (December 2–3, 1992)).

12 It is important to add here that the Hindu Right Wing comprises, among others, of the BJP as its political faction. BJP politician Ram Krishna Advani was highly instrumental in mobilizing the controversial *Ram RathYatra* (1990), a procession undertaken from the state of Gujarat up to Ayodhya, where he was seen as a modern day *Ram*, the Hindu God whose birth place Ayodhya is claimed to be, on a Toyota car decorated like the deity's mythological chariot, with the claim to construct a temple on the spot where the *Babri Masjid* stood. Most BJP politicians including the prime minister Vajpayee have held portfolios of the RSS (RashtriyaSwayamsevakSangh or the National Patriotic/Volunteer Organization) which is termed as the cultural guild of the Hindu Right Wing. Vajpayee's personal trajectory thus as a BJP politician is very crucial to the debate on secularism. Together the BJP and the RSS have historically been ardent in their campaigns for a Hindu nation.

and democracy as against their BJP counterpart. Though both Singh and Rao also speak of a civilizational legacy, and therein attempt to re-project history in producing a present and a future, in Singh's speeches (the two examples stated under the neologism tolerance prove this) secularism is often slipped as an adjective, an aside, understood as another face of pluralism and Indian democracy. Thus, even though the cosmetic set up of the presentation of the paradigm is the same, the style and the intentionality indicates subtle differences.

Another factor which emerges from the analysis is that in many references to the paradigm of secularism, particularly before Ayodhya, the term was used as such with no translated versions, even in speeches which were delivered in the Hindi language (often termed as *Secularvād.*) There has been no term or co-equivalent to 'secularism' in any Indian language (Chatterjee 1998: 345). However, post the events of the demolition of the *Masjid* in Ayodhya, different neologisms were developed in numerous Indian languages. It is in this context that the events of 1992, which formulate a backdrop to this analysis, acquire prime importance. Following a national crisis, when the secular fabric of the country, and in turn its acclaimed unifying ideological red-string came to be questioned, the 'Indian' terminology and archive was developed (or at least, revoked through a selective re-appropriation of history) so as to communicate the term to the perceived Indian audiences. In order to 'save' the idea of secularism and in turn to save the acclaimed founding idea of India itself, the prime ministers have attempted to communicate the message in a language which is understood by their audiences. It is against this backdrop that other neologisms of secularism have emerged in India. One noteworthy term in this context is *Dharna-nirpekshta* (literally meaning 'religious non-bias'). *Dharma* here is the Hindi term for religion though it is widely understood as a 'way of life,' (literally translates to 'duty,') in sync with the ideology of religion-as-faith, as religion is not deemed an appropriate category for grasping the understanding of the numerous Indian faiths.[13]

Vajpayee, in an open address in the North Indian city of Fatehabad, Haryana stated

> We are famous for Dharma-nirpekshta. For us Dharma-nirpekshta is not a negative ideology. It is a positive vision. There should be no biases and discrimination on the basis of religion. People are free to practice the religion of their choice. The Constitution provides a guarantee of complete religious freedom(...).[14]

---

13 For more on this debate see Nandy1998: 321.
14 Vajpayee, Atal Behari, Open Address in Fatehabad, Haryana, (August 19, 1999).

However, the phrase has often been attacked by the Indian academic world[15] as also by several political actors and parties. It was seen as having a negative approach to religion *per se*. Thus, once again, the local atmosphere contributed to a transformation in the explanation of the term secularism. It led instead to the definition of secularism being modified into the paradigm of *Sarva Dharma Sambhava* and the category of *Sampraday* or *Pantha-nirpekshta*. (*Sampraday* and *Pantha* refer to the term 'communal' and thus through this modification secularism has been developed into the derivative of communal non-bias.)[16]

The one collectively agreed upon basis is the identification of religious-diversity and acceptance of religion as a primary life-guiding dictum for Indians. Hence the acknowledgement that secularism in India can never be 'atheistic or irreligious'. However, the 'chutnification'[17] of the term with numerous neo-logisms and derivatives has also produced ambivalences in its concrete understanding. Though clearly stated that the term does not mean that India or Indians are irreligious, it is never really specified by the prime ministers, as to how the State and the religious sphere ought to be separated.

Another decisive derivative to the paradigm which defines the other to the term in the Indian context is *communalism*. In most addresses by *all* the prime ministers, a continuity is maintained whereby secularism is defined vis-à-vis this ideological other. The term has a very *indigenous* connotation in India, described as "conflict, often accompanied with violence, between religious communities, primarily the Hindus and the Muslims, for political and/or economic gains" (Vohra 1997: 2). An enormous thrust has been laid upon defining what secularism entails for Indians by defining what it ought not to be. Thus, in continuity with the attempts to produce a secular India before internal audiences, the profiling of aberrations to this desired ideal-type is also undertaken, often by creating obvious dichotomizations between secularism and communalism.

Rao, attempts the same in the following address given on the occasion of an award ceremony to honour citizens who have epitomized communal harmony in their personal lives

> But of course in a pluralistic society, by definition we have to get over certain tendencies which go against the name of a pluralistic society. And it is here that communalism has

---

15 For e.g. Spivak Gayatri, *The Trajectory of the Subaltern in my Work*, Keynote Lecture at the University of California at Santa Barbara (2004) see online: http://www.youtube.com/watch?v=2ZHH4ALRFHw (accessed on December 16, 2011).
16 It is imperative to note here that the term *communal* and *communalism* have a specific meaning in India which is embedded in the colonial and post-colonial Indian history.
17 The Hindi term *Chutney* refers to a mixture. It has also been used in the English language with regards to an Indianization of the English language.

to be tackled first because we are secular, because we are pluralistic, because historically there is really no need, no reason at all for any communal feeling in this country. This country has welcomed everyone; this country has absorbed everyone who came from outside, people who came as invaders became permanently part of this country. So this is the kind of attraction which India has held for centuries together and there is no reason why it should not be so hereafter.[18]

As evident, once again a shifting re-staging of history which is a specific kind of history, is at work here as a validating hinge for Indian secularism. Secularism is projected as having a life of its own in the country. The phrases 'because historically there is no need for any communal feeling in this country,' and 'it should not be so hereafter,' indicate that the national imagination is rendered complete by secularism acting as the interface between India's rich past and its promising future. The paradigm of secularism is utilized to even explain to Indians- communalism ought to be combated *because* India is secular, because it is an attack on India's very survival. In another address Rao re-iterated the statement of India's first prime minister Jawaharlal Nehru, in stating that "we must have it clearly in our minds and in the mind of the country that the alliance of religion and politics in the shape of communalism is the most dangerous alliance and it yields the most abnormal kind of illegitimate breed."[19] On another occasion, communalism is projected in a metaphor as a 'virus,'[20] which plagues the national fabric of the Indian society. India is thus again profiled as a country "that can never go against religion. But nonetheless needs to protect its identity of those elements that inject its politics with religious fervor or fundamentalism."[21]

The above analyzed derivatives of secularism which are used by the prime ministers to paint a secular India, indeed do project a multi-coloured, accommodating story. Vajpayee, in an address to the Nation in 1996, stated "The first mosque in India was established in Kerala under the rule of a Hindu king and his blessings. Similarly after Jesus's sacrifice and crucifixion, India saw the establishment of its first Church. These different places of worship belong to different religions and are a living example of our secular traditions."[22]

---

18 Indianprime minister, P.V. Narasimha Rao, *Communal Harmony-India's Heritage*, Address at the KabirPuraskar presentation ceremony, New Delhi, (August 13, 1994).
19 Rao, P.V. Narasimha, *Agenda Before the Nation*, Address at the Indian Upper House of Legislature, The Rajya Sabha, (March 11, 1993).
20 Rao, P.V. Narasimha, *Towards a Strong and Vibrant India*, Speech delivered at the first meeting of the reconstituted National Intergration Council, New Delhi, (November 2, 1991).
21 Rao, P.V. Narasimha, *Communal Harmony-India's Heritage*, Address at the KabirPuraskar presentation Ceremony, New Delhi, (August 13, 1994).
22 Vajpayee. A.B., Address to the Nation, (May 19, 1996).

However, some scraping beneath the political rhetoric brings numerous contradictions to light. Whereas, on the surface, the Constitution is projected as propagating the idea of non-intervention in religious affairs and a distancing between the state and the religious domain, an a-religiosity in politics,[23] there exist articles such as those recognizing the rights of religious minorities (Article 30(1) specifically). Unlike all the articles which are applicable to *all* citizens as individuals, such articles are eventually in recognition of community based rights. Besides, there are personal laws or religious codes (especially instrumental in the case of marriage and inheritance of property) which govern the lives of people depending on their religion by birth. Many religious practices have been termed unjust and imply a deprivation of fundamental freedoms guaranteed to the citizens by the Constitution. Thus, the constitutional rights of individuals often come into conflict with personal religious codes. In some instances the state is inevitably pushed to intervene in the 'religious' sphere, thereby technically departing from the principle of a 'strict wall of separation' between religion and state principles.[24]

What emerges from this context is that even though within political rhetoric, the entry of religion into political affairs and vice-versa is condemned, in reality the two spheres do entangle in numerous ways. Thus, notions of what comprises the 'political,' the 'private', the 'public' and the 'religious' remain floating, constantly negotiated and fuzzy in their boundaries. In a remarkable rhetorical strategy, in addresses to internal audiences, these spaces of ambivalence are left loose and never demarcated. It suffices to state that religion ought not to enter the domain of politics and communalism is the avoidable other to Indian secularism. But what really the intervention of one sphere into another means is stra-

---

[23] For example Vajpayee comments "Secular does not mean that we are irreligious or opposed to religion. This is a religious country. But secularism definitely means that religion will not be controlled or run by the state. That the state does not have its own religion. That all religions are equal in the eyes of the state. None shall be discriminated against. Really our secularism is a positive secularism, not negative (...)This is not just a wish but a necessity." (Vajpayee, A.B., Address on the prevalence of normalcy in the state of Jammu and Kashmir, (January 9, 1999)).

[24] The State has in the past actively intervened in the personal laws of the Hindu community. For e.g. abolishing the practice of *Satī*, the dowry system and untouchability. Regardless of the underlying social necessity of the same for the protection of the fundamental rights of those on the receiving side of these personal customs, it is often alleged that this intervention of the state has been particularly more active in the case of the majority Hindu community. However, a similar firmness is not shown by the state with regard to several Muslim personal laws which also come in conflict with fundamental rights of many belonging to the community. This leniency towards a minority community has led to allegations by the Hindu Right and parties such as the Bharatiya Janata Party (BJP) that the Congress is only 'pseudo-secular.'

tegically silenced owing to the ambiguity of the existing distinctions. Instead, the emphasis is diverted on notions of tolerance, communal harmony, pluralism and what is popularly and repetitively termed as the 'Unity in Diversity' master code. This phrase (Unity in Diversity), acquires a special significance in India. Its use is commonplace also in colloquial language. It simultaneously contributes to producing 'India' as well as serving as a justification for its secularism. For example, Singh in an address to a conference on 'Democracy, Development and Inclusiveness,' states before Indian audiences as also external ones "(...)for us in India, democracy is not just a way of life, it is the way of life. For our nation the defining principle has been and will always be 'Unity in Diversity.' This is the idea of India."[25] Noteworthy again here is how in Singh's addresses secularism and its derivates become an adjective, an aside whose meaning is not explicitly explained, by shifting the emphasis to democracy. Silencing is a prominent part of political speech, used in order to communicate with large audiences. In Singh's addresses, this silencing implies an elaborate emphasis on democracy whose co-ordinates are also never really unpacked, rather assumed. Secularism simultaneously is placed next to the words democracy, unity in diversity and pluralism, often within the realm of the same sentence. This may be read as a means to understand which colour and flavor the paradigm of secularism is given sometimes through strategic silencing and on others through strategic highlighting. The following may be read as another example of the same

> In a country of the size and diversity like ours, it is only the concern and care for the sensibilities of each other which can ensure a smooth functioning of the institutions we have created. This is the only way to maintain peace and harmony amongst the people of India... The delicate fabric of our nation woven around democracy and secularism is the only anchor-sheet for our country's existence.[26]

Secularism thus often appears in co-occurrence with democracy.[27] The aforementioned categories of the existing Indian versions of secularism are of course not mutually exclusive.

There are other mechanisms which re-invest the imagination of a 'secular India' with a sense of truth within the addresses. An important constituent of

---

25 Singh, Manmohan, *Democracy- The Way of Life in India*, Address at a Conference on Democracy, Development and Social Inclusion, New Delhi, (December 8, 2005).
26 Rao, P.V. Narasimha, *Countering Communal Forces*, Address to The Nation in the aftermath of Ayodhya, (December 6, 1992).
27 For example in a random sample of 10 speeches collected, the term secularism occurs 29 times whereas the term democracy occurs 24 times, mostly co-occurring and clubbed together in the same paragraph in the speech.

the same is the utilization of 'national' heritage. This implies 'using the past,' and therein also *producing* the past, for the cause of India's pluralist secularity. Memory is revoked by the prime ministers at varying levels for a dual purpose. First, to re-produce the idea of a *common* past, which contributes to the production of a sense of being a sum i.e. a unified national space. Second, to re-create or re-negotiate the same past by inducing it with new imaginations to fit the agenda at stake. Therefore, to produce India as a secular nation, all three prime ministers revoke examples from (i) India's homogenized civilizational past, (ii) Indian mythology and literature, (iii) the first Indian armed struggle for independence in 1857, (iv) the Indian national movement for independence and (v) Indian national heroes who embraced the paradigm of secularism and are stalwarts in Indian history.

Numerous addresses proceed with sweeping statements which make references to India's 'civilizational' past as an illustration of its secularity. For example, the addresses are replete with phrases like

> "The notion of tolerance (...) is powerfully reflected in the history of the civilization of India"[28],
>
> "Our ancient civilization provides a strong base in which to build a model for regulating the interaction of religion and politics,"[29]
>
> "(...) liberal outlook is a distinctive feature of our civilization."[30]

Such opening and closing phrases, which are used before or after discussing the notion of secularism, help advance the idea that the paradigm has a clear history in the country.

In continuation with the same mechanism, illustrations from an abstract, vague and generalized Indian mythology and literature are revoked. It is here that certain literary figures acquire importance. For example, the famous Sufi Saint Kabir is often quoted in the addresses. Kabir's work reflects a combination of the Hindi language with influences of many local North Indian dialects and bears an immense mass appeal for Indian audiences. Besides, as a literary fig-

---

[28] Rao, P.V. Narasimha, *Towards a Strong and Vibrant India*, Speech delivered at the first meeting of the reconstituted National Intergration Council, New Delhi, (November 2, 1991).

[29] Rao, P.V. Narasimha, *Religion- A Unifying Force*, Address at the opening of the International Conference on Religion and Politics, organized by the Rajiv Gandhi Institute for Contemporary Studies, (January 30, 1994).

[30] Rao, P.V. Narasimha, *Religion- A Unifying Force*, Address at the opening of the International Conference on Religion and Politics, organized by the Rajiv Gandhi Institute for Contemporary Studies, (January 30, 1994).

ure, the saint also epitomizes themes of Hindu-Muslim unity and the search for a religion which does not constrain one to a single God or holy book. He is thus used as an example of communal harmony for the audiences.

Similarly, the use of a famous phrase from the Rig Veda "Ekam Sad, Vtpra Bahudha Vadadti" meaning 'Truth is one, sages call it by different names,' is meant to revisit the value of religious tolerance, India's own ancient derivative of secularism.

The above illustration points to another development in the history of some of the religious sects in India: The idea of a singular God, that there is only one Supreme Being, who is worshipped by different names in different religions. These influences of the newer religious worlds, initiated by the likes of the *Bhakti Movement* and some parts of the *Bengal Renaissance*, introduced a new genre of pluralism, which was different from polytheistic Hinduism's everyday acknowledgement and, sometimes even indifference, to the existence of multiple gods who weren't one's own. However, both understandings of pluralism are confused in the addresses under the clubbed category of 'ancient Indian religion' or 'Indian mythology' or 'our ancient scriptures' etc. In pointing out these differences in the meanings of *pluralism*, I do not intend to challenge that one is more relevant or authentic than the other. Rather, I wish to question the assumedhomogeneity and given-ness of the term *religious pluralism* itself, which is seen as synonymous to *secularism* in the Indian context.[31]

However, Memory does not just imply the strategic re-visiting of the past in order to conjure certain elements of a common heritage but also forgetting. In all such examples, which are cited to actualize the theme of national integration, certain elements, counter-examples, are strategically silenced. The history of colonial, and later a newly de-colonized India, is also replete with occasions of communal tensions between the Hindus and the Muslims which found a climax in the actualization of the Partition of British India into India and Pakistan. These tensions have found a continuity in an independent India as well but

---

[31] The above statement derives its inspiration from Wendy Doniger's article in the *Outlook magazine* (titled *All in the big tent: how 'lost' its old stripes in the service of the new Indian state* (special issue January 26, 2014), which discusses pluralism in Hinduism and numerous renunciant sects in India. The author gives enough evidence in the cause of pluralism and its different forms but my own contribution here is in deflecting our attention to how pluralism in itself as an Indian trope of secularism cannot be assumed to have a singular meaning. Thus if the Prime ministers use different excerpts from the words of different religious reformers, the same word pluralism, which is presented as a derivative of secularism, can bear different connotations. These differences are never outlined and a generalized understanding is used to construe the nation as secular (here embedded in its pluralism).

are purposely forgotten when the prime ministers wish to revoke the Indian imagination of a secular nation. A common mechanism adopted by the prime ministers is the strategy of diversion. This is sometimes done explicitly, especially in the face of communal riots (as in the advent of the Babri Masjid-Mandir controversy in 1992 and the Gujarat riots of 2002), when the internal audiences are directly asked to erase the memory of such aberrations. However, it is also pursued implicitly when the theme is rhetorically shifted to a focus on India's economic agenda. It is here that the discourse shifts more categorically to the 'India emerging' story. Thematically the emphasis thus moves to economic reforms and the neo-liberal agenda adopted by the state for India to emerge as an economic powerhouse. Thus, the absence of the discussion on the paradigm of secularism in some addresses, even in the course of conflicts and crises such as Ayodhya and Gujarat, does not imply that the notion is unimportant but points towards its silencing by deflecting the discussion to another pressing agenda-India, the emerging economic power.

Statements such as "The going has never been as good for India in the past as it is now... Our economy has been growing at an impressive pace of over 8 %... Wherever I go, I see our nation on the move,"[32] "Indian is certainly on a march," "There is a visible progress all around," indicate the metaphor of speed which is attached to India.

On some occasions the themes of secularism and India as an emerging power are beautifully brought together under the same umbrella. For example in the following lines Singh states

> It is not only us but the entire world, which is viewing India as an emerging power of these times. The whole world is eagerly watching the manner in which India is making rapid economic progress. And this economic growth is happening within the framework of a liberal democracy. Our country is a multi-cultural, multi-religious, multi-lingual and multi-ethnic nation (...)It is because of this that the entire world's attention is riveted on us.[33]

Here, it is important to note that the discourse of an 'emerging India' takes place within the framework of a liberal 'multi-religious,' 'multi-cultural' democracy. Thus, India's distinctiveness is embedded not only in that it is an emerging power but one that is simultaneously secular and democratic.

---

32 Singh, Manmohan, *India-Marching Steadily Towards New Frontiers*, Address on the occasion of Indian Independence Day, (August 15, 2006).
33 Singh, Manmohan, *A Resurgent India-The Roadmap for Lasting Peace and Prosperity*, Address on the occasion of the Indian Independence Day, (August 15, 2005).

India is on the road to progress. The whole world is watching us with expectation...There comes a time in the history of a nation when it can be said that the time has come to make history. We are today at the threshold of such an era. The world wants us to do well and take our rightful place on the world stage. (...) Let us come together, as one nation, strengthened by our plurality, to work shoulder to shoulder and build a new India.[34]

Another distinct mechanism to cause digression from communal violence, which disturbs the continuity of secularism as a cohesive interface between India's past and its future, is to locate 'real' actors which disturb this ideological continuity. Thus, while communalism is the ideological other projected against secularism, other actors which destroy this imagination of a secular emerging India are situated in a discursive strategy to shift the blame. This refers in some cases (as with Rao specifically) to internal actors[35] and in Vajpayee's case to an external actor that instigates national crevices, most prominently Pakistan.[36]

3 Responding to the Outside – Producing a secular *and* emerging India

The imagination of a secular and an emerging India is at the same time projected for the 'outside.' This raises the obvious question as to why it is imperative for this profile that India be projected as *secular?*

In an address to a joint session of the Parliament on the occasion of the then Russian President, V. Putin's, visit to India in 2000, prime minister Vajpayee states

> We are commemorating this year the fiftieth anniversary of the establishment of our Republic. We have reposed faith in the principles of democracy which are today universal ideals

---

34 Singh, Manmohan, *A Resurgent India-The Roadmap for Lasting Peace and Prosperity*, Address on the occasion of the Indian Independence Day, (August 15, 2005).
35 Rao explicitly relates the Ayodhya crisis with the BJP. "I am sad to state that the BJP-VHP combine has not only failed to respond to my efforts but as a matter of fact have gone about deliberately to not only thwart my efforts but also to mislead the nation (...) What has happened today in Ayodhya where the Babri Masjid structure has been demolished, is a matter of great shame for all Indians."(Rao, PV Narasimha, *Countering Communal Forces*, Address to The Nation in the aftermath of Ayodhya (New Delhi: December 6, 1992)).
36 Given that the Gujarat riots of 2002 occurred when the BJP was in power in the state itself as also at the Centre, the blame is deflected implicitly to 'external forces.' During this period one also finds Vajpayee revoking memory of the Kargil war of 1999 with Pakistan as a deflection mechanism. The history of the Partition, the wars over the disputed state of Jammu and Kashmir and even the ungovernable spread of terrorist attacks are all factors that are repeatedly and most blatantly associated with Pakistan.

providing for the growth of the human being and society. Our democratic structures are rooted in the cardinal values of pluralism, secularism and tolerance.[37]

The underlying idea is to paint and celebrate a multi-religious, multi-linguistic, multi-ethnic India. However, this is done carefully and strategically with a more pressing intentionality to produce an India which is not in conflict with a larger comity of nations, rather in ideological cohesion with themes of democracy and pluralism. In this context, on numerous occasions, the prime ministers are seen as situating India on an ideological common ground with other countries under a larger United Nations umbrella. In the following lines, Vajpayee attempts the same in Washington

> It is the proud privilege of both India and the United States that our two countries are models-one in the East and the other in the West-of democracy as well as unity in diversity. We both [sic.], cherish, preserve and promote universal human rights such as freedom of speech, political choice and religious belief.[38]

In the above lines the prime minister attempts to achieve multiple ends. First an emphasis is placed on the theme of *unity in diversity*, as done also in addresses before internal audiences. Second, Vajpayee locates India in ideological conformity with the United States, which is also projected here as a vibrant diversified democracy. Lastly, this established image of India is also projected as a desired ideal, a 'model' for other nation-states. Another example in the same direction is in the following statement made by Narasimha Rao, much earlier (in 1993) with regard to Indo-UK relations. Rao states

> "Both our governments share a strong commitment to the UN, its basic purposes and principles as enshrined in the UN Charter (...) We recognize the threat to pluralistic and democratic societies and nation states from religious fundamentalism and narrow ethnic chauvinism. These threats need to be firmly countered through a renewed commitment to democracy and secularism.[39]

Here the emphasis is placed not just on the paradigms of democracy and secularism but also on a larger ideological framework of the United Nations. India is

---

[37] Vajpayee, Atal Behari, *A New Chapter in Indo-Russian Relations*, Special Joint Session of the Parliament on occasion of the visit of President of Russia, Vladimir Putin (New Delhi: October 4, 2000).

[38] Vajpayee, Atal Behari, *Gandhiji an Apostle of Peace*, Speech while unveiling the statue of Mahatma Gandhi (Washington: September 16, 2000).

[39] Rao, P.V. Narasimha, *India and the United Kingdom*, Banquet Speech in honour of the British prime minister, Mr. John Major, New Delhi, (January 25, 1993).

thus projected as a responsible secular democracy which embraces ideals that belong to a larger community of nation-states.

An important observation which emerges from *all* the addresses for external audiences is that though secularism as a paradigm is evoked repetitively, the prime ministers do not elaborate upon its underlying meaning in these addresses. Thus, it suffices to state that *India is secular*. However, the semantic contours of the paradigm are not explained. This is done with an underlying awareness that the Indian context may provide for multiple comprehensions which do not necessarily comply with the idea of a strict separation of the religious and the state spheres. Thus to avoid this clash, the addresses usually entail the term and pause, evoking it yet not explaining it, thus maintaining a teleological idea of a 'modern' secular India.

One line of continuation between the addresses delivered before perceived internal and external audiences is the justification offered as to why India ought to be secular. Though in the internal sphere it is re-iterated that there is no other possible environment in which such diversity could thrive, in external settings, the argument is sometimes also co-related to the Jammu and Kashmir conflict. The paradigm of secularism, in such instances, serves two simultaneous purposes- first it is used to defend India's ideational basis- i.e. to explain that 'India' can survive only if its diversity flourishes under secularism; and second to project an other, which is the state of Pakistan. The following lines sketch the same lucidly

> As for Kashmir, it is a part of India (...) Pakistan thinks that Kashmir should go to Pakistan because there is a Muslim majority. My answer and India's answer is that what do we do with some states where there is a Christian majority? Where do we send them? This is an absurd situation. We are a secular state. We have Hindus, Sikhs, Muslims, Christians, Parsis and all the religions of the world are available in India. I can't send people on religious lines to different countries and have only one community or religion in India. That is not my philosophy at all. The basis of the Indian state is secular. If the basis of the Pakistan state is different then I cannot help it (...) Indian history is witness that for thousands of years we have been absorbing cultures from abroad and also sending our own culture outside (...) it is just not possible for any Indian mind to accept that all people belonging to one religious denomination only should be in one country and no one else should come. That's not the philosophy of India.[40]

---

40 Rao, P.V. Narasimha, *Contributing to the New World Vision*, 'Address on Challenge and Opportunity in the Post Cold War Era-An Indian Perspective on the Emerging Structure of Inter-State Relations,' at the French Institute of International Relations, Paris, (September 29, 1992).

As evident, secularism is projected as the paradigm which allows multiple religions to co-exist in India, thus formulating the backbone of a unified national space. However, certain other elements also emanate from the address above. First, Pakistan is projected as the prominent other in that it lays claims on the state of Jammu and Kashmir which is viewed as an integral part of India. Second, the lines reflect why the Indian state's claim on the controversial territory are ever more emphatic- because to accept Pakistan's accession of the state would be a severe blow to India's secular image.[41] Third, the last lines of the quote illustrate how a *pars pro toto* synecdoche is employed here so that the 'Indian mind' may be generalized to epitomize acceptance and a secular outlook.

It is noteworthy that the emphasis on an India of the future is much more prominent in speeches addressing an external audience. The following lines by Manmohan Singh, delivered in Tokyo provide one such illustration

> I invite all of you to a youthful, dynamic, self-confident India, where more than a billion people are seeking socio-economic progress in the framework of a functioning democracy,...I am convinced that the 21st century will be the century of Asia...I invite you to join us to build a new India, a new Asia and a new world.[42]

In fact, this theme *finds* continuity also in a speech by Kamal Nath, Commerce and Industry Minister under Manmohan Singh, when giving a key note address at the 'Asia: An Emerging Giant' Conference in New York in 2006 "India today remains an unbeatable combination of an ancient civilization embracing economic globalization in a context that is open and democratic. And that is what really makes India the emerging giant which it has become."[43]

New themes of economic globalization and democracy are introduced in simultaneity to older ideals embedded in an 'ageless culture,' 'an ancient civilization,' reflecting the ideals of tolerance and secularism. In fact, secularism itself gets re-contextualized by a historical shift from India as a country in a crisis to India as a country 'on the move.' Thus an essential link may be located with market liberalization post 1991. Here the opening up of the Indian economy itself ought to be viewed as a historical process, not an ongoing condition and becomes a context which has contributed tremendously to the nature of the vo-

---

41 This partly also explains why on page 1 I lay emphasis on the *yet* in the statement "India is emerging yet secular and democratic." While 'emerging *yet* democratic' refers to an other being projected implicitly (China), secular is a referent to Pakistan.

42 Singh, Manmohan, *Expanding New Horizons of Indo-Japan Business Opportunities*, Speech at the Indo-Japan Business Luncheon Meeting, Tokyo, (December 15, 2006).

43 Nath, Kamal, *India: An Emerging Giant*, Keynote Address, Columbia University, (October 14, 2006).

cabulary of secularism used for external audiences. This is precisely where the *Emerging India* story engages *explicitly and implicitly* with the re-negotiation of secularism in that not only is secularism employed as a discursive stake in the materialization of a smooth market liberalization and as a diversion mechanism to shift the agenda from a nation struck in religious crisis to one that is secular and democratic and ready to emerge, but also implicitly in that it has also constituted a transformation of the rhetoric also of the Hindu Right wing BJP itself. When at the centre all three governments have forwarded the cause of market liberalization and more recently the BJP has also severely played down its *Hindutva*[44] politics, at least explicitly, and shifted its rhetoric to developmental aims and India's economic emergence. The statements on Indian secularism in the international debates, especially in the new millennium, are meant also to show that India is different from China and Iran, Iraq, Afghanistan, and Pakistan. The latter four become the basis of staging an otherization in terms of Indian secularity specifically in projecting a tolerant and syncretic India whereas in reference to the former, another emergent power, secularism is a convenient aside clubbed with democracy. These are the main competitors and 'India' wants to shine above them. This significant international context ought also to be borne in mind when viewing how secularism is translated by Indian prime ministers for the world audiences. Secularism thus, whether when at the core of the debates, or as an embellishing adjective that furthers the cause of India being a favourable democracy, becomes a window to the larger ongoing shifts in how the Indian state reacts to, re-configures, and even profits from an environment of global processes where the very category of the Nation-State stands thoroughly challenged.

---

[44] In his work on religious nationalism in India, Van der Veer aptly summarizes the meaning of the term, as propagated by the BJP, as follows: "The party's program stresses *Hindutva*, Hinduness, a term explored by the Hindu nationalist leader V. D. Savarkar in the 1920 s: A Hindu means a person who regards this land of Bharat Varsha, from the Indus to the Seas, as his FatherLand as well as his Holy-Land that is the cradle of his religion. The term *Hindutva* equates religious and national identity: an Indian is a Hinduan equation that puts important Indian religious communities, such as Christians and Muslims, outside the nation." (Van der Veer 1994: 1).

4 How silences speak and expressions silence – Conclusions

We have seen how a *secular emerging* India is discursively produced by three Indian prime ministers. In both settings the paradigm finds overlaps: Indian diversity and the idea of secularism are not an invented/imported ideal but one with identifiable roots in an 'Indian' past. However, what is new to this discourse is that in the external scenario, the emphasis shifts more in the direction of maintaining an ideological cohesiveness with the world. Especially in environments that speak to the language of the UN, where democracy, liberalism, secularism and pluralism are much celebrated themes, the prime ministers' addresses provide the additional tinge of conformism. Aware that in the Indian context, ambiguities regarding the very understanding of the term persist vis-à-vis the distinction of the religious sphere from the domain of the state, these addresses meant for the 'outside', while engaging with the theme of secularism, do not indulge in elaborate explanations of the paradigm. In most addresses the prime minister stops after having stated that India is a secular democracy which now seeks its economic destiny of emergence. No advances follow such statements. Thus a silence is strategically maintained. Paradoxically, in the internal setting, there appears to be an over-emphasized elaboration of the explanations, induced almost with a sense of urgency and desperation and a language which employs overloaded 'religious' referents. But here, even though elaborate explanations ensue, the boundaries between the 'religious' and the state are never explicitly explained, rather silenced under the garb of neo-logisms. Thus, the external reflects spaces of silence which inevitably *speak* of a strategic quiet maintained in explaining secularism, while the internal reflects an arena of over-expression which nonetheless *silences* the gray zones of controversy looming large over the paradigm in India. The dual-faced mirror of secularism is thus utilized to reflect only what the resources of the given context allow to be reflected. This mirror of secularism thus, again, becomes an interface reflecting the past and projecting the future.

Within the purview of the speeches of the three politicians, subtle differences between the rhetoric of the BJP leader Vajpayee and the Congress leaders Rao and Singh highlight not just the ambivalences in translating secularism for Indians, but also that certain categories like *Indian civilization, Indian heritage, our traditions, our past*, become shorthand terms, often like secularism itself, presented as un-disputed facts. Though cosmetically the same, the visions behind these terms are different (for Vajpayee more of a Hindu achievement and for Rao/Singh a syncretic mix which also utilizes the archive of other religious resources). What remains important though is that minus these differences, the paradigm of secularism remains an important stake within the discourse of *all three* leaders.[45] In that sense, all three lend their voice to a consistent national master narrative whichbases the idea of India itself within the ideal of secularism.

This chapter has attempted to show how *secularism* is translated by the Indian PMs, in its mostpublic and official version, for audiences within and without. It has elucidated how the primeministers 'speak' the Indian nation *secular*, unleashing its (E)merging faces- that is how the external and internal imaginations of India are made to *merge* in the concept of secularism. At the same time,- the *secular* India *merges* with that of an *emerging* India in the same way as India's past and future arelexically made to *merge* in the addresses to conjure a present which is *emerging*.

References

Bhargava, Rajeev. 2006. "Indian secularism: an alternative trans-cultural ideal" (modified version of "The Distinctiveness of Indian Secularism"). In *The Future of Secularism*, edited by. T.N. Srinivasan, 20–53. New Delhi: Oxford University Press.

Blom Hansen, Thomas.1999. *The Saffron Wave: Democracy and Hindu Nationalism in Modern India*. New Jersey: Princeton University Press.

Chatterjee, Partha. 2005."Secularism and tolerance." In *Secularism and its Critics*, edited by Rajeev Bhargava, 345–79. New Delhi: Oxford University Press.

Hannoum, Abdelmajid. 2008. "What is an order of time?" (review of Hartog, François. 2003 *Régimes d'historicité: Présentisme et Expériences du Temps*. Paris: Seuil). *History and Theory*47: 458–71.

Hartog, François. 2005. "Time and heritage."*Blackwell, Museum International*57, 3:7–18.

Mishra, Balbhadra, and Satyaprakaśa, eds. 1971. *Manaka Angrezī-Hindī-Kośa*. Prayāg: HindīSāhityaSammelana.

Nandy, Ashish. 2005. "The politics of secularism." In *Secularism and Its Critics*, edited by Rajeev Bhargava, 321–43. New Delhi: Oxford University Press.

---

45 In fact, with the general elections for 2014, heated debates on the nature of Indian secularism have returned to the forefront. This especially since the BJP's announcement of its next Prime ministerial candidate, Narendra Modi, Chief Minister of Gujarat, a controversial political figure, who hasremained in power in the state since, and in spite of, the riots in 2002. One of the many controversial statements made by Modi on the topic has been "Secularism to me means India First." Though cloaked in rhetoricin favour of market liberalization which is used to generate promises for a better economic future, the aboveline evokes the prominent question: *Whose* and *which* India is Modi referring to? The electoral campaigning of 2014, at the time of the final reviewing of this contribution,confirms thatthe topic of secularism continues to be an important discursive stake in Indian politics.

Van der Veer, Peter. 1994. *Religious Nationalism*. Berkeley: University of California Press.
Vohra, Ranbeer. 1997. *The Making of India: A Historical Survey.* Armonk-New York-London:ME Sharp Inc.

Beatrice Renzi
Anti-caste Radicalism, Dalit Movements and the Many Critiques of Secular Nationalism in India

> "[...] the imposition of secularism by Nehru, in its inner logic, derived its true force in forestalling social transformation by positing communalism (defined as deviation from secularism) as the main enemy, in effect being, paradoxically, also a recipe for how not to fight communalism as a deeper ordering of social power relations!"
>
> Saroj Giri (2010: 136)

> "There is an overwhelming consensus among scholars and journalists (not to speak of a large section of common people) that India is a nation of Hindus (or a Hindu majority nation), and that the main fight is between communalists and secularists over its definition."
>
> Gail Omvedt (1995: 92)

Why is it that Dalits[1], in their quest for equality, do not abandon religious conversions, which fragment and weaken their claims on the secular nation state? It was with this question that the convener of a conference entitled "Plural Societies and Imperatives of Development: Religions, Communities, Citizenship", held in April 2010 at Jawaharlal Nehru University, New Delhi, concluded his presentation. While the question remained muted at the conference, the search for answers revolves around bitterly antagonistic perspectives on the role of religion in defining the collective identities of marginalized groups and their participation in India's history, democracy and the nation. This paper examines the many and often highly contentious discourses involved in a Dalit critique of secular nationalism and its cultural construction of caste and power in India. The aim is to contextualize these debates historically, so as to unveil how a discourse on sec-

---

[1] 'Dalit', literally means crushed or, in a wider sense, oppressed. As a difference to other terminologies (e.g. *'harijan'*, *'avarna'*, 'untouchable', 'scheduled caste' etc.), which have been used to identify roughly the same group of heterogeneous peoples traditionally excluded from the *chaturvarna* system, the term 'Dalit' projects an identity based on socially constructed systems of exploitation rather than on caste, may it be defined in religious or secular terms. It therefore denounces externally enforced conditions, rather than ascribing qualities to human beings. Nevertheless, also the designation 'Dalit' remains contested both from within and as an external attempt at social categorization and objectification. While an examination of the ideological repertoires at play in the politics of naming goes beyond the scope of this chapter, we consider it important to approach 'Dalit' movements within the larger framework of anti-caste radicalism.

ular nationalism has come to define India's self-conception and its path to development and democratic deepening.

1 Power and 'the Hermeneutics of Interculturality': Rethinking Secular Nationalism across Narrative Orders and Socio-political Agency

Many postcolonial and cultural studies have convincingly demonstrated that even the conceptualization of what is understood as religion is the result of fluctuating historical, political and epistemological processes involving a multiplicity of narrative orders and socio-political agents, often in mutual competition with each other.[2] When approached analytically, these processes draw us into intercultural interpretations which require that meanings and practices be contextualized, taking into account their underlying 'regimes of truth' and the way collective identities are articulated and publicly represented. Intercultural understanding in turn works through dialogical exchanges, resulting from interpretative streams going in both directions. In the present paper, the analysis of discourse will serve to explore "the relations of power which structure the inter-discursivity, or the inter-textuality, of the field of knowledge" (Hall 1996: 136), and which impact on the way power is maintained, reconfigured or subverted in the social order. In so doing, we will be able to pick out the secular as a discursive thread so as to demonstrate its entangled relation to diverse notions of religiosity, its inherently political nature and its far-reaching sociological implications.

It is in this sense that our investigation pursues what Martin Fuchs has termed 'the hermeneutics of interculturality'.[3] Taking the concept of religion and its historical and cultural constructions as examples, Fuchs highlights the difference between 'the hermeneutics of interculturality' as an analytical approach or level of translation and an approach which is premised upon terms of comparison constructed around a predefined matrix of presumed general applicability:

---

[2] See for examples with reference to India: Dalmia 1997, Dirks 2001, Van der Veer 2001 and Mandair & Dressler 2011.
[3] This expression is taken from Fuchs 2004. For further elaborations on related perspectives, see also Fuchs 2009 and 1999.

> "Two different practices of translation become visible through the examples of the 'religionizing' of non-Western cultures: One which sends forth concepts, so as to 'grasp' (or, if necessary, construct) matters and through these concepts the characteristics of a collective; the other, which expresses itself in the possibility of a critical correction of the first form of translation and is informed by the idea of understanding the context, emphasizing situational connotations, pragmatic multivalences and the subjective capability of attributing meaning. For the question of interculturality and the debate on sociological comparison it would be important to bring more clearly to the attention the implications of the different forms of translation, so as to gain clarity over the level of translation which is being addressed and the implications thereof" (Fuchs 2004: 452; translation by the author)[4].

In the first form of translation mentioned above, the notion of religion, constructed as an analytical category beyond situated histories and sociopolitical agencies, is then applied to structure and to represent the lived realities of peoples with respect to given frames of communitarian and national belonging. This approach has served the West in its encounters with non-Western cultures, as much as it has served to legitimize 'universalist' representational claims originating from within the same allegedly integrated cultural context. For Indian secularism, Romila Thapar reminds us that,

> "Because the practice of religion is so closely tied to caste, the nature of religion is not similar to that of Europe, and in the Indian context the secularist dialogue has to include caste, which again makes it different from the European experience. This becomes all the more pertinent since both caste and secularism involve questions of social ethics, access to human rights, and the availability of these to all social groups" (Thapar 2007: 92).

If religion and caste are so intimately intertwined in India, how are we to understand those discourses, both autochthonous and foreign, which frame Indian secularism as the antidote to communalism without addressing the dynamics of socioeconomic and cultural inequalities based on caste? In turn, why do these discourses premised on an essentialized and externalized understanding of communalism tend to gloss over those internal processes which sought to sup-

---

4 "An den Beispielen der 'Religiosisierung' nicht-westlicher Kulturen werden zwei unterschiedliche Praktiken der Übersetzung sichtbar, die eine, die Begriffe aussendet, um Sachverhalte und über diese dann die Charakteristika eines Kollektivs zu 'fassen' (oder notfalls zu konstruieren), die andere, die sich in der Möglichkeit der kritischen Korrektur der ersten Übersetzungsform äußert und von der Idee des Kontextverstehens geprägt ist: dem Akzent auf situationale Konnotationen, pragmatische Polyvalenz und subjektive Bedeutungsgebungsfähigkeit. Für die Frage der Interkulturalität und die Diskussion des soziologischen Vergleichs wäre es wichtig, die Implikationen der verschiedenen Übersetzungsformen deutlicher vor Augen zu führen, um Klarheit darüber zu gewinnen, auf welcher Übersetzungsebene man sich bewegt und was deren Implikationen sind" (Fuchs 2004: 452).

press popular spaces of syncretic or 'Guru-Pir' religiosities that are prevalent among the lower castes? Lastly, how is the nation state, with its dominant coalitions and its nation-building projects (including secularism), implicated in such discourses? And how do they implicate us in terms of the level of translation we pursue in our sociological analysis?

In the light of these questions, we cannot but proceed by examining relations of power between different 'regimes of truth' which are involved in the way Dalits and minorities both engage in and are confronted by the symbolic and material embodiments of religion and secularity. Following Asad (2006, 2003, 1983, 1979), I set out to unpack these embodiments analytically into 'formations' of the secular, understood as an epistemological category, and of secularism, seen as a pattern of political rule (Asad 2006: 228). The investigation is therefore focused on how these formations of secularism and the secular interrelate with the underlying 'regimes of truth' that become manifest in different forms of social cohesion; or in other words, that find expression in the different ways collective identities are articulated into more or less stable communitarian, majoritarian/minoritarian and national belongings.

The literature on India has richly investigated and documented the role of religious-secular constructions in processes of caste/community/national formation in the history of the subcontinent (e.g. Thapar 1985; Dirks 2001; Bayly 1999), taking both a locally circumscribed caste/communitarian angle (e.g. Michelutti 2008; Rawat 2011; Mandair 2011; N. Chatterjee 2011; Rao 2010) and a broad national perspective (e.g. Khilnani 1997; Aloysius 1997; Menon 2006), and highlighting the inextricable link through which these processes are connected to different ideologies of rule and public order and the social forces that propel them. While I shall critically examine and build on some of the approaches offered by this literature, the focus of analysis here lies on the 'ideological field of force' which emerges from dominant and subordinated regimes of truth in mutual competition and which impacts in three crucial ways on formations of secularism and the secular: first, in the way the secular and the religious are constituted as publicly legible and locally contextual spaces; secondly, in the way secularism, defined as the patterns of political rule and public order, is structured and legitimized; and thirdly, in the way processes of collective identification take shape and position themselves in inter- and intra-caste/communitarian, majority/minority and national relations. It is important to highlight that the nation state is not understood here only in its institutional embodiments, but as a public persona with its own symbolic dimension, its own system of meaning that is reflective of the histories of conflict sedimented into the cultural memories of its peoples.[5]

2 *Doing the Secular:* Patterns of Political Rule and the Collective Representation of Dalits in India

From the early 1990s, the Dalit question forcefully re-emerged on to the national scene in India, pushing into the discursive center stage of politics, academia and the media. Over a century before the birth of the nation, during the formative phase of Indian nationalism, radical movements were already questioning the dominant discourse on 'Indian identity' as an essentially Brahmanical cultural construct. For these radicals, opposing Brahmanism and its organicist incorporation of marginalized groups, the Indian nation had to emerge not merely from the fight against British imperialism, but from the struggle against caste and feudal exploitation which the laboring masses had been waging for centuries against upper-caste oppressors, now self-styled as the new nationalist leadership. These anti-Brahmanical movements took shape in the context of fundamental changes, which from the nineteenth century came to articulate the public sphere, particularly in British India. While the colonial state, officially after the revolt of 1857, gradually disengaged from intervening in what it defined as the religious, supposedly apolitical domain of the community, Hindu and Muslim movements increasingly framed hitherto shared popular spaces within essentialized and homogenized political compartments. This was in response to colonial categorization and a three-way polemic with Christian missionary organizations (cf. Menon 2006). According to Rao, "Ironically, colonial intervention accelerated two seemingly contradictory processes: the secularization of caste and its novel association with Hindu religion. The colonial government abdicated direct responsibility for adjudicating issues of ritual status, religious rights, and community standing, though these were important realms of state intervention under the Old Regime. While this produced new openings for challenging caste discipline and Brahmanical norms, the mediation of Brahmanical knowledge (and the secularization of the Brahman's power as state functionary) played an important role in colonial knowledge formation" (Rao 2010: 43; see also Aloy-

---

[5] See in this regard also Wohlrab-Sahr's contribution in The Immanent Frame (www.ssrc.org): Multiple secularities and their normativities as an empirical subject (posted 13.12.2011).

sius 1997: 46, 51). Dirks argues that it was in the course of this process that "Hinduism became increasingly Brahmanic" (Dirks 2001: 151).

A Brahmanical interpretation of Hinduism, involving "bits and pieces from upper caste belief and ritual with one eye on the Christian and Islamic models" (Thapar 1985: 21), was now projected as the natural basis of social organization and national unity by the English-speaking class that came to dominate the pan-Indian public discourse during the anti-colonial struggle. Aloysius states that "The emergent Hinduism was at once Brahmanical as well as national. Nationalism and nationalist consciousness was the context in which the ideology of sacred and secular hierarchy transformed itself into, and articulated itself as, Hinduism" (Aloysius 1997: 104). Thapar notes that such processes were propelled by the rise of a powerful middle class, which "would find it useful to bring into politics a uniform, monolithic, Hinduism created to serve its new requirements" (Thapar 1985: 22). This was a class of urban professionals of mostly Brahman background with links to the rural upper castes, while the anti-Brahmanical movements were headed by leaders from low and untouchable castes. These movements sprung up sporadically in different regions across colonial India, such as Jotirao Phule's (1827–1890) Satyashodak Samaj in the Bombay Presidency, Swami Achhutanand's (1879–1938) Adi-Hindu Depressed Classes Association in the United Provinces and E.V. Ramasami, 'Periyar's' (1879–1973) Dravidian movement in the Madras Presidency. Some espoused radical anti-caste ideologies based on theistic or atheistic belief systems, while others adopted a reformist path following heterodox or devotional *bhakti* traditions. Notwithstanding strong regional variations and fundamental differences between ideological positions vis-à-vis mainstream Hinduism, they all aimed to rally Shudra and untouchable communities around egalitarian and self-dignifying identities set in opposition to Brahmanism while simultaneously raising their awareness of the role of self-representation in the emerging political arenas. Aided by the rise of vernacular print journalism and its potential for 're-presenting' new visions of collective belonging (cf. Anderson 1983: 25–46), increasingly visible groups from the lower castes confronted dominant colonial and nationalist discourses by engaging in polemics and petitions for social recognition. "For one, the very act of history-writing was now appropriated and redeployed by lower-caste groups, jeopardizing the objectivity-claims of history itself. A very large number of lower-caste counter-histories began to be written and published, which defined caste-status – neither as an ancient and immutable tradition nor as a permanent birth-mark on the individual – but as a contingent and arbitrary attribute, acquired by a people at a certain historical moment in the past, at the moment of defeat or fall, so to speak" (Banerjee 2007: 220).

These movements can be seen as part of a tradition of anti-caste radicalism, which also forms the ideological humus for the modern Dalit movements. However, it was not until the introduction of incipient structures of political representation with the Montague-Chelmsford Reforms of 1919 and more decisively with the Government of India Act of 1935 that an autonomous identity for untouchables came to be mobilized on the pan-Indian political scene. Long drawn out processes of identity construction influenced by the social enumeration and categorization of the colonial–cum-Brahmanical administration, as well as by socio-religious reform and Hindu revivalist movements, orientalist scholarship and caste associationism (cf. Bayly 1999 and Dirks 2001), were now greatly accelerated and re-shaped by the contending drives to political representation. The Indian National Congress, the Muslim League and the other parties in the fray increasingly tried to enlist "putative constituencies under the banner of religion" (Copland 2007: 301; cf. also Copland 2000, 2008). What had initially been envisioned as a system of representation based on 'communities of interest' (including non-religious corporate/commercial interests; Tejani 2008: 116) and separate electorates with reserved seats for minority interests was quickly caught into the spiral of 'communal politics' along an ever-hardening Hindu-Muslim divide. Tejani (2008) documents how "between 1928 and 1931 a broad spectrum of political opinion reinforced a meaning for nationalism as the unity of the (Hindu) majority" (Tejani 2008: 264). Under Gandhi's spiritualized leadership and his shift towards mass mobilization, the Congress's cultural-national discourse became increasingly hegemonic.

In the new democratic numbers game, widely scattered untouchable communities, hitherto grouped under regionally diverse categories and often under a non-Hindu label, were now incorporated into the Hindu fold as a unitary political category (Mendelsohn and Vicziany 2000: 2, 28–30, 99). Mani (2005) stresses that, while untouchables continued to be rejected as not being 'of us', the establishment of 'Vedic-Brahmanic nationalism' dictating the arithmetic of incipient popular representation turned untouchability into an exclusively Hindu affair.

> "As untouchables would help the Hindus constitute the majority, he [Gandhi] insisted that untouchability was a 'reproach to Hinduism' rather than to the national culture. Gandhi, on the one hand, insisted [...] that only the 'Hindu members' should be involved in this intra-Hindu affair, and on the other, he tried to present the issue as part of the national, not Hindu, reconstruction, thus making it amply clear that despite his occasional evocation of the secular basis of Indian nationalism, he also equated it with Hindu nationalism" (Mani 2005: 347).

For the emerging Dalit leadership, the question of identity vis-à-vis Hinduism became paramount. In the All-India Depressed Classes Conference of 1920 Ambedkar openly challenged Congress's claims to nationalism. He denounced those untouchable leaders who had been acting as the main spokesmen for these classes for co-opting the latter politically on behalf of Congress and making them subservient to the Gandhian politico-religious agenda. By selectively focusing on the removal of untouchability as a social evil and an upper-caste moral duty, this not only left the ideological and material structure of caste exploitation unchallenged, it re-enforced ascriptive hierarchies separating the lower-caste majority, the touchable caste-Hindu Shudras, from the untouchable Harijans (s. also Ambedkar 1946, 1948; cf. Aloysius 1997: 181). Already in 1935, at the Yeola Conversion Conference, Ambedkar publicly declared his intention to leave Hinduism, exhorting his followers to do the same. It is with the assertion of autonomy from Hinduism that Ambedkar (e.g. 1987), as the independent leader of the untouchable masses, managed to consolidate an autonomous pan-Indian Dalit identity framed in the modern language of rights and self-respect and politically wedged as a key swing constituency into the battleground of dominant upper-caste and Muslim nationalisms. Rao (2010) highlights how, from the 1930s, the rise of "an active, visible Dalit public" (Rao 2010: 88) – now organized in regional associations and mobilized around civic rights, particularly of public access to temples, schools and water tanks – was countered by a colonial jurisprudence and administrative practice which tended to frame these demands "as claims upon private property, enabling a legal defense of caste inequity in the language of liberalism, and *not* in the usual idiom of tradition" (Rao 2010: 116). Colonial governance vested with the mantle of religious non-interference essentially "enabled Hindu majoritarian power" (Rao 2010: 149). In this context, and amidst the rising state-centric nationalism of the Congress, Ambedkar had to focus on securing to the Dalits' "political legibility within a liberal framework" (Rao 2010: 123) by projecting them as a separate political minority, demographically dispersed, socially marginalized and economically deprived (e.g. Ambedkar 1989; cf. Dirks 2001: 257, 270).

By the 1940s, it was evident that Ambedkar's Independent Labor Party (ILP), despite its aim to represent not only Dalits but the toiling masses, was too isolated within the pan-Indian political landscape to be able to lead a shift from a minoritarian Dalit agenda to a transformative project for society as a whole. Significantly, the end of the ILP in 1942 coincided with the creation of the Scheduled Caste Federation (SCF) and the renewed effort to secure, if not separate electorates, then proper recognition of special provisions for the Depressed Classes. As Omvedt argues, the SCF was a "step backward" from the radicalism of the previous decade, functioning "as the political representative of Dalits, as a special interest group within a statist-capitalist democratic structure" (Omvedt 1994: 217–18). There were three sets of factors defining the relationship between the Dalits and potential allies among the anti-Brahman, Muslim and left movements, which impeded the consolidation of a horizontal Dalit-Bahujan alliance or a class-based proletarian–peasant front. First, the anti-Brahman movements, ideologically based on a common collective identity of all lower castes, had since the early stages been politically dominated by the upper strata of influential Shudra castes.[6] Besides often representing dominant landowning groups with conflicting interests to those of untouchable laborers, these caste-Hindu communities, being economically independent and positioned above the ritual pollution line, had been more successful in challenging ascriptive hierarchies and moving upwards without having to mount an all-out critique of the underlying normative system (cf. Michelutti 2004, 2008; Jaffrelot 2003). They were therefore not inclined to forgo the advantages of aligning with the Hindu mainstream for a vastly more onerous 'anti-systemic' alternative. At the latest with the electoral reforms of 1935, 'they realized that the time had come to assimilate or be condemned to the wilderness' (Menon 2006: 20). As they integrated into the Congress system, the erstwhile antagonism towards the upper-caste nationalist project and the radical critique of caste and land relations lost their vigor.

Secondly, it is now more widely acknowledged (e.g. Tejani 2008: 228; Jaffrelot 2003: 24–25; Mani 2005: 351–354) that, as became evident during the confrontation between Gandhi and Ambedkar leading up to the Poona Pact of 1932, Gandhians, Hindu traditionalists and liberals among the leading upper castes were united in their determination to reverse the British Government's decision to establish separate electorates for the Depressed Classes out of a fear that if untouchables were recognized as distinct from Hindus, they would make 'common cause' with the Muslims and threaten caste-Hindu supremacy over the nation.[7] Aloysius (1997: 183–184) suggests that an emerging horizontal formation joining together the lower-caste and Muslim masses had already been

---

6 Deliége (2001: 150–151) and Mendelsohn and Vicziany (2000: 94–95) argue that, since the beginning in both Maharashtra and Tamil Nadu, untouchables played at best a marginal role in the anti-Brahman movements and separated quickly to form independent caste-based movements. Rao (2010: 48–9) highlights how, already in 1895, only five years after Phule's death, Dalit members were banned from the Satyashodak Samaj.

7 See Gandhi's often quoted statement of 21August 1932 in a conversation with the traditionalist Congressman Sardar Vallabhai Patel: "The possible consequences of separate electorates for harijans fill me with horror… [They] do not realize that the separate electorate will create division among Hindus so much that it will lead to bloodshed. 'Untouchable hooligans' will make common cause with 'Muslim hooligans' and kill caste-Hindus." *The Collected Works of Mahatma Gandhi*, vol. 50, Ministry of Information and Broadcasting, Government of India, 1972, p. 469.

shattered by the Non-Cooperation and Khilafat Movements, which, despite their pretensions to seeking Hindu–Muslim unity, were meant to fasten the grip of the two traditional elites over the increasingly intransigent lower orders by shifting the masses' focus from economic and political demands to freshly ignited religious allegiances and vertical identifications. Menon goes further in arguing that the increasing anti-Brahmanical militancy of the lower castes was "temporarily resolved through the projection of united Hindu violence against Muslims" (Menon 2006: 14). Examining the rise of Hindu-Muslim riots from the 1920s in Bengal, he highlights how *bhadralok* parties and politicians purposefully diverted rising low-caste discontent on to an increasingly stigmatized Muslim Other, thereby "killing two birds with one stone – the subaltern castes would be less intractable towards social superiors, and they could act as a militant force, albeit of contingent loyalty" (Menon 2006: 18).

Thirdly, even though banned as a party, the communists, whose aim was to sway the Congress towards the left, had become integrated into the Congress Socialist Party since the latter's formation in 1934 and had progressively withdrawn their support for radical opposition movements outside (Sarkar 1983: 370 – 1, 413; cf. Corbridge and Harriss 2000: 48 – 49, 54). Class struggle and national independence gained a priority over caste-based mobilization, leaving Marxists and other left-leaning Congressmen aloof from the Dalit question, while the Hindu right and traditionalists within the Congress were setting the agenda (Omvedt 1994: 177). Aided by the grassroots activism of Hindu reform organizations, the latter were systematically engaged in 'weakening the organizational base of the lower castes' (Jaffrelot 2003: 492) and establishing their networks and institutions among the Harijans. The Hindu Mahasabha was the first to establish the Depressed Classes Association, followed by the All-India Anti-Untouchability League, later renamed the Harijan Sevak Sangh. The latter was created to promote the Gandhian Congress policy of Harijan 'uplift', which – partly drawing on popular *bhakti* traditions and partly echoing Vivekananda's and other upper-caste Hindu revivalist ideologies – condemned untouchability but proclaimed an assimilative view of society centered on the varna system as the divine and natural order. In this world view, "the redeemed untouchable should be humbly grateful on two counts: first, for having been remade physically and morally into a clean vegetarian teetotaler; and secondly, for being allowed to act as an instrument of repentance and spiritual cleansing for the high-caste benefactors who had 'uplifted' him (her)" (Bayly 1999: 251). Paternalism and condescension notwithstanding, integration within mainstream Hinduism and the upper-caste dominated Congress system was an appealing option to many Dalit leaders, who, often emerging from conditions of deprivation and a prevailing ethos of sanskritization, saw in it not only political and economic opportunities, but genuine reformist possibilities and the rallying call to Hindu national unity.

Besides co-opting Dalit leaders and promoting sanskritized Harijans as a counterweight to independent Dalit movements, traditionalists within the Congress actively used state powers to avert the coming together of an oppositional front.[8] Analyzing the anti-landlord and textile workers' struggles of the late 1930s, which saw the united mass mobilizations of Dalit, Shudra and Muslim peasants under the leadership of Ambedkar and communist and moderate labor leaders, Omvedt (1994: 199) states: "Against all their campaign promises and efforts to maintain a pro-poor image, Congress ministers were considering using Emergency powers to check the growing influence of communists and other radicals, but this proved impossible. Instead, the ministry introduced an Industrial Disputes Bill in the Bombay Legislative Assembly on 2 September 1938. The bill [...] made conciliation compulsory and, under certain very ill-defined conditions, made strikes illegal." According to Aloysius (1997: 196), "The need here [of non-violent Non-Co-Operation] was to edge out the perennial threat of the revolt of the mass of lower caste peasantry and the challenge of more radical ideologies both within and without the Congress." It has been well documented (e.g. Guha 1992) how Gandhian mobilization, even though ostensibly non-violent, relied heavily on control and discipline (if not outright caste coercion as in the earlier Swadesh movement) to give popular legitimacy to leaders of the National Movement and their claim to stand for the nation as a whole.

In the tumultuous atmosphere of the pre-independence phase, amidst rapidly changing international and domestic constellations, caste-Hindu upper classes, whether conservative Tilakites, Gandhians, communists or of other political orientations, were equally ready to rally around what had become the all-important aim of establishing an 'anti-imperialist united front' (Omvedt 1994: 186). From left to right, the Dalit cause and its promoters were being attacked as pro-British, unpatriotic, communal and casteist. Partition and nation-building under a Congress system increasingly dominated by conservatives (after the split of the Congress Socialist Party in 1948) sealed their fate for the decades to come. Dalit politics lost its national prominence and receded into regionally dispersed

---

[8] Since the 1937 elections following the reforms of 1935, the Congress gained power over legislative councils in seven provinces of British India, enabling Congress ministers to control large sections of the administration (Jaffrelot 2003: 11).

movements,⁹ often struggling against internal fragmentation and the endemic odds of resistance to versus assimilation into dominant Hindu alignments and the precariousness of alternative coalitional options.

In the new democratic nation, the Scheduled Castes, now firmly embedded within the Hindu mainstream, were granted special protection by virtue of their backwardness and not by way of recognition of their status as a separate minority. In response to a proposal for electoral reforms in SC-reserved constituencies, which was aimed at strengthening the accountability of SC candidates towards their own electorate, Patel reacted by stating in the constituent assembly:

> "To the Scheduled Castes' friends, I also appeal: 'Let us forget what Dr Ambedkar or his group have done. Let us forget what you did. You have very nearly escaped partition of the country again on your lines. [...] therefore I resist this only because I feel that the vast majority of the Hindu population wish you well. Without them where will you be? [...]'"[10]

Tejani (2008) has documented how, during the pre-partition phase and afterwards in the proceedings of the Constituent Assembly, the purpose of reservation changed from being an instrument to ensure the self-representation of minority groups, defined in terms of religion or caste, to becoming a welfarist policy tool of the new liberal nation state. Notwithstanding significant achievements in raising the SCs' awareness as a political constituency and in improving the socioeconomic level of a section of the Dalit population, in the first instance the reservation system did not, as Ambedkar had envisioned for separate electorates, further the establishment of an autonomous Dalit political force.[11] On the contrary, by secularizing the SCs' dependence upon caste-Hindu power-holders within the liberal democratic framework, it arguably operated as one of the key mechanisms by which the Congress managed to secure its continued hold on power over the first quarter-century of independent India. Claiming for itself the universalist mandate of representing the 'integrated will of the people' (Guha 1992: 71), under Nehru's 'technocratic socialism' and the Gandhian legacy of moral leadership, the Congress and its 'dominant coalition' (Bardhan 1988: 219) of proprietary

---

9 For example, for Maharashtra see the Dalit cultural movement already underway in the first post-independence phase (Guru 1997); for Western Uttar Pradesh see the gradual process of Ambedkarization from the late 1940s and more vigorously in the 1960s (Pai 2002).

10 Speech on 28 August 1947, as quoted in Jaffrelot 2003: 95.

11 It is only from the 1980s, with the emergence of an educated section of public-sector employees who had benefited from SC reservations, that the system can be seen as having contributed in the development of an autonomous Dalit political force, first under BAMCEF and then under BSP leadership.

classes oversaw the demobilization of transformative movements (Kaviraj 1997: 52, 60) and the establishment of an upper-caste bureaucratic state. Besides centralized planning, infrastructural and industrial development, the upper-caste bureaucracy took charge of equality and distributive justice as a matter of public policy 'constituted as a domain outside politics' (Chatterjee 1993: 205) and linked to economistic conceptions of national progress and the secularizing effects of modernity, while keeping 'culture tucked away' in the realm of the private (Chatterjee 1986: 158–9; 1993: 226).

3 Discursive Fields, Epistemic Formations and Dalit/Anti-caste Critiques of Secular Nationalism

Already since the 1950s, if not before (Aloysius 1997: 109, fn. 19; cf. also Dutt 1940), rising Marxist and left scholarship countered official historiography exposing the elitist and 'reactionary' character of Indian nationalism. Yet, with some notable exceptions,[12] it remained part of a 'Left nationalist-Marxist consensus' (Sarkar 1997: 39), which framed Indian nationalism in primarily anti-colonial terms and gave preeminence to class/economic oppositions between the masses and the alliance of imperialism with a 'subordinated feudalism' (Sarkar 1997: 43) over internally more divisive socio-cultural dimensions. Emanating from the radicalism of the 1960s and 1970s, it is the Subaltern Studies Collective, which started publishing in the early 1980s, that is often credited for having been among the major proponents of a shift away from the more traditional Marxist framework towards the study of subaltern groups as autonomous socio-political and cultural agents (cf. Sarkar 1997: 41, 83–86; Vanaik 1997: 181–183). Nevertheless, as Sumit Sarkar, himself a member of the early Collective, concedes, it was in practice rarely able to transcend the parameters of anti-colonial nationalism or the 'fragmentary resistance' and 'derivative discourse' constructed around the dichotomy between the indigenous community or colonized intelligentsia and

---

[12] See, for example, D.D. Kosambi's contribution (1965) to the study of ancient India and, more importantly here, in demystifying some of the narrative constructions of the dominant historiography of post-colonial India, which tended to draw on nineteenth-century Hindu revivalist notions of a diverse but united cultural heritage based on a glorious Vedic-Aryan past, while neglecting the role of pre-Aryan, Naga and Buddhist traditions and the heterogeneous evolution of Brahmanism itself and its impact on the progress of science, statecraft and democracy in India.

the cultural domination of colonial-Western modernity of the later *Subaltern Studies*.[13] As a result, rather than investigating the articulation of collective identities in the light of internal dimensions of power and changing socio-economic relations, thereby giving voice to anti-caste movements as active agents of autonomous cultural traditions representing the nation on equal grounds, the *Subaltern Studies* school has tended to portray subalterns from a class/communitarian angle as resisting colonial and elite exploitation from within the same cultural framework. While the *Subaltern Studies* project has continued to expand and transform itself over the decades (cf. Ludden 2002), a radical critique (e.g. Natrajan 2011, 2008; Aloysius 1997) has highlighted how the project largely failed to explore the implications of the cultural basis of Indian nationalism (centered on Brahmanism as the unitary tradition of the nation), not only for Dalit identity formation and politics, but also for Indian democracy and national identification.

It is from the late 1980s, amidst the growing economic crisis, the general disillusionment with bureaucratic statism and developmentalism, rising tensions around the 'mandir-mandal' conundrum and shifting alignments both within the dominant coalition and with regard to emerging political forces among rich farmers and the lower castes, that religion and caste forcefully re-emerged on to the national political scene. This lead to a reconfiguration of what had hitherto been the established limits of the *problématique politique* (Bourdieu 1981), of those discourses and forms of conduct that the dominant political classes allowed as legitimate in the political field. Dominant upper castes in public affairs, the media and academia had sustained, albeit from often very different left-Marxist, liberal-bourgeois or Hindu traditionalist positions, what came to be termed the 'Nehruvian consensus', embodied by the post-colonial Congress rule and a shared discursive field on the core principles of democracy, secularism and socialism as the pillars of the new nation state (cf. Corbridge and Harriss 2000: 20–22; Vanaik 1997: 274). The disintegration of the 'Nehruvian consensus' has then been seen by many within that group as equal to the crisis of the nation state per se. As a result, mainstream discourses, often theorizing around the binary oppositions of secularism versus communalism, state versus community, Western modernity versus indigenous traditions etc., have tended more or less implicitly to collapse the Nehruvian legacy with that of the state and democracy abstracted from its cultural embeddedness. The debate on the crisis of Indian secularism has been particularly

---

[13] For Sumit Sarkar's critique of Partha Chatterjee's work on the post-colonial state and modernity, see Sarkar 1997: 4, 5, 87–101. For a similar critique, see Vanaik 1997: 181–192, 225–7. For a more sympathetic critique, see Nigam 2006: 53.

prolific in terms of academic production. It has largely been carried out within upper-caste English-language circles and set within the communalism versus secularism framework. Besides other perspectives, such as those from neoliberal tendencies (e.g. Bhagwati and Srinivasan 1993; Bhagwati 2007) and institutional/constitutional views on the uniqueness of Indian secularism (e.g. Bhargava 2007), attention has focused on the confrontation between left-leaning academics positioned roughly within two camps: those supportive of prominent anti-modernist (Nandy 2003, 2007) and anti-'technocratic-state' arguments (Chatterjee 1994), concerned in part with the instrumental misappropriation of the state for Hindu majoritarian interests, and those scholars who are critical of such arguments due to their perceived assonance with Hindu nationalist positions. In particular, what the latter find questionable in such arguments are the assumption of the inherent tolerance of Hindu society, the pre-eminence given to a consensus-based community-driven public policy vis-à-vis that defined by the central state authorities, and the tendency to consider democratic institutions as an imposition of Western modernity rather than as a result of India's very own modern history.[14] Without reviewing this body of literature here, it is necessary for the purpose at hand to sketch the paradigmatic differences of alternative visions that are more in line with a Dalit critique.

According to these perspectives, the mainstream secular-nationalist discourse has been flawed from its inception, much before the crisis of the Nehruvian state, the escalation of aggressive Hindu nationalist politics or the Congress's turn to a 'pale saffron' populism in the 1980s. The very secular-national credentials of the Congress and the Nehruvian state are questioned as the main embodiments of a century-old nationalist project of Hindu majoritarian rule, which has connived or not done enough to avert the continued socio-economic exploitation and cultural annihilation of the lower castes. Aloysius argues that "Their [the dominant castes'] new-found national-secular ideology was neither a replacement of nor antagonistic to, the old Brahmanic sacral ideology of ascriptive superiority, but on the contrary, a combination with it, and in fact a transformed version of the latter, due to historical reasons" (Aloysius 1997: 221). Here, the emphasis does not lie on the failure of the Congress and the Nehruvian system, which in mainstream discourse is often ascribed to forces exogenous to the system, such as those of an externalized communal threat (of colonial/Western modernity or Islamic orientation). A Dalit critique rejects the discourse of an

---

14 For a variety of arguments in this regard see, for example: Vanaik (1997: 40–57, 114, 149, 153–154, *contra* Nandy 175–7, *contra* Chatterjee 184–92, 228–9), Sarkar (1997: 5, 87–101), Giri (2010) and in a different vein also Kaviraj (1997). For a somewhat apologetic reading of Nandy and Chatterjee in this regard, see Nigam (2006: 142–155; in reference to the latter also pp. 299–300).

externalized communalism holding secular institutions under siege. The focus is on the communalism within. Mani notes: "Like them [elitist secularists] many liberal-democrats do not want to see that communalism in India is not confined to strife between Hindus and Muslims but actually has its genesis in the dominant ideology of caste" (Mani 2005: 22). Sharing common ground with a Dalit critique of secular nationalism, Giri specifies: "On the one hand, the Subaltern Studies school externalizes communalism to the effects of the homogenizing, enumerative regimes and constructs of colonial state power carried over into the postcolonial period.[15] [...] On the other hand, left-secular scholars define 'our' culture as composite, secular, and democratic, and view communalism as a force external to the nation, self-referentially taken to be identical to constitutional secularism[16]" (Giri 2010: 131). In her investigation of the debates on secularism in the constituent assembly, Tejani documents how: "secularism became one of the pillars of Indian nationalist thought because the architects of the new nation-state – overwhelmingly middle-class, upper-caste Hindu men – saw it as providing a counterpoint to challenges posed from the margins by Muslim and Dalit communities" (Tejani 2008: 14–15). Going further, Giri contends that secularism has been used systematically in the politics of the postcolonial state and its elite leadership to avert attempts at social transformation and ensure the preservation of the status quo in the new democratic set-up, "so that it [the fight against communalism] could just be the organizing principle and legitimizing basis of state power, provide the basis for the 'unity and integrity' of the nation, and so on. The imposition signified that secularism had to create a need for itself, [...] so that it then becomes the legitimizing principle, a progressive plank for the new political regime" (Giri 2010: 137; see also Vanaik 1997: 31–32).

From these viewpoints, the crisis of secular nationalism is seen as the expression of the inherent communalism of the prevailing order, once again let loose to rescue the dominant castes whenever the horizontal mobilization of the lower castes threatens their rule. In the late 1980s, with the re-emergence on to the national scene of allied Dalit-OBC movements and party political formations and their forceful claims for a greater share of state resources, it is the interposition of an ever-resurgent Muslim threat that is used to rally the united (Hindu) nation and divide anti-Brahmanical forces along vertical identifications. Kothari acknowledges: "Indeed, one interpretation of the Hindutva tirade

---

15 "See for example, Pandey (2006), Chatterjee (1994), Guha (1989), and Kaviraj (1990)" (Giri 2010: 131).
16 "For a liberal version, see Rajeev Bhargava (1994) and Akeel Bilgrami (1994). For a more left (Marxist) version, which will be discussed below, see Aijaz Ahmad (1996) and Sumit Sarkar (1996)" (Giri 2010: 131).

is that it was an almost instant reaction to Mandal in the form of an upper caste Brahmanical backlash against the threat of an OBC-*dalit*-Muslim alignment [...]" (Kothari 1997: 442–3, fn. 2; similarly, Menon 2006).[17] Gail Omvedt shows how the Congress strategy to divide the Dalits and the other backward castes continued unabated in post-independence India and succeeded in warding off the attempts of both camps to re-emerge on to the pan-Indian scene. By working through a system of patronage based on the control of the upper castes over the lower castes against the Shudra middle castes (cf. also Jaffrelot 1999), Congress under both Nehru and Indira Gandhi managed to retain power and halt popular unrest, which was mounting as a result of failed promises on development and land reform and the harshening rural conditions, as public resources were being channeled away from agriculture into industry (Omvedt 1994: 326–332). Within the climate of the heightened cultural and economic radicalism of the 1970s, the spread of education and means of communication among sections of the Dalits and OBCs brought about the revival of strong regional movements[18] and the spread of a 'Dalit consciousness' among an increasingly wide range of emerging social movements (Kothari 1997: 448; Omvedt 1995: 6, 76, 79, 81–2, 86). According to Omvedt (2002: 424), it was at this point that the reservation system came to play a fundamentally different role as an instrument of national politics. During its heyday, the Congress had successfully used reservations as a tool to divide Dalits and OBCs. By frustrating OBC claims towards reservations and pitting them against those of the Dalits, it had preempted their political consolidation and eased the path of Dalit leaders into Congress. It was with the first opposition Janata government and its appointment of the Mandal Commission in 1979 that an attempt was made to use reservations as an instrument for Dalit-OBC unity and for consolidating the growing mobilization of the middle and low castes. Following Omvedt, it was at this juncture that "the Dalit/OBC-upper caste conflict was given a communal twist with the engineering of Hindu-Muslim riots. [...]. After the events in Gujarat [reservation riots of 1981, 1985], the upper castes will never again dare to attack the Dalits and OBCs directly, but rather will attempt to push the ideology of 'Hindu unity' in order to maintain their power" (Omvedt 2002: 425; s. also Ilaiah 1998: 286–287). It was then in the 1980s that Dalits took the lead in forging a Dalit-Bahujan alliance, reviving pre-independence anti-Brahman themes and attempting anew to push a common Dalit/

---

17 Along these lines see also Menon (2006: 8, 14); Vanaik (1997: 52, 274, 301–305, 323–326); Sarkar (1997: 359).
18 On the Dalit Panthers, see Omvedt 1995: 72–81; Zelliot 2001: part IV; Rao 2010: 187–197. On the literature movement, see Brueck 2008, and on the cultural movement in Maharashtra, see Guru 1997.

anti-caste agenda on to the national scene. With BAMCEF and later the BSP, Kanshi Ram succeeded in propelling politically a pan-Indian discourse of Dalit-Bahujan unity and for the first time in bringing Dalits to power in a coalition government with the OBC/Yadav-based Samajwadi Party in the 1993 UP elections.

From the 1990s the discursive high ground has registered visible shifts, incorporating hitherto marginalized arguments from a Dalit critique of secular nationalism into the mainstream of politics, academia and the media. This has been sustained also by the rise of increasingly vocal and interconnected Dalit human rights groups as well as by the growing number of voices within more established circles, who recognize Dalit/anti-caste movements as vital agents of secularization, socio-cultural transformation and liberal democracy in India[19]. Mainstream accounts are now more carefully scrutinized in terms of the role assigned to Dalit/anti-caste forces in history and the nation.[20] At the same time, the idea of India's cultural unity as the basis for national integration within a 'caste-blind' institutional framework has not lost currency in public discourses today. The rhetoric speaks of the progressive dissolution of caste and inequality in public life through the gradual incorporation of the lower castes into the mainstream by way of democratic mechanisms and affirmative action, regardless of the fact that globalization and privatization have relentlessly eroded the share of public-sector jobs in the economy and thereby the significance of reservations. While the everyday humiliation and brutality inflicted on Dalits are often portrayed as epiphenomenal and hardly as constitutive of existing power relations in society and the state, higher castes' frustration continues to be directed at those perceived to be undeserving beneficiaries, who, at the cost of 'merit' and 'efficiency', are given the benefit of government safeguards without abandoning their atavistic ways (Menon 2006; cf. Sukumar 2008).

---

19 For examples of academic contributions in this direction, see: Mangubhai 2014; Rao 2010: 17; Banerjee 2007; Nigam 2006: 39, 52; Vanaik 1997: 31; Kothari 1997: 447, 450–3. Notable is also the role played by those feminist voices and movements positioned at the intersection of caste, class and gender (e.g. Rege 2006, 2005, 1996; Chakravarti 1993; Pawar 2009; Geetha 2007). With regard to the media, see for example the relevant sessions of Aamir Khan's popular talk show Satyamev Jayate (www.satyamevjayate.in).

20 For example, the NCERT textbooks have been thoroughly re-written as part of the National Curriculum Framework 2005. They now provide insights into the richness of Dalit and tribal (*adivasi*) cultural characteristics, and they stimulate students to question the dominant normative system and the practice of untouchability and to re-construct for themselves a rights-based democratic and egalitarian value system (cf. George and Madan 2009; Pathak 2002). See, for example, NCERT, *Textbook for Class VIII: "Social and Political Life"* or other NCERT textbooks, particularly on social and political issues, in http://ncert.nic.in. On historiography, see Sarkar 1997: 359; Nigam 2006: 93–5; Banerjee 2007: 221.

Nigam acknowledges that, "In immaculately secular terms, these elites continued to dominate institutions and assets of society, keeping marginalized groups [...] in perpetual deprivation. 'Merit', 'efficiency', and 'productivity' were its new slogans" (Nigam 2006: 312). For Ilaiah these are not mere slogans of the past: "the discourse has been changed from dharma to merit. The state and the civil society are moulded to suit 'merit' in modern times just as it was moulded to suit dharma in ancient times" (Ilaiah 1996b: 196; s. also Mani 2014).

As Dalit perspectives on secular nationalism are being considered more seriously in scholarly establishments, they are also being re-interpreted and reconciled with dominant discursive lines. Even among critical voices, what emerges is at times an ambiguous, if not self-servingly apologetic or patronizingly elitist assessment of the relationship between secular nationalism and Dalit/anti-caste agency. For example, Nigam (2000, 2006) adopts, with slight variations, the binary framework of the prominent political theorist Partha Chatterjee, who distinguishes between 'civil society' and 'political society' (Chatterjee 2004). Nigam positions the postcolonial Dalit, together with the Hindu right, Muslims and other minorities (Nigam 2006: 320–321), in the "'underground', so to speak— to smoulder in the depths of political society [...]" (76). To him, it is only with the coming apart of the Nehruvian consensus that these "outlawed" forces have broken loose and made their first "appearance on the political stage and in parliament" (2006: 325). In Nigam's terms, these insurrectionary "little selves" have not yet come to interrelate with the state "through the practices of a modern democratic polity" (2000: 4266), as they are still steeped in the primordial identities of religion, caste and ethnicity. In fact, Nigam, preoccupied with Chatterjee and other political theorists of nationalism (2006: 40–65, 306–308), is convinced that the crisis of anti-colonial nationalisms is intrinsic to their very democratic project: "Their impulse of 'inviting the masses into history', repeatedly comes up against their impulse of creating a homogenous national culture" (2006: 76; s. also 2006: 322). It is in this striving for universalism that secular nationalism produced a dominant Hindu culture, though Nigam is keen to stress that this happened only "by default" (2006: 68, 77, 315).[21] He acknowledges that Nehru, as the leading ideologue of secular nationalism and the ethos of national unity, was undergirded by a Hindu nationalism "with its blindness to the question of dalit emancipation" (2006: 69–79). However, what matters most to

---

[21] Elsewhere and somewhat ambiguously Nigam highlights, once again in pursuit of Chatterjee, how the contradiction between modernity (universalisms being what typifies the "emancipator discourses of modernity"; Nigam 2000: 4256) and democracy or "the struggle against modernity" (Nigam 2000: 4267) is peculiar to post-colonial nationalism due to its very colonial experience.

Nigam is to emphasize that these features existed as the natural, almost unavoidable by-product of the otherwise praiseworthy, if at times misconceived, egalitarian secular democratic impulse towards a universal unmarked citizenship (2006: 310–312). In this, the Dalit is choreographed in as the usual 'fragment' (vide Chatterjee), who has become instrumental for a double purpose: in the secularism versus communalism framework, as a bulwark against the rising Hindutva forces (2000: 4256); and as the recalcitrant separatist who, through the discourse of universalism, allows the upper caste moral exculpation. To Nigam, it is not Hindu majoritarianism that Dalit/anti-caste forces reject, but "to be willing parts of the two great artefacts of our modernity, namely, secularism and the nation" (2000: 4258). Even though he occasionally acknowledges "the givenness of the nation, such as was sought to be constructed by the Congress" (2000: 4264), he ultimately goes back to faulting the Dalits for having a "problematic relation with the nation" (2006: 309) or Ambedkar for "resisting the idea of the part being represented in an essential section of the whole" (2000: 4264), conveniently overlooking the fact that the problem does not lie in the part, but by whom and in what way the whole gets to be defined.

It comes as no surprise that Dalit intellectuals adamantly reject not only what they perceive as "patronising or posterior epistemology" (Guru 2002: 5009) and the discursive sophistry of upper-caste theorists, particularly "those middle class ex-radicals for whom the old [Marxist] frameworks have ceased to be charming options" (Guru 2002: 5009). They also condemn how language, canons and protocols are used systematically to exclude Dalits from entering into the high grounds of scholarly establishments and from questioning received knowledge through alternative approaches, especially those that threaten to erode the current "cultural hierarchies that tend to divide social science practice into theoretical brahmans and empirical shudras" (Guru 2002: 5009; see also Mani 2014; Sukumar 2008; V. Kumar 2010; Guru and V. Geetha 2000). More broadly, it is on questions of 'voice' and representation, as well as on the understanding of Dalit epistemology and the nation, that the two sides greatly diverge.

Today, political thinkers, academics and activists, from both Dalit and non-Dalit backgrounds, are working in greater numbers and in a more interconnected fashion on issues of Dalit relevance. They are trying to push for an epistemological revolution, including a new historiography and the reconstruction of alternative cultural traditions (cf. Mani 2014; Sreenivas 2011). The aim is to document a cultural understanding of caste and power which serves a three-fold purpose: (i) to 're-present' new visions of collective belonging based on Dalit knowledge and cultural practices, which have hitherto been marginalized; (ii) to project these collective identities for the Dalits outside what is perceived as a politically consolidated Hinduism and its hierarchical logic; and (iii) to define the nation and its democratic institutions in emancipatory and more representative ways.[22] Within these discourses, the subaltern masses are seen as having been in pursuit of a far more universal and inclusive national project than that imposed by the dominant Brahmanical forces. This understanding of the nation is not based on internally divisive hierarchies or exteriorized threats, but on a more egalitarian representation of the wide multi-culturalism of its peoples. This is what Aloysius terms the homogenization (equal distribution) of social power within culture (Aloysius 1997: 80, 97, 121, 126, 144–146, 151), or what Ilaiah refers to as Dalitization, that is, the universalizing of the principles of labor, democracy and equality (Ilaiah 1998: 291; Ilaiah 2001). In this sense, Dalit intellectuals reject the left's "conceit of universalism" (Guru 2005: 4, 16), which to them hides brutal relations of power behind the discourse of impartiality. "Universalism in its coercive form tends to drag all these particulars that have the potential to become universal at the same time suggesting that it is the only universal that has superior truth and that everyone should fall in line with it for liberation" (Guru 2005: 16). Consequently, they refuse to be portrayed, as in mainstream left narratives, as the long passive masses, whose "real awakening" (Vanaik 1997: 57) coincided with the crisis of secular nationalism and the rise of Hindutva politics. In Dalit historical accounts, it has been neither Gandhi (e.g. Nigam 2000: 4258) nor a latter-day democratic awakening that brought the Dalit masses into politics, but their very own traditions of resistance dating back to pre-modern times (Aloysius 1997: 182, 202–211). "The political nationalists saw themselves as heirs to another tradition of the subcontinent's history – that of resistance, heterodoxy, protest and egalitarianism. The anti-Brahmanic traditions of Buddhism and the Bhakti movements of the pre-modern era were appropriated to express the modern socio-political message of equality" (Aloysius 1997: 165–166).

Partly building on long-standing anti-Brahmanical traditions (Zelliot 2001; Lorenzen 1996 and 1987), new Dalit scholarship has been vigorously pushing for a transformative historiographical project from what are considered hitherto suppressed autochthonous cultural sources emanating from the Dalit-Bahujan[23]

---

[22] See, for example, the work done by organizations such as the Dalit Intellectuals' Collective (DIC), established since 1997 in Mumbai, or the following accounts: Mani 2014, 2005; V. Kumar 2010; Ahmad and Upadhyay 2007; Ilaiah 2007, 2001, 1998, 1996b; Narayan 2009, 2004a, 2004b; Guru and Geetha 2000.

[23] The term 'Dalit-Bahujan' literally means 'the Dalit majority people'. It is generally used to refer to all those groups of people who are considered the victims of Brahmanic oppression and exploitation. These include the Scheduled Castes and Scheduled Tribes, and most often also women and Shudras (who occupy the forth *varna* in the *chaturvarna* system and are roughly equated with the administrative category of OBC). Despite its problems (N. Kumar 2000; Guru

masses (e.g.: Narayan 2009; 2004a, 2004b; Guru and V. Geetha 2000).[24] Following up on earlier attempts to reconstruct an autonomous non-caste/anti-Brahmanical history, it has been at pains to document how, by controlling language, knowledge and written expression, Aryan-Brahman domination managed virtually to obliterate the memory of India's multi-cultural forces (Mani 2005; Ilaiah 2001). Mani is keen to show how, since their arrival, the Aryan-Brahmans have proceeded through violence and obscurantism to destroy, enslave and co-opt the mental and physical energies of the original inhabitants (cf. Phule [1873] 2002), from putting kshatriyahood on sale in exchange for divinely sanctioned *dandanite* (rule by force) and through the brahmanization of entire tribes, to the mystification of the early Buddhist ethos by assimilation into the upanishadic absolutism (cf. Kosambi 1965). Notwithstanding the strong critique of Brahmanism, some (e.g. Omvedt 2008a, 2008b, 2009) inscribe the revolutionary vision of the abolition of caste within the 'radical anti-caste traditions' of Hinduism, which are taken as the basis for the construction of a more genuinely democratic national unity. Other, less conciliatory perspectives (Ilaiah 2009) presage the advent of a 'post-Hindu India', in which the 'scientific technological creativity of the Indian productive masses' is released from the Brahmanical seizure of divinely ordained inequality and ultimately manages to 'inverse the cultural idiom' and to bring Hinduism and its caste system to an end. While a 'Dalit consciousness' is reaching more deeply into the mainstream of public opinion and questioning the policy and scholarly establishments, it is important to note that the challenges to widening its spread also originate from within the Dalit fold. Dalit movements are certainly not monolithic: they are fragmented along caste/class lines[25] or regional and religious affiliations[26] and are often in pursuit of antagonistic ideological and political aims.[27]

---

and Geetha 2000: 131), this terminology is expressive of a discourse which aims to counter the mainstream understanding of Dalits as a minority, as "little selves" (Nigam 2006) or "fragmentary identities" (Chatterjee 1993) etc. It is with the revival and spread of a more radical Dalit consciousness from the 1970 s that such language has given expression to a renewed intent to influence the mainstream normative system and gain political power by consolidating a collective identity comprehensive of numerical strong sections of the oppressed.

24 See in this regard also the role played by the growing field of Dalit autobiographical works (Moon 2001; Chauhan 2004; Ilaiah 1996a; R. Kumar 2010; Kamble 2009; Pawar 2009; Rege 2006).

25 On the problem of *jati* and class identities and their effect on the fragmentation of Dalit forces, particularly between leaders and grassroots activists and between Dalit party political affiliations, see Omvedt 2001; Guru 1999, 1997; V. Kumar 2003, 2010; Pai 2002; J. V. Deshpande 1997.

26 For example, on Dalit Christians in Tamil Nadu, see Fernandes 2010; Deliége 2001: 157–162; Mosse 1994. On Sikhs in Punjab, see Jodhka 2010.

The decades-old controversy over the imposition of UN sanctions against caste-based discrimination is illustrative of the tug-of-war that has been at play between Dalit movements and mainstream forces within public institutions, but also of the challenges of finding a representative popular 'voice' for the Dalit cause. The government of India ratified the UN Convention on the Elimination of Racial Discrimination (CERD) in 1968. However, it has not only been severely lagging in submitting reports to the UN Committee in charge of monitoring states' compliance (eight years delay on the last report) and uncooperative with the UN Special Rapporteur in following up on specific cases, but it has disowned the key principle defining the Convention's application as enshrined in its Article 1.[28] In the reports the government of India has continuously denied the descent-based nature of caste discrimination and has refrained from including therein any mention of abuses against Dalits (CHRGJ&HRW 2007: 3, 22). The same position of the Indian government has been upheld in the context of the United Nations World Conference against Racial Discrimination, Xenophobia and Related Intolerances held in Durban in 2000. During almost two years of preparatory negotiations, Dalit human rights groups report strategies to discredit their claims and of lukewarm support by the media[29] and the larger civil society-based networks (Guru 2001). At the same time, Guru laments the fact that "The Durban initiative was hegemonised more by the opinion makers among dalits based in the metropolis rather than the people's initiative" (Guru 2001). To Guru, these "elite representation", refraining from regular popular consultations and from taking dissenting opinions into account, ended up reproducing the very "exclusionary boundaries" that it had set out to overcome. In the end, observers conclude that: "Despite all the efforts on the part of the Dalit activists [...], no expressions in any way associated with caste discrimination were to be found in the

---

27 Ideological splits in Dalit movements have been often characterized by the contraposition of cultural versus socioeconomic politics; or in other words, of whether to give primacy to caste (religion/culture) versus class (economic) based aspects or the reverse. For a discussion of these issues, see Sahota 2008 and Omvedt 1995. These ideological convictions and also more practical political considerations have been at the root of often diverging dispositions of Dalit forces towards potential allies and coalition partners, both within the party system (see Guru 1997: 27) and with regard to civil-society movements (see V. Kumar 2003, 2010; Omvedt 2001).
28 The interpretation of Article 1 as stated in the General Recommendation XXIX by the UN Committee on the Elimination of Racial Discrimination clarifies that "discrimination based on 'descent' includes discrimination against members of communities based on forms of social stratification such as caste and analogous systems of inherited status" (CHRGJ&HRW 2007: 3, see also pp. 22, 59).
29 The vernacular media hardly carried the story, while the English media was mostly devoid of Dalit voices (Guru 2001).

final document from the Durban Conference, when the negotiations were over" (Hardtmann 2009: 205–6).

The tenor of the confrontation has remained unchanged over the past decade. In 2010, justifying the government's rejection of the latest bid to include caste in a new set of UN guidelines against descent-based discrimination, Indian officials argue: "Besides how can anyone suggest that India's fight against caste-based discrimination will be helped by international attention on the issue? Are we a closed country where debates do not take place and correctives not applied?" (*The Hindu*, Front Page, 31.03.2010). Academics have not stayed out of the controversy. For example, in a meeting with CERD in February 2007 (CERD Report, 23.02.2007), the delegation of the government of India included the renowned sociologist Dipankar Gupta, at that time with Jawaharlal Nehru University. Framing his argument in terms of the non-equivalence of caste and race (s. also Visvanathan 2001; Panini 2001), Professor Gupta substantiated the official line and concluded by saying that the matter was "useful only for getting members of the same nation to *hate one another* (emphasis added)."[30] Whether due to a 'patriarchal morality' or reminiscent of earlier nationalist narratives, issues of caste discrimination are perceived as divisive and as detracting from national unity and pride, and they continue to be sidelined in official discourses.

4 Conclusion

Amidst India's rising economic power and the increasing role of its secular polity in international relations, it is religion and caste that continue forcefully to influence the national political scene. In this context, this paper has investigated how religion and the secular are implicated in constituting the state and the public sphere with its diverse political subjectivities. In particular, the study has assessed the role of Dalits as agents of secularization, socio-cultural transformation and democracy in today's India.

By taking a contextual perspective of religion and the secular as discursive formations enmeshed within the same 'ideological field of force' (Hall 1996: 136), the paper has re-conceptualized secularism beyond binary oppositions of secularism versus communalism, state versus community, or Western modernity versus indigenous traditions. Historically informed investigations have revealed the contingent

---

[30] Professor Gupta's quote is from J.B.S. Haldane in reference to the word 'race'. A summary of Dipankar Gupta's speech at CERD, entitled "Why caste discrimination is not racial discrimination", is available at www.india-seminar.com/2007/572.

nature of secular nationalism shaped by long-standing processes of national, community and majority/minority formations, which have continued to wrangle over systems of legal governance and democratic representation, with their underlying normative systems on religion and secularism. The present study has highlighted the inherently political nature of secular-religious regimes, which not only impact on the way Dalit people come to articulate their collective self-conceptions, but are expressive of local power relations defining society and the state at large.

The paper has also shown how Dalit people, far from being the long passive masses, have desperately attempted to overcome divisive forces so as to forge inter-caste/community alliances and consolidate caste clusters into common collective identities and effectively channel their numerical strength into new political subjectivities. In so doing, the paper has pointed to processes through which secular-religious regimes, with their material and symbolic embodiments, are negotiated, mobilized or subverted from diverse sociopolitical positions; or, in the Gramscian sense, it has shed light on some of the intricate processes through which the 'war(s) of position' inside and between shifting social formations are articulated. Ideological and political contestation marks not only the interrelation of Dalit versus mainstream establishments, but is internal to the very formative processes shaping Dalit identification and representation. It is important to stress that the Dalit field of sociality is marked by a history of violated agency, both in its striving for assimilation and its attempts at subversion, which is also linked to century-old systems depriving Dalit people of the means for public representation, written codification and the development of authoritative guardianships for their own epistemologies. It is only in more recent decades, through an ever-growing historiographical and literary production, that Dalit/anti-caste voices have been able to reduce what is arguably a dearth of ammunition in a struggle for normative self-determination.

By positioning the field of investigation at the intersection between questions of secularism and subalternity, entangled within locally contextual and historically constituted dynamics of power, I have also sought to illustrate how the understanding of secular nationalism changes if it is viewed through the lenses of critical Dalit/anti-caste perspectives and how this view alters our assessment of the potentials and constraints facing democracy and national unity in contemporary India. More significantly here, this has allowed us to highlight how a bottom-up perspective implies more than a shift in standpoint, more than a capsizing of dominant representations of society and the state in India. Rather, it represents a methodological choice which implicates how we conceive meaning in socio-cultural translation and how we seek to contribute to epistemic production.

References

Ahmad, Imtiaz and Shashi Bhushan Upadhyay, eds. 2007. *Dalit Assertion in Society, Literature and History.* Delhi: Deshkal Publication.

Aloysius, G. 1997. *Nationalism without a nation in India.* New Delhi: Oxford University Press.

Ambedkar, Bhimrao Ramji [1916] 2004. "Castes in India: their mechanism, genesis and development", in *Class, Caste, Gender,* ed. Manoranjan Mohanty, 131–135. New Delhi: Sage.

—. [1946] 1970. *Who Were the Shudras? How They Came to be the Fourth Varna in the Indo-Aryan Society.* Bombay: Thackers.

—. 1948. *The Untouchables Who Were They and Why They Became Untouchables?* New Delhi: Amrit Book Co.

—. 1987. "Riddles in Hinduism," in *Writings and Speeches*, vol. 4, Dr. Babasaheb Ambedkar. Bombay: Education Department, Government of Maharashtra.

—. 1989." Untouchables or the children of India's ghetto," in *Writings and Speeches*, vol. 5, Dr. Babasaheb Ambedkar. Bombay: Education Department, Government of Maharashtra.

Anderson, Benedict 1983. *Imagined Communities.* London: Verso.

Arun, Chockalingam Joe 2007. *Constructing Dalit Identity.* Jaipur: Rawat Publications.

Asad, Talal 1979. "Anthropology and the analysis of ideology." *Man*, (n.s.) 14 (4): 607–627.

—. 1983. "Anthropological conceptions of religion." *Man*, (n.s.) 18: 237–59.

—. 2003. *Formations of the Secular.* Stanford: Stanford University Press.

—. 2006. "Responses," in *Powers of the Secular Modern: Talal Asad and his Interlocutors,* eds. David Scott and Charles Hirschkind, 206–242. Stanford: Stanford University Press.

Banerjee, Prathama 2007. "Caste and the writing of history," in *Dalit Assertion in Society, Literature and History,* eds. Imtiaz Ahmad and Shashi Bhushan Upadhyay, 218–242. Delhi: Deshkal Publication.

Bardhan, Pranab 1988. "Dominant proprietary classes and India's democracy," in *India's Democracy: An Analysis of Changing State-Society Relations,* ed. Atul Kohli, 214–224. Princeton, NJ: Princeton University Press.

Bayly, Susan 1999. *Caste, Society and Politics in India.* Cambridge: Cambridge University Press.

Bhagwati, Jagdish 2007. "Secularism in India," in *The Future of Secularism,* ed. Thirukodikaval Nilakanta Srinivasan, 11–19. New Delhi : Oxford University Press.

Bhagwati,Jagdish and Thirukodikaval Nilakanta Srinivasan 1993. *India's Economic Reforms.* Government of India Ministry of Finance Press.

Bhargava, Rajeev 2007. "The distinctiveness of Indian secularism," in Thirukodikaval Nilakanta Srinivasan (ed.) *The Future of Secularism.* New Delhi : Oxford University Press.

—. 2011. "Rehabilitating Secularism," in *Rethinking Secularism,* eds. Craig Calhoun, Mark Juergensmeyer and Jonathan Van Antwerpen, 92–113. New York: Oxford University Press.

Bourdieu, Pierre 1981. "La representation politique." *Actes de la recherche en sciences sociales,* 36–37: 3–24.

Brueck, Laura R. 2008. "Mainstreaming marginalized voices: the Dalit Lekhak Sangh and the negotiations over Hindi Dalit literature," in *Claiming Power from Below,* eds. Manu Bhagavan and Anne Feldhaus, 151–165. New Delhi: Oxford University Press.

Chakravarti, Uma 1993. "Conceptualising Brahmanical patriarchy in early India: gender, caste, class and state." *Economic and Political Weekly,* 28 (14): 579–585.

Chatterjee, Nandini 2011. *The Making of Indian Secularism*. New York: Palgrave.
Chatterjee, Partha 1986. *Nationalist Thought and the Colonial World. A Derivative Discourse?* London: Zed Books.
—. 1993. *The Nation and its Fragments: Colonial and Postcolonial Histories*. Princeton: Princeton University Press.
—. 1994. "Secularism and toleration." *Economic and Political Weekly*, 29 (28): 1768–1777.
—. 2004. *The Politics of the Governed*. New York: Cambridge University Press.
Chauhan, Sevaram 2004. *Sangarsh*. Dewas: unpublished.
CHRGJ & HRW (Centre for Human Rights and Global Justice & Human Rights Watch). 2007. *Hidden Apartheid. Caste Discrimination against India's "Untouchables"*. 19 (3 C). New York: CHRGJ & HRW.
Copland, Ian 2000. "The political geography of religious conflict." *The International Journal of Punjabi Studies*, 7 (1): 1–27.
—. 2007. "The imprint of the past," in *From the Colonial to the Postcolonial: India and Pakistan in Transition*, eds. Dipesh Chakrabarty, Rochona Majumdar, and Andrew Sartori, 287–308. New Delhi: Oxford University Press.
—. 2008. "From *Communitas* to Communalism," in *Colonialism, Modernity and Religious Identities*, ed. Gwilym Beckerlegge, 23–47. New Delhi: Oxford University Press.
Corbridge, Stuart and John Harriss. 2000. *Reinventing India: Liberalization, Hindu Nationalism and Popular Democracy*. Cambridge: Polity Press.
Dalmia, Vasudha 1997. *The Nationalization of Hindu Tradition*. New Delhi: Oxford University Press.
Deliége, Robert 2001. *The Untouchables of India*. Oxford: Berg.
Deshpande, Gobind Purushottam 2002. "Of hope and melancholy. Reading Jotirao Phule in our times," in *Selected Writings of Jotirao Phule*, ed. Gobind Purushottam Deshpande, 1–22. New Delhi: LeftWord Books.
Deshpande, J.V. 1997. "Behind Dalit anger." *Economic and Political Weekly*, 32 (33/34): 2090–2091.
Dirks, Nicholas B. 2001. *Castes of Mind. Colonialism and the Making of India*. Princeton and Oxford: Princeton University Press.
Dutt, Rajani Palme 1940. *India Today*. London: Victor Gollancz.
Fernandes, Walter 2010. "Caste and conversion movements," in *Social Movements I. Issues of Identity*, ed. Tharaileth Koshy Oommen, 95–115. New Delhi: Oxford University Press.
Fuchs, Martin 1999. *Kampf um Differenz*. Frankfurt: Suhrkamp.
—. 2004. "Das Ende der Modelle: Interkulturalität statt (Kultur-)Vergleich," in *Konfigurationen der Moderne*, eds. Shalini Randeria, Martin Fuchs, and Antje Linkenbach, 439–468. Baden-Baden: NOMOS.
—. 2009. "Reaching out; or, nobody exists in one context only: society as translation." *Translation Studies*, 2 (1): 21–40.
Geetha, V. 2007. *Patriarchy*. Calcutta: Stree.
George, Alex M. and Amman Madan. 2009. *Teaching Social Science in Schools*. New Delhi: Sage.
Giri, Saroj 2010. "Hegemonic secularism, dominant communalism." *Rethinking Marxism*, 22 (1):130–147.
Gramsci, Antonio [1975] 2001. *Quaderni del Carcere*. Edizione critica dell'Istituto Gramsci a cura di V. Gerratana, vol. I (1929–1932) & II (1930–1933). Torino: Einaudi.

Guha, Ranajit 1989. "Dominance without hegemony and its historiography," in *Subaltern Studies VI.*, ed. Ranajit Guha, 210–309. New Delhi: Oxford University Press.
—. 1992. "Discipline and Mobilize," in *Subaltern Studies VII*, eds. Partha Chatterjee and Gyanendra Pandey, 69–120. New Delhi: Oxford University Press.
Guru, Gopal 1997. *Dalit Cultural Movements and Dalit Politics in Maharashtra*. Mumbai: Vikas Adhyayan Kendra.
—. 1999. "The Dalit movement in mainstream sociology," in *Dalits in Modern India,* ed. Sebastian Marian Michael, 150–161. New Delhi: Sage.
—. 2001. "Politics of representation." *Seminar*, n.508.
—. 2002. "How egalitarian are the social sciences in India?" *Economic and Political Weekly*, 37 (50): 5003–5009.
—. 2005. "Introduction: athropy in Dalit Politics," in *Athropy in Dalit Politics*, ed. Gopal Guru, 7–28. Mumbai: Vikas Adhyayan Kendra.
Guru, Gopal and V. Geetha. 2000. "New phase of Dalit-Bahujan intellectual activity." *Economic and Political Weekly*, 35 (3): 130–134.
Hall, Stuart 1996. "On postmodernism and articulation," in *Stuart Hall. Critical Dialogues in Cultural Studies*, eds. David Morley and Kuan-Hsing Chen, 131–150. London: Routledge.
Hardtmann, Eva-Maria 2009. *The Dalit Movement in India. Local Practices, Global Connections.* New Delhi: Oxford University Press.
Ilaiah, Kancha 1996a. *Why I am not a Hindu*. Calcutta: Samya.
—. 1996b. "Productive labour, consciousness and history: the Dalitbahujan alternative," in *Subaltern Studies IX. Writings on South Asian History and Society*, eds. Shahid Amin and Dipesh Chakrabarty, 165–200. New Delhi: Oxford University Press.
—. 1998. "Towards the Dalitization of the nation," in *Wages of Freedom. Fifty Years of the Indian Nation-State*, ed. Partha Chatterjee, 267–291. Delhi: Oxford University Press.
—. 2001. "Dalitism vs Brahmanism: the epistemological conflict in history," in *Dalit Identity and Politics. Cultural Subordination and the Dalit Challenge*, vol. 2, ed. Ghanshyam Shah, 108–128. New Delhi: Sage.
—. 2007. *Turning the Pot, Tilling the Land*. New Delhi: Navayana.
—. 2009. *Post-Hindu India*. New Delhi: Sage.
Jaffrelot, Christopher 1999. *The Hindu Nationalist Movement and Indian Politics*. New Delhi: Penguin.
—. 2003. *India's Silent Revolution: The Rise of the Low Castes in North Indian Politics*. Delhi: Permanent Black.
Jodhka, Surinder S. 2010. "Sikhs today: development, disparity and difference," in *Religion, Community and Development*, eds. Gurpreet Mahajan and Surinder Jodhka, 173–202. New Delhi: Routledge.
Kamble, Baby 2009. *The Prisons We Broke*. New Delhi: Orient Blackswan.
Kaviraj, Sudipta 1997. "A critique of passive revolution," in *State and Politics in India*, ed. Partha Chatterjee, 45–88. New Delhi: Oxford University Press.
Khilnani, Sunil 1997. *The Idea of India*. London: Penguin.
Kosambi, Damodar Dharmanand 1965. *The Culture and Civilization of Ancient India*. Delhi: Vikas Publishing House.
Kothari, Rajni 1997. "Rise of the *Dalit*s and the renewed debate on caste," in *State & Politics in India*, ed. Partha Chatterjee, 439–458. New Delhi: Oxford University Press.
Kumar, Narender 2000. "Dalit and Shudra politics and anti-Brahmin movement." *Economic and Political Weekly*, 35 (45): 3977–3979.

Kumar, Raj 2010. *Dalit Personal Narratives. Reading Caste, Nation and Identity.* New Delhi: Orient Blackswan.
Kumar, Vivek 2003. "Dalit movement and Dalit international conferences." *Economic and Political Weekly*, 38 (27): 2799.
—. 2010. "Different shades of Dalit mobilization," in *Social Movements I. Issues of Identity*, ed. Tharaileth Koshy Oommen, 116–136. New Delhi: Oxford University Press.
Lorenzen, David 1987. "Traditions of non-caste Hinduism: the Kabir Panth." *Contributions to Indian Sociology*, (n.s.) 21 (2): 263–284.
—. 1996. "Introduction. The historical vicissitudes of Bhakti religion," in *Bhakti Religion in North India. Community Identity and Political Action*, ed. David Lorenzen, 1–34. New Delhi: Manohar.
Ludden, David 2002. "A brief history of subalternity," in *Reading Subaltern Studies*, ed. David Ludden. London: Anthem Press.
Mandair, Arvind-Pal 2011. "Translation of violence: secularism and religion-making in the discourses of Sikh nationalism," in *Secularism and Religion-Making*, eds. Markus Dressler and Arvind-Pal Mandair, 62–86. Oxford: Oxford University Press.
Mandair, Arvind-Pal and Markus Dressler. 2011. "Modernity, Religion-Making, and the Postsecular," in *Secularism and Religion-Making*, eds. Markus Dressler and Arvind-Pal Mandair. Oxford: Oxford University Press.
Mangubhai, Jayshree P. 2014. *Human Rights as Practice.* New Delhi: Oxford University Press.
Mani, Braj Ranjan 2005. *Debrahminising History.* New Delhi: Manohar.
—. 2014. *Knowledge and Power.* New Delhi: Manohar.
Mendelsohn, Oliver and Marika Vicziany. 2000. *The Untouchables. Subordination, Poverty and the State in Modern India.* New Delhi: Foundation Books.
Menon, Dilip 2006. *The Blindness of Insight.* Pondicherry: Navayana.
Michelutti, Lucia 2004. "'We (Yadavs) are a caste of politicians': caste and modern politics in a north Indian town." *Contributions to Indian Sociology*, (n.s.) 38 (1&2): 43–73.
—. 2008. *The Vernacularisation of Democracy.* New Delhi: Routledge.
Moon, Vasant 2001. *Growing Up Untouchable in India: A Dalit Autobiography.* Lanham: Rowman & Littlefield.
Mosse, David 1994. "Idioms of subordination and styles of protest among Christian and Hindu Harijan castes in Tamil Nadu." *Contributions to Indian Sociology*, 28 (1): 67–106.
Nagaraj, Doddaballapura Ramaiah 2010. *The Flaming Feet.* Ranikhet: Permanent Black.
Nandy, Ashis 2003. *The Romance of the State.* New Delhi: Oxford University Press.
—. 2007. "Closing the debate on secularism," in *The Crisis of Secularism in India*, eds. Anuradha Dingwaney Needham and Rajeswari Sunder Rajan, 107–117. Durham: Duke University Press.
Narayan, Badri 2004a. "Nationalist past and political present." *Economic and Political Weekly*, 39 (31): 3533–3540.
—. 2004b. "Inventing caste history: Dalit mobilisation and nationalist past," in *Caste in Question: Identity or Hierarchy?* ed. Dipankar Gupta, 193–220. New Delhi: Sage.
—. 2009. *Fascinating Hindutva. Saffron Politics and Dalit Mobilization.* New Delhi: Sage.
—. 2011. *The Making of the Dalit Public in North India.* New Delhi: Oxford University Press.
Natrajan, Balmurli 2008. "Cultural values," in *Encyclopedia of Social Problems*, ed. Vincent N. Parrillo, 193–196. New Delhi: Sage.
—. 2011. *Culturalization of Caste in India: Identity and Inequality in a Multicultural Age.* London: Routledge.

Nigam, Aditya 2000. "Secularism, modernity, nation." *Economic and Political Weekly, Special Articles:* 4256–4268.
—. 2006. *The Crisis of Secular-Nationalism in India.* New Delhi: Oxford University Press.
Omvedt, Gail 1994. *Dalits and the Democratic Revolution.* New Delhi: Sage.
—. 1995. *Dalit Vision.* New Delhi: Orient Longman.
—. 2001. "Ambedkar and after: the Dalit movement in India," in *Dalit Identity and Politics,* ed. Ghanshyam Shah, 143–159. New Delhi: Sage.
—. 2002. "The anti-caste movement and the discourse of power," in *Caste and Democratic Politics in India,* ed. Ghanshyam Shah, 413–431. Delhi: Permanent Black.
—. 2008a. *Seeking Begumpura: The social vision of anti-caste intellectuals.* Pondicherry: Navayana.
—. 2008b. The Bhakti radicals and untouchability," in *Speaking Truth to Power,* eds. Manu B. Bhagavan and Anne Feldhaus, 11–29. New Delhi: Oxford University Press.
—. 2009. "Social movements and democracy," in *Challenges to Democracy in India,* ed. Rajesh M. Basrur, 145–166. New Delhi: Oxford University Press.
Pai, Sudha 2002. *Dalit Assertion and the Unfinished Democratic Revolution.* New Delhi: Sage.
Panini, M.N. 2001. "Caste, race and human rights." *Economic and Political Weekly,* 36 (35): 3344–3346.
Pathak, Avijit 2002. *Social Implications of Schooling.* New Delhi: Aakar Publications.
Pawar, Urmila 2009. *The Weave of My Life: A Dalit Woman's Memoirs.* New York: Columbia University Press.
Phule, Jotirao [1873] 2002. "Slavery & the cultivator's whipcord," in *Selected Writings of Jotirao Phule,* ed. Gobind Purushottam Deshpande, 23–190. New Delhi: LeftWord Books.
Rao, Anupama 2010. *Dalits and the politics of modern India.* Ranikhet: Permanent Black.
Rawat, Ramnarayan S. 2011. *Reconsidering Untouchability.* Bloomington: Indiana University Press.
Rege, Sharmila 1996. "Caste and gender: the violence against women in India." *EUI Working Paper Series,* No. 96/17, European University Institute, Badia Fiesolana.
—. 2005. "Dalit women talk differently: A critique of 'Difference'," in *Athropy in Dalit Politics,* ws. Gopal Guru, 39–62. Mumbai: Vikas Adhyayan Kendra.
—. 2006. *Writing Caste/ Writing Gender. Narrating Dalit Women's Testimonios.* New Delhi: Kali for Women.
Sahota, Bali 2008. "The paradoxes of Dalit cultural politics," in *Claiming Power from Below,* eds. Manu B. Bhagavan and Anne Feldhaus, 189–207. New Delhi : Oxford University Press.
Sarkar, Sumit 1983. *Modern India 1885–1947.* New Delhi: Macmillan India Ltd.
—. 1997. *Writing Social History.* New Delhi: Oxford University Press.
Sreenivas, Deepa 2011. "Telling different tales: Possible childhoods in children's literature." *Childhood,* 18 (3): 316–332.
Sukumar, Narayana. 2008. "Living a concept: semiotics of everyday exclusion." *Economic and Political Weekly,* 43 (46): 14–17.
Tejani, Shabnum 2008. *Indian Secularism.* Bloomington: Indiana University Press.
Thapar, Romila 1985. "Syndicated moksha?" *Seminar,* no.313.
—. 2000. *Narratives and the Making of History.* New Delhi: Oxford University Press.
—. 2007. "Is secularism alien to Indian civilization?"in *The Future of Secularism,* ed. Thirukodikaval Nilakanta Srinivasan, 83–108. New Delhi : Oxford University Press.
Vanaik, Achin 1997. *The Furies of Indian Communalism.* London: Verso.

Van der Veer, Peter 2001. *Imperial Encounters. Religion and Modernity in India and Britain*. Princeton: Princeton University Press.
Visvanathan, Shiv 2001. "The race for caste: prolegomena to the Durban Conference." *Economic and Political Weekly*, 36 (27): 2512–2516.
Zelliot, Eleanor 2001. *From Untouchable to Dalit. Essays on the Ambedkar Movement*. New Delhi: Manohar.

Part II: **Nationalism, Islam and Democratization: Secular Dynamics in the Arab World**

Daniel Kinitz
Deviance as a Phenomenon of Secularity: Islam and Deviants in Twentieth-century Egypt—A Search for Sociological Explanations[1]

What is a Muslim scholar to do if he is asked for a fatwa on an originally non-religious topic, say if drinking cola or consuming a certain drug is *ḥalāl* or *ḥarām* (religiously permissible or forbidden)? To reject the question as being outside religious competence might suggest that religion is not universal – especially a problem for Islam, which is constructed as *dīn wa-dunyā* (religion and 'wordly' world) within the discursive tradition of scholars of Islamic law. But instead of practising individual reasoning (*ijtihād*), such scholars have begun to ask technical specialists.[2] In this way, Egyptian scholars have shown how Islam can cope with the modern phenomenon that being an expert in certain field normally includes being a *lay person* in other domains of life.[3] What Peter L. Berger and Thomas Luckmann said about religious laymen proves to be true for religious scholars as well when they are confronted with problems originating from a non-religious social field: the scientific, economic etc. "'lay' member of society no longer knows" how to generate an answer relying merely on his own knowledge, but he "still knows who the specialists [...] are presumed to be" (1991: 130). In the words of the renowned Arab scholar Yūsuf al-Qaraḍāwī concerning contemporary fatwa-giving: "If the doctor says: this is harmful, the Mufti must say: this is *ḥarām*." (2008: 72).

Obviously there are social domains that are clearly separated from religion, but which still do not represent a problem for a religious claim to universality. At least the aforementioned problems can be translated into an Islamic code, enabling Islamic solutions to be offered for what are, technically speaking, non-Is-

---

[1] I thank Monika Wohlrab-Sahr and Marian Burchardt for comments on earlier versions of this article.
[2] In the case of drinking cola, the little-known Grand Mufti ʿAllām Naṣṣār declared it religiously permissible in 1951 after consulting experts from the Ministry of Health (see Skovgaard-Petersen 1997: 171–172).
[3] Contemporary examples include the former Grand Imam of al-Azhar Sayyid Ṭanṭāwī (1928–2010), consulting experts on financial transactions (Skovgaard-Petersen 1997: 302), and the famous scholar Yūsuf al-Qaraḍāwī (b. 1926), who discussed issuing fatwas in the modern world (al-Qaraḍāwī 2008).

lamic questions. Dynamics, sometimes taking the form of a conflict, rather seem to appear at another boundary. We are talking about Muslim scholars and intellectuals who have been excluded as deviants and, at the end of the twentieth century, as "secularists" (*'almānīyūn*) by members of an Islamic establishment.[4]

The present article suggests that this construction of deviance as non- or anti-religious can be understood as a phenomenon of secularity. As has become clear within general debates on the notion of secularity and its different variants, including secularism and secularization, there is a broad field of different understandings. Bringing these varying understandings into a meaningful order has already been attempted.[5] One of the latest suggestions of a general but still precise notion is that put forward by Wohlrab-Sahr and Burchardt, who define secularity as "forms and arrangements of differentiation between religion and other social spheres" (2012: 881), or, as I would generalize it, between the religious and the non-religious.

In the following, I argue how different cases from twentieth-century Egypt can be understood as a challenge to Islam as generated by its establishment.[6] While this challenge is dealt with by constructing a boundary between an 'orthodox'[7] religion and the (claimed) non- or anti-religious deviants, a modern Islamic identity is being generated.

But what exactly challenges Islam and its establishment? To provide an answer, I will apply two theoretical approaches summarizing and explaining cases of (the construction of) deviance in twentieth-century Egypt. The first approach, following Berger and Luckmann as well as Bourdieu, explains deviance as a competing *symbolic universe*. The second approach, following Luhmann's social systems theory, explains deviance as a mere religious construction, being an answer to the challenges of a modern society. Both approaches include the construction of identity as a distinction between self and other. In this way, the

---

4 These periods are roughly consistent with 1924–1952, as well as the period after 1967.
5 Besides Casanova 1994, Dobbelaere 2002, Lübbe 1965 and Swatos, William and Olson 2000, see the recently translated Luhmann 2013, 201–231. For reflections on the notion of secularity and the secular in the context of the Arab world and Islam, see especially Agrama 2010, Asad 2003 and Asad et al. 2009, as well as Schulze 2010 and Tibi 1980.
6 For the argument that the secular (here: secularization) is primarily a problem for religion, see Casanova 1994, 20, and, for a reflection as to why this is the case, Luhmann 2013: 201–231. A similar approach applied to Islam is Roy 2007, though it is based on an ontological equivalence between religion and secularism.
7 Within both Sunni Islam and Islamic studies it is stressed that, instead of speaking of *orthodoxy*, the term *orthopraxy* is to be preferred, since there is no church defining the religious truth but rather a common standard of how to practise religion. As we can see in the following, speaking of orthodoxy may nevertheless make sense.

two sociological understandings of deviance can be summed up as a phenomenon of secularity, not simply referring to something non-religious, but to the construction of a boundary between religion and what is claimed to be non- or anti-religious.

1 Examples from the Twentieth Century

'Deviant' publications in the first half of the twentieth century in Egypt caused smaller or larger scandals or at least attracted disciplinary rebukes. One of the lesser known examples is Muḥammad Abū Zayd's *al-Hidāyah wa-al-ʿirfān fī tafsīr al-Qurʾān bi-al-Qurʾān* (1930) on a self-referential interpretation of the Qurʾān.[8] It was confiscated shortly after its publication or, more precisely, after it had attracted the public attention of potential sympathizers and critics alike. Abū Zayd not only broke with the tradition of leaving aside established commentaries, he also wanted to clean up Qurʾān interpretations of superstitions, relying on reason rather than on standing traditions.[9] Muḥammad Rashīd Riḍā (1865–1935), the famous reformer and editor of the Pan-Islamic journal *al-Manār*, accused him of *ilḥād* or atheism and deviation alike (Riḍā 1931).[10] Some scholars brought the case to court, accusing him of apostasy and calling for separation from his wife, since a non-Muslim cannot be married to a Muslim woman. But a court in Cairo finally decided in Abū Zayd's favor (see Jefferey 1932: 302). Another, politically sensitive interpretation was that of Qurʾān 4:59, requiring the believer to "obey God and obey the messenger and those in charge [or in authority] among you (*ūlī al-amr minkum*)". From the latter, Abū Zayd concluded that a government is supposed to consist of more than one person, which implicitly disqualified the monarchy at that time as not being in accordance with Islam (see Jansen 1980: 88). Still today, copies of this commentary on the Qurʾān are hard to find in Egypt.

In the following, we will not dwell on individual cases, but only give a brief overview, since all examples can be understood as one and the same phenomenon: a challenge to Islam and its establishment. Better known *causes célèbres*

---

8 The work is not easily available to this day; I have had to rely on secondary sources.
9 In this way, the famous night journey (*isrāʾ*) of Mohammed to Jerusalem becomes the Hijra to Medina in Abū Zayd's view, with the consequence that the famous Aqsa mosque (lit.: remote mosque) is not the one in Jerusalem. See Jefferey 1932: 305–306.
10 See Riḍā 1931, the first of four articles on Abū Zayd. Although Riḍā had personal reasons for this emotional reaction, the book was still considered atheistic in the 1970s (see al-Dhahabī [1976] 2000, 2: 390–400).

in which deviants were constructed are connected to 'Alī 'Abd al-Rāziq's *al-Islām wa-uṣūl al-ḥukm* (1925) on an apolitical, spiritual Islam, Ṭāhā Ḥusayn's *Fī al-shi'r al-Jāhilī* (1926) on the inauthenticity of the literary and Islamic traditions, the same author's *Mustaqbal al-thaqāfah fī Miṣr* (1938) on a liberal education program, Muḥammad Aḥmad Khalaf Allāh's *al-Fann al-qiṣaṣī fī al-Qur'ān al-karīm* (1948/51) on a metaphorical understanding of the Qur'ān, and Khālid Muḥammad Khālid's *Min hunā nabda'* (1950) as a critique of a clerical Islam and a plea for the separation of Islam from politics ('Abd al-Rāziq [1925] 1993; Ḥusayn [1926] 2012, [1938] 2011; Khalaf Allāh 1951; Khālid 1974). All these authors had to face sanctions often going beyond the censorship of their aforementioned works. 'Alī 'Abd al-Rāziq was first dismissed from his office as a judge and excluded from the circle of scholars,[11] while Ṭāhā Ḥusayn und Khālid Muḥammad Khālid were sued by conservatives and their 'provocative' publications removed from the market.[12] Ḥusayn was probably only able to retain his job as a professor at the University of Cairo through the patronage of the famous intellectual Aḥmad Luṭfī al-Sayyid, the then rector. 'Alī 'Abd al-Rāziq and Khālid Muḥammad Khālid publicly repudiated their views.[13]

The first group of cases of exclusion can be delimited historically as lying within the period between the abolition of the Islamic Caliphate (1924) and the coup of the Free Officers (1952). In particular, the early cases (about 'Abd al-Rāziq and Ḥusayn) can be regarded as a sign of a changed social and political role for Islam and its scholars, which had apparently become contingent. This also applies to prominent cases of Islam-related deviance in the late twentieth century. After the decline of Nasserism after 1967 and the 'conversion' of a number of Leftist intellectuals to political Islam in the 1970s, a number of heated debates between members of an Islamic establishment and its critics occurred in the late 1980s and 1990s (see especially Flores 1988, 1993, 2012).

Members of that establishment (scholars and intellectuals) in particular argued insistently that the decision was between Islam and what was now called secularism (*al-'almānīyah*) and claimed to be against religion. A sad climax, and

---

[11] See the argumentation and declaration of the Grand Imam of al-Azhar and 24 scholars from 25.08.1925, documented in al-Khaṭīb 1993. Good sources in Arabic include Shāhīn 2001 and Shalabī [1994]; for English and French sources, see Adams 1933: 259–68; Arkoun 1994; Binder 1988: 128–169; Filali-Ansary 1994.

[12] On Ḥusayn's work as well as his role as a critic of society, see Ayalon 2009, Cachia 1956, Gibb 1929, Hourani 1983 and Ibrahim 1992.

[13] While 'Abd al-Rāziq obviously gave in to social pressure, Khālid started to publish works stressing the sovereignty of Islam. Ḥusayn modified his work on pre-Islamic literature, leaving aside some provocative statements.

particularly relevant for our analysis, was the stigmatization of Faraj Fūdah (Fawdah) and Naṣr Ḥāmid Abū Zayd as Islamophobic secularists in the 1990s, accompanied by threats against other intellectuals, which continues to this day.[14] In my view, Faraj Fūdah is the only one of these intellectuals, who – at least in the early 1980s – explicitly professed secularism (al-'almānīyah) as part of a normative political ideology. The controversies connected to Fūdah and Abū Zayd have both been examined in detail and will only briefly be recalled here.[15]

Faraj Fūdah (1945–1992), who holds a PhD in agriculture, was an intellectual and a member of the conservative New Wafd Party. As a public figure, he was actively engaged in criticizing the Islamic establishment, calling at times openly for a secular state, defined by the separation of politics and religion (clerics).[16] In 1992 he openly opposed two famous Azharite scholars, who were simultaneously members of the Muslim Brotherhood, in a public discussion on "Islam and secularism". The same year, Fūdah was publicly accused of *kufr* (unbelief) and anti-Islamic secularism by Azharite scholars, above all 'Umar b. 'Abd al-Raḥmān. Two months later Fūdah was killed by members of the militant al-Jamā'ah al-islāmīyah on the grounds of his being an unbeliever (see Hatina 2007: 47–70).

Naṣr Ḥāmid Abū Zayd (1943–2010) was a professor at the Department of Arabic Language and Literature at Cairo University. In his controversial book *Naqd al-khiṭāb al-dīnī* (1992) he criticized what he called the "religious discourse" (Abū Zayd [1992] 2003). He not only claimed that an Islamic establishment, especially scholars, had monopolized the discourse on Islam, therefore representing some kind of priesthood (2003: 80) – maybe even more provocative was his claim that there is no difference in principle between the discourse of an extremist Islam and the claimed moderation of that very establishment (2003: 67). In the first half of the 1990s, there was not only a controversy about his promotion to full professorship (1992–95): Abū Zayd was also stigmatized as an apostate and forcibly divorced on this ground (1993–96), although he himself was a devout Muslim.[17] Behind the actions taken against Abū Zayd were mem-

---

[14] Death threats made to other intellectuals include the attorney Muḥammad Sa'īd al-'Ashmāwī (1980s), the Leftist politician Rif'at al-Sa'īd, the philosopher Ḥasan Ḥanafī (1990s) and Sayyid Maḥmūd al-Qimnī (in 2005).

[15] For a brief overview of the *causes célèbres* concerning Fūdah, Abū Zayd and others, see Marshall and Shea 2011: 61–82. Further details can be found in Hatina 2007 (on Fūdah) and Thielmann 2003 (on Abū Zayd).

[16] See his political reform program including an explicit commitment to secularity/ secularism (both *al- 'almānīyah* in Arabic), Fūdah 1983: 74.

[17] The best coverage on this case is only available in German: Thielmann 2003.

bers of a conservative establishment, above all ʿAbd al-Ṣabūr Shāhīn (1928–2010), Professor of linguistics at Cairo University and preacher at the famous ʿAmr ibn al-ʿĀṣ mosque.[18]

But what conceptual instruments were used to deal with these 'deviants' in the twentieth century?

2 Concepts of Deviance

The basic concept underlying the construction of deviance is that of a boundary with two (presupposed) clearly opposed sides: Islam and non-Islam. The point here is that this distinction is not a symmetrical one, but made from one side, the side claiming to represent Islam, at the same time excluding what it sees as deviant. This is not only true for modern constructions, but also for Qurʾānic terms such as *ridda/irtidād* (apostasy), *kufr* (disbelief) and *ilḥād* (atheism). In this way, something non-Islamic could be designated and handled from an explicitly Islamic point of view. But this integration of a non-Islamic outside into an Islamic inside is connected with a paradox, since the non-Islamic is incorporated symbolically into Islam.[19] With the evolution of the Arabic term *al-ʿalmānīyah* (secularism, secularity) in the nineteenth century, peaking in the late twentieth century, this paradox has become even more apparent. One of the central modern terms to describe the opposites of Islam or non-Islam respectively cannot be traced back to traditional Islamic sources, but is itself 'secular' in the sense of being of non-religious origin. An early entry in a French-Arabic dictionary, published in the aftermath of Napoleon Bonaparte's *campaign* in Egypt and Syria (1798–1801), roughly marks the birth of a word that was not yet a socially grounded notion[20] and was for a long time without any social relevance. A century later, when European influence had settled in the Middle East, the problem connected to *al-ʿalmānīyah/ secularism* mainly concerned European actors and their paradigms, sometimes quite properly perceived as anti-religious. Prominent examples include "secularist" European schools popular with Arab locals equa-

---

18 One other opponent was the scholar Yūsuf al-Badrī, speaker of the group of lawyers who accused Abū Zayd of being an apostate and, since there was no Egyptian law punishing apostasy, petitioned for a divorce.

19 It can thus be said that the unbeliever, apostate etc. is actually still part of the world of Islam, although he does not belong to it in a strict sense. This paradox is based on the difference between facts and norms.

20 See Bocthor 1827/29, 2:3 on *laïque*, translated as *ʿalmānī*. Bocthor (Buqṭur) was an Egyptian Copt who served as a dragoman during Bonaparte's campaign, migrating to France afterwards.

ted with "unbelief" and "atheism".[21] On the intellectual level one can also find other notions to grasp phenomena at the outside boundary of Islam around 1900. When the Egyptian reformist scholar Muḥammad ʿAbduh (1849–1905) translated and edited a work on non-religious schools of thought – from Socrates to Voltaire to socialism (!) – he preferred the notion of *dahrīyūn* (materialists) in the title of the second edition,[22] using a derivate of the Qurʾānic term *dahr*, signifying *saeculum* as well as the temporal *world*.[23] But the recoined term *al-dahrīyah* (materialism), like the contemporary term *al-ʿalmānīyah*, was not able to gain ground in the following decades. Both, *kufr* (unbelief) and *ilḥād* (atheism) seemed to be the first choice to grasp something on the other side of Islam.[24] But such terms are linked to a modern problem: in a world where tolerance has also become an issue in Islam, detecting unbelief and declaring someone an unbeliever (*takfīr*) has become politically incorrect. Nowadays it is rather militant fundamentalists who openly practice *takfīr*, while Muslim scholars and intellectuals who believe that they represent the views of a broad, moderate center admonish pointing to others not as unbelievers but rather as non-Muslims (*ghayr al-muslimīn*) (e. g. al-Qaraḍāwī 2004: 44). Especially when it comes to 'deviating', anti-Islamist Muslim thinkers, it cannot be ignored that so-called deviants see themselves in a different way – either as neutral or as friendly towards religion – and that they have rather feelings of discomfort about Islamists and scholars appearing as spokesmen for Islam.[25]

During the rise of Islamism in the 1970s, some Islamist thinkers would refer to what they called *al-ʿalmānīyah* (secularism) as the deniable cultural equivalent of the social order, established by French and British rule over Egypt as de-

---

21 See, for example, the letter to and the response by the above-mentioned journal *al-Manār* in 1911, complaining about a popular "secular(ist) non-religious" French school in Beirut (Ḥaffār 1911).
22 This is the famous translation of the Persian original by Pan-Islamic reformist Jamāl al-Dīn al-Afghānī criticizing what he called in Persian the *nayčariyān* (naturalists) summing up different schools of thought (al-Afghānī [1903]). One prominent pre-modern example is the treatise *al-Munqidh min aḍ-ḍalāl* by Abū Ḥāmid al-Ghazālī (1058–1111), accusing *materialists* (*dahrīyūn*) and others of atheism (*ilḥād*).
23 The Qurʾān refers to Arab pagans believing in a cyclical world without a hereafter. The above-mentioned use of *dahrīyah* as materialism is a recoinage.
24 Thus, the above-mentioned work by ʿAbd al-Rāziq was defined as "atheism" in the Egyptian press in 1925 (see al-Khaṭīb 1993: 4).
25 Note that in Arabic the words for *Islamic* and *Islamist* are homonymous (both *islāmī*), which makes it easier to appear as a representative of Islam.

viation from the rule of the Islamic *sharī'a*.²⁶ When in the 1980s and the beginning of the 1990s Islamists debated in public with non-Islamist intellectuals (see Flores 2012), it was mainly the former observing *al-'almānīyah* (secularism) in their accompanying articles and books, whereas the latter saw a problem in the growing social and political dominance of Islam, or more precisely, in its self-proclaimed representatives.²⁷ For the critics of secularism, *al-'almānīyah* became a notion including all they rejected as non- or anti-Islamic: materialism (here: *al-māddīyah*, not the above mentioned ancient *al-dahrīyah*), atheism, Nasserism (which in the view of many Egyptians had failed) and connected to that, nationalism, Marxism or socialism respectively. It is therefore no surprise that at least four of the above-mentioned 'deviating' works and their authors from the early twentieth century are retrospectively discussed and connected explicitly with *secularism*,²⁸ and four of the works are still being re-issued (Khalaf Allāh 1999, 'Abd al-Rāziq 2007, Ḥusayn 2011; Ḥusayn 2012). The point here is that it is mainly the critics of *secularism* who construct what *al-'almānīyah* is and at the same time draw a boundary between Islam and non-Islam.²⁹ To give some examples, when the scholars Yūsuf al-Qaraḍāwī and Muḥammad al-Ghazālī discussed "Islam and secularism" with the philosopher Fu'ād Zakarīyā in a publicly advertised panel discussion in Cairo in 1986, it was al-Qaraḍāwī ([1987] 1997), as a critic of secularism, who felt the need to investigate secularism (in contrast to Islam) further, while Zakarīyā's works focused on the so-called *Islamic awakening* (*al-ṣaḥwah al-islāmīyah*) (1986; 1987).³⁰ When the intellectuals Muḥammad 'Imāra, Faraj Fūdah and others publicly discussed the identity of Egypt "between civil and religious state"³¹ in 1992, it was 'Imāra, again a critic of secularism, who

---

26 As examples, see al-Qaraḍāwī [1977] 1993, as well as al-'Awwā [1975] 2008, who makes a distinction between an Islamic and a secular(ist) *maṣlaḥah* (public interest, welfare).
27 From time to time so-called ‚secularist' intellectuals would more or less admit their affirmative stance to ‚secularity' (in Arabic also *al-'almānīyah*). To my knowledge only Faraj Fūdah would integrate this into a political programme (1983: esp. 74–77), and even then only as one aspect besides others.
28 First of all *al-Islām wa-uṣūl al-ḥukm* and *Fī al-shi'r al-Jāhilī* as well as *Mustabqal al-thaqāfa fī Miṣr* and *Min hunā nabda'*. See in particular 'Imāra [1993]: 39–44 and 45–49; 'Imāra 21.09.2011; 'Imāra 29.09.2011; al-Qaraḍāwī 1993: 47–52 and, less prominent, Shāhīn, 2001, 2005.
29 Within pro-secular, anti-Islamist circles, rather, the notion of *tanwīr* (enlightenment) is to be found in the 1990s.
30 For a description of the panel discussion and the main arguments, see Gallagher 1989.
31 For documentation, see 'Imāra 2011. Note that the official title "Miṣr bayna al-dawla al-madanīyah wa-al-dīnīyah" (Egypt between civil and religious state) – chosen by Fūdah – does not contain the notion *secularity* or *secularism*, but instead *madanī* (civil) in the senses of "not military" or "not theocratic" respectively.

published several books on *al-'almānīyah* and Islam.³² When 'Abd al-Ṣabūr Shāhīn tried to prevent his colleague Naṣr Ḥāmid Abū Zayd from being promoted to a full professorship, it was the former who edited a collection of articles (Shāhīn [1994]) against the "Marxist" Abū Zayd in particular and against secularism in general.

In this respect, *al-'almānīyah/ secularism* was framed by (self-acclaimed) Islamic perspectives as foreign threat to Islam, and therefore to the whole of society, especially in the late 1980s and early 1990s. In this context, Azharite scholars were able to construct the intellectual and political activist Faraj Fūdah as a foreign instrument of postcolonial secularism and insinuate that Fūdah would agitate aggressively against symbols of Islam.³³ In this situation, the renowned journalist Fahmī Huwaydī was able to construct "secularist extremism" (*taṭarruf 'almānī*) and its agents as *muftarūn*, or 'inventors of lies' against religion.³⁴ In this context, the university professor 'Abd al-Ṣabūr Shāhīn was able to construct secularism as subversion (*takhrīb*) of Egyptian society and declare that its "agent" Naṣr Ḥāmid Abū Zayd could be nothing else than a secularist enemy of Islam.³⁵ But how were the perceived deviants dealt with?

3 Dealing with Deviants

In the first half of the twentieth century, sanctions not only included disciplinary actions but were also followed by possible 'reintegration'. 'Abd al-Rāziq repudiated his own ideas by declaring himself temporarily not liable³⁶ and was rehabilitated. Ḥusayn published a version of his work expurgated of religious prov-

---

32 Among the more important ones I count 'Imāra [1992] 1997, since the al-Azhar and the then Grand Imam were involved in the publication of the first edition. Fūdah had only published one small collection of essays (2005), taking the title of the first one, *Ḥiwār ḥawla al-'almānīyah* (Dialogue with secularism), as the title of the book, while the remaining essays dealt with existing problems connected to Islamism and the state.
33 See the anonymous declaration "al-'Almānīyūn adāh gharbīyah... li-tashwīh al-Islām" (01.04.1992). Fūdah was murdered by Islamist militants two months later.
34 This is a derivation of the Qur'ānic *iftirā'*, regularly translated as "inventing a lie", "inventing a falsehood" or "fabricating a lie", namely against God (see e.g. 3:94; 6:21; 7:37).
35 See Shāhīn [1994], esp. 5 and 242. Abū Zayd (1995: 9) himself even claims that Shāhīn had declared him a *kāfir* (unbeliever) during his Friday sermon at the 'Amr ibn al-'Āṣ mosque in April 1994.
36 See 'Abd al-Rāziq's statement that the devil had taken possession of his tongue, documented in al-Khaṭīb 1993: 7.

ocations (1927)[37] and became dean and later minister of education. The giving in to social pressure may serve as an explanation: the 'deviating' ideas of the author just had to be corrected through either a public announcement of his 'review' or appeasement. On the other hand there are obviously cases where intellectuals authentically converted from a 'secular' ideology to political Islam. Khālid Muḥammad Khālid declared that he had been *mistaken*, and advanced the political idea of Islam as *dīn wa-dawla* (religion and state) (see Binder 1988: 159–161).[38] Actions against 'secularist' deviants in the 1990s and beyond seem to have been more threatening: Fūdah was killed, while Naṣr Ḥāmid Abū Zayd was forcibly divorced and died in exile fifteen years later. Others, such as the leftist Rifʿat al-Saʿīd, the attorney Muḥammad Saʿīd al-ʿAshmāwī and the intellectual Sayyid Maḥmūd al-Qimnī, are still under threat. But how can the social construction of deviation and the disciplinary reactions that followed be explained?

4 Conflict and Field (Bourdieu)

In a common sociological view, the examples mentioned above can be reconstructed as a social field in which newcomers ('secularist' outsiders) with relatively little capital (authority in questions of Islam) fight against a dominating establishment holding the most capital specific to this field, with the newcomers trying to overcome the establishment and to become the rulers of the field themselves.[39] Obviously, the externalized deviants are coupled with conservative Islamic scholars and intellectuals, as well as with Islamist militants.[40] The dynamics of the quarrels could be explained using an assumption of early conflict theory: "The closer the relationship, the more intense the conflict" (Coser 1956: 67–72, discussing Georg Simmel). Taking a theory of social fields as a framework for explanation, it can be argued that a conservative Islamic establishment (*orthodox* Azharite scholars as well as anti-secularist intellectuals) dominated the

---

37 However, he still argued that certain poetry, traditionally attributed as *jāhilī* (part of the pre-Islamic era of ignorance or *al-Jāhilīyah*), emerged only after the advent of Islam.
38 Conversions from the second half of the twentieth century, especially after 1967, include Ṭāriq al-Bishrī, Ḥasan Ḥanafī and Muḥammad ʿImāra.
39 Instead of modern sociology (Pierre Bourdieu et al.), see the "Prolegomena" (al-Muqaddimah) by Ibn Khaldūn (1332–1406) on the circulation of power between a sluggish urban establishment and vital Bedouins.
40 They are *coupled*, I would argue, since at least representatives of the establishment think that they are talking about the same thing: Islam.

Egyptian public discourse on Islam, at least in the 1980s and 1990s. This is also indicated by the fact that the Egyptian regime had to use religion for its own purposes but could not prevail against orthodox Azharite scholars and Muslim intellectuals.[41] Within this framework of explanation, the new players ('secularists') are equipped with less capital (religious authority). In this respect, it may be argued that a revoking or, in the case of Ṭāhā Ḥusayn, a modification of his book on Jāhilīyah poetry ([1927] 1933) constitutes a concession to the discursive dominance of an Islamic establishment. But it can also be seen as a shrewd move to accustom the Egyptian public to *liberal* ideas on Islam at a pace that is seemingly more successful in the long term than the distribution of idiosyncratic and therefore irritating views (see Ayalon 2009: 121). Another example: when the 'deviant' Sayyid al-Qimnī (b. 1947) publicly declared that he would stop writing in 2005 (documented in Ismāʿīl 2005: 13), he did not change his views but obviously only gave in to death threats by militant Islamists – just to publish a whole series of critical works again after some time spent waiting.[42] Obviously the conflict is asymmetrical in relation to authority, but it also asymmetrical in other respects.

The construction of opponents depends on what and whom an Islamic establishment and Islamists observe as being *deviant*, non-Islamic or even anti-Islamic. In principle, this construction of deviation can come from whoever makes Islam explicit within the Egyptian public sphere, first of all major institutions such as the al-Azhar and its scholars, the Fatwa council (*Dār al-Iftāʾ*) and the Muslim Brotherhood. The fact that some Azharite scholars, first of all the Grand Imam, as well as intellectuals close to the Muslim Brotherhood warned of a secularist danger at the beginning of the 1990s[43] can be interpreted as actors threatened by a potential loss of power.

Additionally, it can be argued that the so-called secularists become deviants only from a certain Islamic perspective; as well as that the situation is perceived as competitive or as conflict primarily from a certain Islamic point of view. Theoretically speaking, against the background of encountering "symbolic universes", the construction of social reality, as well as its cognitive and normative certainties, is jeopardized fundamentally by deviants representing doubts with or

---

41 But since the publication of views not only belongs to a religious but also intellectual field, grounded on technical reproduction, the state can exercise influence on publishers or run its own publishing houses (see González-Quijano 1998).
42 See his critical series of essays against scholars and the Muslim Brotherhood with titles such as "Get out of our mosques!" (al-Qimnī 2007).
43 In addition to the above-mentioned article in *al-Nūr*, see al-Qaraḍāwī 1993, Quṭb 1994 and al-Maṭʿanī 2006.

without expressing them.⁴⁴ But the perceived challenge of the 'secularists' does not itself constitute a claim to power; rather, critics of an established Islam and its discourse undermine the rules of the social field (see Kinitz, in preparation). Therefore, the question is how such seemingly subversive deviations are dealt with. Taking the field approach mentioned above, one can argue that the established owners of the field-specific capital tend to conservation strategies and create a kind of Islamic, anti-secularist orthodoxy.⁴⁵ Under the name of *al-'almānīyah* as an identity-generating demarcation scheme, this has especially been the case in the late twentieth century.

5 Modifications of the Symbolic Universe

One essential aspect of creating an Islamic 'orthodoxy' is the modification of established Islamic semantics. Deviant terms have to be translated (decoded) into an 'authentic' Islamic language to make them useable for a self-acclaimed orthodox perspective.⁴⁶ In the last decades of the twentieth century, this decoding could subsequently follow patterns of thinking developed by founders of modern Islamism, above all Sayyid Quṭb (1906–1966). In a discursive engagement with Western ('wordly') ideas on the political order of society, Quṭb tried to reconstruct an Islamic identity of the *umma*, the nation of Islam, by decoding its most important features as *authentic* Islamic concepts. According to him, *jinsīyah* (nationality) can be plausibly reconstructed as *'aqīda* (credo), *waṭan* (homeland, nation) as *dār al-Islām* (house/ land of Islam), the *ḥākim* (ruler) as *Allāh*, and the *dustūr* (constitution) as the *Qur'ān*.⁴⁷

---

44 In other words: "The appearance of an alternative symbolic universe poses a threat because its very existence demonstrates empirically that one's own universe is less than inevitable." (Berger and Luckmann 1991: 126).
45 See the observation in Bourdieu [1984] 1995: 73: "Heresy, heterodoxy, functioning as a critical break with doxa (and often associated with a crisis), is what brings the dominant agents out of their silence and forces them to produce the defensive discourse of orthodoxy, the right thinking, right-wing thought that is aimed at restoring the equivalent of silent assent to doxa."
46 See the observation in Berger and Luckmann 1991: 133: "Second, nihilation involves the more ambitious attempt to account for all deviant definitions of reality in terms of concepts belonging to one's own universe. In a theological frame of reference, this entails the transition from heresiology to apologetics. The deviant conceptions are not merely assigned a negative status, they are grappled with theoretically in detail."
47 See Quṭb's famous *Ma'ālim fī al-ṭarīq* ([1964] 1979: 146) adopting ideas by Ḥasan al-Bannā. In this respect Quṭb defends a universality of Islam (not necessarily its exclusivity), which is rather a defense of Muslim societies against 'foreign' cultural supremacy.

Common Islamic apologetics against secularism and the West come close to this self-assertion: Islam is claimed naturally to include modern achievements such as freedom and democracy. In other words: Islam does not have to be modernized since its principles always have been modern. And it seems to be the same with the notion and phenomenon al-'almānīyah: since Islam does not have a church, as critics of secularism claim, it cannot be secularized.[48] Hence, making modernity and secularism an issue in Muslim societies is supposed to be something artificial.[49] But, why has secularism or al-'almānīyah been such a challenge if Islam as such is claimed to be modern? In other words, what problems are coped with when an explicitly *Islamic* perspective observes *secularism* as foreign and deviant?

Assuming that deviations from Islam as well as secularism are constructed from without – deviants as well as secularists would normally not call themselves such – it is likely that discussing the content of 'secularist' works will not produce new findings on secularism as such. Rather, deviations appear in the eyes of an established 'Islamic' beholder who observes these works. From a sociological point of view it can be suggested first that what is perceived as deviant does not correspond to the traditional, prevailing (established) world view and its socially constructed truths and norms.[50] This includes examples mentioned above such as 'Abd al-Rāziq's spiritual Islam, Ḥusayn's historically only partially authentic Qur'ān in the early twentieth century, and Faraj Fūdah's and Naṣr Ḥāmid Abū Zayd's critique of an Islamic establishment in the late twentieth century. The perceived deviation of such perspectives on Islam seemed to have been so irritating to the Islamic 'holders of truth' that they provoked an explication of 'orthodox' premises. The general argument in creating an Islamic orthodoxy is denying the deviant's right to have a reasonable claim to truth by trying to detect fallacies. Here, one can think of all the publications that defend Islam against secularism (see Flores 2012; Kinitz, in prep.). Another option is to claim that the 'deviant' ultimately knows that he is ignoring the truth and that in any case he would be up to no good.[51] Though insincerity cannot be demonstrat-

---

48 But see the above-mentioned Abū Zayd 2003: 80, observing a contradiction between the scholar's claim and the reality of a priesthood in Islam.
49 In this respect, the artificiality either consists of secularism as foreign (e. g. Jād al-Ḥaqq: *Taqdīm*, in 'Imāra 1997: 8; Quṭb 1994: 31) or, from an affirmative perspective, as something already contained in Islam (Ḥanafī [1989]: 304; al-Bannā 20.10.2011).
50 There is no doubt that personal disputes as well as power struggles are often involved at the same time.
51 In the words of Berger and Luckmann (1991: 133): "One need, therefore, only search their statements carefully to discover the defensiveness and bad faith of their position. Whatever

ed directly (see Luhmann [1984] 1995: 150), making an issue out of it can rather lead to suspicions – in this case, that the question is not about truth, but about moral devaluation. The point here is not that the activists of an Islamic establishment are running out of arguments, but that religious truth is actually reduced to a mere *claim* within a modern public sphere. It can dominate the public opinion, but it does not have any monopoly.

Since mass media give room not only for established Islamic views but also for 'deviant' or 'secular(ist)' view, every spokesman for Islam has to remember that 'deviations' from an established Islam are published as truths as well. Consequently, even if an established Islamic authority tries to correct deviant views in public by drawing a boundary between *right* and *wrong* Islam, it remains one, but not the only voice of Islam. Thus, establishing the boundary of Islam by explicating what it is not is apparently associated with a claim to exclusive access to absolute truth. Following this pattern, the Grand scholars (*kibār al- 'ulamā'*) who excluded 'Alī 'Abd al-Rāziq from the 'group of scholars' (*zumrat al-'ulamā'*) in 1925 had to claim to know what Islam is, as well as what it is not.[52] Their exclusive claim to truth was revealed in the fact that, whoever represented an opinion perceived by them as deviant could not know the truth and thus could not be a scholar.[53] In this way, a contradiction becomes apparent: while scholars handled the truth as being one and as referring to something absolute, the social act of exclusion indicated that religious truth is in fact contingent and bound socially.[54] In other words, the modern plurality of contradicting truths becomes a problem for anyone claiming to have access to an absolute, exclusive truth. Therefore any deviant claim to truth represents a potential challenge.

Cases from the early twentieth century ('Abd al-Rāziq, Ḥusayn) show how it is possible to deal 'successfully' with such a challenge by disciplining actual deviants and warning potential ones. For the late twentieth century, public and private disciplining, such as death threats by militant Islamists, can be interpreted as a mean to keep potential deviants within the "institutionalized definitions of

---

they say in this matter can thus be translated [...]. In a theological frame of reference the same procedure demonstrates [...], that all unbelief is but unconscious dishonesty, even that the atheist is *really* a believer."

52 That this was not a foregone conclusion was evidenced by the fact that they were, after all, trying to refute central arguments by 'Abd al-Rāziq on several pages (al-Khaṭīb 1993: 15–45).
53 See the declaration on the exclusion (*ikhrāj*) of scholars from the community (Ibid: 46).
54 This social dimension already becomes apparent when looking at the main sources of Sunni law: whenever a clear rule is missing in the Qur'ān and *sunna*, the consensus (*ijmā'*) of religious authorities or even of the *umma* can be referred to.

reality" (Berger and Luckmann [1966] 1991: 130). As a result, the concerned intellectuals have to live in fear or seek refuge under the protection of bodyguards – or, in the case of Sayyid al-Qimnī in 2005, declare they will stop writing. The case of al-Qimnī is also of interest because, in contrast to cases from the 1990s, it is again a case of a public surrender. Al-Qimnī declared his "regret" for his publications after a serious death threat by the militant group al-Jihād him of disbelief and blasphemy, giving him one week to announce his "repentance".

6 Making a Boundary of Islam Explicit

In my opinion, the case of the Muslim intellectual Jamāl al-Bannā (1920–2013) shows what can be said just yet, his views indicating boundaries of Islam, without being excluded as *secularist*.[55] Al-Bannā expresses the views outside of an accepted mainstream Islam such as permitting smoking in Ramadan (!) or condoning the exchange of kisses among the unmarried, especially among teenagers and young adults, provoking reactions from prominent official and unofficial speakers of Islam in the years between 2005 and 2008.[56] In 2006 he published an article which showed how to mark out the boundary of Islam using established arguments. In his weekly column in the daily newspaper *al-Miṣrī al-yawm* (2006–2013) he stated that there is "No life without religion... and no life with religion alone" (18.10.2006): adding "sports, play and amusement", in short, very *wordly* affairs, to social life was a matter of indifference to religion. Interestingly, this provoked no scandal as the former statements on smoking and kissing did, although this time it came at the end of Ramadan, when general public attention to religious issues is greater than the rest of the year. What were his arguments? Al-Bannā himself points out that: "If I want a society to be confined to religion, then there will be no human life as God has intended. Rather there is [or will be] human life as religious institutions and the men of religion want it to be [...], meaning nothing but the backwardness of society [...]."[57] (18.10.2006)

---

[55] This was the case, although al-Bannā himself sometimes, but always carefully, speaks of some of his views as being secular(istic).
[56] On al-Bannā as Islamic thinker (*mufakkir islāmī*) and his arguments, see Kinitz, in preparation.
[57] The Arabic original reads:

فإذا أريد للمجتمع أن يقتصر على الدين، فلن توجد حياة إنسانية كما أرادها الله، وإنما توجد حياة إنسانية كما تريدها المؤسسات الدينية ورجال الدين [...]، ولا يعنى هذا إلا تأخر المجتمع [...].

It is remarkable here how al-Bannā combines a critique of religious structures with common arguments. When he denies the authority of the al-Azhar and its scholars by insinuating *unwordliness*, he is attacking them with their own weapons: since an established argument claims that Islam is religion and *dunyā*, the temporal, actual ('wordly') world, in al-Bannās view they do not have enough knowledge of Islam in the broadest sense. The point here is that al-Bannā uses an argument from established Islamic discourse, which is also used against *secularism*, namely that Islam is more than religion (*dīn*). In short, al-Bannā arouses interest by using a provocative title but showing at the same time that his statements are based on an Islamic discursive tradition that is even accepted by the scholars he criticizes. More than once al-Bannā has been described as religiously unqualified, but to my knowledge he has never been stigmatized as deviant or secularist by established scholars or intellectuals.

7 The Differentiation of a Modern Society

If one analyzes the social position of those who are stigmatized as secularists or as opponents of Islam (the micro-level), one can come to the conclusion that an Islamic establishment holds the power to define what 'true' Islam is.[58] The focus, however, can also be placed on the challenge deviants pose for established opinions in the context of a modern society (macro-level).

In traditional societies without mass media a common world view could be taken for granted, and a difference of opinions could be bypassed or ended through geographical separation or social exclusion. Strangers could be successfully treated as *barbarians* and their existence treated as socially irrelevant (or waged war on), since they were outside the community (Berger and Luckmann 1991: 123). In Muslim history, at least from an established Sunni perspective, one could stylize the representatives of other interests and truths as disbelievers, who accordingly belonged to a different group (in a cognitive and normative sense) and therefore could not belong to the community of actual believers.[59] Another option was to integrate non-Muslims as "people of the book" into an Is-

---

58 This especially refers to al-Azhar. The Grand Imam of al-Azhar is de jure the highest authority on questions on Islam in Egypt. The Azharite Islamic Research Academy recommends which publications on Islam are to be banned and confiscated. Additionally, al-Azhar received constitutional status in 2012.
59 Just think of the dissensions after the death of Mohammed, accompanied by the formation of different groups (Sunnites, Shiites, Kharidjites, etc).

lamic society, since in practice they did not thwart the *authentic* world view – and if so, they could be left aside, treated by force or bound by contract, that is, by establishing social norms based on mutual expectations. In this sense, *non-Islamic* was something that could exist within one's own community, explicitly decoded as something somehow connected to Islam, for example, Jews and Christians. In cases of conflict, deviants could be geographically and socially externalized. In contrast, it can be argued, deviants cannot be socially excluded completely from all domains of a modern society – at least not by one actor.[60] And another problem arises: modern mass media cannot be controlled completely by one instance. In Egypt, where the al-Azhar recommends which publications concerning Islam are to be banned, prohibition can make a book even better known. Media reports on the ban arouse public curiosity, and forbidden books can be imported from Lebanon. This means that the power of specific actors cannot bypass the general structure of functional differentiation, including the functional logic of the media system.

This is even true for the rare cases of murder. The assassination of Faraj Fūdah by means of Islamist vigilantism in 1992 demonstrates not only a fundamentalist doubt over whether Egyptian law really corresponds to (their) Islam, it also shows that violence was obviously the last resort to try to exclude a 'deviant' from Egyptian society. But at the same time it promoted the author Faraj Fūdah and transformed his person as well as his thoughts into a symbol within social communication, reproduced as living by public remembrance in liberal newspapers, as well as by reprints of his books (Fūdah [1985] 2004, [1986] 2005, [1988] 2007).[61] Actors with the aim of fighting 'deviants' who are supposed to be enemies of Islam have to search for modern ways to cope with that.

In the case of ʿAlī ʿAbd al-Rāziq (1925), the scholars referred to the official law of the al-Azhar, enacted by the 'worldy' ruler ʿAbbās Ḥilmī II. By applying Article 101 of the law, decoding ʿAbd al-Rāziq's views as being not "appropriate with the description of scholarship" and therefore excluding him *legally*,[62] they transformed a question of religious truth into a question of law. In the contem-

---

60 This assumption, obviously following the approach of social systems theory, does not contradict two extreme cases: (1) murder would mean the annihilation of physical existence (as a precondition for social participation); (2) deprivation of citizenship could still include (lawfully illegal) social existence, including economic or other social interaction. One possible exception might be the banishment of citizens by the state, but in this case it could be argued that the banishment is concerned only with one national society, not with "world society" (in Luhmann's sense) as such.
61 Examples of articles about him in the liberal press are Ḥasan 08.06.2010 and ʿAbd al-Wahhāb 28.03.2013.
62 The law has been documented in *al-Manār* in three parts. For Article 101, see 8 (1911): 610.

porary case of Naṣr Ḥāmid Abū Zayd, legal action was begun especially in 1993, and in doing so, the final decision was left to the legal system. One can even find scholars like Yūsuf al-Badrī who regularly take deviations to court or Islamists like Muntaṣir al-Zayyāt who work as attorneys defending militant groups. In other words, the existence of functional differentiation between the religious and the legal systems has been accepted implicitly even by the conservatives and, partly, by revolutionaries. So, as mentioned in the beginning, the challenge for a (conservative) Islam does not lie in functional differentiation, or, so to speak, in a de facto secularization as such.

8 Conclusion

What is the challenge that deviants pose for Islam and its establishment in twentieth-century Egypt? As we have seen, deviants were not simply competitors of the capital of religious authority; rather, their very existence showed how traditional authority is being subverted (see Kinitz, in preparation). One (re)action of the Islamic establishment in handling this perceived problem of deviance was to create an 'orthodox' Islam, thereby justifying the exclusion. I would argue that the more deviance is criticized, the more important it becomes to create an orthodox religious identity.[63] In this way, deviance as something excluded becomes, so to speak, coupled to religion – exclusion of and explicit opposition to it is no successful way of getting rid of it.

One of the most general notions of exclusion is represented by the historically relatively new term *al-'ālmānīyah*, coined by its critics anti-Islamic secularism. At least in the 1990s, someone could be stigmatized by labeling him secularist (*'almānī*).[64] For twentieth-century Egypt it seems to be true that whoever challenges an exclusive claim, especially by showing the fallacies of an Islam socially bound to Muslims, must expect to be confronted with the stigma of deviation as well as with disciplinary action. This is much more than the power of an Islamic establishment, challenged by what its representatives claim to be deviant. It is the fact that the unity of a modern society cannot be brought to terms with a traditional Islam relying on a binary scheme of one concrete and exclusive truth.

---

[63] And both sides, 'true' Islam as well as 'deviance', are constructed by one and the same observer: the critics of deviance and, nowadays, "secularism".
[64] While today some critics of political Islam are trying to re-launch the term by means of the partly provocative confession of being a "secular [not necessarily secularist] Muslim" (*muslim 'almānī*).

The dissident Naṣr Ḥāmid Abū Zayd (1943–2010), mentioned above, constructed this problem of unity (oneness) versus pluralism as a problem of "the unification of thought and religion" (*tawḥīd al-fikr wa-al-dīn*) within what he calls the established "religious discourse", stating that:

[...] this insisting on the existence of one Islam and rejecting actual pluralism leads to two results, regardless of the intentions of this or that writer. The first result is that there is one stable meaning of Islam not affected by the movement of history, not affected by the difference of societies, as well as a pluralism of groups on the grounds of different interests within one society. The second result is that this one stable meaning is owned by a group of humans – they are categorically clerics – and that the members of this group are free from natural human passions and prejudices.[65] (2003: 79).

Here, Abū Zayd's call for Islamic pluralism touches one crucial point in our search for theoretical explanations: the question of the unity of religion within a modern society, since in a complex society, unity and its description have to be more abstract and depersonalized. One concrete truth controlled by an establishment can dominate, but it is obviously not alone within the public space. Rather, I would argue, a modern media system treats established truths as well as 'deviations' as formally equal. The functional logic of the media system leaves room for religious and anti-Islamist deviants (dissent as news), as well as for statements by renowned scholars and intellectuals (prominence as news). The social order of functional differentiation subverts any exclusive claim to represent the whole of society.

Within the media system, speakers *for* Islam become more or less speakers *on* Islam. In other words, in a modern society, speaking in the name of religion or representing it is reduced to a mere claim to truth. This implies not only the decline of the religious authority of traditional scholarship, but a de-ontologization of truth (see Luhmann 1962), disavowing any exclusive claim to it. Speaking on Islam as a mere claim to truth means the loss of a traditionally given authority who could speak for Islam from an exclusive standpoint. For Islam in Egypt, the differentiation of a modern society is therefore not something happening at the outside boundary of religion. Since deviants and so-called secularists are coupled with religion as a religious problem, the quarrels with deviants are dynamics happening at a boundary, where religious identity is constructed. This

---

65 The Arabic original reads:

ولكن هذا الإصرار على وجود إسلام واحد ، ورفض التعددية الفعلية يؤدى إلى نتيجتين بصرف النظر عن نوايا هذا الكاتب أو ذاك. النتيجة الأولى : أن للإسلام معنى واحداً ثابتاً لا تؤثر فيه حركة التاريخ ، ولا يؤثر باختلاف المجتمعات ، فضلا عن تعدد الجماعات بسبب اختلاف المصالح داخل المجتمع الواحد النتيجة الثانية : أن هذا المعنى الواحد الثابت يمتلكه جماعة من البشر – هم علماء الدين قطعاً – وأن أعضاء هذه الجماعة مبرأون من الأهواء والتحيزات الانسانية الطبيعية.

boundary might appear as an outside boundary of Islam, but from a sociological perspective its construction can be observed as being a differentiation inside religion. In other words, within a modern society – at least in the cases discussed here – the construction of religious identity has to cope with the paradox that it must include the different (see Luhmann [1997] 2013: 293–305). We therefore need not observe the construction of deviance only as a modern search for religious identity. Since this identity is constructed by using the distinction between religion and non-religion, it also makes sense to designate it as a phenomenon of secularity, understood as a notion that is merely getting to terms with societal reality but not representing it. Understood in this way, the notion of secularity is the form of a theoretical distinction: it does not refer to something non-religious as such. Rather, it treats the non-religious as something indeterminate, regardless of its 'religious' description of it as *secular(ist)* or otherwise.[66] In this way, deviance can be understood as a phenomenon of secularity.

Literature

N.N. 01.04.1992. "al-'Almānīyūn adāh gharbīyah... li-tashwīh al-Islām." *al-Nūr.*
'Abd al-Wahhāb, Islām. 28.03.2013. "Faraj Fūdah... man ya'ish ḥurran lā yamut..." *al-Miṣrī al-yawm:* 12.
'Abd al-Rāziq, 'Alī. [1925] 1993. *al-Islām wa-uṣūl al-ḥukm.* [Introduction by Jābir 'Aṣfūr]. [Cairo]: al-Hay'a al-miṣrīyah al-'āmma lil-kitāb.
——. [1925] 2000. *al-Islām wa-uṣūl al-ḥukm* [edited by Muḥammad 'Imāra]. Beirut: al-Mu'assasa al-'arabīyah lil-dirāsāt wa-al-nashr.
——. [1925] 2007. *al-Islām wa-uṣūl al-ḥukm.* Cairo: al-Hay'ah al-miṣrīyah al-'āmma lil-kitāb.
Abū Zayd, Muḥammad. 1930. *al-Hidāyah wa-al-'irfān.* Cairo: Muṣṭafá al-Bābī al-Ḥalabī.
Abū Zayd, Naṣr Ḥāmid. 1995. *al-Tafkīr fī zaman al-takfīr. Ḍidd al-juhl wa-al-zayf wa-al-khurāfah.* Cairo: Madbūlī.
——. [1992] 2003. *Naqd al-khiṭāb al-dīnī.* Cairo: Madbūlī.
——. 2005. *Naḥw manhaj islāmī jadīd lil-ta'wīl.* www.ibn-rushd.org/arabic/Rede-AbuZaid-A.htm.
Adams, Charles C. 1933. *Islam and Modernism in Egypt: A Study of the Modern Reform Movement Inaugurated by Muḥammad 'Abduh.* London: Oxford University Press.
al-Afghānī, Jamāl al-Dīn. [1903]. *al-Radd 'alā al-dahrīyīn.* [Cairo]: N.p.
Agrama, Hussein Ali. 2010. "Secularism, sovereignty, indeterminacy: is Egypt a secular or a religious state?" *Comparative Studies in Society and History* 3: 495–523.
Arkoun, Mohammed. 1994. "La leçon d'Ali Abd al-Rāziq," *Qantara:* 8–9.
Asad, Talal. 2003. *Formations of the Secular: Christianity, Islam, Modernity.* Stanford: Stanford University Press.

---

66 See the observation of indeterminacy in Agrama 2010, as well as the suggestion that *secularization* should be treated as a notion of second-order observation in Luhmann 2013: 201–231.

Asad, Talal, Wendy Brown, Judith Butler, and Saba Mahmood, eds. 2009. *Is Critique Secular? Blasphemy, Injury, and Free Speech*. Berkeley, Calif.: Townsend Center for the Humanities.
al-'Awwā, Muḥammad Salīm. [1975] 2008. *Fī al-niẓām al-siyāsī lil-dawlah al-islāmīyah*. Cairo: Dār al-shurūq.
Ayalon, Yaron. 2009. "Revisiting Ṭāhā Ḥusayn's *Fī al-Shi'r al-Jāhilī* and its sequel." *Die Welt des Islams* 1: 98–121.
al-Bannā, Jamāl. 18.10.2006. "La ḥayāh bidūn dīn... wa-lā ḥayāh bi-al-dīn waḥduhu." *al-Miṣrī al-yawm*: 13.
—. 20.10.2011. "al-Islām wa-al-ḥurrīyah wa-al-'almānīyah (4/5)." *al-Miṣrī al-yawm*: 14.
Berger, Peter L. and Thomas Luckmann. [1966] 1991. *The Social Construction of Reality: a Treatise in the Sociology of Knowledge*. London: Penguin.
Binder, Leonard. 1988. *Islamic Liberalism: a Critique of Development Ideologies*. Chicago, London: The University of Chicago Press.
Bocthor, Ellious. 1827/29. *Dictionnaire français-arabe*. vol. 2. Paris: Didot.
Bourdieu, Pierre. [1984] 1995. *Sociology in Question*. London: Sage.
Cachia, Pierre. 1956. *Taha Husayn: his Place in the Egyptian Literary Renaissance*. London: Luzac.
Casanova, José. 1994. *Public Religions in the Modern World*. Chicago: The University of Chicago Press.
Coser, Lewis A. 1956. *The Functions Of Social Conflict*. London: Routledge.
al-Dhahabī, Muḥammad Ḥusayn. [1976] 2000. *al-Tafsīr wa-al-mufassirūn*. 3 vols. Cairo: Maktabat Wahbah.
Dobbelaere, Karel. 2002. *Secularization: an Analysis at Three Levels*. Bruxelles: PIE Lang,
Esposito, John L. and Azzam Tamimi, eds. 2000. *Islam and Secularism in the Middle East*. London: Hurst.
Filali-Ansary, Abdou. 1994. "Ali Abderraziq et le projet de remise en ordre de la conscience islamique." *Égypte/Monde arabe* 20: 185–201.
Flores, Alexander. 1988. "Egypt: a new secularism?" *Middle East Report*, 153: 27–30.
—. 1993. "Secularism, Integralism and Political Islam: The Egyptian Debate." *Middle East Report*, 183: 32–38.
—. 2012. *Säkularismus und Islam in Ägypten: Die Debatte der 1980er Jahre*. Berlin: Lit.
Fūdah [Fawdah], Faraj. 1983. *al-Wafd wa-al-mustaqbal*. Cairo: Maṭābi' sijill al-'arab.
—. [1985] 2004. *Qabl al-suqūṭ*. Cairo: Dār wa-maṭābi' al-mustaqbal.
—. [1986] 2005. *Ḥiwār ḥawla al-'almānīyah*. Cairo: Dār wa-maṭābi' al-mustaqbal.
—. [1988] 2007. *al-Irhāb*. Cairo: Dār wa-maṭābi' al-mustaqbal.
Gallagher, Nancy E. 1989. "Islam v. Secularism in Cairo: An Account of the Dar al-Hikma Debate." *Middle Eastern Studies* 2: 208–215.
Gibb, H. A. R. 1929. "Studies in contemporary Arabic literature." *Bulletin of the School of Oriental Studies* 3: 445–466.
González-Quijano, Yves. 1998. *Les gens du livre: Édition et champ intellectuel dans l'Égypte républicaine*. Paris: CNRS Éd.
Ḥaffār, Muḥammad Najīb. 1911. "al-Ilḥād fī al-madāris al-'almānīyah" [and the commentary by al-Manār]. *al-Manār* 7: 544–548.
Khalaf Allāh, Muḥammad Aḥmad. 1951. *al-Fann al-qiṣaṣī fī al-Qur'ān al-karīm*. Cairo: Maktabat al-nahḍa al-miṣrīyah. [Reprint 1999. Cairo: Sīnā'].
Khālid, Khālid Muḥammad. [1950] 1974. *Min hunā nabda'*. Beirut: Dār al-kitāb al-'arabī.

Ḥanafī, Ḥasan. [1989]. *al-Yamīn wa-al-yasār fī al-fikr al-dīnī*. Vol. 7 [within the series], *al-Dīn wa-al-thawrah fī Miṣr 1952–1981*. Cairo: Maktabat Madbūlī.
Ḥasan, Māhir. 08.06.2010. "Ughtīla al-Duktūr Faraj Fūdah." *al-Miṣrī al-yawm*: 2.
al-Khaṭīb, ʿAlī Aḥmad, ed. 1414 AH/1993. *Radd hayʾat kibār al-ʿulamāʾ ʿalā kitāb al-Islām wa-uṣūl al-ḥukm lil-Shaykh ʿAlī ʿAbd al-Rāziq*. Supplement to *Majāllat al-Azhar* 3.
Hatina, Meir. 2007. *Identity Politics in the Middle East: Liberal Thought and Islamic Challenge in Egypt*. London, New York: Tauris Academic Studies.
Hourani, Albert. 1983. *Arabic Thought in the Liberal Age, 1798–1939*. Cambridge: Cambridge University Press.
Ḥusayn, Ṭāhā. [1927] 1933. *Fī al-adab al-Jāhilī*. Cairo: Maṭbaʿat Fārūq.
—. [1938] 2011. *Mustaqbal al-thaqāfah fī Miṣr*. Cairo: Dār al-kutub wa-al-wathāʾiq al-qawmīyah.
—. [1926] 2012. *Fī al-shiʿr al-Jāhilī*. Cairo: al-Dār al-miṣrīyah al-lubnānīyah.
Huwaydī, Fahmī. 2004. *Muwāṭinūn lā dhimmīyūn*. Cairo: Dār al-shurūq.
Ibrahim, Ibrahim. 1992. "Taha Husayn: the critical spirit," in *Problems of the Modern Middle East in Historical Perspective: Essays in Honour of Albert Hourani*, ed. John P. Spagnolo, 105–118. Reading: Ithaca Press.
ʿImāra, Muḥammad. [1993]. *Fikr at-tanwīr bayna al-ʿalmānīyīn wa-al-islāmīyīn*. N.p.: Jamʿīyat al-markaz al-ʿālamī lil-tawthīq.
—. [1992] 1997. *al-Islām wa-al-siyāsa. Al-Radd ʿalā shubuhāt al-ʿalmānīyīn*. Cairo: Dār al-Rashād.
—. 21.09.2011. "al-Inqilāb ʿalá al-gharb al-ʿalmānī." *almesryoon.com*.
—. 29.09.2011. "Matā yufīq al-ʿalmānīyūn." *al-Wafd* (online).
Ismāʿīl, Ḥasan, ed. 2005. *Miswaddat waṭan*. Cairo: Dār wa-maktabat al-ḥurrīyah.
Jansen, Johannes J.G. 1980. *The Interpretation of the Koran in Modern Egypt*. Leiden: Brill.
Jefferey, Arthur. 1932. "The suppressed Qurʾan commentary of Muhammad Abû Zaid", *Der Islam* 20: 301–308.
Kinitz, Daniel. in prep. *Die andere Seite des Islam: Säkularismus-Diskurs und Islamischer Denker im modernen Ägypten*. Unpublished PhD thesis, University of Leipzig.
Lübbe, Herrmann. 1965. *Säkularisierung: Geschichte eines ideenpolitischen Begriffs*. München: Karl Alber.
Luhmann, Niklas. 1962. "Wahrheit und Ideologie: Vorschläge zur Wiederaufnahme der Diskussion." *Der Staat* 1: 431–448 [re-published in *Soziologische Aufklärung*, vol. 1].
—. [1984] 1995. *Social Systems*, translated by John Bednarz, Jr., with Dirk Baecker. Stanford, Calif.: Stanford University Press.
—. [1997] 2013. *Theory of Society, Volume 2*, translated by Rhodes Barrett. Stanford, Calif.: Stanford University Press.
—. [2000] 2013. *A Systems Theory of Religion*, transl. David A. Brenner. Stanford, Calif.: Stanford University Press.
Marshall, Paul and Nina Shea. 2011. *Silenced: How Apostasy and Blasphemy Codes are Choking Freedom Worldwide*. Oxford, New York: Oxford University Press.
al-Maṭʿanī, ʿAbd al-ʿAẓīm. 2006. *al-ʿIlmānīyah wa mawqifuhā min al-ʿaqīdah wa-al-sharīʿah*. Cairo: Dār al-Fārūq.
al-Qaraḍāwī, Yūsuf. [1977] 1993. *al-Ḥulūl al-mustawradah wa-kayfa janat ʿalā ummatinā*. Cairo: Maktabat Wahbah.
—. [1987] 1997. *al-Islām wa-al-ʿilmānīyah wajhan li-wajhin*. Cairo: Maktabat Wahbah.
—. 2004. *Khiṭābunā al-islāmī fī ʿaṣr al-ʿawlama*. Cairo: Dār al-shurūq.

—. 2008. *Mūjibāt taghayyur al-fatwá fī 'aṣrinā*. Cairo: Dār al-shurūq.
al-Qimnī, Sayyid Maḥmūd. 2007. *Ukhrujū min masājidinā!!* Cairo: Dār wa-maktabat al-ḥurrīyah.
Quṭb, Muḥammad. 1994. *al-'Almānīyūn wa-l-Islām*. Cairo: Dār al-shurūq.
Quṭb, Sayyid. [1964] 1979. *Ma'ālim fī al-ṭarīq*. Cairo: Dār al-shurūq.
Riḍā, Muḥammad Rashīd. 1931. "al-Ilḥād fī al-Qur'ān (1/4)." *al-Manār* 9: 673–697.
Roy, Olivier. 2007. *Secularism Confronts Islam*. New York: Columbia University Press.
Shāhīn, 'Abd al-Ṣabūr, ed. [1994]. *Qiṣṣat Abū Zayd wa-al-inḥisār al-'almānīyah fī Jāmi'at al-Qāhira*. Cairo: Dār al-i'tiṣām.
Shāhīn, Ilhām Muḥāmmad. 2001. *al-'Almānīyah fī Miṣr wa-ashhur ma'ārikuhā. 1 – Ma'rakat kitāb al-Islām wa-uṣūl al-ḥukm*. Cairo: Dār hārmūnī.
—. 2005. *al-'Almānīyah fī Miṣr wa-ashhur ma'ārikuhā. 2 – Ma'rakat kitāb "Fī al-shi'r al-Jāhilī" lil-Duktūr Ṭāhā Ḥusayn wa-ma'rakat kitāb "Min hunā nabda'" lil-Ustādh Khālid Muḥammad Khālid*. Cairo: al-Muqaṭṭam.
Shalabī, Khayrī. [1994]. *Muḥākamat Ṭāhā Ḥusayn*. Cairo: Dār al-mustaqbal.
Schulze, Reinhard. 2010. "Die Dritte Unterscheidung: Islam, Religion und Säkularität," in *Religionen – Wahrheitsansprüche – Konflikte: Theologische* Perspektiven, ed. Walter Dietrich and Wolfgang Lienemann, 147–205. Zürich: TVZ Theologischer Verlag.
Skovgaard-Petersen, Jakob. 1997. *Defining Islam for the Egyptian State: Muftis and Fatwas of the Dār al-Iftā* (Leiden: Brill)
Swatos Jr., William H., and Daniel V. A. Olson, eds. 2000. *The Secularization Debate*. Lanham: Rowman & Littlefield Publishers.
Thielmann, Jörn. 2003. *Naṣr Ḥāmid Abū Zaid und die wiedererfundene ḥisba: Šarī'a und Qānūn im heutigen Ägypten*. Würzburg: Ergon.
Tibi, Bassam. 1980. "Islam and secularization: religion and the functional differentiation of the social system." *Archiv für Rechts- und Sozialphilosophie*, 2: 207–222.
Wohlrab-Sahr, Monika and Marian Burchardt. 2012. "Multiple secularities: toward a cultural sociology of secular modernities." *Comparative Sociology* 6: 875–909.
Zakarīyā, Fu'ād. 1986. *al-Ḥaqīqah wa-al-wahm fī al-ḥarakah al-islāmīyah al-mu'āṣirah*. Cairo: Dār al-fikr.
—. 1987. *al-Ṣaḥwah al-islāmīyah fī mīzān al-'aql*. Cairo: Dār al-fikr al-mu'āṣir.

Gudrun Krämer
Secularity Contested: Religion, Identity and the Public Order in the Arab Middle East

The Arab Middle East has long been seen as an exception to broader political and intellectual trends, especially those coming from the West and associated with liberal democracy, from citizenship and human rights to gender equality. Globally speaking, however, it is not so exceptional really. With regard to secularity, the Arab case lends further weight to the argument that (secularist) accounts of modernity as secular, with religion being either irrelevant or reactive (in the forms of nativism, cultural nationalism and identity politics), are culturally biased and fail to describe global realities (Casanova 2008; Taylor 2009; Warner, Vanantwerpen, and Calhoun 2010; Esposito and Tamimi 2000). The Arab Middle East is thus not alone in *not* following the path described by Charles Taylor in 'A Secular Age' for the North Atlantic world, or Latin Christendom at large (Taylor 2007). In the Arab Middle East today, it is not belief (or faith or religion) that has to defend itself as rational and legitimate but it is religious doubt, critique and indifference. Faith is not just prevalent in society but specific expressions of faith are imposed by the state, enshrined in constitutions, applied in important legal fields, and widely shared among the population. As a result, the public sphere is ruled by moral norms defined by conservative Muslims and Christians alike, while critics and sceptics have been largely relegated to virtual space and the private sphere.

Developments in the Arab Middle East have often been explained with reference to culture and religion, or to be more precise, to Islam as the majority religion in the region. This approach renders the debate on multiple modernities (or alternatively, varieties of modernity, global modernity) all the more interesting as the proponents of 'multiple modernities' also posit culture(s), or civilization(s), with their specific practices and institutions, as major factors in shaping historical potentials and trajectories.[1] There can be no doubt that culture and religion

---

[1] This is not the place to go into the debate on global modernity, varieties of modernity and multiple modernities. The chief proponent of the concept of multiple modernities is, of course, Shmuel Eisenstadt (esp. Eisenstadt 2000). The concept has been frequently critiqued, notably by Volker H. Schmidt (2006), who suggests speaking of 'varieties of modernity,' and Arif Dirlik (2007), who proposes to think in terms of 'global modernity.' Both critics use capitalism (a global phenomenon with regional and/or cultural varieties) as a point of reference.

matter to the issue of secularity. But so do state policies, market forces and transnational flows and influences, all of which intersect with local understandings of culture and religion, modifying them and being modified by them. Interestingly, state policies, market forces and transnational flows do not figure prominently in Casanova's and Taylor's influential readings of secularity.

1 Notions of the Secular

The emphasis on *secularity* rather than on *secularism* (the conscious policy of separating between religion, state and politics and the institutional arrangements resulting from this policy) helps to refine the analysis (see Wohlrab-Sahr and Burchardt 2012). Secularity foregrounds the social functions and cultural meanings attached to different kinds of differentiation between religious and non-religious domains, their articulations in various fields (and not just state politics), and the institutional arrangements created to express them. Differentiation between religious and non-religious domains has occurred in the Arab Middle East as much as in other parts of the Muslim world, and in many instances it amounts to secularization. A closer look at modern political thought and practice (including notably Islamic or Islamist discourse), economics, law, art and education would reveal that secularization processes form an integral part of the Middle Eastern experience, and not just the Arab one. The question is (and here the focus on secularity proves itself particularly useful) to what extent these processes have been perceived as legitimate, productive and desirable, and by whom, and whether taken together, they constitute more than the specificity that is characteristic of any kind of secularity, be it Polish or Peruvian.

To speak of secularity rather than secularism, however, does not necessarily solve the familiar conundrum: 'The secular' can refer to an epistemological stance, entailing 'neutral' or 'non-religious standards of reason' (Asad 2003), or alternatively, to a 'lay' or 'worldly' (non-religious, non-clerical) agent or institution, irrespective of the epistemology, project and ideology this agent or institution might pursue. To give an example relevant to Middle Eastern contexts: if greater weight is given to the agent rather than the project, a non-clerical state body applying religious law such as Islamic Sharia or Jewish Halakha can be seen as engaging in an act of secularization. Terminological fuzziness (which of course is not just terminological but also conceptual) is especially acute in contemporary Arab debates: Modern Arabic usage does distinguish between 'lay' (*madani*) and 'clerical' (*dini*) actors and institutions, even though the term *madani* again covers a broad semantic range, from civil to civic to civilized.² But it does not systematically differentiate between secularization, secularism and secularity. The term *la-diniyya*, which for some time was used for both secularity and secularism, refers to the 'absence' or 'denial' of religion. The term most commonly employed today, *'almaniyya*, is less reductive but still fails to capture the multiple dimensions of secularity. The etymology of the term is not entirely clear. Some link it to *'alam*, 'world.' Others pronounce it *'ilmaniyya* and associate it with *'ilm*, 'knowledge.' This is not entirely convincing linguistically, not to mention the fact that at least in the pre-modern era, *'ilm* usually referred to religious learning. No matter whether spelled with an 'a' or an 'i', *'almani / 'ilmani* covers many things from non-religious to agnostic to anti-religious, and from secular to secularist, and is commonly understood to signal distance from, if not hostility to, religion. (It is important to note that in the present context, religion equals not just Islam but includes Christianity and Judaism as members of the family of 'Abrahamic religions' which in contrast to, say, Buddhism and Hinduism are described as 'heavenly religions' in Islamic theology and jurisprudence.)

In spite of his declared focus on the Western experience, I would like to structure my argument according to José Casanova's discussion of three dimensions of secularism and of secularization as the ensemble of historical developments leading to it (Casanova 1994, 2008). They can be summed up as functional differentiation, religious decline, and privatization of religion. Individually and in conjunction they modify an existing religious-secular divide and by the same token, they affect the relationship between 'religion' and 'state.' Needless to say, these terms are culturally embedded and hence cannot be easily transposed from one context to another. Thus the concept of religion that undergirds most discussions of the Western experience cannot be generalized. However, it is relevant to Muslims, Christians and Jews with their belief in a personal God. 'Functional differentiation,' which concerns the institutional and constitutional separation of 'religion' or 'church' and 'state,' is perhaps easiest to study. 'Religious decline,' which relates to religion's diminishing relevance with respect to how groups and individuals interpret the world and live their lives, a process which may (but need not) lead to professed agnosticism or even atheism, is more complicated. 'Privatization of religion,' which entails the relegation or

---

2 Historically, civilization (here Ar. *tamaddun*) in the sense of 'being civilized' or 'cultured' was associated with urban life (the term *tamaddun* is related to Ar. *madina*, 'city') and contrasted with the existence of nomads and barbarians. The association of civil and civilized is still present in modern parlance but the emphasis has moved elsewhere: it now distinguishes 'civil' from 'clerical' on the one hand and 'military' on the other.

withdrawal of religion to the private sphere, poses considerable difficulties conceptually and empirically. Not only do relegation and withdrawal result from very different power constellations; they can also lead to diverse institutional arrangements. What is more, notions of public and private are contingent on time, place, gender and social context and thus cannot be taken as sociocultural givens.

Casanova has done much to refute facile assumptions concerning the 'privatization of religion,' and it is no coincidence that his 1994 monograph was entitled 'Public Religions.' Significantly, Charles Taylor largely ignores the public-private divide to concentrate on what he calls the 'conditions of belief,' particularly a condition in which belief in God or a transcendent truth more generally, is no longer the only option to embrace (Taylor 2007; for critical debate, see Warner, Vanantwerpen, and Calhoun 2010). The various dimensions discussed by Casanova, Taylor and others are ideal types in the Weberian sense, designed to invite conceptual clarity and empirical rigour. They do not 'mirror' reality, a reality that in the Arab Middle East as much as elsewhere, tends to be less neat and well defined.

2 Functional Differentiation: Clergy and State

Contrary to widespread assumptions, religion, law and politics have rarely been as closely intertwined in the Middle East, or 'in Islam,' as it is often claimed, especially by present-day Islamists and their critics (and the latter are not restricted to the West). At the theoretical level, special caution is needed when speaking about God's rule or theocracy, for like secularity, theocracy covers a broad semantic range (Trampedach and Pečar 2013; Krämer 2013). If understood as the unmediated rule of God, taking place before the end of time ('identitarian' or 'eschatological theocracy'), theocracy has never been conceptualized by Muslim thinkers. According to the theologians, God is king and lord; he can intervene in cosmic and human affairs at any time; and he sent out messengers of whom Muhammad is the last. But God does not stand at the head of the Muslim polity. If, in contrast, theocracy is defined as governance *in the name of* God, exerted by princes, prophets, saints and scholars who act in the light of divine guidance, as obtained through the foundational texts of Islam or through divine inspiration ('representative theocracy'), then it has been widely practised in Muslim contexts, including the Arab Middle East. Still, I would argue that with the possible exception of the prophet Muhammad's charismatic leadership of the Muslim community, in the early part of the seventh century Common Era (C.E.), religion and state have never been fused in 'Islamic' societies and that the link between religion and politics was not fundamentally different from that found in contemporary 'Christian' Europe.

Having said that, it is of course important to study the configuration of actors in Middle Eastern contexts, which differed in several ways from European ones. To begin with, there is no church in Islam in the sense of a hierarchical institution with established doctrinal authority similar to the Catholic Church, and operating largely independently of the state. Neither Sunni nor Shi'i Islam has ever developed such a church, not even in the Islamic Republic of Iran or the Islamist emirates that emerged in various parts of the Muslim world, from Mali to Syria and Chechnya. However, like in Judaism, there emerged a 'class' of religious and legal scholars (Ar. pl. *'ulama'* and *fuqaha'*) who, sociologically speaking, fulfilled the functions of a clergy without being mediators of salvation (see Iogna-Prat and Veinstein 2003; Gaborieau and Zeghal 2004; Krämer and Schmidtke 2006). Their chief task was to interpret the normative texts (i.e., the Qur'an and the Prophetic Traditions, or Sunna, which is made up of individual reports, or Hadiths) and the canon of authoritative writings based on these texts, and to apply their knowledge to the fields of education, law and worship. A different role was played by saints, Sufis and dervishes representing the mystical 'paths' and brotherhoods which spread from the twelfth century C.E. onward, and antinomian expressions of religiosity, all of which claimed authority on the basis of spiritual experiences or supernatural powers rather than textual knowledge.

Like other rulers, the (Sunni) caliphs portrayed themselves as 'God's shadow on earth,' and the principle of divine right featured prominently among royal strategies of legitimation (Trampedach and Pečar 2013; Krämer 2013). Yet the caliphs had no part in the prophetic mission, which ended with Muhammad as 'the seal of the prophets.' (The Twelver Shia developed specific notions of the imamate which, however, were of limited practical relevance until the modern period.) (See Arjomand 1984) Like the Sunni caliphs, Muslim rulers had to protect religion by defending and if possible expanding, the 'abode of Islam' (Ar. *dar al-islam*). They were responsible for the maintenance of law and order, and for enforcing Sharia (which was, however, chiefly developed by the religious and legal scholars). Within their realm, they exercised a certain control over legal and educational institutions. At least in the major cities, they appointed the judges, intervened in the assignment of teaching posts at the more important institutions of higher Islamic learning (Ar. *madrasas*), and patronized religious scholars, saints and Sufis as well as their institutions. Hence, directly or indirectly, they influenced the spread or marginalization of theological and legal schools. As 'guardians of the faith' they were furthermore charged with the suppression of heresy, apostasy and un-Islamic practices more generally. In spite of these powers, even the caliphs failed to establish themselves as ultimate arbiters in matters of creed and religious law: Faced with caliphal claims to religious authority, the Sunni 'ulama' declared themselves the 'heirs to the prophets.'

In spite of clear tendencies towards 'state' control over the religious field, to borrow Bourdieu's term, the result was not a 'state religion.' True, the ruling elites were Muslims; the Sharia was considered the prime (albeit not necessarily the only) source of normativity; and it was chiefly Islamic scholars and institutions that benefited from royal patronage. But Sharia norms were not translated into positive law, and 'state' control of the religious field was never complete, partly because there was no church which would have facilitated such control. What is more, the subject population often differed from the beliefs of their rulers: in many cases including the early caliphate and the Ottoman Empire up until the sixteenth century, the majority were non-Muslims; in others they followed another branch, or 'confession,' of Islam. The principle of *cuius regio, eius religio*, which was established in the wake of the Peace of Augsburg (1555) in order to end religious war in Europe, and according to which subjects had to follow the confession of their sovereign or leave the realm, was the exception rather than the rule. The conversion of Safavid Iran to Twelver Shi'ism in the sixteenth century may still be the nearest thing to a state religion in pre-modern Islam. Yet Safavid rule is no more representative of Muslim polities than is Byzantine or Russian caesaropapist rule of Christian Europe as a whole.

Since the modernizing reforms of the nineteenth and twentieth centuries, Arab governments have been secular in the sense of being non-clerical and making no claims to religious authority. This includes the Saudi monarchs who have gone furthest in emphasizing the Islamic character of the Saudi state, law and constitution. The only exception left today is the Moroccan king who, based on his claims to descent from the prophet Muhammad (which he shares with the Jordanian monarch and millions of other Muslims) and his own powers of blessing (Ar. *baraka*), is credited with religious authority, at least within Morocco (see Hammoudi 1997). While this claim has long been used to strengthen his authoritarian rule, it has also been employed to enact legislation aimed at improving the status of women. Significantly, then, the one contemporary Arab ruler credited with religious authority has used it not to implement Sharia but to adapt it to modern conditions, a policy widely acclaimed by secular human rights activists.

3 Law and Public Order

In an Islamic context, it is not so much the relation between clergy ('church') and state that matters to the configuration of secularity, but rather the link between Islamic law or normativity (Sharia) and public order (*ordre public*). The introduction of Article 2 in the Egyptian constitution which in 1971 and 1980 respectively, made 'the principles of Islamic Sharia' first 'a main source' and then 'the chief source' of legislation epitomizes this link and illustrates its wider sociocultural and political repercussions (see notably Duprêt 2000; Lombardi 2006; Agrama 2012). Among other things, the Egyptian example has revealed the ambiguities of the Sharia project: in amending the constitution the state authorities yielded to the combined pressure of the Islamic religious establishment and the Islamist opposition (Krämer forthcoming). Yet they did everything to block the actual codification of Sharia outside the domain of personal status affairs where it had already been in force. The reasons for this seemingly contradictory policy were political as well as technical.

Many observers fail to recognize the complexity of Islamic law and its intricate relations with tradition, custom and convention. They underestimate the fact that Sharia does not constitute a code but is as it were dispersed in the vast body of texts that constitute Islamic jurisprudence, or *fiqh*; that *fiqh* is not unified but represented in a number of Sunni and Shi'i schools of law (Ar. *madhhab*, pl. *madhahib*, 'path'); that these law schools are internally plural; that the methods of legal reasoning are both varied and disputed; and that at least since the late nineteenth century, the authorities 'implementing' Sharia rules have not necessarily been religious in the sense of clerical (*'ulama'* and *fuqaha'*) but rather political (rulers, governments and parliaments). For this reason, some scholars have considered the implementation of Islamic law by the modern state as secularization of this law (see notably Bälz 1997; Duprêt 2000).

The Sharia has often been described as unchanging, representing the essence of Islam and by the same token unifying the Muslim community across the boundaries of status, ethnicity and political affiliation. For the same reason, it is perceived by many as a guarantee of social justice and cohesion. This perception is flawed, politically as well as technically: Even explicit textual references in the Qur'an and Sunna which according to Islamic legal and theological teachings, should be beyond human interpretation have in fact been hotly debated and variously applied. The principles invoked to justify interpretation include the discretionary power of the ruler to order public affairs in accordance with the broad guidelines of Sharia (Ar. *siyasa shar'iyya*); the legal concept of necessity (Ar. *darura*); notions of the public good (Ar. *maslaha 'amma*) and, most far-reaching of all, the overarching aims or 'finality' of Sharia (Ar. *maqasid al-shari'a*). Muslim scholars and bureaucrats have always differed as to how much change (adjustment, adaptation, or even innovation) could be tolerated, and whether change thus rationalized was intrinsically valid or merely concessional.

Again contrary to widespread assumptions, Sharia was in fact not applied completely and exclusively in the pre-colonial period. Local custom as well as princely rulings often served as alternative sources of adjudication. In the Ottoman period, sultanic status law was known as *qanun* (from Lat. *canon*) and was applied in the official court system alongside Islamic law. In many Arab and Muslim-majority countries today, rules and norms derived from the Qur'an and Sunna and identified with Sharia (technically speaking, they mostly represent jurists' law or *fiqh*) inform personal status and family law. Only a few states enact (elements of) Islamic criminal, maritime and commercial law (see notably Na'im 2002; Peters 2005; Otto 2010). With few exceptions, Sharia (and again it has to be remembered that much of it is in fact *fiqh*) is neither fully applied nor openly suspended or abrogated. Rather, most governments pursue strategies of evasion and avoidance which restrict the binding force of Sharia norms either substantially or procedurally. This includes Egypt. Yet public controversy over Islamic law, particularly criminal law, has not obliterated the symbolic function of Sharia, or the 'Islamic frame of reference,' as a safeguard of stability and justice that is at the same time authentic, divinely sanctioned and beyond the reach of despotic rulers.

"A Civil State with Religious References"

The well-known Islamist claim that 'Islam is religion and state' (Ar. *al-islam din wa-dawla*) seems to preclude any distinction between religious and secular domains. Any separation of religion and state was and to a large extent, still is portrayed as an offence against Islam as well as a violation of Muslim identity. The linkage of religion, identity and authenticity is crucial here. For decades, Islamists have asserted that Islam is an all-embracing system of norms and values that must shape individual conduct and public order and that the Sharia is fundamentally unchanging and beyond human intervention, an argument clearly directed at authoritarian claims to power and thus attractive to many who otherwise have no Islamist leanings. However, there have been important changes in Islamist discourse over the past few years, and they were enhanced, at least temporarily, by the wave of democratic protest triggered in 2010–11 and widely known as the Arab Spring.

After years of calling for the 'application of Sharia' as the determining factor that made a system Islamically valid and legitimate, Islamists like the Egyptian Muslim Brothers and the Tunisian Nahda Movement decided not to highlight Sharia in their drive to win broader segments of the public and perhaps also to dissipate concerns among wider non-Muslim audiences. Instead, they spoke of a 'civil state' (*dawla madaniyya*) with an 'Islamic frame of references' (*marja'iyya islamiyya*) (see e.g., Abu 'Ajjur 2012; Krämer 2013; Krämer forthcoming), suggesting modified thinking not only about democracy but also about secularity. Despite this change in terminology, the majority of Muslims and non-Muslims alike continued to identify the 'Islamic frame of references' with Sharia. So did the Islamists as the electoral platforms of their parties and presidential candidates, notably Muhammad Mursi in Egypt, and the Egyptian Constitution of December 2012 in which they had a major say, made abundantly clear. As suggested above, the Sharia is not only amenable to interpretation but in constant need of it. It cannot be applied without a continuous process of selection and interpretation. The principles elaborated in the scholarly literature, from necessity to the common good to the finality of the Sharia, are still employed by legal experts and state judiciaries today and in many instances, given wider scope than previously (see e.g., Lombardi 2006). Outside limited circles that are usually labelled Salafist today, even many Islamists differentiate between a 'stable,' unchanging core of the Sharia and its 'flexible' elements that can be adapted to changing conditions (Ar. *al-thabit wa-l-mutaghayyir*), thus allowing for more elasticity and variation than is widely thought, and perhaps is even clear to these authors. However, this recognition does not alter their conviction that the public and the private sphere must be structured according to Islamic rules which they identify with Sharia. The implications of this conviction for the articulation of secularity are obvious.

4 Privatization of Religion

Most Muslims take it for granted that Islam entails more than belief in the One God and his messenger Muhammad: Islam is not just faith but religion. (The Arabic language clearly distinguishes between the two, with the former being *iman* and the latter *din*. The term '*aqida* refers to doctrine and belief.) By the same token, they will assert that faith calls for deeds that attest to its truth before the world (this is the meaning of Ar. *shahada* for the Muslim creed), and that as a religion, Islam establishes a way of life ('*din*') that translates religious principles into daily actions and bodily practices. Islam is a public religion par excellence, perhaps more so than Christianity, Judaism or Buddhism. Here, visibility tends to merge into hegemony, giving shape to the deeply rooted sense that Islam is power and that it must not be subdued. The Islamic claim to hegemony in 'Islamic lands' is expressed positively, in enjoining the public performance of Islamic rites and negatively, in restricting the religious freedom of Muslims as well as of non-Muslims, sceptics and agnostics.

Not only in the Arab world, core elements of Muslim worship, such as Friday prayer and the pilgrimage to Mecca (Ar. *hajj*) are performed in public, as visible and audible confirmations of both faith and belonging. In most Muslim-majority contexts, the call to prayer is a public proclamation of the truth of Islam. By contrast, the religious practices of other religious communities are heavily constrained, if they are admitted at all. Their right to construct or renovate religious buildings in Muslim-majority areas is disputed. At the same time, non-Muslim places of worship and identifying markers, such as headgear, dress and tattoos, have been a normal part of life in most Muslim-majority societies outside what is now Saudi Arabia and other areas controlled by particularly rigid interpretations of Islam.

With regard to religious freedom, three prohibitions stand out: prohibition of non-Muslim mission, of Muslim conversion to another religion, and of blasphemy – not because they are frequent occurrences but because they highlight the binding power of religious norms in the public *and* the private sphere. According to classical *fiqh*, a Muslim's denial of core elements of creed and rite, or declaration of non-faith, or change of religion classify as apostasy and must be sanctioned (see Saeed and Saeed 2004; also Wils 2007). The principle rests on weak foundations for the Qur'an describes apostasy as a sin that will be punished in the hereafter but it does not prescribe a specific sanction here on earth; the relevant Prophetic Traditions (or Hadiths) are of debatable status. It still remains that the majority of Muslim jurists have always considered a Muslim's change of religion or (public) declaration of non-faith as illegitimate and tantamount to treason; many have demanded the death sentence for Muslim males, and imprisonment combined with beatings for females. The problem is compounded by the loose definition of 'apostasy' which can range from blasphemous speech and acts to the disrespectful handling of the Qur'an, as a physical object containing the word of God. According to Islamic law, blaspheming the prophet Muhammad or for that matter, any prophet recognized by Islam, including Moses and Jesus, ranks with the crime of apostasy and calls for the corresponding legal sanctions.

The Rushdie Affair of the late 1980s and the Danish cartoon controversy of 2005/6 have highlighted the emotions that are released (or roused by interested parties) if it is felt that Islam has been offended. The emotional dimension is of great importance here. And while it is true that many Arab states have signed the

1948 UN Declaration of Human Rights and subsequent human rights conventions, and that many constitutions guarantee the religious freedom of their citizens, they continue to restrict it in a variety of ways. A common practice is to limit freedom to the *inner forum* (freedom of thought and conscience) and to sanction public expression of doubt and dissent or of beliefs and practices considered contrary to Islam and the 'heavenly religions' (free exercise of religion). In Egypt for instance, 'respect' for Islam or religion more generally, has been made part of the *ordre public*. In the process, Islam has been finally transformed into a state religion, with unclear consequences for citizenship rights.

Still, it is important to note that while the public expression of social deviance and of religious doubt, critique and dissent has never been encouraged in Middle Eastern societies, neither has their public repression. Prevailing attitudes have been rather Victorian: Many pre-modern governments did in fact tolerate illicit practices, such as the consumption of drugs and alcohol, prostitution or homoeroticism provided they remained behind closed doors, or were restricted to non-Muslim space. Even religious dissent, agnosticism and atheism could thus be tolerated provided they did not enter the public domain. The same is still true of most Arab governments today, although not necessarily of their 'clerical' establishment and Islamist opposition. In a way, this constitutes an inversion of the public-private divide associated with secularization for religion has not been relegated to, or withdrawn to, the private sphere. On the contrary, it is private space that allows for critique and deviance, whereas public space is expected to conform to Islamic or religious norms more generally.

This divide may well be in flux, too. With the expansion of cyberspace and the social media the distinction between public and private is becoming increasingly blurred. This literally opens up space for artistic expression, religious debate and political critique, especially in the more restrictive Gulf countries. While political activity continues to be tightly controlled, the past few years have witnessed an extraordinary upsurge of cultural creativity in countries such as Saudi Arabia and the United Arab Emirates (see e.g., Freitag 2010). Still, even in relatively liberal societies such as Tunisia or Lebanon there is as yet no free religious market comparable to what is found in Canada, the United States or most parts of Europe, not only because governments prevent its emergence but because large sections of the population do not regard such a market as desirable. The latter is especially relevant in light of Taylor's 'conditions of belief,' which turn around the availability of alternative modes of thought and life that are not faith-based.

Moral Politics and Market Islam

'Public morality' has been of crucial importance to the so-called application of the Sharia. It affects not only 'immoral' lifestyles, sexual preferences and unconventional patterns of behaviour more generally, but also the freedom of expression, art and science. Moral politics have been a recurrent feature of Muslim societies (and of course not only Muslim societies) across time and place. In the modern period, conservative understandings of modesty that, rightly or wrongly, are traced back to religion have become hegemonic, easily censored by state and other authorities and hence difficult to challenge publicly. Again it has to be remembered that local Christian understandings of religious freedom, modesty and decency do not differ greatly from prevailing Muslim ones. For Muslims, the core issues have always been abstention from alcohol; separation of the sexes in public; and 'modest clothing,' particularly the veil in its diverse forms. It is here that the blending of Sharia with custom, convention and even fashion becomes most readily apparent as the veil can take many forms, from the shapeless body cover to the decidedly chic headscarf. 'Believing with belonging' is expressed in compliance with religious duties (the so-called pillars of Islam: profession of faith, ritual prayer, almsgiving, fasting during the month of Ramadan, and pilgrimage to Mecca) and the observance of certain dietary rules and dress codes, which, contrary to the convictions of many who propagate and fulfil them, are not necessarily laid down in the Qur'an or Sunna exactly as they are currently practised.

Since the 1980s and 1990s, the Arab world has witnessed a spectacular proliferation of Islamic associations, activities and accessories. Today, the 'Islamic revival' or 'awakening' (Ar. *al-sahwa al-islamiyya*; in Western sources often described as Islamization) appears to encompass virtually all aspects of public and private life: everyday speech and conduct, Islamic ethics and aesthetics, charity, business and commerce (of which veiling is just one example). As a result, it has Islamized the landscapes of sound and sight (see notably Haenni 2005; Abaza 2006; Pink 2009; Van Nieuwkerk 2013). The 'Islamic trend' (*al-tayyar al-islami*) now ranges from moderate or pragmatic Islamists (some of whom identify themselves as 'centrist,' or *wasati*) to Salafis and militant Jihadis of various persuasions, and from the 'new Islamic thinkers' and 'new Islamic preachers' to the (largely female) piety movement (for the latter, see Mahmood 2005; Hafez 2011), all with their diverse activities and cross-links at home and abroad. Articulations of piety vary accordingly, from what has been called 'Islam light' to ultra-rigid Salafism. Islamic institutions serving the mission (*da'wa*) broadly understood include mosques, prayer rooms and religious salons; Islamic associations, religious schools and welfare institutions, from health clinics to literacy classes. 'Islamo-business' has expanded rapidly, producing not only religious commodities but also street wear and fashion (Haenni 2005; Tripp 2006; Pink 2009). Islamization has made a remarkable impact on the media, beginning with publishing and the press, which Muslim reformers had been using very successfully from the late nineteenth century onward, moving to cassettes, TV and satellite channels to virtual space and the social media. In the field of art and leisure, or 'edutainment,' 'pious art' developed at an unprecedented pace (Haenni 2005; Hirschkind 2006; Van Nieuwkerk 2013). The fact that music proved particularly attractive has been interpreted in light of Muslim preferences of aural over visual cultures. The only segments not greatly affected by 'Islamization' are those having to do with exposing the body in public, first and foremost sports and dance.

The spread of 'Islamic' media, 'Islamic' business, 'Islamic' self-improvement, and an 'Islamic' mass and consumer culture highlight the close connection between (technical) modernity and public religiosity. At the same time, they reveal the impact of market forces and of transnational flows of money, goods and people, on shaping local configurations of secularity in a way that is certainly not unaffected by state policies but also not primarily directed by them. Moving beyond the fields of law and constitution helps to counter a prevalent trend to over-state the state in analysing, or 'deconstructing,' secularization processes in the Arab Middle East and beyond (for this trend, see notably Agrama 2012). To the extent that religion, or rather *reference to* religion, has permeated domains that are for the most part not immediately relevant to the state and its hold on power (albeit relevant to the broader issue of governance), creating 'pious' patterns of production, consumption and betterment, both spiritual and economic, one might even speak of a fourth dimension of secularity, to be added to those discussed by Casanova, Taylor and others.

5 The Decline of Religion

The above should serve as ample evidence that in spite of profound socioeconomic change and identifiable processes of secularization, religion has not declined in the Arab Middle East. Empirical surveys of religious affiliation, faith and practice support this observation (see e.g., Bertelsmann 2008). Yet Islamists as the most vocal and visible socio-political force today have been calling for *more* religion rather than less. The question therefore is not whether Muslims can live in a secular environment (millions of Muslims do) but whether they view secularity as a legitimate and desirable principle to regulate (an Islamic) state and society.

There is a tradition of secular thought and indeed of secularism in the Arab Middle East going back to the early twentieth century if not beyond. Prominent intellectuals have given voice to it (see Kassab 2010; Al-Azm 2014). Still, secular thought continues to be largely identified with leftist, European (and hence 'unauthentic') thought. It is true that national liberation movements like the Egyptian Wafd, formed after World War I, or the pan-Arab movements of the 1940s and 1950s did call for national unity across religious boundaries (best known as the 'unity of crescent and cross'), and advocated the modern notion of citizenship. This stance gave them historical credibility but it did not develop into principled secularity, accepted by broad segments of the intellectual elite and the general population. Whereas nationalism made the transition from ('Christian') Europe to the Arab Middle East, and was even absorbed into Islamist discourse, secularity or to be more precise, secularism did not.

It has been argued that this is in part a result of limited demand (Hashemi 2009). Accordingly, the pre-modern Middle East witnessed religious conflict among followers of various branches of Islam and less importantly, among different groups of Muslims and non-Muslims, too, but it was never existentially threatened by religious warfare as were parts of early modern Europe. Unlike in early modern Europe, secularity was not elaborated and institutionalized as a framework to contain inter-communal violence and re-establish social peace, lending it historical depth and weight. (As a critical aside it should be said that while in the long run early modern solutions such as the principle of *cuius regio, eius religio* may have contributed to secular thinking their immediate results were 'state' control of religious affiliation and spatial segregation along religious lines.) In the nineteenth and twentieth centuries, socio-religious tension morphed into what is commonly called 'sectarian conflict,' which was exacerbated by European intervention albeit not solely caused by it. Lebanon, Syria and Iraq are prime examples of such inter-communal ('sectarian') violence, and even Egypt, where the very notion of majority and minority continues to be denounced as alien and harmful to national unity, has witnessed violent conflict between Muslims and Copts.

For that reason, one would expect secularity to be debated as a suitable framework for peaceful conflict resolution. As the Arab Spring has shown, important segments of the (middle-class, urban) public do in fact advocate functional differentiation at the political and constitutional levels, not least in the hope that it might contain the political use of religion and curb violence committed in the name of religion. Critical voices include 'centrist' or 'progressive' Islamists who emerged well before the Arab Spring, such as the Tunisian group of Progressive Islamists or the Egyptian Wasat Party. But they are faced with opponents who continue to reject secularity as culturally alien and politically taint-ed. The critique of secularism as godless and immoral is of course thoroughly familiar from many sociocultural contexts. Another argument is specific to the post-colonial Arab Middle East: Here, secularization is widely portrayed as the centre-piece of a modernizing project imposed from outside and/or above, by colonial and post-colonial authoritarian regimes, one that jeopardizes the identity of Muslims to the benefit of their enemies. I would argue that the political argument – secularism as a tool of colonization and cultural alienation, and secularists as agents of foreign and despotic powers – carries as much weight as fears of a decline of religion. None of this flows, as it were, naturally from the Qur'an and Sunna. Rather, it derives from a specifically modern reading of these texts and Islamic teachings at large.

6 Multiple Secularities?

It is still too early to assess the long-term impact of the Arab Spring. Calls for good governance, freedom and participation demonstrate that like nationalism, these principles have been adopted by important segments of an Arab public as universally valid, irrespective of the fact that they have been forcefully propagated by the West. Rather than being denounced as 'imported,' these principles have been authenticated as genuinely Islamic, or at least fully compatible with Islam, highlighting the processes of entanglement and connectedness that characterize the present state of accelerated globalization. With regard to core concepts of political liberalism, then, the thesis of an Arab, or Islamic, exceptionalism has to be modified. It still remains that for political as much as for cultural reasons, secularism continues to be anathema to broad sections of the Arab public and not just the Islamists. Distinctions between public and private and among different spheres or subsystems with their specific functional logic (politics, the economy, education, family, public morality) exist. These distinctions are not always consistent and of course they are subject to change. In spite of the tangible effects of secularization on all fields, a secular approach continues to be widely seen in negative terms, as a loss of coherence and integrity rather than positively, as a means to liberate creative energies and to enhance social and national integration. That makes the Arab Middle East a specific case among the various articulations of secularity but not an exceptional one.

Bibliography

Abaza, Mona. 2006. The Changing Consumer Cultures of Modern Egypt. Cairo's Urban Reshaping. Leiden and Boston: Brill.
Abu ʿAjjur, Muhammad Muhammad. 2012. Al-dawla al-madaniyya allati nurid. Al-Mansura: Dar al-Kalima li-l-Nashr wa-l-Tawziʿ.
Agrama, Hussein Ali. 2012. Questioning Secularism. Islam, Sovereignty, and the Rule Of Law in Modern Egypt. Chicago: University of Chicago Press.
Al-Azm, Sadik J. 2014. Is Islam Secularizable? Challenging Political and Religious Taboos. Berlin: Gerlach Press.
Arjomand, Said. 1984. The Shadow of God and the Hidden Imam. Religion, Political Order, and Societal Change in Shiʾite Iran from the Beginning to 1890. Chicago and London: Chicago University Press.
Asad, Talal. 2003. Formations of the Secular. Christianity, Islam, Modernity. Stanford: Stanford University Press.
Bälz, Kilian. 1997. "Submitting faith to judicial scrutiny through the family trial: the 'Abū Zayd case.'" Die Welt des Islams 37.2: 135–155.
Bertelsmann Stiftung. 2008. Religionsmonitor 2008. Gütersloh: Bertelsmann.
Bhargava, Rajeev, ed. 1999. Secularism and its Critics. New Delhi: Oxford University Press.
Casanova, José. 1994. Public Religions in the Modern World. Chicago: University of Chicago Press.
Casanova, José. 2008. "Public religions revisited," in Religion: Beyond a Concept, ed. Hent de Vries, 101–119. New York: Fordham University Press.
Dirlik, Arif. 2007. Global Modernity. Modernity in the Age of Global Capitalism. Boulder CO: Paradigm Publishers.
Duprêt, Baudouin. 2000. Au nom de quel droit? Répertoires juridiques et référence religieuse dans la société égyptienne musulmane contemporaine. Paris: Maison des sciences de l'homme.
Eisenstadt, S.D. 2000. "Multiple modernities." Daedalus 129.1: 1–29.
Esposito, John L., and Azzam Tamimi, eds. 2000. Islam and Secularism in the Middle East. New York: New York University Press.
Freitag, Ulrike, ed. 2010. Saudi-Arabien. Ein Königreich im Wandel? Paderborn: Schöningh.
Gaborieau, Marc, and Malika Zeghal, eds. 2004. Autorités religieuses en Islam (=Archives de Sciences Sociales des Religions 49/125).
Haenni, Patrick. 2005. L'islam de marché. L'autre révolution conservatrice. Paris: Seuil.
Hafez, Sherine. 2011. An Islam of Her Own. Reconsidering Religion and Secularism in Women's Islamic Movements. New York and London: New York University Press.
Hammoudi, Abdellah. 1997. Master and Disciple. The Cultural Foundations of Moroccan Authoritarianism. Chicago: Chicago University Press.
Hashemi, Nader. 2009. Islam, Secularism, and Liberal Democracy. Toward a Democratic Theory for Muslim Societies. Oxford: Oxford University Press.
Hirschkind, Charles. 2006. The Ethical Soundscape. Cassette Sermons and Islamic Counterpublics. New York: Columbia University Press.
Iogna-Prat, Dominique, and Gilles Veinstein, eds. 2003. Histoires des hommes de dieu dans l'islam et le christianisme. Paris: Flammarion.

Joas, Hans, and Klaus Wiegandt, eds. 2009. Secularization and the World Religions. Liverpool: Liverpool University Press.

Kassab, Elizabeth S. 2010. Contemporary Arab Thought. Cultural Critique in Comparative Perspective. New York: Columbia University Press.

Krämer, Gudrun. 2013. "Gottes-Recht bricht Menschen-Recht. Theokratische Entwürfe im zeitgenössischen Islam," in Theokratie und theokratischer Diskurs, ed. Kai Trampedach and Andreas Pečar, 493–515. Tübingen: Mohr Siebeck.

Krämer, Gudrun. forthcoming. "Piety, politics and identity: configurations of secularity in Egypt," in 'A Secular Age' Beyond the West, ed. Mirjam Künkler, John Madeley, and Shylashri Shankar.

Krämer, Gudrun, and Sabine Schmidtke, eds. 2006. Speaking for Islam. Religious Authorities in Muslim Societies. Leiden and Boston: Brill.

Lombardi, Clark B. 2006. State Law as Islamic Law in Modern Egypt. The Incorporation of the Sharī'a into Egyptian Constitutional Law. Leiden and Boston: Brill.

Mahmood, Saba. 2005. Politics of Piety. The Islamic Revival and the Feminist Subject. Princeton: Princeton University Press.

Na'im, Abdullahi, ed. 2002. Islamic Family Law in a Changing World. A Global Resource Book. London: Zed.

Otto, Michiel-Jan, ed. 2010. Sharia Incorporated. A Comparative Overview of the Legal Systems of Twelve Muslim Countries in Past and Present. Leiden and Boston: Brill.

Peters, Rudolph. 2005. Crime and Punishment in Islamic Law. Theory and Practice From the Sixteenth to the Twenty-First Century. Cambridge: Cambridge University Press.

Pink, Johanna, ed. 2009. Muslim Societies in the Age of Mass Consumption. Politics, Culture and Identity between the Local and the Global. Cambridge: Cambridge Scholars Publishing.

Saeed, Abdullah, and Hassan Saeed. 2004. Freedom of Religion, Apostasy and Islam. Aldershot: Ashgate.

Schmidt, Volker H. 2006. "Multiple modernities or varieties of modernity?" Current Sociology 54: 77–97.

Taylor, Charles. 2007. A Secular Age. Cambridge MA and London: Belknap Press.

Taylor, Charles. 2009. "The polysemy of the secular." Social Research 76.4: 1143–1166.

Trampedach, Kai, and Andreas Pečar, eds. 2013. Theokratie und theokratischer Diskurs. Tübingen: Mohr Siebeck.

Tripp, Charles. 2006. Islam and the Moral Economy. The Challenge of Capitalism. Cambridge: Cambridge University Press.

Van Nieuwkerk, Karin. 2013. Performing Piety. Singers and Actors in Egypt's Islamic Revival. Austin: University of Texas Press.

Warner, Michael, Jonathan Vanantwerpen, and Craig Calhoun, eds. 2010. Varieties of Secularism in a Secular Age. Cambridge MA and London: Cambridge University Press.

Wils, Jean-Pierre. 2007. Gotteslästerung. Frankfurt am Main and Leipzig: Verlag der Weltreligionen.

Wohlrab-Sahr, Monika, and Marian Burchardt. 2012. "Multiple secularities: toward a cultural sociology of secular modernities." Comparative Sociology 11.6: 875–909.

Part III: **Secularities in East Asia**

Mark R. Mullins
Japanese Responses to Imperialist Secularization:
The Postwar Movement to Restore Shinto in the Public Sphere

The world has changed dramatically since Jürgen Habermas initiated scholarly debate about the nature of the public sphere over half a century ago. At the time, religion was regarded as largely irrelevant for understanding the nature of the bourgeois public sphere in modern Europe since it had already been reduced to personal piety or to the private sphere of familial relations in the wake of the Reformation.[1] Habermas was hardly alone in assuming that "privatization" was the inevitable fate of religion in modern societies. This was a central element of many secularization theories advanced in the West and taken-for-granted for most of the twentieth-century.

Over the past couple of decades, however, it has become the focus of serious criticism. In *Public Religions in the Modern World* (1994), for example, José Casanova highlighted the fact that religions around the world were breaking out of the restricted role they had been assigned in the private sphere and were again making claims about public life and institutions. This rediscovery of a "public role" by many established religious traditions—which he identifies as the process of "deprivatization"—refers to "the fact that religious traditions throughout the world are refusing to accept the marginal and privatized role which theories of modernity as well as theories of secularization had reserved from them" (1994: 5).

In recent years, Habermas (2006: 1) has acknowledged that "religious traditions and communities of faith have gained a new, hitherto unexpected political importance," and must be included in our consideration of the public sphere. Nevertheless, his approach, as Michelle Dillon explains, is still dominated by the "highly cognitive and rational approach to social life" that is embedded in his theory of communicative action. For that reason, he "ultimately gives short shrift to all those nonrational but highly significant sources of action and meaning in everyday life, all those things that spring from emotion and tradition" (2012: 250–251). If the public sphere is an area of social life where individuals

---

[1] According to Habermas, the process of "privatization" was already rather advanced by the end of the eighteenth century ([1989] 1991: 11–12).

can gather and freely share their views and concerns and formulate some agenda for political action, then it is hardly limited to the types of gatherings with which Habermas was preoccupied in the European context, i.e., discursive arenas such as salons and coffee houses where non-religious citizens engaged in debate and discussed matters of common concern.

It is significant that this problem highlighted by Dillon—who is primarily concerned with the deficiencies of Habermas's approach to religion in Western societies—also appears in Eiko Ikegami's (2000, 2005) revision of public sphere analysis for the Japanese cultural context. Ikegami is similarly critical of Habermas's preoccupation with the "liberal public sphere" and his neglect of the "nondiscursive, nonrational, or other counterpublics" (2000: 990, 1023). She makes the case for a "plurality of publics" and provides a broader framework that takes seriously a range of social groups—women, racial minorities, and religious groups, for example—which have been largely excluded from consideration in Eurocentric studies of the public sphere. Although her approach was developed initially to clarify the role of Tokugawa "apolitical" aesthetic circles and associations, her perspective can be usefully extended to a consideration of the role of religion beyond the private sphere in modern Japanese society.

The significance of Japanese religions for the public sphere has recently received focused attention in relation to the response of various groups to the 2011 "triple disaster" of earthquake, tsunami, and nuclear accident in Fukushima. A number of scholars have drawn attention to the many new initiatives undertaken by Buddhist institutions and new religions in disaster relief, spiritual counseling, social involvement with environmental and nuclear issues, and in critical engagement with the government's energy policy.[2] Given the emergency situation of northeastern Japan, these are important new developments and, to borrow Ikegami's terminology, represent emerging "counterpublics" that could eventually influence the political process and help determine the shape of public life and institutions.

My concern in this chapter, however, is with the Shinto-related efforts to restore influence in the public sphere—a movement that began over half a century ago soon after the end of the Allied Occupation of Japan (1945–1952). This case study of Shinto will indicate how a tradition—even if an "invented one" from just over a century ago—continues to provide a vision for how life in the public sphere should be shaped and still retains the power to mobilize individuals and groups for political action.

---

[2] On these recent developments, see Shimazono (2012, 2013), Inaba and Kurosaki (2013), and McLaughlin (2013a, 2013b).

In his contribution to the recent volume, *Rethinking Secularism*, Richard Madsen makes an interesting claim that is closely related to our consideration of the public sphere and secularization outside of the modern West. Madsen writes that:

> The secular form of Asian political institutions often *masks a religious spirit*. Japan, for example, has a secular constitution, but many of its government leaders have felt compelled to pray for the spirits of the war dead at the Yasukuni shrine, in the face of strong criticism from China, South Korea, and many other Asian countries, not to mention the United States. The pressure to visit the shrine comes from nationalistic constituencies within Japan, but it is, indeed, a pressure to worship at a Shinto shrine, presided over by a priest, which purports not just to memorialize the names of the dead but actually to contain their spirits. (2011: 249, emphasis mine)

This chapter seeks to provide the background necessary to understand Madsen's claim that institutions often thought to be secular may in fact contain a hidden religious dimension. At the same time, I hope to clarify how some major changes in Japanese religion and society over the past century relate to the theoretical debates about secularization.

1 Modernization, Secularization, and Japanese Religions

The inherited wisdom from the West on the relationship between modernization and religion has been largely framed in negative terms with theories of secularization. Following Max Weber, it has been generally assumed that the necessary concomitant of modernization is the "disenchantment of the world" through rationalization and, ultimately, secularization. In the master narrative, this is interpreted as religious decline at multiple levels—a decline in individual religiosity (belief, ritual practice), a decline in religious institutions, and a decline in the power of religion to integrate societies around one frame of meaning. In the case of Western Europe, the power of the "sacred canopy" provided by medieval Catholicism began to disintegrate under the impact of the Protestant Reformation, the spread of industrial capitalism and modern science, and through the formation of the modern nation-state (Peter Berger [1967] 1969). In short, the modernization process in the West involved a shrinking of the sacred canopy and the replacement of a religious monopoly by a market situation in which various subworlds were forced to compete. It is usually understood that this increasingly pluralistic situation leads to privatization and removal of religion from the public sphere.

In *A General Theory of Secularization*, David Martin provided a more cautious and nuanced analysis of the secularization process that identified variations depending upon a number of factors, including whether a country is monopolistic, pluralistic, Catholic or Protestant, for example, and whether key events in the history of a country included revolution—either united against an external force or conflict between various groups in the same society (his postulate of "frame"; 1978: 15). Based on a consideration of these variables interacting in distinctive ways, Martin identified different patterns of secularization, which he referred to as the American, English, Scandinavian, Mixed, Latin, Statist (right), Statist (Left), and Nationalist (1978: 59). Given that "multiple secularities" emerged in Western societies, we should not be surprised to find that the process of secularization in Japan has a distinctive pattern of its own.

As we will see below, an accurate understanding of the situation in Japan requires that we move beyond the framework of an isolated nation state and take into account the global interconnectedness that has shaped both the Japanese understanding of religion and some of the responses to the process of secularization. One difficulty that must be recognized at the outset in approaching this topic is that there is no consensus in either scholarly or popular discourse on the meaning and use of the concept of "religion" (*shūkyō*) in Japan. Even though the term was imported from the West in the late nineteenth century and has sometimes been viewed as an artificial construct that is inapplicable to the Japanese situation, it has been adopted and adapted by scholars and used widely over the past century—even by the government for official and legal purposes.[3]

Another aspect of the global interconnectedness that has shaped the development of religion in modern Japan is closely related to the strategies developed by political and religious leaders to address the "threat" represented by European and American excursions and empire-building initiatives in the nineteenth century. One central point that I hope will become clear is that the sociologic regarding modernization and secularization developed on the basis of European history does not fit the case of Japan. This is not to say that Japanese are particularly religious or that Japan is unique, but simply to point out that modernization has "ambivalent effects" on religion (Munakata 1976: 99). It may lead to secularization—understood by many scholars to involve the decline of religious beliefs, practices, or institutions—but at the same time it may reinvigorate others and even create an environment in which new forms of religion can flourish. In a

---

[3] The issue of terminology is a complicated one and cannot be pursued here. See Isomae (2003, 2005), Thal (2002), Josephson (2012), and Krämer (2013) for detailed treatment of how the term 'religion' has been used and adapted in the Japanese context.

word, a unilinear conception of modernization and religious decline cannot adequately account for the situation in some non-Western regions of the world. Over the past two decades, of course, this perspective has also been critically revised by scholars focused on the study of religion in a variety of Western contexts.[4]

2 Japan's Modernization and the Creation of a Sacred Canopy

The master narrative of secularization mentioned above has been a compelling one, but it does not easily fit the Japanese experience. Japan's political and religious response to modernization from the nineteenth century was initially shaped internally by the disintegration of the Tokugawa feudal order and externally by the threat of Western imperialism. Meiji Restoration leaders recognized that a unified nation was needed to face this crisis and religious resources were mobilized for this cause. Prior to the restoration of imperial rule, Japan was composed of numerous groups divided by diverse commitments, including clans, politicized Buddhist sects, as well as protest groups comprised of peasants and small landowners. Politically, Japan was divided into 270 political domains (*bakuhan*), each ruled by a regional feudal lord. According to Maruyama Masao (1974: 327), it was not until the Meiji Restoration that national consciousness truly developed and led to "a sense of political solidarity and national unity." There was also an important religious dimension to this situation. While the common people were monitored and controlled by the Buddhist temple system during the Tokugawa period (1603–1868), they were hardly integrated under a sacred canopy. In the premodern period, in fact, a large majority of the Japanese populace were divided into particularistic village communities and united around local Shinto cults (Davis 1977: 63–64). Shinto, therefore, primarily functioned as the legitimizer of sub-worlds throughout Japan.

It was only after the Restoration that a national form of Shinto was created by leaders in the new government in an effort to unify and integrate a heterogeneous population and mobilize the people for nation-building, modernization,

---

[4] This now constitutes a substantial literature that we cannot consider here, but see Wohlrab-Sahr and Burchardt (2012) for a helpful review framed in terms of "multiple modernities" and "multiple secularities."

and military expansion.⁵ In order to deal with the problems of internal chaos and the threat of Western imperialism, the restoration government pursued a policy of uniting the people under the canopy of a state-sponsored and emperor-centered civil religion.⁶ The family-state ideology articulated by the Meiji Constitution and the Imperial Rescript on Education (1890) was justified with reference to the divine origin of the emperor and the people of Japan. These documents not only reinforced the traditional Confucian virtues of loyalty and filial piety, but also were used to forge a strong national identity. This meant that Buddhism lost the state patronage it had enjoyed during the Tokugawa period and a new form of Shinto was created to provide the foundation for a new political order. Here we see both the secularization of established Buddhism—including the loss of power and prestige of priests, and destruction of properties—and the sacralization process at work in the development of State Shinto. This new form of Shinto was eventually understood and defined by the government as a natural and "non-religious" Way that bound all Japanese together and transcended other organized religions. In spite of the government's claims, Sarah Thal (2002: 110) reminds us that "the rhetoric of Shinto as 'not a religion' was never entirely convincing. Because even state-supported shrines relied for most of their income on the donations of worshipers and the purchase of amulets, questions repeatedly arose concerning the religiosity of even the most public, nationally ranked shrines." In spite of the government's position, there were Japanese priests and scholars who continued to recognize the "religious" character of Shinto shrines during these years.⁷

---

5 There is a substantial literature on the development of this new form of 'State Shinto'; representative works include Holtom ([1943] 1963), Murakami (1970, 1982), Hardacre (1989), and Shimazono (2010).

6 As Richard Rubenstein (1989: 116–117) has observed, "the West initiated modernization with a rejection of the highest religious and political authorities, not excluding regicide, and tended to equate modernization with secularization," whereas "Japan undertook modernization under the authority of its supreme religio-political authority and in defense of the values of its traditional civilization."

7 Miyaji Naokazu (1886–1949) is one prominent figure that affirmed this interpretation. Miyaji had served in the Ministry of Home Affairs as head of the Shinto Bureau's Research Department (Jinjakyoku Kōshōka) prior to his appointment to the Chair for Shinto Studies at the Imperial University in Tokyo, a position he held from 1938 to 1945. He subsequently served as an adviser to Jinja Honchō (Association of Shinto Shrines), the main umbrella shrine organization of the postwar period. In a 1946 interview conducted soon after the Occupation began, he explained: "In my opinion religion is intercourse between human beings and what is superhuman. Therefore, all shrines naturally fall into the category of religion. . . . The government did not negate the religious activities of the shrines even when it did not regard the shrines as religion" (Miyaji 1946: 143).

The new national religion created by the restoration bureaucrats differed considerably from the previous forms of Shinto belief and practice. It was largely an "invention of tradition" projected back on Japanese history, rather than a true restoration (Hobsbawm 1983: 1–14; Hardacre 1989: 4). In order to shift the allegiance of the majority of the population from particularistic local communities to the Emperor and the national community, a major effort of re-socialization was required on the part of the government. Eventually this transformation was achieved through the effective use of the public school system, military conscription, and control of mass media.[8]

By the 1930s this civil religion became increasingly totalitarian and members of every religious group were required to conform to the state-defined orthodoxy. In 1939, in fact, the Diet enacted the Religious Organizations Law, giving the state authority to disband any group whose teachings were in conflict with "the Imperial Way." This rather restrictive environment for religious minorities continued until the end of the Second World War and the arrival of the occupation forces.

3 Imperialist Secularization and the Restructuring of Religion and Society

Just as the perceived threat from the West generated a crisis that helped launch the creation of a new national civil religion, it was the defeat and Occupation of Japan by the Allied Powers in August 1945 that also led to its rapid deconstruction. On 15 December of that year, the Supreme Commander for the Allied Powers (SCAP) issued the Directive for the Disestablishment of State Shinto and set in motion policies that effectively reduced Shinto to the status of a voluntary organization and fundamentally restructured Japanese religion and society. Shinto's "public" role was essentially privatized by the strict enforcement of the separation of religion and state. In addition to ending government financial support for and administration of Shinto shrines, the Directive instructed the Japanese government to remove Shinto elements from all public institutions. This included taking *kamidana* (Shinto altars) out of schools and public offices, eliminating

---

[8] The role of public education was particularly important in the forging of a new national identity connected to the imperial household and symbolized by the new national shrines. On this point see Murakami (1982: 46–49). For a more focused treatment of the place of Shinto and Yasukuni Shrine in textbooks for elementary school children during this period, see Irie (2001: 73–78).

Shinto elements from textbooks and curriculum, and terminating of forced shrine visits (*sanpai*) on the part of students, teachers, and government officials.

The Emperor-centric Shinto tradition was also secularized through the abolishment of the Imperial Rescript on Education (*Kyōiku Chokugo*) and the Diet's passing of a new bill for education in 1947. At the time, both the Emperor and the Imperial Rescript were regarded as "sacred" (*shinsei*) and understood to be the standard and source of both individual and social morality (Fukuda 1993: 538–39). The Occupation authorities thought that the continued propagation of such views in public schools was in fundamental tension with the larger goal of democratization and encouraged the Japanese government to prepare a new education policy and guidelines. The new law eliminated references to filial piety and loyalty to the Emperor, as well as the exhortations to offer oneself to the State on behalf of the Imperial Throne. Through these various reforms and the strict application of the separation of religion and state, Shinto was largely removed from the public sphere. Shrines were allowed to continue in the private sphere—like other religious bodies (Buddhist, Christian, and New Religions)—only if militaristic and ultranationalistic elements were abandoned.

The profound changes brought about by the Occupation authorities provide a good example of what N.J. Demerath (2007: 72–76) has designated as "imperialist secularization," which is the coercive and top-down removal of religion from public institutions by a foreign power. This is a very different process from the one outlined in most versions of secularization, that is, the gradual decline of religion with the advance of modernization. As far as imperialist secularization is concerned, we should note that it may or may not bring about the secularization of consciousness on the part of practitioners of a given religion. In this particular case, many religious and political leaders continued to believe that Shinto should play a central role in society and in due course would act on that conviction.

The Occupation policies clearly secularized Shinto by removing it from the public sphere. At the same time, the disestablishment of State Shinto and abolishment of the wartime laws regulating religion, which were framed in articles 20 and 89 of the postwar Constitution (1947), created a free-market religious economy in which all forms of religion were allowed to exist without interference from agents of the state. In the early decades of the postwar period, therefore, we also see a surge of new religious movements, which contributed to the ongoing pluralization and growth of the institutional dimension of religion in Japan. This occurred, I should add, when Japan was focused on rebuilding a devastated country and going through a second major period of modernization.

Here, again, we see the "ambivalent effects" of modernization and very different patterns of secularization depending on the level or dimension of analysis.

During the Occupation and early decades of postwar Japan, for example, we see secularization at the societal level—with the removal of Shinto from the public sphere—but at the same time dynamic movements of resacralization may be seen in the emergence of literally hundreds of new religious movements. I do not want to over-emphasize the social significance of new religions here— since probably less than 10 percent of the Japanese belong to one of these movements today—but it is remarkable, as Max Eger (1980: 18) noted years ago, that Japan "gave evidence of an unparalleled growth in its 'religious population' at precisely the same time as its most recent 'modernization.' Even though the growth of the new religious movements has since tapered off, this coincidence of 'modernization' and 'religious growth' constitutes a remarkable confutation of the Western idea that modernization goes hand in hand with secularization." It should be remembered that Eger wrote this assessment several decades ago when there were still many signs of growth and vitality, which is very different than the situation today.

While national statistics indicate that organized religion still has a significant presence today, it is well documented that many of these institutions are in serious trouble. Most organized forms of religion have been struggling with basic demographic realities. In the early postwar period, for example, older established Shinto and Buddhist institutions—disproportionately concentrated in rural areas or small towns—struggled with the impact of urbanization, while a number of new religious movements emerged and initially benefited from the population shift. Today all organized forms of religion are beginning to feel the impact of the low birthrate and aging population. While some religious groups (notably New Religions and Christian Churches) have grown over the past century as a result of active membership recruitment, most religious organizations depend on natural growth, which is based on births to members and effective religious socialization. A fertility rate below 2.1 points to population decline and Japan's birthrate, which had been declining for decades, was only 1.41 in 2012. While there will undoubtedly be winners and losers in the shrinking religious market, it seems likely that most religious groups for the foreseeable future will be struggling to maintain their institutions and activities as the number of active clergy and members continues to decline.[9]

---

9 See Reader (2012) for a recent assessment of the case for secularization that gives particular attention to the institutional data on religion.

4 Deprivatization and the Reappearance of Public Religion

Recent evidence from the institutional level of analysis supports the interpretation of serious decline, but what about the societal dimension or the role of Japanese religion in the public sphere? Some years ago Peter Berger ([1967] 1969: 107–108) defined secularization as "the process by which sectors of society and culture are removed from the domination of religious institutions and symbols." In other words, it refers not just to institutional decline and a weakening of individual belief and practice, but also involves the "privatization or religion" or the removal of religion as a significant force or influence in the "public sphere." Is this the inevitable and irreversible fate of religion in modern societies?

As noted above, José Casanova (1994) challenged this understanding of secularization through an examination of socially engaged religious movements that had emerged over the course of several decades. On the basis of these case studies in multiple national contexts, he argued that it was clear by the 1980s that religions around the world were breaking out of the restricted role they had been assigned in the private sphere and were again making claims about public life and institutions. In contrast to the earlier assumptions regarding the inevitability of privatization, Casanova argues that this process depends in part on how religious groups interpret their religious tradition and context. "Privatization and deprivatization are, therefore, historical options for religion in the modern world. Some religions will be induced by tradition, principle, and historical circumstances to remain basically private religions of individual salvation. Certain cultural traditions, religious doctrinal principles, and historical circumstances, by contrast will induce other religions to enter, at least occasionally, the public sphere" (221).

Several decades ago Richard K. Fenn (1978: xii) elaborated a perspective on secularization that anticipated in some ways the argument advanced by Casanova, arguing that "individuals and groups are responsible for secularization: not impersonal or abstract forces like technology or education, but living and active human agents." Secularization occurs, he explained, as individuals and groups redefine and negotiate the boundary between the sacred and the profane. It is this changing "definition of the situation" that shapes the path toward either secularization or desecularization. According to Fenn's framework, the process of desecularization is, in fact, theoretically possible if religious groups "assign wide scope to the sacred and require high levels of integration between personal and corporate values" (1978: 139). Religious groups that define the sacred in broader terms represent a potential force for desecularization if they are able effectively mobilize their members to engage the public sphere.[10] It is possible for groups—which for decades may have been largely concerned with personal piety and content a with religious life in community or congregation "separate from the world"—to discover a larger vision and adopt the view that it is their duty to engage society and influence the broader sphere of public life. This can be seen, for example, in the transformation of some fundamentalist and evangelical Protestants in the late 1970s from "separatists"—preoccupied with individual salvation and personal piety—into the "Moral Majority"—a social movement that actively sought to shape electoral politics, public schools, and legislation in America.

Although Casanova documented his claims about deprivatization through case studies of "public religion" in the West (including Catholic and Protestant movements in Spain, Poland, Brazil, and the United States), he argued that "the deprivatization of religion is indeed a global phenomenon" (1994: 10). As it turns out, there is considerable evidence from Japanese religions in the postwar period to support Casanova's claims. It is well known that Sōka Gakkai, the largest Buddhist new religion in postwar Japan, for example, was not content to cultivate the piety of its followers in the private sphere, but formed its own political party, the Kōmeito, with a vision of shaping public life according to its principles and ideals. By making claims about public life and institutions, this movement challenged the assumption that modernization inevitably leads to the privatization of religion. Sōka Gakkai's political engagement has been the focus of considerable criticism and public debate, as well as scholarly research.[11] Another new religion, Kōfuku no Kagaku, recently organized its own political party, the Happiness Realization Party (*Kōfuku Jitsugen Tō*) in 2009, and expressed a concern to shape public life through electoral politics. Less widely known—particularly outside of Japan—are the Shinto-related movements that have been actively engaged in efforts to reshape the public sphere for decades, which is my particular concern here.

---

10 This contingency model is very different from the earlier perspectives on secularization represented by such scholars as Peter Berger and Brian Wilson for whom it was an inevitable and irreversible process. At least in Berger's earlier work, desecularization appeared to be theoretically possible only by a return to a pre-modern and pre-industrial form of society.
11 For two recent treatments, see Okuyama Michiaki 2010 and Erica Baffeli 2010; for a more detailed analysis of Sōka Gakkai's and Kōmeito, see Ehrhardt et al. (forthcoming).

5 The Return of Shinto to the Public Sphere

As we have seen, the privatization of Shinto occurred not as a result of modernization per se, but due to its forced removal from the public sphere as a result of the directives issued by the Supreme Commander of Allied Powers and implemented by the Japanese government. Under these circumstances, it is not surprising that the process of deprivatization in the postwar period is closely connected to the Shinto-related neonationalistic response to the imposition of a foreign social order on Japan.[12] As soon as the Occupation ended, religious and political leaders quickly mobilized forces to restore Shinto to public life and institutions.

What is it that motivates and mobilizes religious groups to re-engage the public sphere? Casanova's case studies revealed that what seems to precipitate the involvement of religious groups "are different types of state intervention and administrative colonization of the life world and the private sphere." Protestant fundamentalists in the United States became politically mobilized, for example, in response "to state rulings coming from the Supreme Court, the Internal Revenue Service, and Congress" (Casanova 1994: 227). In the Japanese context, we can similarly observe that mobilization of people in a variety of Shinto-related movements in postwar Japan was precipitated by the "intervention and administrative colonization" by the Allied Occupation and the perceived (and actual) loss of influence in the public sphere.[13]

The movement to revive or recover what had been destroyed during the Occupation can be traced back to the early 1950s. The Association of Shinto Shrines (Jinja Honchō), which had been organized in 1946 as a way for shrines to survive as religious bodies during the Occupation, began to work actively on numerous fronts to restore Shinto influence in public life and institutions (Ueda 1979: 304–305). In the postwar period, in fact, this religious association has been "primarily active as a political force in Japan. Its political aim is to revive State Shinto by promoting nationalism and reverence for the Emperor" (Shimazono 2007: 706).

The significance of the Association of Shinto Shrines as a force for deprivatization in the postwar period can be illustrated through an examination of the

---

[12] Not all forms of religious nationalism are expressed in a way that has significance in the public sphere. See Shimazono (2001: 88–137) for a consideration of religious nationalisms that are largely "spiritual" or "cultural" and those that have political significance.
[13] This interpretation is supported by Ueda Kenji (1979), the late Shinto scholar, as well as the account of the postwar period provided by Jinja Shinpōsha, ed., *Shintō Shirei to Sengo no Shintō* (1971).

Shinto Seiji Renmei, the main political arm of the Association, which was established in 1969. At one time it was known as "the League Promoting Ties between Politics and Shinto," but is better known today as the "Shinto Association of Spiritual Leadership" (hereafter referred to as Shinseiren). Over the years it has worked especially closely with the Liberal Democratic Party (LDP) in order to gain national attention for their concerns and to bring their agenda and various initiatives to the Diet for action. As explained on the home-page and in numerous publications, the Shinto spirit provides the foundation for Shinseiren's political vision and activities.[14] According to these official sources, the central aims of Shinseiren are 1) to nuture support for the Imperial Household and to guard its dignity or majesty (*kōshitsu no songen goji*); 2) to work for a revised Constitution that will be the pride of the Japanese people; 3) to reestablish as a 'national rite' the care of the Shōwa martyrs enshrined in Yasukuni Shrine ; and 4) to put in place a education system that will cultivate the heart of young people and give them hope for the future (this is elaborated in various places in terms of a restoration of moral and patriotic education, which resembles the *shūshin* curriculum of the prewar period).

According to the history of this political group, in 1984 there were some 945 shrines scattered across all the country's prefectures included in the list of supporting institutions (Shintō Seiji Renmei, ed. 1984: 167–184). Although a current list of supporting shrines is unavailable, a close relationship remains between Shinseiren and many shrines affiliated with the Association of Shinto Shrines. The Association provides office space in Tokyo for the group and for its local branches in Jinja Hochō prefectural headquarters throughout Japan. A link to the Shinseiren home-page is also maintained on the Association's website.[15] Over the decades, Shinseiren has continued to gain support among politicians, particularly those from the Liberal Democratic Party. Its political clout, in fact, is related closely to its affiliated "debating club" known as the Shinto Seiji Renmei Kokkai Gi'in Kondankai, an association of Diet members who support the aims of Shinseiren. This is essentially a round-table discussion group for Diet members, which supports the broad goal of restoring the public role of Shinto. In 1984 only 44 Diet members were listed as members (Shintō Seiji Renmei, ed., 1984: 151–

---

14 See http://www.sinseiren.org/index_menu.html for a number of Shinseiren position statements on key issues of concern. For a historical account of their first fifteen years and an overview of their key activities, see Shintō Seiji Renmei, ed. (1984).
15 See http://www.jinjahoncho.or.jp/honcho/index4.html (most recent access 4–28–2014).

152), but it has steadily grown over the decades and by 2010 some 157 of 722 Diet members belonged to this group and worked to advance its goals.[16]

The close relationship between the Association of Shinto Shrines, Shinto Seiji Renmei, and politicians today can be clearly illustrated with reference to Yamatani Eriko, one of the darlings of Shinseiren and a person who represents the far right of the Liberal Democratic Party. Yamatani is a popular speaker and regularly appears at of Shinseiren study meetings and gatherings held across the country. She has also served as the chief secretary of a group of Diet members who support Yasukuni Shrine and is strong advocate of "official visits" (*kōshiki sanpai*) to the shrine by the prime minister.[17] She is also a strong supporter of the Imperial Household and has recently been promoting group tours and pilgrimages to Ise Shrine in order to cultivate a deeper appreciation for the Imperial Household, gratitude for Japanese identity, and worship of Amaterasu Omikami, the ultimate source of the nation.[18] Finally, the fact that she has a re-election office within the shrine precincts of Katori Jingu, in Katori City, Chiba Prefecture—with her campaign posters prominently displayed there—indicate how closely Shrine Shinto is linked to Shinseiren politicians.[19]

Early efforts to restore Shinto in the public sphere by Shinseiren and its affliated politicians, includes the movement to promote "official visits" (*kōshiki sanpai*) to Yasukuni Shrine and efforts to renationalize the shrine (Shintō Seiji Renmei, ed. 1984: 45–56). From 1969 to 1974, the Liberal Democratic Party worked hard to pass the *Yasukuni jinja hōan*, a bill to restore direct financial support to the shrine, which had been eliminated by the Shinto Directive in the early days of the Occupation. These efforts generated widespread protests by religious minorities and other activists groups that were concerned to preserve a clear separation of religion and state, and, ultimately, ended in failure. Other initiatives promoted by Shinseiren include movements to reclaim the ideals of the Imperial Rescript on Education and thereby restore proper moral and patriotic education in the public schools, the creation of new textbooks that would support such a curriculum, and promotion of the policy to have public schools use the national

---

16 See John Breen and Mark Teeuwen (2010: 201–202) and the Shinto Seiji Renmei homepage (http://www.sinseiren.org/) for additional information on Shinseirin membership, political agenda, and current publications.
17 The Diet group in support of Yasukuni Shrine is known as "Heiwa o Negai Shin no Kokueki o Kangaeru Yasukuni Sanpai o Shiji Suru Wakate Kokkai Giin no Kai."
18 See the following videos for Yamatani's explanation of her May 2010 promotion of Ise Shrine pilgrimages:
http://www.nicovideo.jp/watch/1271036516; http://www.nicovideo.jp/watch/1275963427.
19 Reported in *Shūkan kinyōbi* , No. 797 (30 April 2010): 36–37.

flag and anthem for official ceremonies (Shintō Seiji Renmei, ed., 1984: 66–75). Another goal of Shinseiren was to revise the Constitution and replace the one imposed during the Occupation—which sought to 'weaken the nation'—with one that would renew respect for Japanese traditions and restore pride and strength to the nation (Shintō Seiji Renmei, ed., 1984: 76–78). One early success story was the reign-name legalization movement, which was achieved with the passing of the Reign-Name Law (*Gengōhō*) in 1979, and restored the Japanese calendar based on the reign of the Emperor (Ruoff 2001: 158–201).

Reviewing these various movements and initiatives in the 1980s, K. Peter Takayama (1988) argued that they collectively represented an attempt to revitalize Japan's prewar civil religion. At the time, however, very little had actually been achieved by Shinseiren and its supporters. Many of the restoration initiatives have been the focus of renewed attention since the mid-1990s and today there is considerably more evidence to support Takayama's claims that religion is returning to the public sphere through Shinto-based civil religious initiatives. These new efforts are closely related to a resurgence of neonationalism in the wake of the social crisis precipitated by the Kobe earthquake and sarin gas attack on the Tokyo subway system by followers of Aum Shinrikyō (Mullins 2012a). In the post-Aum environment, a number of new groups were formed, such as the "Japanese Society for History Textbook Reform" (Atarashii Rekishi Kyōkasho o Tsukuru Kai), organized in 1996, and the Nippon Kaigi, founded in 1997, which provided additional support for the initiatives that had been promoted by Shinseiren for several decades.

6 Contemporary Developments

As may be seen in Table 1, a number of the key concerns advanced by Shinseiren for several decades have received renewed attention and promotion over the course of seven LDP administrations since 1998. When considered in isolation, some of the developments noted below may appear unrelated to religion—and they probably are without religious significance for many individuals whose lives are subsequently shaped by the new policies (in public schools, for example)—but when taken all together and seen in relation to the political agenda and goals of the Association of Shinto Shrines and Shinseiren, they are clearly a part of a civil religious vision for Japanese society. At the very least, this is how many individuals on the secular left and some religious minorities perceive these initiatives. Here I can only highlight a few key developments during the administrations of several LDP Prime Ministers to illustrate the reappearance of religion in what is often regarded as the "secular" public sphere. While one could certainly argue that not all of the developments noted below are explicitly "religious," it would be difficult to interpret them within a purely "secular" frame.

Table 1. LDP Prime Ministers and Restoration Initiatives, 1998–2013.[20]

Name	Term in Office	Initiative/Legislation Promoted or Passed
Obuchi Keizō (1937–2000)	30 July 1998–5 April 2000	Diet passed a bill to provide official and legal recognition of the National Flag (Hinomaru) and Anthem (Kimigayo) in 1999.
		Ministry of Education issues guidelines and instructions for all public schools to sing the national anthem and use the flag for official events, such as entrance and graduation ceremonies.
		On 5 April 2001—the last day of Obuchi's term and first day of Mori's term—the Ministry of Education approves the new revisionist textbook for junior high schools, which was prepared by the "Japanese Society for History Textbook Reform" (Atarashii Rekishi Kyōkasho o Tsukuru Kai).
Mori Yoshirō (1937–)	5 April 2000- April 26, 2001	Prime Minister Mori Yoshirō's address at the celebration of the thirtieth anniversary of Shinto Seiji Renmei refers to Japan as a "divine nation" (*kami no kuni*) centered on the Emperor (15 May 2000).
Koizumi Jun'ichirō (1942–)	April 26, 2001–26 September 2005	Fulfilling his promise to supporters that he would visit Yasukuni if elected as Prime Minister, Koizumi participates in *kōshiki sanpai* on a number of occasions between 2001 and 2005.
		Kokoro no no-to, patriotic moral education texts, distributed to elementary and junior high schools by Ministry of Education (2002).
		LDP makes public draft proposal for New Constitution, including revisions to articles 20 and 89 that pertain to religion, which would clearly weaken the clear separation of religion and state (2005).
Abe Shinzō (1954–)	26 September 2005–26 September 2007	Revision of Fundamental Education Law (*Kyōiku Kihon Hō*, 2006).
		Pro-Yasukuni Anime DVD "Pride" (*Hokori*), produced by Nihon Seinen Kaigisho for the Ministry of Education, distributed for viewing in 93 locations across Japan (2007).

---

20 Official data for each Prime Minister is available at the government home-page: http://www.kantei.go.jp/jp/rekidaisouri-index.html; http://www.kantei.go.jp/jp/rekidai/ichiran.html; additional information has been gleaned from multiple sources.

Name	Term in Office	Initiative/Legislation Promoted or Passed
Fukuda Yasuo (1936–)	26 September 2007 – 24 September 2008	Regulation banning school visits to Yasukuni Shrine and *gokoku jinja* (state-protecting shrines) ruled no longer valid by Minister of Education (March 27, 2008). Ministry of Education provides orientation of new policy allowing school visits to shrines during the summer of 2008.
Asō Tarō (1940–)	24September, 2008- September 16, 2009	On his personal home-page Asō promotes a proposal to make Yasukuni Shrine a special category organization, eliminating its current status as *shūkyō hōjin* (religious corporation), which would allow direct financial support by the government.
Abe Shinzō (1954–)	26 December 2012-	Abe renews call to revise the Constitution and on 1 May 2013 proposes revision of Article 96 to allow amendments to be passed by simple majority in the Diet rather than a two-thirds majority. Reiterates his stance that a revision of the Constitution is indispensible for true liberation from the postwar regime. Initially avoids visiting Yasukuni Shrine as Prime Minister, but makes offerings for the Spring Festival and 15 August; indicates that whether or not Cabinet members participate in Yasukuni Shrine rites should be decided by the individuals concerned; makes official visit on 26 December 2013.

First, let us consider the impact of legislation regarding the national flag and anthem on public schools, which was passed while Obuchi Keizō was Prime Minister. Since the use of the flag and anthem had been restricted and discouraged during the Occupation period, these symbols have only gradually been re-integrated into public life during the postwar decades. In 1949, the Supreme Commander of Allied Powers (SCAP) rescinded the restriction and General MacArthur announced in his New Year message that the Japanese people could once again freely use the flag and anthem (Cripps 1996: 81). The following year, Amano Teiyū, the Minister of Education, issued a statement that it was desirable that the flag be raised and anthem sung on national holidays. From that time, their use in schools and public life was encouraged and began to expand.

It was in 1958 that the Ministry of Education first instructed (*gakushū shidōryō*) public schools that it was "desirable" for the flag to be raised and the anthem sung at official school events (entrance and graduation ceremonies). Under these soft guidelines, however, compliance rates were not too impressive. While the flag reappeared and was used regularly in parades and was waved proudly in the 1964 Tokyo Olympics, considerable opposition remained in the schools and the teachers' union, Nikkyōso, and other critics argued that these symbols were unsuitable for use in the schools since they had been used for the mobilization of both teachers and students in wartime Japan.

Over the years conflicts erupted in many schools across Japan when school administrators attempted to enforce the Ministry of Education policy, but it was the suicide of a high school principal over the issue that focused the nation's attention and contributed in part to the government's effort to legalize these symbols. Ishikawa Toshihiro, Principal of Sera Senior High School in Hiroshima Prefecture, committed suicide by hanging himself on 28 February 1999 after difficult negotiations with teachers in an effort to persuade them to go along with the directives from the Ministry of Education and Prefectural Education Board.

Although widely accepted as Japan's national symbols from years of use, the Hinomaru (flag) and Kimigayo (anthem) had never been officially approved as such by any government administration. Some political leaders reasoned that the problems surrounding use of these symbols in public life could be resolved if they were "officially" recognized by passing legislation in the Diet. In 1999, after considerable debate, the Diet finally approved the Kimigayo and Hinomaru as the official symbols of the nation.[21] At the time this legislation was being debated in the Diet, Prime Minister Obuchi clearly stated on June 29 that freedom of conscience would be protected and no coercion would ever be involved in public institutions if the bill passed.[22]

In spite of such assurances, many religious leaders and public intellectuals raised serious concerns about this legislation. The Catholic Council on Justice and Peace, for example, sent a letter of appeal to Prime Minister Obuchi on 12 March 1999, which expressed opposition to the government's rushed efforts to legalize the flag and anthem. According to the Council's interpretation, the Hinomaru is a symbol of Japan's military aggression and invasion in Asia. Likewise, the lyrics of the Kimigayo express praise for the Emperor as the ruler of Japan, which violates Japan's postwar Constitution that placed the government clearly in the hands of the people. Rather than approving these as the symbols of the nation, the letter urges government representatives to consider a new flag and

---

[21] Even though the bill was passed by the Diet, it did not actually represent the view of the majority of Japanese on this issue. When the national flag and anthem legislation was being debated, for example, an opinion poll conducted by the *Mainichi Shinbun* (14 July 1999) found that 43 percent were in favor of official recognition of the *Hinomaru* as the national flag, while some 52 percent were opposed or in favor of a more careful debate and discussion; similarly, 36 percent were in favor of official recognition of *Kimigayo*, while some 58 percent were opposed or in favor of more serious debate.

[22] For the original Japanese record of Prime Minister Obuchi's explanation on 29 June 1969, see http://sdaigo.cocolog-nifty.com/kokkikokkasingirokushoroku.pdf.

anthem that will reflect the principles of peace and democratic values that are foundational to Japan's Constitution.[23]

Before the end of the year, the Ministry of Education reaffirmed its instructions to require all public schools to use the legal symbols for official events, such as entrance and graduation ceremonies, and worked closely with School Boards to see that the rules were enforced. The passing of this legislation clearly strengthened the position of politicians and educators who felt it was their duty to have all teachers and staff lead students by example in singing the national anthem before the flag for important school ceremonies. Even before the intensification of "guidance" from the Ministry of Education, a number of teachers had already been disciplined for failing to comply with the 1989 guidelines.[24] The situation only became more difficult for teachers after 1999.

It was the passing of this legislation that strengthened the position of politicians and educators who felt it was their duty to have all teachers and staff lead students by example in singing the national anthem before the flag for important school ceremonies. The Ministry of Education subsequently re-issued guidelines and instructions for all public schools to sing the national anthem and use the flag for official events, such as entrance and graduation ceremonies. There were many protests against the strengthening of the Ministry policies by both teachers and students in various schools across the nation, but the widespread resistance quickly subsided. A number of teachers, however, continued to refuse to stand or lead students in what they regard to be oppressive patriotic rituals that will recreate an educational environment that too closely resembles that of wartime Japan. Takahashi Seiju (2004: 177), a teacher in the Tokyo Metropolitan school system, has reached back to the Tokugawa period to find another parallel, comparing this policy to the one used by the authorities centuries ago to force followers of the Catholic Church (*Kirishitan*) to deny their faith by trampling upon a sacred object (*fumie*) in public. Required participation in these patriotic rituals, Takahashi explains, "is like forcing teachers and staff to step on a *fumie* before students, and it is absolutely unforgiveable."

For those enforcing the Ministry of Education policy, the primary concern is to preserve the social harmony (*wa*) of the school community and to promote patriotism and pride in country. Those teachers refusing to participate are viewed as selfish (*wagamama*) and excessively individualistic. For the small minority of

---

[23] The 12 March 1999 Appeal Regarding Hinomaru and Kimigayo is available online: http://www.cbcj.catholic.jp/jpn/doc/doc_bsps.htm#syukyo; http://www.cbcj.catholic.jp/jpn/doc/cbcj/061102.htm

[24] In 1990, for example, 118 teachers were disciplined for refusing to comply and in 1991 some 220 (see Niioka 2004: 241).

teachers—whether members of the more critical left teachers union (Nikkyōso) or Christians—the new policy is a clear sign of Japan's rightward shift and represents a return to the wartime educational policy of coercion. While those imposing the new patriotic rituals do not regard them as religious and some who participate may gain a sense of well-being and Japanese pride through the experience, others forced to participate regard them as oppressive and linked to the wartime civil religion that required public school teachers to participate in rituals of respect toward the Imperial Rescript of Education, singing of the national anthem, and shrine visits (*sanpai*). Today there are over 700 plaintiffs (teachers) at various stages of appeal with District Courts and the Supreme Court to either reverse or prevent future disciplinary action by the Boards of Education in Tokyo and Osaka for their refusal to lead students in what they regard as civil religious rites.

The increased pressure on teachers and staff to comply with the Ministry of Education's instructions is no doubt related to the revision of the Fundamental Education Law (*Kyōiku kihon hō*), which restored patriotic moral education as a central component of public education. The movement to revise the education law can be traced back to discussions that began in the 1960s, but it was Prime Minister Abe Shinzō, a well-known nationalistic leader and member of both Shinseiren and Nippon Kaigi, who finally pushed the legislation through the Diet on 28 April 2006.

Let me offer a concrete example to illustrate why some observers still regard patriotic education and singing of the anthem as fundamentally religious. In a speech to Diet members at the Shinto-related Shinseiren political gathering on 15 May 2000, Prime Minister Mori Yoshirō gave full expression to the civil religious vision and agenda that drives the Association of Shinto Shrines and other restorationist groups, stating that "Japan was a divine nation centered on the Emperor" (*kami no kuni*). This statement was interpreted by many observers to be in fundamental tension with the postwar Constitution, which placed power and authority with the people and defined the Emperor as a "symbol"—i.e., without political power. After his remarks were widely circulated by the media, Mori found himself in a difficult press conference in which he was forced to clarify his position. Mori affirmed the freedom of religion as guaranteed by the constitution and claimed that he had no interest in restoring Shinto as the State Religion. His statement, *Tennō o chūshin to suru kami no kuni* [the nation with the Emperor at its heart in the land of deities], he explained, was made "in the context of describing the activities of the Council of the Shinto Political Federation of Diet Members" (that is, *Shinseiren*). After apologizing for causing such a misunderstanding, he concluded with a very revealing statement: "What I most intended to express in my statement at the Council of the Shinto

Political Federation of Diet Members meeting was that, as we have seen again and again criminal cases committed by youths in which it is clear that they pay little regard to human life, we must educate our children to understand the invaluable importance of human life, while deepening their *natural religiousness*" (emphasis mine).[25] This statement clearly reveals that Mori and the Shinseiren have a religious agenda for public institutions. While Mori apologized for the misunderstanding caused by his statement, he refused to retract it.

It seems apparent—notwithstanding claims to the contrary—that it is this civil religious vision at the foundation for the restoration initiatives and educational reforms aimed at nurturing patriotism and morality. Mori's concluding statement is representative of a widespread understanding of Shinto as something "non-religious" (in the sectarian sense, that is), but still regarded as something that is essential for defining what it means to be Japanese. This perspective, which Thal (2002: 112) notes "pervaded public discourse until at least 1945," has clearly been revived and cultivated in the postwar period and is central to the postwar initiatives of Shinseiren.

The return of the Liberal Democratic Party to power in December 2012 under Prime Minister Abe has brought with it a renewed focus on the neo-nationalistic agenda of strengthening patriotic education, promotion of Yasukuni Shrine, and efforts to revise the Constitution. Gotō Toshihiko, the chairperson of Shinseiren, recently heralded the return of Abe and the LDP in the organization's monthly magazine, *Kokoro*, and expressed his hope there was, at last, the leadership needed for the rebirth and restoration of Japan.[26] While Gotō acknowledged that the victory of the LDP in December was due more to the utter failure of the Democratic Party and disappointment of the people than to a genuine trust and hope in the LDP, he noted that Abe—as a leading member of the Shinto Seiji Renmei Kokkai Gi'in Kondankai—truly shared the values of the Shinto world and would work for their restoration in public life.

Abe's overarching goal is to restore national pride and create a beautiful Japan—a concern succinctly captured in the title of his best-selling book *Utsukushi Nippon e* (2006)—and this, he maintains, will only be possible if the

---

[25] Both the original Japanese and English translation of Mori's 26 May 2000 press conference remarks may be found online at: http://www.kantei.go.jp/jp/morisouri/mori_speech/2000/0526kaiken.html and
http://www.kantei.go.jp/foreign/souri/mori/2000/0526press.html (access 15 August 2011).
[26] In *Kokoro*, No. 184, 1 February 2013, 1–2. This issue of the magazine also provides a report on the lower house elections in December and a list of the 218 candidates recommended by Shinseiren and elected for office, which represents a substantial block out of the total number of 722 Diet members.

laws and Constitution that were put in place during the Occupation period are fundamentally reformed (28–9). [27] Abe has recently renewed the call for revision of the Constitution and on 1 May 2013 proposed a revision of Article 96 to allow amendments to be passed by simple majority in the Diet rather than a two-thirds majority. The overwhelming victory of the LDP in the July 2013 elections means that Abe has another opportunity to push through his agenda of constitutional revision (recall that his first chance was cut short by illness and fall from power in 2007). Given the impact of legalization of the flag and anthem in 1999, and the revision of the Fundamental Education Law in 2006, religious minorities are particularly concerned about possible revision of Article 20 and 89, which clearly define and protect religious freedom and the separation of religion and state.

Following the 2011 "triple disaster" and return of the Liberal Democratic Party under Abe's leadership, there has been another significant increase in support for Shinseiren, with some 204 Diet members now affiliated and supporting their agenda. Shiseiren members are also well represented on Abe's new Cabinet formed in December 2012, and many also belong to a range of other neonationalistic groups. As may be seen in Table 2, a significant percentage of the 19 Cabinet members are actively involved in these associations. Given the orientation and composition of his Cabinet members and the dominance of the LDP in the Diet, it could be that Abe will be more successful in pushing through his agenda this time around.

Table 2. Affiliation of Cabinet Members with Neonationalistic Associations (2012). [28]

Number and Percentage of Cabinet Members	Neonationalistic Associations
14 (73.7 %)	Shinseiren
13 (68.4 %)	The Japan Conference (Nippon Kaigi)

---

27 In addition to this popular book, see the policy paper posted on his home-page, which also explains that the "postwar regime" established by the Occupation of Japan can only be escaped by Constitutional Revision ("*sengo reji-mu kara no dakkyaku o nashitogeru tame ni wa kenpō kaisei ga fukaketsu desu;*" see http://www.s-abe.or.jp/policy/consutitution_policy).

28 See "The Abe Cabinet: An Ideological Breakdown," 28 January 2013, prepared by the Children and Textbooks Japan Network 21 [Kodomo to Kyōkasho Zenkoku Netto 21], an NGO organized in 1998 to critically engage the revisionist textbook movement, and translated by Matthew Penny. This is available on both the NGO homepage and the *Japan Focus* site (see http://www.ne.jp/asahi/kyokasho/net21/20130128-abecabinet.htm and http://www.japanfocus.org/events/view/170).

Number and Percentage of Cabinet Members	Neonationalistic Associations
12 (63.2 %)	Diet Member Alliance for Promoting the Assessment of a New Constitution (Kenpō chōsa suishin giin renmei), organized in 1997 to promote revision of the Constitution, especially Article 9.
15 (78.9 %)	Association of Diet Members for Worshipping at Yasukuni Shrine Together (Minna de Yasukuni Jinja ni sanpai suru giin no kai), established in 1981.
9 (47.4 %)	Diet Member Group for Considering Japan's Future and History Textbooks (Nippon no zento to rekishi kyōkasho o kangaeru giin no kai)

The significant shift to the right can also be seen in the increasing number of Diet members visiting Yasukuni Shrine on August 15, which almost doubled from 55 in 2012 to 102 in 2013. Although Abe avoided Yasukuni visits during his first term as Prime Minister (2006–2007)—a decision he later regretted—he could not resist this past year and made his way to the shrine for an official visit on 26 December 2013. There have already been some serious repercussions from this shrine visit—both internationally and domestically—as it drew strong condemnations from South Korea and China, and even the unexpected public expression of "disappointment" by the United States. Abe's problems in connection with Yasukuni Shrine will not be disappearing anytime soon. In April 2014, two lawsuits were launched against the government by citizens' groups in Osaka and Tokyo, which together have some 800 plaintiffs bringing Abe's shrine visit before the court on grounds that it violated the constitutional separation of religion and state, and they are seeking compensation for the psychological stress it caused.[29]

---

29 Reported in the *Asahi Shinbun* on April 12 and 22, 2014. In this political climate, it is highly unlikely that proposals for the re-nationalization of the shrine will be launched, though this is the ultimate goal of many restorationists. The last Prime Minister to advocate this was Asō Tarō, who proposed that Yasukuni Shrine be registered under a new 'special' category of organization —removing it from its current status as a religious corporation, which would allow the shrine to be financially supported by the government again (see his personal home-page: http://www.aso-taro.jp/lecture/talk/060811.html).

7 Conclusion

In spite of many clear indicators of secularization in Japanese society today, particularly with reference to individual religiosity and religious organizations, the evidence reviewed here indicates that there is a Japanese version of secular society in the making today that does indeed, as Madsen suggested, "mask a religious spirit." This blurring of the line between religious-secular phenomena is apparent in various social locations in contemporary Japan. At the communal level, as Porcu's study in this volume shows, non-religious neighborhood associations (*chōnaikai*) continue to play a significant role in the preservation of sacred sites and shrines and in the organization of important festivals and ritual events in urban Japan. A similar blurring of the line between religious-secular, I have argued, is now occurring in public institutions as well.

Given the reappearance of Shinto in the public sphere, we may need to examine more carefully how religious values and rituals are reappearing in what we often regard as secular terrain. Whether shrine visits will again become a part of the public school system remains to be seen. The patriotic rituals and moral education that have been reintroduced into public schools in just one decade, however, indicates that it may be time to devote more serious attention to the study of educational institutions in order to accurately grasp the nature of "secularity" or "religiosity" in contemporary Japan. It could be, in fact, that "the school system," as Fitzgerald (1993: 316) suggested some years ago," turns out to be "more important than even the shrines and temples for understanding the religiosity of the Japanese people." In light of recent developments in the public sphere, in any case, it would be premature to consider secularization as a *fait accompli* as far as Japanese society is concerned.

Our studies reveal conflicting "emic" interpretations of what is involved in both communal events and public institutions. Some prefer to use the language of civic duty and customary practices with regard to their participation in a range of ritual events, while others identify these practices as "religious" and their promotion by local and national civic and political leaders as actions that clearly violate the constitutional separation of religion and state. Given the pluralistic nature of postwar Japanese society, it is not surprising that these neonationalistic movements and legislative victories have been widely contested by many intellectuals, the teachers' union (Nikkyōso), and a variety of religious leaders and groups. Future studies will need to take into consideration these "counterpublics" (Ikegami 2000)—whether secular or religious groups—which have emerged to represent the interests of other stakeholders in Japanese society. They are critically engaging the Shinto-related initiatives and recent gains in the public sphere and remain unconvinced that the restorationist vision is either "non-religious" or "essential" for their own identity as Japanese.

References

Abe Shinzō 安倍晋三. 2006. *Utsukushii kuni e* 美しい国へ. Tokyo: Bungei Shunju.
Baffelli, Erica. 2010. "Sōka Gakkai and politics in Japan." *Religion Compass*. Vol. 4, Issue 12: 746–756.
Berger, Peter L. [1967] 1969. *The Sacred Canopy: Elements of a Sociological Theory of Religion*. New York: Anchor Books.
Breen, John and Mark Teeuwen. 2010. *A New History of Shinto*. Chichester: Wiley-Blackwell.
Casanova, José. 1994. *Public Religions in the Modern World*. Chicago: University of Chicago Press.
Cripps, Denise. 1996. "Flags and fanfares: the Hinomaru flag and Kimigayo anthem," in *Case Studies on Human Rights in Japan*, eds. Roger Goodman and Ian Neary, 76–108. Richmond, Surrey: Curzon Press/Japan Library.
Davis, Winston. 1977. *Toward Modernity: A Developmental Typology of Popular Religious Affiliations in Japan*, East Asia Papers Series. Ithaca, NY: Cornell University Press.
Demerath, N.J. 2007. "Secularization and sacralization deconstructed and reconstructed," in *The Sage Handbook of the Sociology of Religion*, eds. James Beckford and N.J. Demerath III, 57–80. London, Los Angeles: Sage Publications.
Dillon, Michele. 2012. "Jürgen Habermas and the post-secular appropriation of religion: a sociological critique," in *The Post-Secular in Question*, eds. Philip Gorski, David Kyuman Kim, and John Torpey, 249–278. New York: NYU Press.
Eger, Max. 1980. "Modernization and secularization in Japan: a polemical essay." *Japanese Journal of Religious Studies* 7(1): 7–24.
Ehrhardt, George, Axel Klein, Levi McLaughlin, and Steven R. Reed, eds. (forthcoming). *Komeito: Religion and Politics in Japan*. Berkeley: Institute of East Asian Studies, University of California.
Fenn, Richard K. 1978. *Toward a Theory of Secularization*. Society for the Scientific Study of Religion, Monograph Series Number 1. Ellington, Connecticut: K & K Printers.
Fitzgerald, Timothy. 1993. "Japanese religion as ritual order." *Religion* 23: 315–341.
Forfar, David. 1996. "Individuals against the state? The politics of opposition to the re-emergence of state Shintō," in *Case Studies on Human Rights in Japan*, ed. Roger Goodman and Ian Neary, 245–246. Richmond, Surrey: Curzon Press/Japan Library.
Fukuda Shigeru. 1993. "Kenshō: GHQ no shūkyō seisaku," in *Senryō to Nihon Shūkyō*, ed. Ikado Fujio, 521–60. Tokyo: Miraisha.
Habermas, Jürgen. [1989] 1991. *The Structural Transformation of the Public Sphere: An Inquiry into a Category of Bourgeois Society*. Translated by Thomas Burger with the assistance of Frederick Lawrence. Cambridge, Mass.: MIT Press (paperback edition).
——. 2006. "Religion in the public sphere." *European Journal of Philosophy*, 14/1: 1–25.
Hardacre, Helen. 1989. *Shintō and the State, 1968–1988*. Princeton: Princeton University Press.
Hishiki Masaharu. 2007. *Shiminteki jiyū no kiki to shūkyō—kenpō, Yasukuni Jinja, seikyō bunri*. Tokyo: Hakutakusha.

Hobsbawm, Eric. 1983. "Introduction: inventing traditions," in *The Invention of Tradition*, eds. Eric Hobsbawm and Terence Ranger, 1–14. Cambridge: Cambridge University Press.

Holtom, Daniel C. [1943] 1963. *Modern Japan and Shinto Nationalism: A Study of Present-Day Trends in Japanese Religions.* Orig. pub. University of Chicago Press, 1943; revised edition 1947. New York: Paragon Book Reprint Corp.

Ikegami, Eiko. 2000. "A sociological theory of publics: identity and culture as emergent properties in networks," *Social Networks*, Vol. 67, No. 4: 989–1029.

—. 2005. *Bonds of Civility: Aesthetic Networks and the Political Origins of Japanese Culture.* New York: Cambridge University Press.

Inaba, Keishin and Hiroyuki Kurosaki. 2013. *Shinsai Fukkō to Shūkyō.* Tokyo: Akashi Shoten.

Irie, Yōko. 2001. *Nihon ga "Kami no Kuni" Datta Jidai: Kokumin Gakkō no Kyōkasho o Yomu.* Tokyo: Iwanami Shoten.

Isomae, Jun'ichi. 2003. *Kindai Nihon no Shūkyō gensetsu to sono keifū: Shūkyō, Kokka, Shintō.* Tokyo: Iwanami.

Jinja Shinpōsha, ed. 1971. *Shintō Shirei to Sengo no Shintō.* Tokyo: Jinja Shinpōsha.

Josephson, Jason Ānanda. 2012. *The Invention of Religion in Japan.* Chicago: University of Chicago Press.

Krämer, Hans Martin. 2013."How 'religion' came to be translated as *Shūkyō*: Shimaji Mokurai and the appropriation of religion in early modern Japan." *Japan Review* 25: 89–111.

Madsen, Richard. 2011. "Secularism, religious change, and social conflict in Asia," in *Rethinking Secularism*, eds. Craig Calhoun, Mark Juergensmeyer, and Jonathan Van Antwerpen, 248–269. Oxford University Press.

Martin, David. 1978. *A General Theory of Secularization.* New York: Harper and Row.

Maruyama Masao. 1974. *Studies in the Intellectual History of Tokugawa Japan.* Trans. Mikiso Hane. Princeton: Princeton University Press.

McLaughlin, Levi. 2013a. "What have religious groups done after 3.11? Part 1: A brief survey of religious mobilization after the great East Japan earthquake disasters." *Religion Compass* 7/8: 294–308.

—. 2013b. "What have religious groups done after 3.11? Part 2: From religious mobilization to 'spiritual care'." *Religion Compass* 7/8: 309–325.

Miyaji Naokazu. [1946] 1966. "An interview with Dr. Naokazu Miyaji" (by William P. Woodard on 15 October 1946, and recorded by Dr. Hiyane Antei). *Contemporary Religions in Japan* 7:2 (1966): 143–53.

Mullins, Mark R. 2010a. "From 'departures' to 'Yasukuni Shrine': caring for the dead and bereaved in contemporary Japanese society." *Japanese Religions* 35(1–2): 101–112.

—. 2010b. "How Yasukuni Shrine survived the occupation: a critical examination of popular claims." *Monumenta Nipponica* 65(1): 89–136.

—. 2011. "Religion in contemporary Japanese lives," in *Routledge Handbook on Japanese Culture and Society*, eds. Theodore C. Bestor and Victoria Lyon Bestor, 63–74. Abingdon, Oxon: Routledge.

—. 2012a. "The neonationlist response to the Aum crisis: a return of civil religion and coercion in the public sphere?" *Japanese Journal of Religious Studies*, vol. 39, no. 1: 99–125.

—. 2012b. "Secularization, deprivatization, and the reappearance of 'public religion' in Japanese society." *Journal of Religion in Japan* 1/1: 61–82.

Munakata Iwao. 1976. "The ambivalent effects of modernization on traditional folk religion." *Japanese Journal of Religious Studies* 3(2–3): 99–126.

Murakami Shigenori. 1970. *Kokka Shintō*. Tokyo: Iwanami.
——. 1982. *Kokka Shintō to Minshū Shūkyō*. Tokyo: Yoshikawa Kōbunkan.
Niioka Masayuki. 2004. "Gakkō ni okeru 'Hinomaru' 'Kimigayo' Mondai no Kenpō-Kyōiku Hōgakutaki Kentō." *Hokkaido Department of Law Junior Research Journal*, No. 10: 235–264.
Okuyama Michiaki. 2010. "Soka Gakkai as a challenge to Japanese society and politics." *Politics and Religion* Vol. 4, No. 1: 83–96.
Reader, Ian. 2012. "Secularisation R.I.P.? Nonsense!: The 'rush hour away from the gods' and the decline of religion in contemporary Japan." *Journal of Religion in Japan*, Vol. 1, No. 1: 7–36.
Rubenstein, Richard L. 1989. "Japan and biblical religion: the religious significance of the Japanese economic challenge," in *Social Consequences of Religious Belief*, ed. William Reace Garrett, 116–17. New York: Paragon House.
Ruoff, Kenneth J. 2001. *The People's Emperor: Democray and the Japanese Monarchy, 1945–1995*. Cambridge: Harvard University Asia Center.
Seraphim, Franziska. 2000. *War Memory and Social Politics in Japan, 1945–2005*. Cambridge: Harvard University Asia Center.
Shimazono Susumu. 2001. *Posutomodan no Shinshūkyō: Gendai Nihon no Seishin Jōkyō no Teiryū*. Tokyo: Tokyodo.
——. 2007. "State Shinto and religion in post-war Japan," in *The Sage Handbook of the Sociology of Religion*, eds. James A. Beckford and N. J. Demerath III, 697–709. London: Sage Publications.
——. 2010. *Kokka Shintō to Nihonjinron*. Iwanami Shoten.
——. 2012. "Japanese Buddhism and the public sphere: from the end of World War II to the post-great east Japan earthquake and nuclear power plant accident." *Journal of Religion in Japan* ½: 203–225.
——. 2013. *Nihon Bukkyō no Shakai Rinri*. Tokyo: Iwanami Shoten.
Shintō Seiji Renmei, ed. 1984. *Shinseiren Jūgonenshi*. Tokyo: Shintō Seiji Renmei Chūō Honbu.
Takahashi Seiju. 2004. "Kyōsei no saki ni mieru mono," in *Ryōshinteki "Hino-maru-Kimigayo" kyohi*, eds. "Hinomaru-Kimigayo" Futō Shobun Tekkai o Motomeru Hishobunsha no Kai, 176–79. Tokyo: Akashi.
Takayama, K. Peter. 1988. "The revitalization of Japanese civil religion." *Sociological Analysis* 48/4: 328–41.
Thal, Sarah. 2002. "A religion that was not a religion," in *The Invention of Religion: Rethinking Belief in Politics and History*, eds. Derek R. Peterson and Darren R. Walhof, 100–114. New Brunswick, New Jersey: Rutgers University Press.
Ueda Kenji. 1979. "Contemporary social change and Shinto traditions." *Japanese Journal of Religious Studies* 6/1–2: 303–327.
Wohlrab-Sahr, Monika and Marian Burchardt. 2012. "Multiple secularities: toward a cultural sociology of secular modernities." *Comparative Sociology* 11: 875–909.
Young, Issac. 2009. "Shut up and sing: the rights of Japanese teachers in an era of conservative educational reform." *Cornell International Law Journal* 42: 157–192.

Elisabetta Porcu
The Religious-Secular Divide at the Community Level in Contemporary Japan

The first gathering of the year of the neighborhood association in downtown Kyoto (where I live) took place in January 2014. About twenty members of the association (*chōnaikai*) were present and participated in the Atagokō ritual, which was held at the association's assembly house (*chōya*). Here, we received religious-related objects including sacred sake (*miki*) and rice and an amulet (*mamori fuda*) from the Atago Shrine.[1] It was as if we had paid a ritual visit (*sanpai*) to the shrine without ever leaving the neighborhood. The ritual was followed by the customary shinnenkai, or New Year's party, in a restaurant in the vicinity. Such a mixture of secular and religious elements in the activities of neighborhood associations seems to be at odds with the common self-description of Japanese people as "non religious" (*mushūkyō*). As a matter of fact, there is a high degree of participation in Japan in certain rituals and religious events, such as visiting temples and shrines at New Year's, ancestor veneration, taking care of the neighborhood's street votive shrine, and organizing festivals.[2] In this chapter, I analyze how the borders between the secular and the religious are perceived and blurred at the community level in Kyoto. What emerges from the fieldwork I conducted in the city from 2004 to 2010, and more recently, since September 2013, is the ambiguous attitude of Japanese people towards the articulation of the secular at the local level, despite, or perhaps also because of, their self-description as "non-religious."

In this chapter, I will focus on how the religious-secular divide manifests itself and how its boundaries blur at the community level in a highly urbanized environment such as that of downtown Kyoto. In particular, I will focus on the major festival in Kyoto, the Gion *matsuri*, which attracts crowds of tourists from all over Japan, as well as from abroad. The Gion *matsuri* provides an opportunity to analyze the intermingling of religion and tourism, religion and local government, and the shifting borders between the religious and the secular in

---

[1] The shrine is located on Mt. Atago, in the northwest part of Kyoto. It is linked to the deity known as Atago Daigongen, or Shōgun Jizō, and it is the site of the well-known *sennichi mairi* pilgrimage that takes place on the night of July 31st for protection against fire (see Bouchy 1987: 255).
[2] This does not mean, however, that religion is thriving in Japan or that Japanese society is religious, or that it is immune from secularization processes. See also the special issue of the *Journal of Religion in Japan* dedicated to the religious and the secular in Japan (Porcu and Watt 2012).

an urban setting that has been transformed into an international stage. I will also explore the religious activities carried out within the neighborhood associations, including the distribution of sacred objects from shrines and others related to the Jizō festival (*Jizōbon*).

1 Religion and Community in Kyoto: Festivals and Neighborhood Associations

Local festivals play a prominent role within the context of community life in Japan and neighborhood associations (*chōnaikai*) are fundamental in their organization. In the case of the Gion festival, although they are formally separated, the *chōnaikai* and various associations for the preservation of the floats that participate in the festival[3] are closely intermingled. They overlap so much, in fact, that I was told by some residents that they hardly make any distinction between *chōnaikai* and *hozonkai*.[4] Each household and members of the *chōnaikai* are required to pay monthly fees that are used for all *chōnaikai* activities. These include a variety of activities such as the annual "sports day," i.e., a competition among different *chōnaikai*; communication among residents through the *kairanban* system, i.e., a clipboard distributed to each family with news from the municipality and the police; announcements of births and deaths in the neighborhood; various flyers; and the community newsletter. The *chōnaikai* activities also include fire safety, the organization of festivals, and disaster prevention activities.[5] In the case of the neighborhoods within the Gion festival area, a portion of the fees paid by the residents to the *chōnaikai* are used for the festival in which residents and people linked to the *chōnai* actively take part. With regard to the *hozonkai*, its members do not need to be residents, and, in the case of the neighborhood where I am living, its president does not reside in the neighborhood, though this has been the site of his business company since the postwar period.

---

3 *Yama and hoko*, or "floats and halberds," are the two types of floats participating in the festival. See more below. The Associations for the preservation of these floats are called Yamaboko or Yamahoko Hozonkai (hereafter, *hozonkai*).
4 The *hozonkai* became formally independent from chōnaikai as the organizing bodies of the *yamaboko* procession after World War II, after some troubles arose with regard to the authority and responsibility in the creation of the decorative altar within the assembly house (Ochi 2008: 6).
5 I discussed these activities and the *chōnaikai* in more details in Porcu 2012.

Neighborhood associations, many of which are linked to a Shintō shrine in what is known as the ujiko-*ujigami* system,[6] have been considered sub-groups of this system. Their religious involvement in the activities of the *ujigami* shrine has been highlighted (Sonoda 1975: 123). This involvement, although prohibited after World War II, as we will see below, still continues today, as *chōnaikai* remain the most important agencies for social mobilization of the participants.[7] According to Sonoda (1975: 135), this is because the neighborhood association represents the only collectivity in an urban environment that still keeps its "traditional character as a territorially defined community." In this regard, as one of my informants put it, the neighborhood remains "a village within the city." Thus, although there are legal restrictions that do not allow for the intervention of public bodies in religious practices in present-day Japan, the running of the neighborhood festivals is considered to be part of the civic role of *chōnaikai* (Ashkenazi 1993: 87). This can raise the question of the separation of state and religion in Japan, and can lead to legal actions by citizens who claim such activities are unconstitutional.

Before moving to an analysis of the Gion festival and its significance for our discussion on religious and secular dimensions in an urban space, I will first discuss the role of neighborhood associations within Japanese society and see how they can be considered as fruitful examples of the blurring between these two domains.

1.1 The Religious-Secular Divide within Neighborhood Associations

In the past, neighborhood associations served as powerful instruments of governmental control. In the Edo period (1603–1868), for example, they also played a role in controlling the system of temple registration (*terauke seido*) and the ban on Christianity.[8] In more recent times, from the end of 1930 until the end of

---

6 *Uji* means "clan," and *ujiko*, literally means "children of the clan" (Sonoda 1975: 104). The *ujiko* is a family unit association that is centered around a shrine and based on this system. The *ujigami* is a community deity and the ujiko are the people under its protection (see Nakamaki 2003: 40). The *ujigami* is a symbol of the "superordinate system of the community" (Sonoda 1975: 104).
7 See Sonoda (1975: 120, 123). Although Sonoda's article is dated 1975, this attitude can still be seen today.
8 See Bestor (1989: 52–53, 294); and Williams (2009: 18, 142). I am referring here to the *gonin gumi* (five-household group) that were responsible to supervise adherence to the law, and reg-

World War II, they served the cause of war and militarism through a massive mobilization of the population. With the establishment of the neighborhood associations being enforced at the national level in 1940 (Steiner 1965: 219), their transformation into governmental agents (Aoyagi 1983: 96) and their consolidation into a "nationally centralized system" (Bestor 1989: 70) took place. Although neighborhood associations were formally dissolved in 1947 by the Japanese government under the direction of the Supreme Commander for the Allied Powers, they remained active after the war under new guises until 1951, when the ban was abolished and many new associations appeared (Bestor 1989: 75–76).[9] This clearly shows the strong link between neighborhood associations and the government and indicates why it is relevant to look into their activities in a chapter dedicated to the religious-secular divide in urban Japan. In particular, the link between *chōnaikai* and religious activities and local shrines is worthy of analysis.

In this regard, the postwar period saw two important events: the abolition of State Shintō (one of the products of Meiji policy), and the ratification of the new Japanese constitution, which endorsed the separation of state and religion (*seikyō bunri*). In the same years, the directives issued by the Supreme Commander for the Allied Powers (SCAP) limited the connection between *chōnaikai* and Shintō organizations, including festivals, which were among the activities carried out by the neighborhood associations (see also Aoyagi 1983: 96). The separation of religion and state as legally sanctioned by the postwar constitution is therefore, in this form, a relatively recent development in Japan.[10] Yet the two categories of religious and non-religious have been distinct at various other times in Japanese history, from at least the 8th century onwards (see, for example, the *ōbō-buppō*, or imperial law and Buddhist law, dichotomy).[11] As Christoph Kleine underlines, however, "this distinction was

---

ulate their constituent households. They were abolished by the Meiji government (1868–1912) in its efforts to modernize Japan.

9 For more details on this topic see also Porcu 2012.

10 However, we should consider that the separation of religion as linked to the private sphere, and the secular sphere of morality linked to the public sphere, was a product of the Japanese government's policy that started in the Meiji period. This was sanctioned by Article 28 of the Constitution of the Empire of Japan (1890–1947): "Japanese subjects shall, within limits not prejudicial to peace and order, and not antagonistic to their duties as subjects, enjoy freedom of religious belief" (Kokuritsu Kokkai Toshokan 2003–2004); and was aimed at not threatening the Emperor's system and, later, at ensuring the power of State Shintō, or *kokka shintō* (cf. Isomae 2007: 93; Ama 2005: 31). Here, Shintō was redefined as not having religious characters, but was only linked to imperial rituals.

11 See, for example, Reader (2004) and Kleine (2013).

not terminologically represented by terms entirely equivalent to 'our' terms 'religion' and 'secular'" (Kleine 2013: 5).

In present-day Kyoto, some activities promoted by the *chōnaikai*, such as taking care of the neighborhood's small votive shrine for the bodhisattva Jizō (Jizō-dō), are presented and interpreted by the residents as "non-religious," even though they involve cleaning the shrine, changing flowers, and offering water to the bodhisattva. In order to better understand what I mean by religious activities promoted by these associations,[12] a brief clarification is needed. In this chapter, while I am aware of the problems related to the term "religion" (*shūkyō*) in the Japanese context,[13] I use it in a comprehensive sense that indicates not only doctrines and belief, but also "participation, custom, ritual, action, practice, and belonging" (see Reader and Tanabe 1998: 5–6). Seen in this light, despite being perceived by the local residents as merely pertaining to the communal sphere and a part of the *chōnai* identity, I would argue that the activities involving the care of the Jizō shrine, for example, fall within the category of religion to the extent that they are related to a sacred space, the Jizō-dō being a shrine itself, and involve acts (such as offerings) directed to a divinity, the bodhisattva Jizō. This does not at all exclude their communal aspects, or their being considered a 'custom.'[14] However, if one does not rely on emic interpretations and tries to analyze religious phenomena in Japan from a broad perspective that takes into account several aspects connected with religion, taking care of a votive shrine that hosts a bodhisattva, or organizing a festival dedicated to him (as in the case of *Jizōbon* when a Buddhist ritual is performed) cannot simply be reduced to a non-religious act.[15]

---

12 It is interesting to note that official descriptions of *chōnaikai* do not mention religious activities, but rather highlight cooperation among residents, as well as the creation of a comfortable living environment. This can be seen also as a sign of the ambiguous character of these organizations.
13 See, for example, Isomae (2003; 2007), Kleine (2013), Krämer (2013), Amstutz (2014).
14 This is the word (*shūkan* in Japanese) commonly used by the local people to refer to these rituals, visits to temples and shrines, participation in festivals, etc.
15 Moreover, phenomena, such as praying before the Jizō-dō or taking care of the votive shrine, may make sense within the interpretative framework offered by Jan Platvoet, who defines religion as a communication process between the "believers as empirical persons and putative 'unseen beings' whom the believers accept as real persons" (Platvoet 1999: 262). He speaks, in this regard, of "beings whose existence and activity cannot be verified or falsified but whom the believers believe to exist and to be active, directly or indirectly, in their lives and environment" (Platvoet 1990: 195). In this regard, see, for instance, the suffix *-san/-sama* added to Jizō or Kannon, which makes such "unseen beings" to some extent 'real.' In addition, I would avoid speculating whether people actually think they are acting religiously when they ring the bell of a temple or a shrine, or offer coins, in order for us to decide whether or not these acts are religious.

1.2 The Gion Festival: Between the Religious and the Secular

Chōnaikai and *hozonkai*, together with other associations, such as those related to the organization of the *mikoshi* (portable shrines) parade, are fundamental in the overall management of the Gion *matsuri*. This festival has been considered not a "single" festival, but rather the sum of different festivals and organizing groups. For example, the float procession is coordinated by the Yamaboko Junkō Rengōkai (Association for the Preservation of the Yamaboko Procession), but it is also carried out by the individual neighborhoods hosting the floats (*yamabokochō*) (see Yoneyama 1986: 21–22). These, in turn, are composed of both the *hozonkai* and the *chōnaikai*.

The Gion *matsuri* dates back to the Heian Period (794–1185) as a *goryō-e* ritual to placate departed spirits (*goryō*) and disease-divinities (*ekijin*) that traditionally caused calamities and disease through a curse on the present world (see also McMullin 1988: 272; and Wakita 1999: 2–14). The festival takes place during the entire month of July in Kyoto and is one of the three main festivals in Japan. It starts and ends with two religious rituals: the *kippu-iri*, or start of rituals official opening ceremony, which is performed on July 1st, and the *nagoshi no harae*, or summer purification ritual, which takes place on July 31st. The former, a Shintō offering and prayer for safety during the festival, takes place in the assembly hall of the various *yamaboko* neighborhoods. During the purification ritual *nagoshi no harae*, which is held within the precincts of the Yasaka Shrine, visitors pass through a large wreath made of miscanthus reed (*chinowa*) and receive an amulet for protection from illness and misfortune. Religious-related events and rituals during the festival are numerous and, although intermingled with its cultural and entertaining aspects, they should not be overlooked. In this regard, what characterizes traditional festivals in Japan is the invitation of one or more deities to the festival (cf. Inoue et al. 1979: 164). These deities, in the case of the Gion *matsuri*, are Susanoo-no-mikoto, his consort Kushiinadahime-no-mikoto, and their eight offspring deities, the Yahashira-no-mikogami. They are all enshrined in the Yasaka Shrine, which is located in a strategically central position and is one of the most visited Shintō shrines in the city.

The *Gion matsuri* is organized by 32 *chōnaikai/hozonkai* linked to the Yasaka Shrine.[16] These neighborhoods fall within an area between Aneyakōji and Matsubara Street on the north and south and Higashinotōin and Aburanokōji Street

---

This approach is not only unnecessary for our analysis of religious phenomena, but also is not suitable to the work of scholars of religions, who should investigate the observable world and not assess "non-perceptible realm(s)" (Platvoet 1990: 185).

16 As of July 2014, with the addition of the restored *ōfune hoko*, there will be 33 floats.

on the east and west. Each *chōnai* has its own deities and floats, and many *chōnai* place their deities on their floats for the main procession. The area is a commercial and business district in the center of a big city, and businesses located in *yamaboko chōnai* make financial contributions to the festival (see also Aoyagi 1983: 100), as do the city of Kyoto and Kyoto prefecture.

During the full month-long duration of the festival many events take place, but its climax is reached on the 17th with the procession of floats (*yamaboko junkō*) along three main streets in central Kyoto (Shijō, Kawaramachi, and Oike).[17] Two formal ceremonies related to the float procession are worthy of mention since they clearly reveal how the boundaries between the religious and the secular are blurred: the *kujitori shiki* (drawing lots ceremony) that takes place at Kyoto City Hall on July 2nd, and the *kuji aratame* (presenting of lot), held on July 17th on Shijō Street. During the *kujitori shiki*, the order of the floats is decided by means of a lottery under the supervision of the mayor. This order has to be confirmed on the day of the procession when representatives of each float present their lot to the mayor to prove that their float is placed in the correct order. The fact that the order of the floats is decided under the supervision of the mayor, i.e., a government officer, in an overtly secular space such as that of the city hall, would not be significant if the floats were not connected to religious elements. In the case of the Gion *matsuri*, however, the floats themselves, both the *yama* and *hoko* types, are sacred spaces that enshrine one or more tutelary deities (*go-shintai*). That after the *kujitori shiki* the representatives of the floats pay a ritual visit to the Yasaka Shrine to pray and receive a blessing for a safe festival is also significant.

Another interesting aspect of the festival is the *o-tabisho*, or the temporary shrine where the deities can rest (cf. also Sonoda 1975: 109). During the *shinkō-sai* on July 17th, the *kami* are transferred through portable shrines (*mikoshi*) from the Yasaka Shrine to the temporary shrine. Here they stay until the 24th, when they will be brought back to the Yasaka Shrine (*kankō-sai*). The *Yasaka Jinja o-tabisho* is located on Shijō Street, one of the most commercial streets in Kyoto. On this occasion, a souvenir shop, significantly renamed in September 2013 *O-tabi Kyoto*[18] is dismantled and transformed into the *o-tabisho*, that is, into a sacred place where objects related to the festival are sold, offerings are placed, and the portable shrines (*mikoshi*) with the deities are kept for one week. The *o-tabisho* is hosted within a highly commercialized and secularized

---

17 As of July 2014, with the reinstatement of the *ato no matsuri* (24th), there will be two processions, on the 17th and on the 24th.
18 This was originally named *Shijō sentā*.

space that is closely connected with tourism and the commercialization of souvenir items. This secularized space acquires a religious status through the festival itself. The Gion *matsuri* plays a prominent role in this shop. Pictures of the *mikoshi* are displayed and the name itself is clearly linked to the temporary shrine space. This patently hints at and reinforces an all-year-round continuum between the secular (commercialized) space and the sacred space of the temporary shrine. This is even more relevant if we consider that the *o-tabisho* is thought to have been the original "true ceremonial" space, while the main shrine was merely used for storing *mikoshi* (Inoue et al. 1997). The fact that its location has been obtained from a souvenir shop devoid of all its merchandise and furniture, filled with sacred items and (temporarily) dwelled in by deities, sheds significant light on how religious festivals and events need to cope with structural changes in the urban space and carve out a niche for themselves in an area already occupied by business activities and secular enterprises. Conversely, as seen above, the shop itself is taking advantage of a sacred space linked to a successful religious event/festival that can also be seen as one of Kyoto's "branding" symbols.[19]

Let us turn our attention back to the Gion festival and briefly mention the significance of festivals at the community level and as identity markers. It is relevant to note that before the end of World War II, festivals were a monopoly of the *ujiko*, that is, members of the community linked to a Shintō shrine. However, after the war, festivals and *chōnaikai* changed and festivals lost this feature. Participants, such as tourists and observers, came from outside the *ujiko* and festivals received support from local businesses and companies (see Aoyagi 1983: 97). This is also what happened with the Gion *matsuri*, where the number of tourists and volunteers involved is much larger than that of residents. However, with regard to the participation of volunteers as pullers and carriers of floats, we might recall here that from the beginning, the Gion *matsuri* was a "contracted" festival, that is, the *yamaboko* hired pullers and carriers from various agricultural regions or occupational guilds. It was in the postwar period, (due to dramatic changes that included a diminished religious attachment to Gion), that the recruitment system needed to be changed. First, it became common to hire college students. They did not prove reliable, however, due to their mobility. Therefore, in 1983, a campaign to recruit volunteers began and in 2007, this organization, the Kyoto Gion Matsuri Volunteer 21, was responsible for hiring

---

19 Closely connected with this, and highly interesting in the analysis of dynamics related to the intermingling of the religious and the secular at the urban level, is the transformation of sacred spaces in the city due to urbanization processes (cf. Akino 2013; Ishii 2013; Nelson 2013).

21 out of 32 *yamaboko* (Fukami 2008: 7–8).[20] As for the remaining floats, seven hire college students and four are paraded by the groups traditionally involved (see Fukami 2008: 7–8). Therefore, the active participation of external members (i.e., those who do not belong to the *ujiko*) in the festival and its link to business activities are important parts of the festival itself. At the same time, the massive participation of "non-*ujiko*" people may serve to reinforce the awareness of community members of being part of an important (national and international) event, which might make their own *chōnai* identity stronger (see also Porcu 2012: 99–101).

With regard to the secularized aspects of the Gion *matsuri*, especially in relation to tourism, it is interesting to note that as early as 1955, in conjunction with the proposal to change the route of the *saki no matsuri* (July 17th),[21] there arose a discussion of whether the festival was still related to belief (*shinkō*) or whether it was tourism (*kankō*) that dictated its developments (Yoneyama 1986: 7). Recently, this concern has been expressed by Yagi Toru, a professor at Bukkyō University,[22] when he commented that the festival had given priority to tourism and in so doing, lost its connection with religion. Toru wished for a "return to its original shape as an event based on faith" (Hinatani 2011: 23). It is probably not by chance that this comment was made after the 3/11 disasters, i.e., the earthquake, the tsunami, and the Fukushima nuclear power plant accident that devastated the northeastern part of Japan and have had consequences for the entire country. In the 2011 edition of the Gion *matsuri*, the original "religious" meaning of the festival was emphasized and its function as a deterrent of calamities was highlighted by various representatives.[23]

Tourism-related and cultural policies have played a fundamental role in the developments of the Gion festival and the number of its tourists increased

---

20 See the *Kyōto Gion matsuri yamahoko junkō hikite borantia boshū*, where male volunteers between the age of 18 and 40 are sought. They should either belong to the youth division of the association Kyoto Gion Matsuri Volunteer 21 (Kyōto Gion Matsuri Borantia 21) or be interested in and have sufficient knowledge of the basic tenets of the festival, as well as being prepared to take part in the orientation sessions. See http://www.gionmatsuri.jp/volunteer/hikite/index.html (accessed 27 February 2014). Some of the floats hire their own pullers and carriers. Interestingly, among the requirements for the Tsuki boko, are a "normal" hairstyle (no long or dyed hair), as well as no tattoos or piercing. A simple style is also a requirement for the recruitment for *miko* (shrine maidens) (see http://www.tsukihoko.or.jp/bosyu/, accessed 27 February 2014).
21 This was followed by protests from the local residents (Yoneyama 1986: 7).
22 This is a Buddhist university in Kyoto affiliated with the Jōdoshū (Pure Land) denomination.
23 For more details on this point, see Porcu (2012: 102–104).

exponentially (cf. Yoneyama 1986: 7).[24] In 1959, according to the Act on Protection of Cultural Properties *(bunkazai hogohō)*, the Gion *matsuri* was chosen as an Intangible Folk Cultural Property *(mukei minzoku bunkazai)*. In 1962, the *yama* and *hoko* floats were designated as Important Tangible Folk Cultural Property *(jūyō yūkei minzoku bunkazai)* and in 1979, the float ceremony *(yamahoko gyōji)* was designated as an Important Intangible Folk Cultural Property *(jūyō mukei minzoku bunkazai)*. In 2009, the float ceremony was inscribed in the inventory of the UNESCO Representative List of the Intangible Cultural Heritage of Humanity *(Yunesuko mukei bunka isan)*. The fundamental role of the community/ *chōnai* in the organization of the festival is highlighted in the UNESCO "Nomination for inscription on the Representative List in 2009" submitted by the Japanese Agency for Cultural Affairs.[25] While the cultural aspects of the festival are highlighted in the promotional video produced by the Foundation for Gion Festival Preservation Associations on the occasion of the aforementioned designation and available on the UNESCO official website, the video is devoid of the festival's religious features. Here, all Shintō rituals at the Yasaka Shrine, the procession of the portable shrines, the fact that the floats are portable shrines in themselves, are omitted.[26] This may be explained as a strategic move in order to fulfill the criteria for obtaining the "Intangible Cultural Heritage of Humanity" designation. Miyata Shigeyuki, the then Director of the Department of Intangible Cultural Heritage (Tokyo National Research Institute for Cultural Properties), made a statement that is relevant to the omission of the religious aspects from the video. He claimed that the government cannot promote religious rituals, (therefore they are not listed on the Japanese inventories), but that it can preserve aspects of Intangible Cultural Heritage to which communities "may or may not attach religious significance."[27] The strong secular intervention in a fes-

---

[24] There are cases in Japan where new festivals have been created for touristic purposes. See, for example, the Namahage Sedo Matsuri. This was created in 1964 through the merging of the Namahage (a New Year's Eve ritual) motif with elements of an existing shrine festival, in order to promote the winter season tourism in Akita prefecture (Foster 2013: 316–319).

[25] See the "Nomination for inscription on the Representative List in 2009 (Reference No. 00269)" at http://www.unesco.org/culture/ich/index.php?lg=en&pg=00011&RL=00269 (accessed 27 February 2014). For a perspective on cultural policies related to UNESCO, see, for example, Sano (2005).

[26] In this regard, see also the Okunchi festival in Nagasaki, where the guiding principle of the Nagasaki Organization for the Promotion of Traditional Performing Arts, which takes care of the festival, is to fully promote its touristic aspects and not to "touch" its rituals (Nelson 1996: 138). Similar patterns are to be found in the case of pilgrimages (see Reader 2012).

[27] See, for example, Asia/Pacific Cultural Centre for UNESCO (ACCU) (2009: 17). See also Fukami (2008: 8–9), where the importance of the religious aspects is mentioned, but in the end the

tival that is distinguished by clear religious traits (combined with entertaining aspects[28]) comes to the forefront in these examples.

2 Other Religious Activities at the Community Level in Downtown Kyoto

In this section, I will take into account a few more religious-related events that are organized and performed within *chōnaikai*. The care of the Jizō votive shrine and the organization of the festival dedicated to this bodhisattva are among the main activities. It is customary for each household to take turns caring for this street votive shrine. For this task, we received a bucket with the writing *Chōnai o-Jizō* san (neighborhood Jizō), and some cleaning tools. Our tasks included buying and changing the flowers; changing the offering water every one or two days; cleaning the votive shrine; and collecting the offering by passers-by and residents. It was quite common for people to ring the bell of the Jizō shrine, make a prayer, and then offer some coins. Sometimes *o-mamori* (amulets) were placed in the shrine as well. Before receiving the Jizō-dō task, we had been approached by a *chōnaikai* delegation (who probably feared we might have had objections to doing it) and we were assured by its president (incidentally, a Shintō priest) that we did not have to be worried because this was not a religious activity that could interfere with our—alleged—Catholic faith (as Italians). In this case, apart from what was said earlier regarding emic perceptions of the "religious"/"non-religious" paradigm, we might also argue that, seen as a civil duty for the benefit of the community, taking care of the Jizō shrine should be 'universally' accepted; that is, by all members regardless of their nationality or their own religious convictions (if any). It therefore needs to be presented as free from religious fetters that would otherwise disrupt shift schedules, or create inconvenience to the other neighbors and thus impede their 'harmonious coexistence,' the maintenance of which is one of the main tasks of the *chōnaikai*.

Many rituals and religious activities, especially those related to Shintō, are promoted in the neighborhoods throughout the year. Some of the activities in-

---

cultural aspect of the *yamahoko* (or *yamaboko*) procession prevails when he points out that the Gion Matsuri Yamahoko Rengōkai strives to "preserve and pass on the *yamahoko* procession of the Gion Matsuri as cultural property of the Japanese people."

28 See also Schnell's analysis of the Furukawa *matsuri* in connection with tourism (Schnell 1999: 267–273). The touristic and entertaining aspect of festivals is not new and has historical roots. See for example, the excellent analysis of Asakusa Sensōji in the Edo period by Namlin Hur (2000).

clude gathering of *o-fuda* (wooden tablets) from shrines for the protection of the household, organizing the *shichi-go-san* (seven-five-three) visits to the shrine, and distributing sacred objects from shrines, such as Heian Jingū *shugo* (Protection from the Heian Shrine) or the above-mentioned amulet from the Atago Shrine. Buddhist rituals are also performed within the *chōnai*. One of the main religious events of the year is the summer festival dedicated to the bodhisattva Jizō (*Jizōbon*).[29] Here, scriptures, such as the *Amidakyō* (*Smaller Sukhāvatīvyūha sūtra*) are chanted by a Buddhist priest, and the *juzu mawashi* is performed. On this occasion, the children of the neighborhood sit in a circle and pass around a huge rosary while uttering the *nenbutsu* (Namu Amida Butsu). At the administrative level, the expenses for religious activities constitute a significant part of the budget of the *chōnaikai*. For example, the expenses for the *Jizōbon* festival in our neighborhood, which constitute the largest part of the whole budget, were about 386,000 yen in 2009 and the income for *Jizōbon* (donations, etc.) was 333,000. *Chōnaikai* fees amounted to 877,000 yen. The organization of such religious events—in particular those related to Shintō—has raised criticism from followers of other religious traditions.[30] In some cases they refuse to join the association or pay the required fees for the Shintō festivals. One of the critiques by those who are against the close connection between *chōnaikai* and Shintō, is based on the fact that activities and (religious) services linked with Shintō within the *chōnaikai* are generally considered to pertain only to communal life. Therefore, donations to and participation in such activities are not related to one's own religion and thinking—but are considered something done exclusively for the sake of communal life.[31] Such positions are surely in the minority in Japan and usually the local residents contribute to the expenses of the *chōnaikai* and festivals. The separation of the activities promoted by neighborhood associations from the religious sphere was the same point the president

---

29 *Jizōbon* takes place mainly in the Kansai region. This festival is officially on 24 August, since the 24th of each month is the day dedicated to Jizō. However, the various neighborhood associations organize it during the weekend nearest to that date. Originally this festival was intended as a sign of gratitude towards Jizō in his role of protector of both children and the recent dead of a neighborhood; later the main emphasis was placed on the children (see Yamada 1991: 83). In the Gion *matsuri* area, the Gion festival is undoubtedly the main event of the year.
30 This is in particular true for Shin Buddhist adherents, Sōka Gakkai and Christian-based groups. In the former case, this attitude towards Shintō is related to the non-acceptance of the worship of *kami* in Shin Buddhism, although *kami* worship is not uncommon among the followers who, for example, pay visits to shrines or have a *kamidana* (Shintō family altar) at home.
31 See, for example, a comment by a Shin Buddhist priest in "Chōnaikai to jinja no mondai" (The issue of *chōnaikai* and shrines) http://www.akinet.ne.jp/saikouji/machinoyasukuni.htm (accessed 10 August 2011). (Cf. Porcu 2012).

of our *chōnaikai* highlighted when he introduced the task related to the care of the votive shrine dedicated to the bodhisattva Jizō.

Such activities carried out by the *chōnaikai* raise a very sensitive question regarding the separation of state and religion as expressed in Article 20 of the Japanese Constitution, where it states that "The State and its organs shall refrain from religious education or any other religious activity." The case of the neighborhood associations is borderline because, as mentioned earlier, they are not officially governmental institutions (like they were until the end of World War II). However, the link with governmental offices remains and is visible, for example, in communications and items that are distributed to the residents through the *kairanban* system.[32]

At this point, it is interesting to briefly mention a case that occurred in the 1990s when a Christian citizen of Dazaifu City (Fukuoka prefecture) complained that the *kairanban* was used by the president of her ward association (*kuchō*) to circulate information about a religious event—on the occasion of the royal wedding of the Crown Prince and Owada Masako—to be held at the Tenmangū Shrine in her city. According to her, this clearly violated Article 20 of the Constitution (Forfar 1996). Interestingly, the *kuchō* in Dazaifu City were at the same time presidents of the *jichikai* (self-governing associations similar to *chōnaikai*)[33] and could circulate such Shintō-related information if they did so in their latter roles, thus remaining legally free from local government connection. Moreover, once elected, all *kuchō* automatically became members of a Tenmangū Shrine organization, the Sankyōkai, which met to plan major events and organize fundraising campaigns (Forfar 1996: 248–249).[34] This case did not go to court, but the complainant, Mrs. Maeyama, and the Nihon Kirisuto Kyōdan (United Church of Christ in Japan, Japan's largest Protestant group) managed to change the relationship between the Tenmangū Shrine and city administration. The mayor instructed the various *kuchō* about their role in connection with the separation of state and religion, which prompted the shrine to try to change the status of the Sankyōkai by creating a new organization that was not linked with the gov-

---

32 A clear example of the link between the *chōnaikai* and local authorities are the procedures for renting flats that are administered by the city government of Kyoto. Among the several documents necessary for the rental contract, residents are required to sign an agreement through which they commit themselves to enter the *chōnaikai* and actively participate in its activities.
33 *Jichikai*, or self-governing association, is usually composed of the residents of a housing project, while the *chōnaikai* is based on the division of the city or village into blocks (Imamura 1987: 8).
34 To complicate the situation, there were donations made by the shrines to the city office to be used by the neighborhood association (Forfar 1996).

ernment officers, in order to promote both the shrine and the culture of the city (Forfar 1996: 254).

This case, among others, clearly reveals how the sensitive boundaries between the religious and the secular in Japan are variously interpreted and trespassed, and how these boundaries raise legal questions that are often very difficult to solve.

3 Conclusions

In this chapter, I have analyzed how the religious-secular divide manifests itself in a Japanese urban context through the exploration of religious-related activities carried out at the local level. In particular, I explored the role of the neighborhood associations, or *chōnaikai*, and the organization of festivals, notably the Gion *matsuri*, the latter undoubtedly considered one of the symbols of Kyoto.

In the case of this festival, that is, an event with a long history that has developed into a major tourist attraction for visitors from Japan and abroad, we have observed how sacred spaces, like the temporary shrine, have been hosted in a secular location that has been dismantled and adapted to the occasion in order to suit the needs of the deities. At the same time, the secular space of the *O-tabi Kyoto* shop has gained reinforcement through the religious event (as its new name indicates). The transformation of sacred spaces has been related to other phenomena in an urban setting, where religious institutions have to cope with changes at the spatial level and adapt themselves within areas that are increasingly occupied by secular enterprises and businesses. We have also seen various aspects of the festival related to religion, from its origins to the several religious events performed during the duration of the festival. The omission of its religious aspects in favor of highlighting its cultural image has come to the forefront in relation to the float procession recognition as a UNESCO "Intangible Cultural Heritage of Humanity." This can be identified as a strategic move to gain recognition. Moreover, this is due to the fact that the government, in view of the separation of state and religion as sanctioned by the constitution, is not authorized to promote religious rituals, but can promote aspects of Intangible Cultural Heritage to which communities are free to assign religious meaning.

The strong involvement of neighborhood associations in the organization of religious events and everyday religious practices has surfaced despite the fact that these activities are very often presented as pure "tradition" and customs by the local residents, and therefore their religious connotation is neutralized. In the case of the events promoted by the *chōnaikai*, we have seen how these can raise very sensitive issues regarding the separation of state and religion, and how these are closely related to the ambiguous character of the *chōnaikai*, in so far as they are officially no longer governmental institutions. Yet, they are de facto and to some extent still linked with the government, as is evident, for example, from items and communications that circulate in the neighborhood through the *kairanban* system.

We have argued that activities like taking care of the street votive shrine dedicated to the bodhisattva Jizō or organizing the summer festival dedicated to him (*Jizōbon*) cannot be simply reduced to non-religious acts if one does not take emic interpretations at face value but rather evaluates religious phenomena in Japan from a broad perspective that considers religion to include not only belief and doctrines, but also other characteristics, such as custom, ritual, and participation, as well as ludic and entertaining dimensions.

Bibliography

Akino Jun'ichi. 2013. "Shibuya' no chiisana kamigami," in *Shibuya no kamigami*, ed. Ishii Kenji, 269–302. Tokyo: Yūzankaku.

Ama, Toshimaro. 2005. *Why are the Japanese Non-Religious?* Lanham: University Press of America.

Amstutz, Galen. 2014. "How was the concept of religion invented in Japan?" *Journal of Religion in Japan* 3/1: 47–60.

Aoyagi, Kiyotaka. 1983. "Viable traditions in urban Japan: Matsuri and Chonaikai," in *Town-Talk: The Dynamics of Urban Anthropology*, ed. Ghaus Ansari and P. Nas, 96–111. Leiden: Brill.

Ashkenazi, Michael. 1993. *Matsuri: Festivals of a Japanese Town*. Honolulu: University of Hawaii Press.

Asia/Pacific Cultural Centre for UNESCO (ACCU). 2009. "Final report of the International Partnership Programme for Safeguarding of Intangible Cultural Heritage 2009–10. 3rd training course for safeguarding of intangible cultural heritage." Tokyo: ACCU, 17. http://www.accu.or.jp/ich/en/training/curriculum/third/pdf/2009–10TrainingCourseFinalReport.pdf (accessed 12 September 2011).

Bestor, Theodore C. 1989. *Neighborhood Tokyo*. Stanford: Stanford University Press.

Bouchy, Anne-Marie. 1987. "The cult of Mount Atago and the Atago confraternities." *The Journal of Asian Studies* 46(2): 255–277.

Brumann, Christoph. 2012. *Tradition, Democracy and the Townscape of Kyoto: Claiming a Right to the Past*. London and New York: Routledge.

Burchardt, Marian and Monika, Wohlrab-Sahr. 2013. "'Multiple secularities: religion and modernity in the global age – introduction." *International Sociology* 28: 605–611.

Forfar, David. 1996. "Individual against the state? the politics of opposition to the re-emergence of state Shintō," in *Case Studies on Human Rights in Japan*, ed. Roger Goodman and Ian Neary, 245–276. London: Routledge.

Foster, Michael Dylan. 2013. "Inviting the uninvited guest: ritual, festival, tourism, and the Namahage of Japan." *The Journal of American Folklore* 126(501): 302–334.

Fukami, Shigeru. 2008.1.25. "Gion matsuri yamahoko gyōji no iji keishō no tame ni," in *Mukei bunka isan no shisutemu ni kansuru ichi nyūmon hen*. [available in English. "Lecture 8: activities for maintaining and succeeding tradition of the Gion festival Yamahoko events," in *Introduction to Systems of Safeguarding ICH – UNESCO's Convention and Law for the Protection of Cultural Properties in Japan*]. Tokyo, Osaka, Kyoto: ACCU. http://www.accu.or.jp/ich/jp/training/curriculum/curriculum_8.html (accessed 2 September 2011).

Hinatani, Yū. 2011. "'Koto no kaze' (113) fukkatsu naru ka yamahoko junkō 'ato matsuri' [rensai]". *Yomiuri Shinbun* 2011.07.24: 23.

Hur, Nam-li. 2000. *Prayer and Play in Late Tokugawa Japan: Asakusa Sensōji and Edo Society*. Boston: Harvard University Asia Center.

Imamura, Anne E. 1987. *Urban Japanese Housewives: At Home and in the Community*. Honolulu: University of Hawaii Press.

Inoue, Nobutaka, Kōmoto Mitsugu, Nakamaki Hirochika, Shioya Masanori, Uno Masato, and Yamazaki Yoshie. 1979. "A festival with anonymous Kami: the Kobe Matsuri." *Japanese Journal of Religious Studies* 6(1–2): 163–185.

——. 1997. "Basic terms of Shinto," http://www2.kokugakuin.ac.jp/ijcc/wp/bts/bts_o.html#o-tabisho (accessed 2 September 2011).

Ishii Kenji. 2013. "Shibuya Kirisutokyō," in Shibuya no kamigami, ed. Ishii Kenji, 229–248. Tokyo: Yūzankaku.

Isomae Jun'ichi. 2003. *Kindai Nihon no shūkyō gensetsu to sono keifu: Shūkyō, kokka, Shintō*. Tokyo: Iwanami.

——. 2007. "The formative process of state Shinto in relation to the westernization of Japan: the concept of 'religion' and 'Shinto,'" in *Religion and the Secular: Historical and Colonial Formation*, ed. Timothy Fitzgerald, 93–101. London: Equinox Publishing.

Kawashima, Masao. 2010. *Gion matsuri: Shukusai no miyako*. Tokyo: Yoshikawa Kōbunkan.

Kleine, Christoph. 2013. "Religion and the secular in premodern Japan from the viewpoint of systems theory." *Journal of Religion in Japan* 2/1: 1–34.

Kokuritsu Kokkai Toshokan. 2003–2004. "The Constitution of the Empire of Japan." Translated by Ito Miyoji. http://www.ndl.go.jp/constitution/e/etc/c02.html#s2 (accessed 3 December 2011).

Krämer, Hans Martin. 2013. "How 'religion' came to be translated as 'Shūkyō': Shimaji Mokurai and the appropriation of religion in early Meiji Japan." *Japan Review* 25: 89–111.

Kyōtoshi Jichi Hyaku Shūnen Kinen Tokubetsu Ten "Gion matsuri no bi: matsuri o sasaeta hito to waza" Jikkō Iinkai. 1998. Gion matsuri no bi: matsuri o sasaeta hito to waza. Kyoto: Jikkō Iinkai.

McMullin, Neil. 1988. "On Placating the god and pacifying the populace: the case of the Gion 'Goryō' cult." *History of Religions* 27(3): 270–293.

Nakamaki, Hirochika. 2003. *Japanese Religions at Home and Abroad: Anthropological Perspectives*. London: Routledge.

Nelson, John K. 1996. *A Year in the Life of a Shinto Shrine*. Seattle and London: University of Washington Press.

——. 2012. "Japanese secularities and the decline of temple Buddhism." *Journal of Religion in Japan* 1(1): 37–60.

——. 2013. *Experimental Buddhism: Innovation and Activism in Contemporary Japan*. Honolulu: University of Hawaii Press.

Ochi, Miwa. 2008. "Gion matsuri yamaboko junkō no genjō." *Shintō kenkyū shūroku* 22: 1–13.
Platvoet, Jan. 1990. "The definers defined: traditions in the definition of religion." *Method & Theory in the Study of Religion* 2(2): 180–212.
——. 1999. "To define or not to define: the problem of the definition of religion;" in *The Pragmatics of Defining Religion: Contexts, Concepts, and Contests*, ed. Jan Platvoet and Arie L. Molendijk, 245–265. Leiden: Brill.
Porcu, Elisabetta. 2012. "Observations on the blurring of the religious and the secular in a Japanese urban setting." *Journal of Religion in Japan* 1/1: 83–106.
Porcu, Elisabetta and Paul Watt, eds. 2012. "Religion and the secular in Japan." *Journal of Religion in Japan* 1/1, Special issue.
Reader, Ian. 2004. "Ideology, academic inventions and mystical anthropology: responding to Fitzgerald's errors and misguided polemics." *Electronic Journal of Contemporary Japanese Studies.* http://www.japanesestudies.org.uk/discussionpapers/Reader.html (accessed 5 December 2011).
——. 2012. "Secularisation, R.I.P.? Nonsense! The 'rush hour away from the gods' and the decline of religion in contemporary Japan." *Journal of Religion in Japan* 1(1): 7–36.
Reader, Ian and George J. Tanabe Jr. 1998. *Practically Religious: Worldly Benefits and the Common Religion of Japan*. Honolulu: University of Hawaii Press.
Sano, Mayuko. 2005. "International recognition and the future of traditional culture: a view from and towards UNESCO," in *Traditional Japanese Arts and Crafts in the 21st Century: Reconsidering the Future from an International Perspective*, eds. Inaga Shigemi and Patricia Fister, 365–385. Kyoto: International Research Center for Japanese Studies.
Schnell, Scott. 1999. *The Rousing Drum: Ritual Practice in a Japanese Community*. Honolulu: University of Hawaii Press.
Sonoda, Minoru. 1975. "The traditional festival in urban society." *Japanese Journal of Religious Studies* 2(2–3): 103–136.
Steiner, Kurt. 1965. *Local Government in Japan*. Stanford: Stanford University Press.
Wakita, Haruko. 1999. *Chūsei Kyōto to Gion matsuri: Ekijin to toshi no seikatsu*. Tokyo: Chūkō Shinsho.
Williams, Duncan Ryūken. 2009. *The Other Side of Zen: A Social History of Sōtō Zen Buddhism in Tokugawa Japan*. Princeton: Princeton University Press.
Yamada, Patricia. 1991. "A friend in need: the Bodhisattva Jizō." *Japanese Religions* 16(3): 76–92.
Yoneyama, Toshinao. 1974. *Gion matsuri: Toshi jinruigaku no koto hajime*. Tokyo: Chūō Kōronsha.
——. 1986. *Dokyumento Gion matsuri: Toshi to matsuri to minshū to*. Tokyo: Nihon Hōsō Shuppan Kyōkai.

Part IV: **African Scenarios:
(Post-)Colonial Secularity vs.
African Religiosity?**

Paul S. Landau
Moments of Insurgency: Christianity in South African Politics, from the 18th Century to Today

Only a few years ago, President Jacob Zuma addressed a big crowd in the Eastern Cape, speaking in isiZulu, which he knew people would immediately understand better than English.

> When you vote for the ANC [the African National Congress, South Africa's ruling party], you are also choosing to go to heaven. When you don't vote for the ANC you should know that you are choosing that man who carries a fork, who cooks people. When you are carrying an ANC membership card, you are blessed. When you get up there, there are different cards used but when you have an ANC card, you will be let through to go to heaven.[1]

It might come as a surprise to note that this is nothing new. In fact, the history of South African people's politics is filled with religious language, as recorded in some of the earliest sustained Khoekhoe interactions with Europeans (Viljoen 1994) up to the present. President Zuma's words and posture have ample precedents in South Africa's popular politics. In this case, and similar ones, President Zuma invokes salvation or damnation, a way of thinking initiated with Christian missionaries in the nineteenth century. And he is invoking this dialectical pairing as descriptive of worldly politics. At the same time, the words that express these notions were alive and well in African people's vernaculars not only among Christians but long before any missionaries had arrived in southernmost Africa. What did those words originally mean (Smith 1982)?[2] How might we find out? Why does one find religion in ordinary people's mobilizations in various eras, including our own?

---

[1] "Vote ANC, go to heaven': South African President Jacob Zuma accused of blasphemy after claiming supporters will be rewarded in afterlife," *Daily Mail* (UK), Feb. 8, 2011: http://www.dailymail.co.uk/news/article-1354564/South-African-President-Jacob-Zuma-accused-blasphemy-vote-ANC-heaven.html, accessed in July, 2012. See also provincial ANC leader John Block's language ("God is with the ANC ... [the ANC is] your mother and your father," http://www.dailymaverick.co.za/article/2013 – 10 – 24-anc-northern-cape-john-block-is-still-the-gods-choice#.UnwgXyh9mwI, accessed Nov., 2013).

[2] It is by no means certain that *any* "kind" of distinction (religion–secular) will be identifiable in every era, as Jonathan Z. Smith points out.

In general, missionaries' early appraisal of southern Africans (after some years of exposure) was that they possessed no religious worship at all. They had no "beliefs" in a spiritual domain, and certainly no "belief system" involving a spiritual domain. It was only later, as Terence Ranger, David Chidester, and I have each argued[3], when there arose the need for a non-political but map-able "system," an institution useful for ruling people, that imperially sponsored research "discovered" belief-systems. That was tribal religion or "African Traditional Religion,"[4] or "ATR," its purported vocabulary being just those terms and dispositions that had been moved into Christianity (but beheld in their supposedly pre-Christian sense(s)). ATR was not, however, all of a piece in its home-grown matrix: it was paraphyletic, i.e. not contiguous within "itself".

For decades, Africanists simply accepted a muddy version of missionaries' triumphant transformation of Africans' history into static, errant beliefs (ATR). The view that Africans were steeped in religion was in the 1960s standardized and defended against challenge by Divinity scholars (African and Africanist) who put forth Africans' peculiar religiosity as a positive virtue. It is not for this essay but for others to trace this vein out to a larger flow of writing and thinking about and by Africans.[5] Historians have even recently discussed the African "reality" (as they put it) of spirits, featuring (it is claimed) spirits-as-agents in the real world. Or that Africans live in imaginary "worlds" filled with deflectable but usually dangerous "forces".[6] By implication, religion was always Africans' condition, and missionaries' initial views that Africans had no beliefs are seen as especially "biased" (Landau 2010b, ch. 3; Landau 1999).[7] Mainstream historical work continues, however questioningly, to deploy theological, quasi-

---

[3] See Chidester 1996, and Terence Ranger, mainly in his shorter writings on peasant consciousness and peasant "religion," but also and still more accessibly in Ranger 1993 and 1999; and see Jeater 2005.

[4] Shaw 1990: "What I wish to explore here is not merely the creation of images of African religions. It is the creation and maintenance, through the academic study of religion, of a new form of life," 339. For us, it is rather the creation and maintenance, through the divergent practices in life, of new forms of sociality (that never quite fit the either-or of "religion and secularity").

[5] A single provocation: Achille Mbembe, *Critique de la raison nègre* (Paris: La Decouverte 2013) (Mbembe 2013).

[6] Ellis and ter Haar 2004; Ellis and Bayart 2009, esp. Ellis, Bayart, and Hibou, "From Kleptocracy to the Felonious State, 21; Gordon, 2012 is an excellent account of the Lumpa Church movement.

[7] It is shown in these two texts that missionaries, by using Christian ideas as if they were the controlling mechanisms for every interaction, produced "the falsity of analogous practices," which while they often did not reside together in their original settings, "together became a single entity (religion) as a result" (Landau 1999: 8).

Eliadean categories, including a "spirit world," which are inappropriate to (at the least) much of sub-Saharan Africa. As a last preliminary, we note also that some scholars argue religion is a way of understanding, of navigating and predicting, the real world; but certainly (as Emile Durkheim long ago argued), if that were the case, religion would be very bad at what it is most essentially supposed to do.[8]

A minority tradition among historians of religion, led by Jonathan Z. Smith (i.e. 1982) and lately and most clearly by Talal Asad (1973, 1983), have therefore rejected the very idea of religion as a basic category of human behavior. They no longer use the term as an a priori given, on the above grounds; and if it is not such, then change cannot transform it. Here we have to freshly credit Marx: in particular, Marx's understanding (present in *The German Ideology* and in later writings) that ideologies are produced day by day, and hour by hour; that one ideology or religion does not become transformed in a continuous history into another religion. We do not have a text called "religion" before Christianity; we have only a way of looking back on the past, from a position in which Christianity already exists, i.e. after we have completed the repurposing of certain powerful words as components of Christianity.

Now, to be sure, it is not that there were no moments or spaces in which African passers-by were enjoined to hush their voices, or look down, or run off quickly, as if trespassing – the forge, the funeral, the marriage, the initiation. We may (with J.Z. Smith) call these moments "sacred" if we want, but such are aspects of political life everywhere: the antechamber, the spotlight, cordons and guards of any major "event." The evidence from the 1700s for more than this – that ordinary people experienced their ancestors as volitional "spirits," for instance – is flimsy and contradicted by better evidence. Most likely people understood ancestral force as compulsion to risk their personal gain for the wider human polity (also [putatively] descended from the same "ancestor") (Freud 1989; Landau 2010b, ch. 1). For the individual, release from the ancestor(s)'s claims was often a heartfelt goal.

As those elements of past political life requiring self-control and respect are reimagined as religious rituals, European settler rule over Africans is marked as a secularity. We accept with Charles Taylor that if (a) religion has to be made from the common clay, so does (a) secularity, with positive and diverse attributes

---

[8] Mircea Eliade's oeuvre, based in Eastern religions, is alluded to; and Robin Horton's "intellectualist" approach (e.g. in Horton 1967a, 1967b), siding with Durkheim, *Elementary Forms* (Durkheim 1995 [translated by Karen Fields]), esp. Bk. 2, chs. 1–2, on totems; and see Fields, 2002, for her comparison of race-craft discourses to witchcraft ones, also developed in Fields and Fields 2012.

beyond the "absence of religion." It is precisely due to the motivated, and largely Western (colonial, evangelical) reframing of African interactions as religious, that complementary secular domains were set to work in Europeans' overrule (Taylor 2007). After 1926 in South Africa, it became illegal for more than ten Africans to convoke a meeting together for any purpose except "religious" matters or "tribal" affairs, which were themselves religious, so this tendency was reinforced. The state built more and more bureaus to deploy its power on behalf of racist employers. In the countryside the law specified a "tribal" structure of chiefs (with counselors), funded and ensnared in an apparatus of "custom," and an ur-chiefship vested in the Secretary of Native Affairs, who recognized (and funded) all other chiefs, and guided them by his cool expertise. Later this authority would be extended to urban areas and further underwritten by universities and their African Studies programs (Dubow 1989, 1995; Evans 1997). The entirety of African life was reimagined, all of it, as subject to blind faith, or in other words, tribal custom. The making of religiously self-contained Africans (as a state-of-being prior to becoming Christian) underwrote Europeans' confidence that Europeans, in their clean-scrubbed, secular space, should rule. Their "secularity" relied not only on a mastery of bureaucracy, but also on the cult of the singular, Rugby-educated District Officer, thrown on his own resources and good sense.[9]

For southern Africans in reality, the work of making religion proceeded in this way. People were enjoined to imagine and reimagine what constituted a distinctly un-ordinary realm, that was then being set apart – one in which old words would be spoken with new and mostly static effects. That new realm had, first of all, a set apart space, the church, built as a roofed seating gallery, in which powerful words were intoned. Whatever one might call ideology in early South Africa, only later 1800 was there an assertion of the overriding importance of some other place and time besides the lived present, and it occurred in church. Soon every town and village had their built space devoted to an "other" world.

The development of the religious and the secular, and subsequently of the Bible-patterned religious in the political world, was a creative project immediately subject to unique stresses in Africa. Occupation, naming, and control must be fathomed as part of its story (Landau 2012a, 2013b). That a variety of discernible kinds of secularity can be described, is gleaned from Wohlrab-Sahr and Burchardt, the fundaments of whose model derive from Max Weber and ultimately ref-

---

[9] As much a product of fiction, to be sure, as of historical writing of any kind.

erence the enlightenment.[10] Burchardt's and Wohlrab-Sahr's account reads secularities in multiple situations and dimensions, recognizing that people in different places and periods take different paths (c.f. Anderson 2010).

At the same time, Burchardt and Wohlrab-Sahr do not fully incorporate the logic of Talal Asad's rejection of (a) prior religion (or "religion") at the bottom of the analysis.[11] This "religion," sharing a genealogy with "the spiritual," a personal confrontation with inner conflict, and a path toward some form of enlightenment, hails from the Protestant Reformation and the age of exploration and colonialism, especially the 15th to the 17th centuries (Asad 1993). It is not a history-less axiom for all time. As a comparative vision this religion – not just the performance of "religion" or a coloration of a space already religious – comes into being in history.[12] Contextualizing it, Asad suggests (thinking with Ludwig Wittgenstein) that rather than witnessing change in this or that predetermined rubric, we see a "series of untheorized shifts in ways of living," producing new meaning (Asad 2011: 47).[13] Like other ordinary-language thinkers such as V.O. Quine and Stanley Caville, Asad recognizes the variety of those shifts, that they need not collectively share any defining features.[14]

One could therefore argue convincingly that the essential idea of the spiritual was imported to southern Africa. Where all our perspectives converge, however, is in seeing the subsequent inception and then reformation of religious and secular spaces, as a culturally inflected process. The initial building of religion can be recently dated; before it, people lived in ways that did not closely echo the religious-secular divide, but instead featured different, and to them equally profound (if "untheorized") divisions of experience. As I have elsewhere written (Landau 1995), as have others (Rafael 1993; Hallan and Sodipo 1997), this situation is important to understand in grasping the problems afflicting missionaries in their attempts to make manifest "the word of God." The approach adopted

---

[10] Albeit disrupted by totalitarianism, from which lessons have been drawn. Wohlrab-Sahr and Burchardt 2012, discussed here. Nor does Robert Bellah in his important book *Religion in Human Evolution* (Bellah 2011) entirely problematize the notion of religion in examining forms of *its* "simplification".
[11] M. Burchardt, personal communication.
[12] F. Nietzsche, *On the Genealogy of Morals* (1887), "Good and Evil," para 13.
[13] Originally on-line in 2008, a response to Taylor, 2007 (*A Secular Age*).
[14] In contrast, Burchardt's and Wohlrab-Sahr's thinking draws on the axiomatic formulation of the sacred versus secular(ities), a universalist axis.

here is to take history as primary, so that we can make out the birthing of secular spaces and domains of the religious in the past centuries in South Africa.[15]

Several things might be intended by the religious. First there is the spiritual realm as a domain: in which Christ rules as King; or God; or no one, because there is no God, but there are nonetheless invisible forces interacting obliquely with one another and with human beings. Also, the spiritual domain in the more prosaic sense is a habit of mind, or a disposition of contemplation, or reverence. Next, the religious is the communal, the ceremonial, the ritual. Related the religious in ordinary usage is also, still, the *regimented*, the requirement that one devote time to postures of subordination, that this devotion not necessarily be comfortable, that such ave mari on the calendar relative to life cycles. Most of all, the religious is the invisible: it is that which cannot be perceived directly or at will. And that means that causes as well as effects are unseen: that actions begin and end with representational (devotional) behavior. These senses emerged over time with Christian usages, especially after the dispossession of African chiefdoms from the land at the end of the nineteenth century.

In South Africa, apparently religious language erupts in moments of crisis. Why? The elements in a vocabulary that work on "both" a political and religious level do so because their unity predates the early modern European development of the religious-vs.-secular(ity) model. Those old elements were parsed and separated according to colonial requirements for seeing ruled-over people as simple. Africans' fidelity to Christian locutions was ensured by the overlap between education and Christian training in South Africa. Finally, and most importantly, the religious was almost compelled, by the repeated criminalization of secular spaces for groups of Africans in South Africa. White sovereignty meant Africans were debarred from secular politics. Thus John Dube, the first president of the African National Congress (ANC), was first ordained in Brooklyn in 1899, as a pastor (Hughes 2011: 87), and Chief Albert Lutuli, the president of the ANC in the 1950s, was also a pastor and, according to his recent biographer, was permanently "bound by faith" (Couper 2009).[16] There was rarely legal secular space for Africans to organize in: labor unions and the ANC both borrowed spaces from

---

[15] Again, drawing especially on Asad 1973; 2003, and esp. 1983, in which Asad argues that Geertz's (and similar cognitive) models of religion are based on the Christian analogy and distrusts (with Rodney Needham) the notion of "belief."
[16] See also Lutuli's famous, "Road to Freedom is Via the Cross" speech, http://www.anc.org.za/show.php?id=4646.

churches, civic societies, sausage-vendors and dry cleaners (Landau 2010b, ch. 5; Landau 2012b).[17]

1 The Construction of the Christian Religion amid Strife and War

The specific history of the development of the Christian vocabulary and its deployment in South Africa was this. The agents of Christian language, missionaries, congregants, and young teachers, beginning to use existing African lexicons to express their ideas, found that the vocabulary of *chiefship*, i.e of leading, making war, belonging, and mobilizing for greatness, was most suitable and available. Political lexicons featured the morpheme "*****rozi**" mostly used with a locative, hence *rozi-place (or *rotse*-place), to name the preeminent affiliation on the highveld (arable land higher than a thousand meters in altitude) in South Africa. *Rozi -place chiefdoms were of the oldest "prestige [-place] association" surviving in the nineteenth and twentieth centuries, since their roots went back to at least the 17th century on the Zimbabwean highlands and the South African highveld and the Drakensberg range. *Rozi-place as a political idea was related to those fighting men (*vanyai*) deployed under the command of Dombo, a militia leader from south of the Limpopo, who were called the ***rozvi***. Meanwhile, on the highveld of what would be called South Africa proper, one found among the mobilized ranked militias the emergence of "ha-***rootzie***" (*rotse* or *rozi*) and twinned-court *barolong* authority (Landau 2010b, ch. 2; Mazarire 2009; Mudenge 1988).[18]

Throughout the South African highveld martial men allied themselves to one another under a titular, ceremonial authority or two (one inferior, one superior). They ranked themselves in near-equality under a (perhaps apocryphal) ancestor, and carried complementary connections to powerful outsiders. The "prestige-place" multi-lingual agro-pastoral centers developed into stone or earthen-

---

17 Criminalizations of African political meetings date from 1914, 1926–7, 1950 (covering the Communist Party everywhere, and the African National Congress in the Eastern Cape), and 1960–63 (with nationwide laws).

18 The ts – z shift occurs moving from the highveld north toward Kalanga languages or east toward Nguni ones. See also S.I.G. Mudenge, forthcoming. In many accounts, instead of this, one reads of the "coming of the Hurutshe tribe.") Among the historians whose work lays the grounds for my outline but who might nonetheless disagree with me are Peter Delius, Neil Parsons, Phil Bonner, Paul la Hausse Lalouvier, Elizabeth Eldredge, Carolyn Hamilton, and Shula Marks.

walled towns after 1600, threaded with mazes of lanes and demarcated into wards, the oldest quarters the most ingrown with residential subdivisions and resident immigrants. A twin court was popularly imagined in lore as the origin of most of the ruling houses; twin courts are also made into theory by the repeated presence of Tebele and Tebeyane (or similarly named) "twins" in ruling houses' genealogies.

The prestige-place orders were not the only modes of organizing. Highveld- and coastal grasslands-dwellers also belonged to ancient patrilineal associations linked to an animal or a thing, each with their own style of rank: crocodile, hippopotamus, snake, so-called "totems." (These are scarcely totems in the Durkheimian sense, not associated with celebratory catharsis, but carrying limited taboos.) Authority was spoken of under the sign of the lion, i.e. the king. In the early nineteenth century especially, many men not born into chiefships became chiefs. This happened in Lesotho, to "Barozi" (MmaKololo), in boPedi, to bathlaping, in Butua/Rozvi, and very likely with several reputed "Lions" (or Tau's) unifying a barolong regime on the highveld. Each of these polities entailed opportunistic men and partnerships of some kind, and contained multi-ethnic, quasi-urban centers (Landau 2013b). In addition, ordinary highveld men also battled one another in competing for power, and so it is no surprise that the language adopted by Christianity in turn possessed a violent component (Landau 2010b, chs. 2 and 3; Morton 2010; Macdougle 2007: 32; Allina 2011).[19]

The late 1810s–1820s were as is well known difficult times on the highveld and the grasslands in the east. The tumult, which was real if not entirely unprecedented, is today known as the *mfecane* (or *difaqane* in its highveld form) by historians of South Africa. It entailed a heightened military mobilization of young men in a time of widespread hardship and incipient slaving, and for about eighteen months (1822–3), a terrible famine. During that time missionaries created a narrative space (the spiritual or religious domain) premised on political nostalgia. In it, an imaginary place, they reconstructed the prosperous towns and just rule of the past; but reaching this place required either death, or the experience of the apocalypse. Christians' words made sense in predicting an imminent return to order in the turbulent environment, and as for their supreme authority, when he was not *ancestor* they just called him *chief of chiefs*.

Missionaries encountered and then directly provoked the yearning for a ***rozi**-place (*ha-rotse*) restoration, for just and powerful chiefs (or an "ancestor") with benevolent powers, functions popularly associated with chiefships of the

---

[19] Allina cites Dos Santos, *Ethiopia Oriental*, Volume 1, pp. 229–30, n.d. (Theal 1883), 292–314, all referring first hand to the start of the seventeenth century.

past. The preaching work of Robert Moffat, the translator of the first South African-language Bible, developed in his attempt to control the content and practice of Christianity (especially after 1827) in this uneasy environment. Not only was chiefship used to describe and evoke of the majesty of God, in Moffat's discourse, but the very definition of justice (in the kingdom of God) was informed from the normal apprehension of chiefship. In his evangelism Moffat painted a picture of what Christ's future kingdom on earth would be like, and portrayed it as infused with the meetings of the *kgotla* (the central kraal and chief's outdoor official court), and good harvests, plentiful wealth, and growth.

In this frame he openly mused about restoring a powerful chiefdom that warfare had toppled, using the *rotse-* (***rozi***) designation. If restoration was the issue, the question of who would be the ultimate "ruler" of the restored domain became a central one. The pioneering Methodists wanted *Jehovah*, and Moffat briefly favored "Great One" (probably *Mogolo* or *Mogologolo*), but they were reversed by African people who liked and understood the idea of seniority by ancestry, and who chose "ancestor" as their analogue to God: "modimo".[20] In Moffat's bible's language, sinners were those "left behind" (*lathega*), and a turn from grace produced a "stray heifer" (*timelo*), whereas, to be saved would be to be gathered together like chiefs collected wards and refugees in making their early 19th century polities (Landau 2010b: 106). And he accepted "ancestor."

We are now ready to consider how a mobile intersection, a kind of dance, between chiefship and Christianity, gave rise to new zones of religion and new zones of secularity as the institution of chiefship went into decline, and land was lost. Religious expression resulted from deliberately distorted translations, but translations that were never absolutely complete, because not all the old usages die. Ultimately it was *conquest* that allowed God to emerge as a notion entirely separate from ancestors; and later, it was ambitious mobilization that brought the concepts together again.

2 Seven Moments of Insurgency

We will look at seven (1–7) moments, or "snapshots," each relating expressive acts, each act mobilizing people into a better, or more readied community, while simultaneously articulating religious concerns.

---

[20] Of course nonliterate people did not capitalize words. Along with James Brownlee with his manuscript work in isiXhosa (Roger Levine, personal communication, June, 2010), Robert Moffat is widely understood to be one of the seminal figures in the making of South African Christianity.

Let us begin by sampling a few instances of translation that occur early on in the involvement of Christians and non-Christians. As we will see, the non-Christians and novitiate Christians in early contexts still exhibited the previous, uncontradicted usages that Christians now wished to make part of their faith. And, they still saw the land as theirs. First (1), listen in on the Rev. James Hepburn (Hepburn 1895: 47), relaying a sentiment from an unpublished letter from his subaltern, Diphukwe, a "native evangelist" preaching near Maun, in the Kalahari Desert, in central Botswana.[21] There had been scarcely any Christianity in the Maun environs in which Diphukwe worked, and so, if not chronologically earliest, the interaction was new in that place. According to Diphukwe, after he started talking about ancestor, i.e. *modimo*, the old men there told him this (Hepburn 1895: 221):

> We expected, said they, to hear about white people and white people's customs, and you spoke to us about our own customs and about ourselves – strange words such as we had never dreamed of hearing.

Diphukwe did tell them about themselves. Of necessity he spoke not about "God" but of (an/the) ancestor, i.e., among ancestors, one of theirs, and who as such was already represented to these interrelated people in their own speech, which mentioned him in contexts of fear, or honor, or communal mobilization. In other words Diphukwe said "ancestor" and attributed all (Christian) knowledge to him: to *their own* common forebear. Immediately Diphukwe took in his interlocutors's speech as metaphorical and not direct, i.e. as operating in the realm of religion, not the pragmatic here and now. "[Y]ou spoke to us about ... ourselves" in particular he interpreted as a statement about how Christianity is only made relevant when people's real situation is taken into account. But it meant more than that, as an ancestor he was (a) past chief.

A second prefatory moment witnesses this same about-to-vanish unity in a nearly contemporaneous (perhaps even earlier) record of a few sentences captured from "Mmopi, an old man of the *Bakwena* [people of a "crocodile" chiefdom north of the Molopo River in Botswana], the father of Seboni," who had (in 1890) "long since died." In "Secwana," the missionary A.J. Wookey told the readers of the newspaper *Mahoko a Becwana,* he (Wookey) "wrote the words as he [Mmopi] was talking." This is what this retiring missionary thought proper and important to put in an African newspaper – in Mmopi's own phrasing (Volz and Mgadla 2006) (2):

---

[21] See Landau 1995, 133, n.10. This occurred in 1880.

Our forefathers had ancestor/God (*modimo*), and when they build a house, the people went into the house (domesticity: *montlong*). Ancestor/God remained outside and closed them in. When they were taken out, they looked for him and said, where is ancestor/God (*modimo*)? They said he is in the earth (*hatshe*); they couldn't say the sky (*legodimo*[ng]), they said he was just in the earth (*hatshe*). And there were connected lineages of black people then, spread all over the black country (*lehatshe*[ng]).²²

This moment is the crystallization of incipient difference: the difference between a congregation and the world left out of it. The old man Mmopi explicitly attacks the *church*, not usually recognized as a target of epistemological critique. Even if Wookey scarcely grasps this, Mmobi condemns him. He says the church is that enclosure which shuts out (denies) the genuine nature of (an) ancestor, (a) *modimo*. The old man succinctly regrets the diremption of a single "domain" – that of untheorized real life – into two: "the sensuous" real (Marx [1845] 1998: 569 – 77),²³ and a disposition toward "up" or the "air." The latter aspect would prevail to the same measure that black people and their lineages (ancestors) no longer lived freely on the land.

Let us move southward into South Africa's southern highveld in the early 1900s. The mixed farmers of this agrarian, acacia scrubland terrain were undergoing a profound material and experiential transformation (Landau 2010a). They were losing their rights to fields, to markets, and to control their own labor. Samuel Moroka was a leader of a multi-ethnic and multi-racial collectivity, a chiefdom seen by some as the *de facto* "senior" one in the southern highveld (alongside Lesotho). Chief Samuel's following had its roots in a twin-court dual-chief settlement, Thaba Nchu. The Samuelites, in their political behavior, continued

---

22 Volz and Mgadla captured this from the pages of the journal *Mahoko a Becwana*, an early African newspaper, published in Setswana in August of 1890. The original comments arrived in a letter from Alfred Wookey, a prominent London Missionary Society policy maker, translator, and compiler of highveld folklore (pp. 276 – 7); I have altered Volz and Mgadla's translation, and in providing the Setswana, below, I have put a lower case premier letter in *modimo* to reflect spoken speech and changed "stood" to "remained" for *ema*. I have however left in their decisive "God."
Bo rra etsho ba le ba na le modimo [were with or had an/the ancestor], me ba re ba aga ntlo, me batho ba tsena mo ntlong. Modimo oa ema kwa ntle, oa ba tswalela mo teng. Mme jana ba rile ba ewa [iwa?], ba o batla, ba re, modimo o ha kae? Ba re, o ha hatshe [low, i.e. fa fatshe]; ba tlhaela legodimo [to fail to make or come short of heaven], ba re, o ha hatshe hela [he is just in the ground]. Mme ga nna ditshika [sing. *losika*, "vein, artery, sinew, family, generation"] tsa batho ba banntsho, ba anama [spread, increase] mo lehatshing ye lentsho …
Go anama means spread as "tree roots" but *go anama le lehatse yotlhe* is a Biblical sounding phrase, "to spread abroad into all the world": See Brown [1875] 1925, Tom Brown's and A.J. Wookey's edition of the *Tswana-English Dictionary*, orig. 1875 (Johannesburg: Ecumenical 1977).
23 Marx, *Theses on Feuerbach*, in *The German Ideology*.

to follow the previous era's alliances, joining different ethnic types together, ranking them under an appropriate, heralded ur-ancestor tied into networks of ranked chiefs. The Samuelites and other movements also incorporated American-focused ideas, Garveyite notions, and the millenarian expectations nourished by the organization begun by Clements Kadalie, the "I – See – You" (ICU: International and Commercial Workers Union). Their convocations registered the possible *coming power* as a mysterious force, person or event, or implausible restoration. Their movements united households from different origins, and the Samuelites even brought together "Natives" (Africans, Bantu-speakers) and "Coloureds" (to dismay of the Orange Free State police department's CID).

After the British finally defeated the Boer republics, during the reconstruction period and as the future Union of South Africa was hatched, Samuel Moroka arranged a move for thousands of people to what looked like promising land, a place called the "Tati District," in the eastern corner of Botswana. This was in fact an lawless zone of white farmers – men and women akin to Rhodesians and Kenyans (Ranger 1985), but poorer, with fewer resources and no political voice – and black sharecroppers, and tenant farm laborers. There were a few traders, and an adjacent "Native Reserve," where Samuel and his followers rented a less-than-viable expanse of land as an ostensibly semi-autonomous chiefdom. Although they would later on try to purchase further land in Tati District for more people, in 1908, when Samuel wrote plaintively to British and South African authorities, he asked (several times) to return to his natal home, Thaba Nchu, now absorbed by the Orange Free State. He begged to be allowed to reconstitute a chiefship *there*. British personnel prepared to vacate the powerful offices created after the South African War, but there was yet no fully self-governing Union of South Africa (Landau 2010b: 189) (3):

> Your petitioner, as a British Subject [Samuel wrote to the High Commissioner in 1908,] [has] availed himself of all psychological moments to pray for permission to return to the country of [my] birth and people ... in the event of your Lordship being unable to grant this prayer ... submit ... [it] to Lord Elgin, praying that this prayer be laid before His Most Excellent majesty King Edward VII.

What is important here, first, is "the country" of my "birth and people". No recognition of private ownership is ventured. Ceremony and "custom" (religion) would, the colonial administration understood, soon become the proper province of African chiefs. Samuel reached up and out of this religious domain to intrude on the secular space policed by the vested officials of the British Empire (Cohn 1996; Fabian 2002). The request is simple: to assume further rights under the Union Jack. Yet inextricable from religion, and present here, is subservience – the posture of "prayer." The "psychological" dimension of requesting is a way to tell the secular rulers of the intensity of prayer. *Wanting* is here a state of being. At the same time there is no spirit realm, no cosmic media, no ether for carrying messages: there is only a chain of command. The inadequacy of the separation (in times of crisis) between the two complementary, emergent domains, is thereby revealed.

Nearly a decade later, in 1918, eight years after the Act of Union (for South Africa) brought a coalition of white people to power in South Africa, the gold-bearing Reef underneath Johannesburg was producing great wealth. Legislation aimed at Free State landlords encouraged them to transform Africans with access to land to tenants, or force them to move on.[24] Africans in fact then settled in Johannesburg and their politics changed quickly.

Under the Riotous Assemblies Act of 1914, the Secretary of the Native Affairs Department (SNAD) could forbid these Africans from assembling in mass meetings, by his simple decree. Theophilus Shepstone had pioneered the key aspect of the role in Natal: the SNAD was registered as a supreme chief, a figure whose intervention would be both absolutely rational (within the mechanics of government), and yet perhaps absolutely arbitrary (this was allowable) from Africans' point of view. Indeed the SNAD tended intervene on the Liberal side in the 1920s and '30s, favoring "progressive," Christian African farmers (3 % of the population?) over the masses on white farms even though Boer landlords were despised. The 1914 "my word is law" rule was an absolutely critical patriarchic component.

Thousands of incoming rural Africans lived in a cramped and unhygienic settlement near the public sewer in Johannesburg. The post-British dispensation looked increasingly meagre to many of them even before they were mobilized to support the Allies in the first world war; that war made life much more difficult, and the Congress (ANC) leadership publically struggled with the icon of British authority, the Union Jack, debating the meaning of their loyalty. The *actual flag*, as Emile Durkheim suggested long ago, appears often as a dual-natured phenomenon, seeming to "embody" nationalism within it while maintaining its own materiality. British imperial "citizenship" was the half-promise the Union Jack signalled (Durkheim 1995: 231).[25] The flag was waived around on parade, or alternately rent to pieces on stage and stamped under foot.

---

[24] Clifton Crais pointed out some time ago that market forces and ordinary masters and servants legislation explained most of the post-1913 land loss for African farmers, and Harvey Fineberg has a work-in-progress which demonstrates that the Natives' Land Act of 1913 was in fact scarcely enforced.

[25] For this promise, see Chas Reed's forthcoming work.

This was a period of radicalism among working men elsewhere in the world (Limb 2009; van der Walt 2007), of course, as well. The same currents affected South African organizers. In the immediate aftermath of world war, when the most radical parties tried to organize the swiftly growing workforce of Africans (from metals miners to domestic workers), often they used Biblical Christian expressions in their rhetoric. At the same time, on Sunday, some African Methodist Episcopal (AME) preachers demanded the justice that Christian rhetoric seemed to hint at (Campbell 1998; Comaroff and Comaroff 1998). Briefly, for a small window, it appeared that white socialists would work together with the still fairly new organization, the ANC; and that the masses and all Africans would *at once assert themselves in a general stay-at-home strike.* The state had just criminalized striking by sentencing a score of sanitation workers to hard labor in chains merely for asking for a higher wage. Organizing a mass strike would it was felt be dealt with very harshly.

In this tense political environment, Mrs. Charlotte Maxeke (1872–1939), founder of the precursor of the African National Congress's Women's League, addressed a public assembly. Maxeke was a woman with rural roots and family memories of land: for her and she knew for many of her listeners, the restoration of free access to the land remained a cherished ideal. She was also an African Methodist Episcopal – AME – Church pioneer (Landau 2012a) (4):

> [H]ere in South Africa we will suffer to the last day if we do not unite, and there is a thing leading us astray. It is a whiteman [sic] who came to preach the Gospel of God to natives [sic]. When he came [to] South Africa, he [said] there is a land of Great Pleasure, that land is in heaven. He said we must never mind of this land. This land has got sins. We should not depend on it because we will lose a place in heaven if we do. He told us that money is sin, we should not think of money at all because money will stop us from seeing the kingdom of God. We should only think of heaven alone. Now what do you think of them? Were they not only blinding us so they can take our land from us easy? Are they not after our country now? Are they thinking for only a second about the land beyond the skies? Are they not after money? Are they praying to that God they told us about? Are they doing anything to shew you that there is really a place beyond the skies?[26]

Again note the nomenclature: "our country." There are at the start two layers of meaning in "Are they doing anything to shew you" there is a Heaven – Maxeke's artful joining of heaven's invisibility, with the sense that one is not convinced by

---

[26] Maxeke is recorded in her conversation by a spy, speaking at an ANC meeting also covered by the newspaper *Abantu-Batho*, South African National Archives, Pretoria, JUS 446/17/48, Transvaal CID to Director Native Labour, 22 June 1918; Signed Mbusani, taken 21 June 1918 by Sergeant J. Bland, Interpreter Henry; and Signed. J. J. Jordan, Constable, similar; and signed G. J. Broodryk, Constable, taken by J. Bland, Sergeant, 21 June 1918. Thanks to Peter Limb and Grant Christison.

missionaries' model behavior. Maxeke in refashioning her immediate political domain, is creating a secularity, in direct opposition to the religiosity said to inhabit African social life. She does this by correctly associating the invention of a "spiritual" or hyperreal space or "country" with her and her people's loss of land, and seeking to undo the effect. The result is an African secularity, a reattachment of the basic concerns of the self (explored in Christianity, Maxeka would aver) to this world here, under our touch. An African secularity which ruptured the naturalism of the division between supposedly religious African agitation, and the secularized space of colonial administration.

The urge to find a grand chief or ancestor with agency and immediacy had not been spent. In the 1920s, a world movement arose based on the esteem for a person and a set of very general ideas held in his name: Marcus Garvey (Vinson 2012: esp. 70; Bradford 1988). The Universal Negro Improvement Association (UNIA) was Garveyism's international vehicle, preached in churches and auditoriums, paid for in subscriptions. Garvey's intended reign over Africa was modeled in part on Irish nationalist organizations' claims for Eamon Valera; and yet, especially because (unlike Valera) Garvey held no public or party office, his ideas entered the ebb and flow of African expositions, and freely inhabited expanding spaces in church and in Friday night gatherings with Christian themes. Not only did black churches, among them the aging AME ones, spread the message of Black unity (and 80 % of Garveyism unfolded in the United States). There was in Garveyism in Africa, however, as well as America in the 1920s, something which was criticized by the visiting publisher and intellectual H. Selby Msimang, a member of the African National Congress's (ANC's) Cape leadership. Here (5a) Msimang laments (Vinson 2012: 91) that in his visits to Cape Town he is

> "pestered with questions concerning the 'Back to Africa' movement by people who seemed to sleep in *happy dreams of the coming of a Messiah* in the person of Marcus Garvey and his army to restore the status quo of the Bantu *in the land of their ancestors.*"[27]

In time, the American logic was wound into ANC meetings, especially at the hands of Comrade Thaele, but the ANC could not embrace the precise prophecy that Black Americans were coming overseas by airplane, to drive white people away with bombs, and recreate a proper kingdom on earth. The most apparent, even garish, reflection of the entwinement of Christianity and the language of mobilization (***rozi**), was the implausible and millenarian promise of a mass re-colonization of Africa. That plan was as a set of ideas to be repeated and pro-

---

[27] Quote: Vinson 2012: 73. My *italics*.

claimed, rather than a serious strategy. Garvey's fortunes declined, and fearing a direct attack from the colonial apparatus, he became more and more conservative, such that he drew ridicule and attacks from Right and Left; and at the same time, his positions could be read increasingly as matters of faith. According to Robert Vinson, the pro-Garvey newspaper, *The Black Man,* against Garvey's critics, "fired back immediately" against Msimang that the UNIA (United Negro Improvement Association) was (Vinson 2012: 73) (5b)

> "[an] organization *in which the hand of God has made itself felt for the return of His children,* whom he thought fit should be hewers of wood and drawers of water until such times as now when He shall *call them back to Africa* whence they were taken."

The "country" is now "*Africa*" and a return of the diaspora is the eschaton. The end-of-time, and the fulfillment of prophecy, the joining of the past with the present, are said to be waiting for them in Africa. This kind of reoccupation of millenarian prophecy with this-worldly political desire was, to reiterate, not uncommon elsewhere in South Africa. Again the religiosity of the African political form only reveals itself because of creative emotional framings that seek the widest resonances among the public. Yet still an unintentional congruence formed between the mobilization of African men under a distant chief's name, long endemic to highveld politics, with the already-declining world movement. UNIA's local avatar, Wellington Buthelezi, was prosecuted for fraud in South Africa, and Garvey himself was imprisoned on similar grounds; such however only led his South African devotees to hold fund-raising "Marcus Garvey Days" on the first Sunday of each month – in church. From such a matrix the Garveyite-"church" founded by the West Indian Robert Athlyi Rogers extruded a group of devotees who became the Ras Tafarians of Jamaica.[28] Agitation for Garvey and for Wellington continued calls for the elevation of "a King who will reign wisely" on people's "own land," an aspect of many rural movements in South Africa, reflecting the unity of politics before the bifurcation of space into religious and secular. The coming of a powerful lord over everyone was a common promise. People wanted reasonable relations of production and propriety.

The UNIA organization was not the only one to try to call transformation into being with words, or rather, to call people to rise up and save themselves in the here and now (Vinson 2012: 91), – Because It Must Be! The real fulfillment of prophecy was this: Africans' politics were now self-consciously invested with faith, in order to recapture and deploy the full range of assertions in chiefship. That such millenarian sentiments recur should not surprise us when we remem-

---

[28] Bobby Hill, personal communication, 2000.

ber two things: that early missionaries themselves promulgated an apocalyptic vision, and that no public assemblies of a non-religious and non-tribal nature were officially allowed (without prior permission obtained from the hierarchy of Native Experts). We should not, however, attribute it to a natural African orientation toward religiosity.

The sixth and seventh moments in time I wish to transport us to are proper to the post-war, urban world of busy streets, storefronts, and union shops. By the late 1950s, in South Africa, one must think about the modern city, in which jobs had been opened for Africans by another world war, and toward which the entire human geography then shifted, such that cities became (the tipping point is sometime in the late 1950s) home to more families of Africans than rural places. The African National Congress and the Communist Party organized big urban-based mass demonstrations and acts of civil disobedience in the 1950s. The ANC was a member-driven organization, unused to holding meetings attended by vast crowds, more at home with familiar branch groupings at a time when numbers of African families stabilized themselves in neighborhoods as stand-holders.[29] In many small towns and rural outposts, the ANC branches, in their regularity, familiarity, and fealty to bylaws, constructed a secularity as almost a mirror image of religious habit. There was in many rustic Congress meetings the sense that complaint itself should be privileged, repeated, conveyed anew to one another, to the Branch secretary, or the government authorities: the act of "asking" translated as prayer. Mweli Skota, who helped draft the constitution of S.A.N.N.C. (the ANC), later drafted the constitution of his church. They are very similar documents.[30] Yet no one would make the mistake of thinking the ANC a religious body.

A fresh radicalism brewed in the mines and union halls in Johannesburg and Cape Town and Port Elizabeth, reflected in the Youth League of the ANC (dominated by the rural-origin intellectual Anton Lembede) and the direct actions of ANC "Volunteers." The government in this context by piecemeal police action and legislation criminalized all coordinated movements among Africans undertaken to protest its behavior, culminating with the "Treason Trial" of the (up to then) non-violent ANC and its (mostly union and/or Communist) allies.[31] The government also placed under house arrest (beginning in 1952) dozens and ultimately hundreds of union organizers and ANC leaders, under special legislation

---

[29] E.g. Bonner and Nieftagodien, 2001; more of Bonner's work on Soweto is forthcoming.
[30] Mweli Skota Papers, pers. manuscripts, Historical Manuscripts, Cullen Library, University of Witwatersrand, Johannesburg.
[31] South African National Archives, "Evidence Boxes," Treason Trial, un-catalogued (only *some* are duplicated in Historical Manuscripts, Cullen Library, University of Witwatersrand).

designed to circumvent the judicial system. Some factions in this context directly wished the ANC to change its tactics, to lead a nationalist force against the state itself. Nelson Mandela and Walter Sisulu (his mentor) discussed guerilla war as early as 1953. The core of the younger membership were all Lembede-ist nationalists in the 1940s, but while most of them leaned increasingly toward cooperation with the Communist Party, some urban Africans (for instance in Langa, outside Cape Town) were opposed to cooperation with the White Left and broke away, forming the Pan Africanist Congress (PAC). The government banned both the ANC and PAC in 1960 after the Sharpeville massacre.

It is often forgotten that the PAC then moved swiftly toward dramatic, direct confrontations. The Communist Party was already prepared to back the actions of saboteurs, conceiving of this however as "armed propaganda," i.e. subordinate to political control in an environment of demonstration and pressure. All these groups, ultimately including the remnants of the ANC, thrown prematurely into contestation with a government empowered by a self-proclaimed state of emergency, wished to move the population to more fully support massive political change. All of them used apparently religious ideas and language to frame and inform their message (Kelley 1991: 5–24). The PAC's primary leader, a schoolteacher and an ambitious intellectual, was Robert Sobukwe, but there were always plenty of leaders to share the stage with him.

According to Peter Rodda, a reporter in Orlando Township at the PAC's maiden convention, of April 4–6, 1959 (Rodda [1959] 2011) (6),

> Sobukwe delivered a weighty theoretical address to the conference at its opening session [April 4th], but in the events leading up to his address clues to the less philosophical elements of Africanism had been revealed. [This is Rodda's editorializing. P.L.] First, an emotional and sometimes eccentric and exclusive Christianity. Three ministers graced the platform, and in prayers and addresses they referred to '*the hooligans of Europe who killed our God and have never been convicted*' and the legend of *Christ's education in Africa*, while cheers greeted the *salute to 'a black man, Simon of Arabia, who carried Jesus from the Cross'*. A rather sinister post-conference article in *The World* discusses the formation of an *African national church* which 'would play a leading role in Africanist affairs, just as the Dutch Reformed Church did in Nationalist Party affairs'.[32]

The dream of a national church (here shown in Rodda's dystopic vision) resonates throughout South Africa's non-whites' history. It can be found among independent "Ethiopianist" congregations in southern Africa and in the speeches

---

[32] Peter Rodda's original report is reprinted in *Africa South: Viewpoints, 1956–1961*, ed. M.J. Daymond and Corinne Sandwith (Pietermaritzburg: University of KwaZulu-Natal Press 2011), 228), with my added *italics*.

and sermons of the leaders of the Dutch Reformed Church. The fitting of a church for each African "tribe" was also not new. Nehemia Tile founded a chuch in Thembuland in 1881 to be coterminous with the Thembu chiefship (Saunders [1970] 1971). This was an idea Apartheid could also embrace: an analogue to the tribal meeting but with more women paying attention. However, an African *national* church, for "black men," would reclaim sovereignty from the theocrats using their same vocabulary in a dangerously this-worldly manner. That was something else.

Before thinking further here, how stream of Christian radical rhetoric gathered force after 1960, a stream of black scholarly theological thinking in South Africa, with ties to universities and intellectuals overseas. The so-called Black Consciousness (BC) movement in South Africa, associated for most people with Steve Biko, formed in this milieu. The BC movement celebrated the Black body and strove to bring about a "consciousness" required for change, as well as change itself. BC was also a turning inward, along the path laid down by the South African invention of religion so many decades before. BC drew eclectically, in fact, on many strands of thought: from Kenneth Kaunda and Kwame Nkrumah; from South African theologians such as Manas Buthelezi; from Joseph Mbiti, an orchestrator of the "African Traditional Religion" concept; and even the Black Panthers of Chicago, Illinois. Most of all, Christian liberationist sentiment emerged (Magaziner 2010: 42, 122). The 1972 Black People's Convention, in some ways the movement's epitome, reflected the centrality of Christianity to BC. The Convention fell under the interim presidency of Mashwabada Mayatula, a pastor of an independent African church. In his moment of insurgency this is what he had to say (Magaziner 2010: 118) (7):

> I am grateful that today we begin to open the first page in the history book of the newly resurrected Black nation in S[outh] [Africa]. At long last, the LIBERATOR, namely, the promised Black Messiah, 'the very God of the very God' has come. He has freely given us what we prayed for . . . the HOLY SPIRIT – the 'Spirit' of Black Consciousness, of Black Solidarity and Black [U]nity.

How "literally" are we to take this return to the equation of *modimo* (ancestor) with a/the black man? The standard thing to do has been to see statements such as this as a species of rhetorical flourish, ancillary to genuine political (national) streams of history. Recent work however shows that most speakers and listeners took this very seriously. It won't do to impose our metaphorical constructs on them. African organization, denied land – "the country" – and criminalized outside Christian services or ethnic associations, again expands by infusing its permitted domain (religion) with new life. It becomes possible to speak of "the Black nation."[33]

The untranslated notion adopted as "[s]pirit of Black conciousness," namely *moyo*, or *mowa*, or *umoya*, originally meant a unity of action and body: one's breath, which was one's life, and which also projected meaning in and through one, and which disappeared at death. The Christians made it into the soul, but Black Consciousness brought it back, again, into connection with suffering bodies. Meanwhile the police had been professionalized in the 1960s and a new, purposeful apparatus of investigation and interrogation had been put into place, drawing in part on Algerian and American interrogation techniques. Alongside the Black Consciousness exaltation of the black sufferer and the Spirit unifying people's aspirations, the secular enforcement apparatus focused more and more on beating and wounding Black bodies in small rooms. Again, in moments of insurgency, Christianity, permitted to Africans by habit, seemed to reveal itself and color their political claims. Both Sobukwe and B.C. put redemption and salvation back together with liberation, collapsing secularity and religion in the semi-translated figure of "the black man." Ultimately for leaders such as Mayatula, Onkgopotse Abraham Tiro, and Tshenuwani Simon Farisani, lesser known but influential Black Consciousness leaders, the *Black Messiah*'s suffering could merge with the reality of black suffering under apartheid, in its apparently "original" (re-euhemerized) unity, *sans* "spirit" of any ghostly kind. As Christians, in this model, *surviving life's blows* was to be not like Christ but to *be Christ*.

Here we see a forgotten set of usages connected again to *un*translated and singular concepts that Christians from Robert Moffat's time forward had reshaped. One may choose whether one calls the deep interconnections of religion and politics in South Africa's history a weakness or a strength, but there is a singular force behind it: these are not only variations on the familiar dyad, the secular and the religious. The invention of domains of secularity, as important as the invention of domains of religion, emerged unevenly through translation and enforcement. When people acted in emergency situations, however, they still reached back to their oldest usages and their contexts as they had once been: undivided.

It is true that the apparently religious modality has sometimes fallen into eclipse, partly because of the rise of the militant (and military) Left in and, especially, *outside* South Africa from the early 1960s through the 1980s. Communist and ANC led camps in Tanzania, Zambia, and Algeria did not traffic much in Christian ideas; further, the timidity of many Christian leaders in challenging in-

---

[33] Two interactions with Steven Feierman long ago, lie behind this point.

justice, and the duplicity of Allen Boesak, a major Christian "Coloured" cleric and politician, further drew the curtain over political Christianity *per se*. That said, deeper streams still flowed. Every unit of ANC soldiers in their barracks had a political commissar, who functioned like a combination pastor and sergeant. The "Truth and Reconciliation Commission" model as pioneered in South Africa was overtly Christian and confessional. The political function of funerals in South Africa, especially after Michael Diradeng's murder and funeral attended by over ten thousand in Alexandra in 1986, would require a separate treatise. It is enough to note that from time to time, the millenarian vision gathers together the old tropes and expectations from existing African life and thrusts them forward defiantly as an effort to remake this world.

3 Conclusion

The process of making religion was a substitution of gestural, emotive, non-active behaviors for men's agentive action, in the course of using and hearing the same phrases (about destiny, wealth, greatness, belonging, and merging as allies). Religious expressions were deployed in controlled situations, congregations, in which the beseeching of authority was repeated without having an ordinary effect. Because static containment, compliance, and gestures without any real effect were what Native Affairs desired from African chiefs, and because religiosity was tacitly understood as a natural (uncultured) condition, Africans' politics were marked as religious in contradistinction to the overrule of Africans by whites – which proliferated a field of secularity, one of bureaucratic memory and "expertise." The switch-over in "meaning" of prayer words and other terms, the creation and maintenance of these situations, developed *over the same decades* (ca. 1810s–1880s) in which Africans conquered and reorganized other Africans, and then *were* conquered and reorganized in terms of their relationship to production by whites, the decades in which they entered the colonial archive as named tribes or "peoples" given to religious and ethnic (ritual) concerns. Not only in the mind of the South African police in the development of the Apartheid security state, but ironically, in the understanding of scholars, this became Africans' default configuration. But their actual agency in talking and doing having been repeatedly muted, Africans thenceforth recited the same words, over and over again, in Christian ceremonies.

Here our case has been that religion was manifested in crises in public life, not as a deflection of people's political, this-worldly intent toward irrelevance; nor as an atavistic return to a submerged religious or superstitious resting place; but rather, as an occupation, in moments of insurgency, of specially allocated religious space, in any and all ways. We have seen how "the country," meaning actual space – the real world – also manifested itself in these moments. Uttering mobilizing words in their original or near-original contexts, one's agency was again simultaneously Christian and political, irreversibly oriented toward a single path that made no distinction – even if one challenged the behavior of Christians in the process.

South Africa's President Jacob Zuma was immediately attacked by other political parties and church groups alike in South Africa for crossing a line and claiming too much when he spoke of heaven and the ANC. In response Zuma's subordinates defended him by asserting that he had been speaking "figuratively," for instance when he said, "When you are carrying an ANC membership card, you are blessed." We know that in rural places the *idea* of a reference book or *Dompas* often did become a metaphorical vehicle for understanding power, so perhaps this is so. In fact however President Zuma had said that a vote for the ANC was a ticket to heaven, and was ordained to be so by God, when he was Deputy Secretary of the Congress; and he conveyed similar ideas again, after being ordained a pastor in an independent church, in 2007. The ANC, he famously said at that august occasion, would rule "until Jesus returns."[34]

References

Allina, Eric. 2011. "The Zimba, the Portuguese, and other cannibals in late sixteenth-century Southeast Africa." *Journal of Southern African Studies*, 37, 2: 211–227.
Anderson, Kevin B. 2010. *Marx at the Margins: On Nationalism, Ethnicity, and Non-Western Societies*. Chicago: University of Chicago Press.
Asad, Talal. 1973. *Anthropology and the Colonial Encounter*. Ithaca: Cornell.
—. 1983. "Anthropological conceptions of religion: reflections of Geertz." *Man*, 18: 327–59.
—. 1993. *Genealogies of Religion: Discipline and Reasons of Power in Christianity and Islam*. Baltimore: Johns Hopkins University Press.
—. 2003. *Formations of the Secular: Christianity, Islam, Modernity*. Stanford: Stanford University Press.
—. 2011. "Thinking about religious belief and politics," in *The Cambridge Companion to Religious Studies*, ed. Robert A. Orsi, 36–57. Cambridge: Cambridge University Press.
Bellah, Robert 2011. *Religion in Human Evolution, From the Paleolithic to the Axial Age*. Cambridge: Harvard.
Bonner, Phil and Noor Nieftagodien. 2001. *Kathrus: A History*. London: Maskew Miller Longman.

---

34 'Vote ANC, go to heaven': See note 1.

Bradford, Helen. 1988. *A Taste of Freedom: The ICU in Rural South Africa, 1924–1930*. New Haven: Yale University Press.

Brown, Tom, and A.J. Wookey, eds. [1875] 1925, 1977. *Tswana-English Dictionary*. Gaborone: London Missionary Society, 1925; Johannesburg: Ecumenical, 1977.

Campbell, James. 1998. *Songs of Zion: The African Methodist Episcopal Church in the United States and South Africa*. Durham, NC: University of North Carolina.

Chidester, David. 1996. *Savage Systems: Colonialism and Comparative Religion in Southern Africa*. (*Studies in Religion and Culture*). Charlottesville: University of Virginia.

Cohn, Bernard. 1996. *Colonialism and Its Forms of Knowledge*. Princeton: Princeton University Press.

Comaroff, Jean, and John L. Comaroff 1998. *Of Revelation and Revolution, Vol. 1*. Chicago: University of Chicago Press.

Couper, Scott. 2009. *Albert Luthuli: Bound by Faith*. Pietermaritzburg: University of Kwazulu-Natal Press.

Dos Santos. n.d. *Ethiopia Oriental*, Volume 1, 229–30, as cited in Theal 1883.

Dubow, Saul. 1989. *Racial Segregation and the Origins of Apartheid in South Africa, 1919–36*. Oxford: Macmillan.

——. 1995. *Scientific Racism in Modern South Africa*. Cambridge: Cambridge University Press.

Durkheim, Emile. 1995. *Elementary Forms of Religious Life,* trans. Karen Fields, Introduction by Karen Fields. New York: Free Press.

Ellis, Stephen, and J.-F. Bayart. 2009. *The Criminalization of the State in Africa*, esp. Ellis, Bayart, and Beatrice Hibou "From kleptocracy to the felonious state, 1–32. Bloomington: Indiana University Press.

Ellis, Stephen, and Gerrie ter Haar. 2004. *Worlds of Power: Religious Thought and Political Practice in Africa*. Oxford: Oxford University Press.

Evans, Ivan. 1997. *Bureaucracy and Race: Native Administration in South Africa*. Los Angeles: University of California Press.

Fabian, Johannes. 2002. *Time and the Other: How Anthropology Makes Its Object*. New York: Columbia University Press.

Fields, Karen. 2002. "Witchcraft and racecraft: invisible ontology and its sensible manifestations," in *Witchcraft Dialogues: Anthropological and Philosophical Exchanges*, ed. George Clement Bond and Diane M. Ciekawy, 283–315. Athens: Ohio University Press.

Fields, Karen, and Barbara Fields. 2012. *Racecraft: the Soul of Inequality in American Life*. New York: Verso.

Freud, Sigmund. 1989. *Civilisation and Its Discontents*. New York: Norton.

Gordon, David. 2012. *Invisible Agents: Spirits in a Central African History*. Athens: Ohio University Press.

Hallan, Barry, and U. Olubi Sodipo. 1997. *Knowledge, Belief, and Witchcraft: Analytic Experiments in African Philosophy*, 2d ed. Stanford: Stanford University Press.

Hepburn, James. 1895. *Twenty Years in Khama's Country and Pioneering Among the Batuana of Lake Ngami*. London: Lyall.

Horton, Robin. 1967a. "African traditional thought and western science." *Africa: Journal of the International African Institute*, 37, 1 (Jan.): 50–71.

——. 1967b. "African traditional thought and western science." *Africa: Journal of the International African Institute*, 37, 2 (Apr.): 155–87

Hughes, Heather. 2011. *First President: A Life of John L. Dube, Founding President of the ANC*. Cape Town: Jacana.

Jeater, Diana. 2005. "Imagining Africans: scholarship, fantasy, and science in colonial administration, 1920s Southern Rhodesia." *International Journal of African Historical Studies*, 38, 1, online.

Kelley, Robin D. 1991. "The religious odyssey of African radicals: notes on the Communist Party of South Africa, 1921–1934." *Radical History Review* 51: 5–24.

Landau, Paul S. 1995. *The Realm of the Word: Language, Gender, and Christianity in a Southern African Kingdom*. Portsmouth, NH: Heinemann.

——. 1999: "'Religion' and Christian conversion in African history: a new model." *Journal of Religious History*, 23, 1: 8–30.

——. 2010a. "Transformations in consciousness," in *The Cambridge History of South Africa, Vol. 1, chap. 8*, ed. Carolyn Hamilton, Bernard Mbenga, and Robert Ross, 392–448, Cambridge: Cambridge University Press.

——. 2010b. *Popular Politics in the History of South Africa, 1400 to 1948*. New York: Cambridge University Press,.

——. 2012a "Religion in human evolution: colonialism's religious domain," http://blogs.ssrc.org/tif/2012/07/10/colonialisms-religious-domain/

——. 2012b. "'Johannesburg in flames': The 1918 shilling campaign, *Abantu-Batho*, and early African nationalism in South Africa," in *The People's Paper: Abantu-Batho and the African National Congress*, ed. Peter Limb, 255–81. Johannesburg: University of Witwatersrand Press.

——. 2013a "Holy Hustlers," review of Richard Werbner, Holy Hustlers, Schism, and Prophecy: Apostolic Reformation in Botswana (Berkeley: University of Cal. Press, 2011). *History of Religions*, 53, 1 (August): 100–3.

——. 2013b. "'The First Evangelism, Part One,' the Christian States of the Early Nineteenth Century in South Africa," Gaborone, Botswana, South African Historical Association Conference, June 25, 2013.

Limb, Peter. 2009. *The ANC's Early Years: Nation, Class and Place in South Africa before 1940*. Pretoria: UNISA Press, 2009.

Macdougle, Elizabeth 2007. *Crafting Identity in Zimbabwe and Mozambique*. University of Rochester Press.

Magaziner, Daniel. 2010. *The Law and the Prophets: Black Consciousness in South Africa, 1968–1977*. Athens: Ohio University Press.

Marx, Karl [1845] 1998. "Theses on Feuerbach," in *The German Ideology, 569–77*. New York: Prometheus Books.

Mazarire, Gerald Chikozho 2009. "'Reflections on pre-colonial Zimbabwe,' c. 850–1880s," in *Becoming Zimbabwe: A History from the Precolonial Period to 2008*, eds. Brian Raftopoulos and Alois Mlambo, 1–39. Harare and Johannesburg: Weaver and Jacana.

Mbembe, Achille. 2013. *Critique de la raison nègre*. Paris: La Decouverte.

Morton, Fred 2010. *When Rustling Became an Art: Pilane's Kgatla and the Transvaal Frontier 1820–1902*. Cape Town: David Philip.

Mudenge, S.I.G 1988. *A Political History of the Munhumutapa, c. 1400–1902*. Harare: Zimbabwe Publishing House.

——. forthcoming: Work on the Rozvi.

Nietzsche, F. 1887. "Good and Evil," in *On the Genealogy of Morals*, para 13.

Rafael, Vincente L. 1993. *Contracting Colonialism: Translation and Christian Conversion in Tagalog Society Under Early Spanish Rule.* Durham, NC: Duke University Press.

Ranger, Terence. 1985. *Peasant Consciousness and Guerilla War in Zimbabwe: A Comparative Study.* Berkeley: University of California Press.

——. 1993. "The invention of tradition revisited: the case of colonial Africa," in *Legitimacy and the State in Twentieth-Century Africa: Essays in Honour of A. H. M. Kirk-Greene*, eds. Terence Ranger and Olufemi Vaughan, 62–111. London: Macmillan.

——. 1999. *Voices from the Rocks: Nature, Culture and History in the Matopos Hills of Zimbabwe.* Harare: Baobab.

Rodda, Peter. [1959] 2011. "The Africanists cut loose." *Africa, South*, 3, 4 (July–September 1959), reprinted in *Africa South: Viewpoints, 1956–1961*, ed. M.J. Daymond and Corinne Sandwith, 227–30. Pietermaritzburg: University of KwaZulu-Natal Press.

Saunders, Christopher. [1970] 1971. *Tile and the Thembu Church: Politics and Independency on the Cape Eastern Frontier in the Late Nineteenth Century,"* reprint [1970] Abe Bailey Institute of Interracial Studies, University of Cape Town.

Shaw, Rosalind. 1990. "The invention of 'African traditional religion.'" *Religion*, 20, 4: 339–353.

Smith, Jonathan Z. 1982. *Imagining Religion: From Babylon to Jonestown.* Chicago: University of Chicago.

Taylor, Charles. 2007. *A Secular Age.* Cambridge, MA.: Harvard.

Theal, George M. 1883. *Basutoland Records, I.* Cape Town: Government Printer.

van der Walt, Lucien. 2007. "Anarchism and syndicalism in South Africa, 1904–1921: rethinking the history of labour and the left," Ph.D. thesis, History, University of the Witwatersrand.

Viljoen, Russell. 1994. "'Revelation of a Revolution,' the Prophecies of Jan Parel, alias *Onse Liewe Heer*, a Khoisan Prophet and Cape Rebel." *Kronos*, 21 (Nov. 1994): 1–21.

Vinson, Robert. 2012. *The Americans are Coming: Dreams of African American Liberation in Segregationist South Africa.* Athens: Ohio University Press.

Volz, Steve, and Part Themba Mgadla, trans. and eds. 2006. *Words of Batswana: Letters to Mahoko oa Becwana, 1883–1896.* Cape Town: Van Riebeeck Soc.

Wohlrab-Sahr, Monika and Marian Burchardt. 2012. "Multiple secularities: toward a cultural sociology of secular modernities." *Comparative Sociology*, 11, 6: 875–912.

Rijk van Dijk
After Pentecostalism? Exploring Intellectualism, Secularization and Guiding Sentiments in Africa

With the exception of just a few studies (see, for example, Burchardt, Wohlrab-Sahr, and Wegert 2013; Laguda 2013; Swidler 2010; Leatt 2007; Morier-Genoud 2007; Loimeier 1996), the exploration of processes of secularization in Sub-Saharan Africa is either completely lacking in the literature or in a state of infancy. While there is little empirical evidence to substantiate the claim that 'Africans are notoriously religious' (Mbiti 1969), this lack of attention to processes of secularization in Africa may also be the result of an essentialized differentiation between 'us and the other' whereby such processes are predominantly perceived as belonging to a kind of 'European exceptionalism' that cannot be imported into other cultural domains. This contribution questions how religion can be co-productive and co-constitutive of the manner in which, in Casanova's (2011) terms, separate social spheres arise and where religion starts to play less of a role in informing identities. This will be approached from a perspective informed by ideas of sentiment and emotion. I propose that, by building on Wohlrab-Sahr and Burchardt's (2012) notion of studying secularization processes through the guiding ideas that inspire people and groups to engage with this 'work' of separation, we also need to consider the rise of guiding sentiments, that is, emotions that inspire people to view religion differently. This ties the understanding of the experience of secularization to the sensual and the sensitive, and allows for the importation and transportability of Charles Taylor's emotional understanding of the process into Africa. In her brilliant review of Taylor's *A Secular Age*, Hurd (2007, 2008) highlights the difficulty Taylor has in acknowledging that some people in the current age neither endorse religion in any of its manifestations nor eschew any form of metaphysics or humanism. Instead, she points out that Taylor consigns these groups, who seem to adhere to a level of radical or fundamental immanence, to living in a universe cloaked in darkness. She points to his *Unbehagen*[1] about this development by showing how he sees that 'a race of humans has arisen which has managed to experience this world entirely as imma-

---

[1] I am using the German term *Unbehagen* so as to indicate a register of sentiments of unease, anxiety and discomfort that, in their combination, are otherwise difficult to translate in English.

nent [which] we may judge as a victory of darkness (...) a remarkable achievement nonetheless' (Taylor 2007: 376).

Neither Taylor nor Hurd may have realized how relevant this statement is in the context of understanding the development of a particular secularization process in Sub-Saharan Africa. It is indeed a statement that allows for an emic and empirical exploration of the sensuous meaning of notions of darkness and of immanence in contexts where Christianity has been feeding understandings of these. I refer here to the rise of a form of charismatic Pentecostalism that has been sweeping many countries in Sub-Saharan Africa and the feelings of *Unbehagen* that have grown with it. This form of Christianity has become immensely popular over the last two decades, particularly among the emergent middle-class, well-educated, urban sections of the population in countries such as Ghana and Nigeria, as well as in southern Africa, in Zambia, Zimbabwe and South Africa. Often related to groups of university graduates who were taking up leadership positions in the development of these Pentecostal mega-churches, the emphasis on a battle with the forces of darkness seems to belong to an intellectual attractiveness of this form of Christianity (Lauterbach 2010).

In a sense this form of Christianity began introducing a religious modernity (cf. Casanova 1994, 2011; Meyer 2012), that is, an understanding of the modern person as a believer armed with spiritual and moral powers to fight the forces of darkness. While the term 'modernity' must be understood as a condition that creates sharp dichotomies between the modern and the traditional, the superior and the inferior, the immanent and the transcendent, the term 'religious modernity' is used here for the condition that places the creation of these dichotomies in the context of religious thought and praxis. The struggle over the creation of dichotomies in Pentecostalism has often taken the form of a 'break with the past' (Meyer 1998; Van Dijk 1998; Engelke 2010), which has become a dictum for Pentecostal believers in scrutinizing their involvement in customary and traditional practices and declaring these as not befitting a modern engagement with society. While in many places in Africa educated circles have adopted this new form of Pentecostalism in formulating these dichotomies, they also feed the ways in which Pentecostalism embraces the immanent. Supporting intellectual traditions of reading and writing, it is common for leaders to express their thoughts in books and leaflets, with written products focusing on the realities of life – the economic aspects of making a living, running a business and positioning oneself in public domains and circles of intellectual exchange – while becoming successful in social and marital relationships too. This has become a rich body of Pentecostal thought on how the here and now of a believer's everyday, mundane life exhibits the power of the faith in this-worldly success, prosperity and intellectual development (Gifford 2004).

Contrary to Taylor's dark perceptions of people experiencing the world as entirely immanent, here is a religious intellectual development that expresses its belief in the immanent, in the this-worldly nature of its interests in divine power. The second step that this chapter will discuss is the growing disillusionment of some of the educated with the Pentecostal immanent, a rising sentiment of *Unbehagen* with the claims and practices of this form of Pentecostalism that these classes have previously been so supportive of. How can developments in African societies, where Pentecostalism has become truly dominant in the public domain, yet some are increasingly showing unease with a faith they once supported so strongly, be understood? Is this an African secularization of the immanent? Clearly the search for or experience of a form of secularization here, as described by Taylor, is *not* inspired by the pursuit of this-worldly and immanent interests, as these were already part of the Pentecostal faith. How should we interpret a turning away from this faith in the immanent, often inspired by circles in Africa that are becoming critical of the faith, its virulent religious practices, the personality cult of its leaders and its demands regarding the economic resources of its adherents? By focusing on cases from Africa – Ghana and Botswana in particular – this contribution to the discussion asks whether a new space is emerging 'after Pentecostalism', an indeterminate and inchoate space that is ideologically intellectual but not necessarily secular in a Taylorian way. Nor is this space 'post-secular' in the way a number of authors (see, for example, Beaumont and Baker 2011; Molendijk, Beaument, and Jedan 2010) writing on western (urban) spaces have intended, since this European exceptionalism requires to be de-centred in a proper understanding of its inchoate quality.

1 Producing Multiple Religious Modernities?

Embedded in the African Pentecostal quest for religious modernity is a fundamental critique of the mainline missionary churches that first introduced Christianity into African societies. In Botswana, for example, Christianity was introduced as early as 1870, and many of the educated classes were educated in mission schools, treated in mission hospitals and/or were married in these churches. The intellectual and civic public domain is a result of the influence of the mission churches, and their contribution to the development of the nation state has been undisputable. The secular Botswana nation state is related to Christianity in the multifaceted and common way in which secular and religious ritual are intertwined on public occasions. For example, the official in charge of the Registrar of Marriages and the official procedures related to weddings will counsel couples in a public session using verses taken from the Bible, irrespective of the couple's religious beliefs, as public functions are expected to be embellished with an explicit statement pertaining to the Christian faith.

Yet, while the development of the educated classes depended on the mission churches, the significance of this dependence on the mission churches themselves came to be contested by the new (charismatic) Pentecostal churches that started emerging from the 1970s. In Pentecostal circles, the mainline churches were often perceived as offering 'lukewarm' Christianity, as churches lacking divine inspiration and unable to fight the forces of darkness that haunt the lives of many, simply because they do not stop their members from partaking in traditional rituals and do not issue strong moral injunctions *vis-à-vis* personal lifestyles where it comes to drinking, smoking or illicit sexual relations. Becoming a modern believer has come to mean being a born-again believer. In many African countries, this popularity has been connected to the location of prominent members of the educated elite in these countries' public domains.

However, it is clear that the educated classes are turning away from this involvement in the Pentecostal faith. Increasingly criticism is being voiced of the 'too-muchness' of its ideological and moral demands, as well as dissatisfaction being expressed with the Pentecostal fascination with ecstatic ritual display, frantic emotionalism and the unchallenged spiritual and economic power of Pentecostal leaders. The question is how a new post-Pentecostal separation is being fuelled and informed by this criticism and sentiment.

Clearly those who are dissatisfied are not abandoning the notions of the dark forces that may present themselves in life, but nonetheless returning to the mainline Christian traditions that some have left in exchange for the new Pentecostal denominations is not an option. At the same time, opting for a (public) position as a non-believer is usually not viable either, as this would conjure up the perspective of darkness, as Taylor indicated. This is a subjectivity that, with its focus on the immanent, appears to be an easy target for demonic powers and thus becomes highly suspect.

A host of literature argues that, while the notion of a religious modernity should be perceived as oxymoronic, religion is back in processes of modern state-formation. I agree with the position of Wohlrab-Sahr and Burchardt (2012), who argue that, although the non-West demonstrates the relevance of speaking of religious modernities as a culturally and historically pluralized experience of the co-production of religion and secularism, we must also consider multiple secularities on similar grounds. They take particular issue with statements by Casanova (2008) and Berger, Davie, and Fokas (2008), who view the process of secularization, seen as the differentiation of the religious and non-religious social spheres – including the decline in the social significance of religious participation – as being the exclusive preserve of Western and/or European development. The concept of multiple secularities allows a culturally diversified understanding of how societies, groups, classes and individuals produce different paths into differentiating religious and non-religious social spheres. By implication they also challenge the monochrome notion that there is a single process into the 'post-secular' (Beaumont and Baker 2011; Molendijk, Beaumont and Jedan 2010) that is universally applicable. Interestingly, these authors are designing a concept of 'guiding ideas' (Wohlrab-Sahr and Burchardt 2012: 881) in understanding how such processes of differentiation are voiced, argued, justified and made (morally) acceptable. Even though many of these ideas of individuality, tolerance, enlightenment, autonomy and rationality can be located squarely in the genealogy of Western and other modernities, I would like to add the notion of 'guiding sentiments' to this conceptual development. How can we interpret an intellectual *Unbehagen* in this process (see also Atherton, Graham, and Steedman 2011 for a similar concern with economy, religion and sentiment) through which new differentiations between religious and non-religious social spheres are emerging, generating a decline in religious participation in a dominant form of religious life in the way Casanova (1994, 2011) defined it?

First, in terms of different pathways in secularization beyond the Western world and of the proverbial 'European exceptionalism', we need to note that the emergence of a so-called post-secular modern nation state has not been identified in Sub-Saharan African (see Loimeier 1996; Swidler 2010; Burchardt, Wohlrab-Sahr, and Wegert 2013 for notable exceptions). This is not, I would argue, because African nation states 'never became modern', but more because of the modernizing tendencies that form part of the position that religion has been taking all along. Leaving aside a discussion of the religious 'I' in African contexts (see Olivier de Sardan 1992 on this point), the arrival of Christianity and its subsequent translations and appropriations on the continent have been part of what Van der Veer (1995) called a 'conversion to modernities'. While the various forms of Christianity were shaping public domains through the establishment of educational institutions, hospitals and political elite formation, their impact on changing social relations has been equally profound. Comaroff and Comaroff (1997) show how the introduction of Christianity into Southern African societies changed social arrangements at the everyday level by becoming part of daily phenomena such as housing, clothing styles, weddings and initiation.

More than the state, organized and institutionalized religion is the site of the production of modernities (in the plural because of its many local cultural refractions, as well the extensive varieties of paths into a modern condition), as became manifest in the refashioning of the self, relationships, forms of governance and forms of elite positioning. Christianity in Africa modernized itself not only through the emergence of new and Africanized forms of practice and expression – as in the many African Independent Churches – but also through its continuous repositioning in the public domains of emerging African nation states. In fact, many of the independent African churches that were established in the 1920s and 1930s later became important 'producers' of the new national leaderships that came to play an essential role in the move towards independence. These forms of Christianity fed into nascent political life, like the formation of the pre-independence 'native associations', some of which transformed themselves into fully fledged political parties or unions at or around independence. But the route of religious modernity did not stop there.

Starting in the 1970s, and growing in the 1980s, Pentecostalism became a powerful social force in countries such as Nigeria, Ghana, Kenya, Zimbabwe and Zambia, emphasizing diametrically opposed ideas of how a religious modernity can be achieved. In many cases, Pentecostalism penetrated the highest levels of nation-state governance, influencing state policy and political debate in the public domain, and engaging in an international world of interaction with Western governments and large global players.

Many Pentecostals in these African situations started to take issue with the emphasis in the former missionary, mainline churches on asceticism in their shaping of a religious modernity and in their religious practices, an emphasis that declared poverty to be a holy state of being and that stressed an other-worldly orientation for devotees' life-styles. The Pentecostal contestation of this position often emphasized that God's benevolence must become apparent in immanent success and prosperity. The linkages of Pentecostalism with forms of (religious) entrepreneurship quickly became multifaceted, and a whole literature is emerging on the ways in which a new religious market is developing in Africa (Maxwell 1998; Pfeiffer 2005; Van Dijk 2009; Smith 2001). Much of the literature on economic notions of the faith focuses on what Gifford (2004) has termed the 'prosperity gospel'. This particular brand of Pentecostalism has gained public attention because Pentecostal leaders and preachers emphasize 'God's wonder-working power' in providing people with abundant wealth and immediate success (Comaroff and Comaroff 2000, 2001). Claiming that progress can be attained by a pro-active break and/or a critical engagement with traditions (Meyer 1998, Van Dijk 1997, 1998), Pentecostal groups linked up with the market by teaching their followers that a modern believer is a competitive believer who can conquer risks and challenges (Van Dijk 2003, 2009).

This new Pentecostalism began emphasizing a new form of intellectualism as well – new, that is, compared to the teachings of the mainline churches and the educational systems, as well as to the religious history of Pentecostalism itself, where the emphasis had always been on divine revelation as a source of knowledge. Many of the new Pentecostal leaders began emphasizing study, scholarship and the reading of particular books, leaflets and pamphlets, as well as developing a pride in fostering 'sanitized' forms of African thought and a philosophy rooted in Pan-Africanism (Van Dijk 2004). This development not only showed in the marked increase in publications by African Pentecostal leaders, it was also evidenced in the arrival of new Bible schools and Pentecostal universities. As a result a new kind of Pentecostal scholarship has emerged that is interested not only in promoting a kind of 'message for the black race', as the well-known Pentecostal intellectual Mensa Otabil from Ghana calls it (Van Dijk 2004), but also a 'life science' that is interested in developing normativities, ethics and moralities to guide the lives of the modern believer. Many publications address issues such as how to make one's marriage a success, organize one's family life, understand the nation state and the meaning of governance, and so on. Much of this Pentecostal intellectualist development situates itself as highly juxtaposed to Western forms of knowledge of these phenomena. The future of Africa should be in the hands of Pentecostal-inspired thinkers and leadership, and new knowledge about how to live one's life in a modern African context can and should only be produced by those who have the moral legitimacy to pronounce on it. This African Pentecostal intellectualism became critical of missionary teachings and, in places such as Ghana and Botswana, fought to gain greater influence over educational and cultural policies. What Meyer (2004) has called a pentecostalization of the public domain quickly became one of its objectives.

2 The Pentecostalization of an Educated Public

When I began researching the rise of the new charismatic Pentecostal movements in Malawi in the late 1980s and early 1990s, I was struck by the fact that Pentecostal fellowship and prayer meetings were held in secondary schools and in places like Chancellor College in Zomba. Attending a number of these student meetings, I learned how important it was for the students to turn the space of a classroom or lecture hall into a place of worship serving the 'outpouring' of the Holy Spirit, healing and deliverance. Others too have noticed this remarkable religious occupation of educational spaces by these groups, which seemed to turn spaces of learning and intellectual exchange into sites for ecstatic forms of religious experience. Ojo (1998) also located the birth of important Pentecostal movements in Nigeria in interdenominational student organizations in the 1970s. Sadgrove (2007) noticed this as well in her research on student life in Uganda: Pentecostal moral ideologies had become important in Kampala in shaping relationships and ideas of sexual behaviour, as well as the centrality of participating in students' fellowship and prayer meetings. Akoko (2007: 54) recounts not only how the new Pentecostal movements' adherents in Cameroon came to consist of university and secondary-school students, but also how, in the name of 'campus peace', the University of Buea banned the activities of its Pentecostal students' union as early as 1995.

In the classrooms I visited in and around Blantyre in Malawi, charismatic groups began manifesting their presence with loud prayers, singing and preaching. In addition to their presence in the 'soundscape' of the school or university, there were banners, posters and advertisements to announce the meetings they were planning. In many instances these pamphlets included an announcement of the arrival of an important Pentecostal preacher who had been invited to address the students and hold a prayer meeting, including a deliverance session. The Pentecostal world outside these educational institutions was thus invited to enter the school or university, thereby creating a space for the direct involvement of Pentecostal churches with the 'interior' of the institution. Many of the prominent leaders of the Pentecostal movements in Malawi and Ghana had been trained in secondary school and university and became involved in fellowship and prayer meetings in the early years of their educational careers. The personal histories of well-known Pentecostal leaders such as Madalitso Mbewe in Malawi or Dag Heward Mills in Ghana demonstrate how formative these years of student life were for them, catapulting them into their religious careers and the rapidly expanding organizations and churches they established. In the case of Dag Heward Mills, who was trained as a doctor and then started the international Lighthouse Chapel in Ghana, this trajectory of becoming a well-trained (medical) specialist while also being involved in the development of Pentecostalism is seen by many of his followers as highly inspirational and as a model for personal life and destiny.

Lighthouse Chapel, starting from its headquarters near the Korle Bu central hospital in Accra, has branched out to places beyond Ghana[2] since it was established in the late 1980s, and its missionaries also went to Botswana. While conducting fieldwork not far from Gaborone, Botswana, I met a young Ghanaian doctor who was a general practitioner in the town, who also came to the country to support this Ghanaian Pentecostal church there. Operating from the main headquarters of the church in Botswana in a peri-urban quarter of Gaborone, he did not work within the 'soft' life of the country's capital but instead engaged with the people in this somewhat remote, dusty and certainly less luxurious

---

[2] Their website claims to have over 1300 branches worldwide.

town on the edge of the Kalahari Desert. This idea of combining a medical profession with a Pentecostal missionary effort emulates the image of its leader Dag Heward Mills. There is an intellectual interest, if not obligation, to share (medical and moral) knowledge and understanding with a local population, and thus to fight 'ignorance'. The notion of ignorance among a local population that the arrival and activities of a charismatic Pentecostal church could help overcome is a common trope in many Pentecostal messages. It suggests the conviction that, in and through adherence to the Pentecostal faith, things may become clear, transparent and understandable in the social, moral and spiritual lives of individuals that would otherwise remain hidden and unacknowledged and that could potentially become problematic in their lives and fortunes. Pentecostal practice is thus related to revealing the hidden truths about the dark spiritual forces and dynamics that may be present in people's everyday situations. Pentecostals often talk of the need to have a 'spirit of discernment', meaning that knowledge is required to understand why, as a confirmed Pentecostal believer, one is not supposed to visit a traditional healer or be involved in socio-ritual practices where ancestral spirits can make their presence felt. This is an important matter in what well-educated Pentecostals like this doctor seem to be referring to in proclaiming a struggle against ignorance. A medical practice is bio-medically, morally and spiritually superior to the local healing traditions that they see many people turning to, possibly exposing them to demonic powers with dire consequences.

It is in this sense that the idea of a Pentecostal medical pursuit presents a *double entendre* whereby on one level the God-given superiority of biomedical treatment can be demonstrated, whereas at another level a moral fight can be staged against (healing) traditions that engage with what, from a manecheastic point of view, can be seen as the 'powers of darkness' (Meyer 1998). In other words, a doctor like him is situated in a medical and religious moral campaign for which strong convictions are held about the need to make sacrifices, such as giving up the comforts of home and being active in a faraway and unknown place such as Botswana.[3] Although one could interpret this form of medical missionization as a continuation of earlier mainline churches' efforts of the likes of Dr David Livingstone in their attempts to convert a local population to Christianity, the clear point at which a Pentecostal modernity breaks out here is that, instead of a rejection of evil spiritual powers as mere superstition, Pentecostals acknowledge their existence, their ancestry, their innate nature, and the need for knowledge and understanding of their powers and efficacy. This is not a 'second

---

[3] Such South-South religious transnational connections have so far received scant attention in (anthropological) research, but for an exception, see van de Kamp and van Dijk (2010).

naivety' in the way Ricoeur (1967: 351) interpreted the rebirth of a new fascination for the world of religious and spiritual powers in the West. Instead the Pentecostals attack what, in their eyes, is itself a dangerous form of naivety in the dogma and practices of the mainline churches in not taking seriously what these powers entail and how one should be fully conscious of their evil machinations. In other words, there is no excuse for remaining ignorant about the true workings of what the mainline churches reject as mere superstition.

While Pentecostalism thus combines a spiritual focus with the pursuit of knowledge (which are not constructed as being antithetical to one another), we need to return to the question of why Pentecostal faith and practice have been so explicitly located in the intellectual domain of the school and the university as one of the most important cradles from which they developed. Many reasons can be given, all of which show that the modernity of the faith also supports an intellectualist orientation.

Institutions of (higher) education obviously allow for distinction. In colonial times it was the mainline missionary churches that fostered the educational domain in many places in Africa and that were pivotal in forming an educated class from which a new (national) leadership sprang, and that shaped exposure to an external international and transnational world of educational career-making. For Pentecostals, this became even more important. As has been demonstrated, the rise of Pentecostalism in many parts of Africa – unlike Latin America – was driven by the new middle and upper-middle classes that emerged in the 1970s and 1980s in many African cities (Englund 2003; Gifford 2004; Freeman 2012; van de Kamp 2012). Within schools and universities there was a new need not only for inter-class-based distinction, that is, an educated elite distinguishing itself from other sections of the population, but for an intra-class-based distinction as well, that is, a way for Pentecostals to distinguish themselves from those educated at missionary or other educational facilities by claiming the higher moral ground. The Pentecostal fellowships and prayer groups that I spoke to in schools in Malawi in the early years of the rise of this new charismatic movement claimed that they represented a 'better' form of Christianity, a more developed one that would lead – almost automatically – to a higher form of moral leadership. Even when operating in the former mainline (Presbyterian and Roman Catholic) missionary schools, their form of Christianity, student life and intellectual discussion were considered to be of a much higher standing than the student groups that were founded by members of one of the mainline churches. While it was clear that the education received in such schools would lead all students to middle-class positions in Malawian society, the Pentecostal fellowship activities were an attempt to create further distinctions. This resonates clearly with statements made later by international Pentecostal leaders like Mensa Otabil, when he called for Pentecostal churches to acknowledge their responsibility for creating a new moral leadership that would be superior to that which had been gone before (Gifford 2004; De Witte 2011).

One explanation for the intertwining of Pentecostalism with intellectual domains, such as education, is based on the notion of the faith's role in both reflecting *and* producing social stratification. This ties directly into a discussion of secularization understood as a process of the dwindling socio-structural significance of religious formations: the Pentecostal option for thinking about social stratification took the form of a socio-moral hierarchization that creates an awareness of distance and alternative. This was certainly the case in a country such as Malawi, where social stratification in the post-colonial period was directly dependent on the mainline churches' domination of the educational system and the creation of its national leadership.[4] The insertion of a Pentecostal moral stratification has reduced, weakened and distorted this position, opening up a critical perspective of how leadership has come about, and implying that making any claim regarding a Christian standing of leadership is meaningless unless its true Christian nature can be shown. As Meyer (2012) has pointed out, the Pentecostalization of the public domain in Ghana creates, as its flip side, the notion of publics that are not Pentecostal, that cannot be classified as living up to the high standards that Pentecostals set themselves, and that tend to make any claim to a Christian origin, frame of reference or basis of authority doubtful in the minds of many.

The larger Pentecostal churches have been opening their own (Bible) schools and private universities. In terms of the production of an alternative moral stratification of society, this places the creation of a new moral leadership squarely within the context of its own Pentecostalite educational domain. In other words, the process of secularization this fosters is based in the creation of contesting counter-images of leadership placed in public domains, one of which can be qualified as Christian and the other cannot, since it will never be able to live up to the standards that the faith dictates.

A second exploration as to why Pentecostalism sought the educational domain as one of its cradles lies in the fact that schools and universities operate as places of experimentation. As a growing literature shows, schools and universities are social spaces of experimentation in the field of relationships, sexuality and gender roles (see, for example for Ghana, Bochow 2008; for Uganda, Sad-

---

[4] In addition to the Roman Catholic Church, the Church of Central African Presbyterian (CCAP) has a long record of producing leaders, having produced the first president of post-independence Malawi.

grove 2007; Gusman 2009). This literature demonstrates that the school and the university offer a space to students outside and beyond parental control and supervision, bringing the sexes into direct contact with one another and allowing the exchange of intimacies in a setting of peers that is not easily found outside the structures of such institutions. Culturally speaking, schools are seen as platforms where it is easy to exchange knowledge about sexuality and intimacy, and they provide breaks with cultural traditions of initiation and instruction on such matters, which tend to be in the hands of the elderly or relatives in communal ritual forms. Yet the school as a site of experimentation also relates to the often overlooked domain of the spiritual, which is unsupervised from the school's perspective. The Pentecostal fellowships in schools mark out a space of religious experimentation where students are exposed to different forms of religious and spiritual life from those at home. The religious emotions and ecstasy that came to be part of the student Pentecostal fellowships' mode of expression was part of a search to find a new religious expression, to do things differently from their parents or their teachers at Roman Catholic, Presbyterian or government-run schools (Van Dijk 1992). Within these fellowships and prayer meetings, new songs were sung, and the young people themselves started preaching, engaged with the manifestation of the Holy Spirit (in the singular and as opposed to any other spiritual manifestation) and voiced the moralities that should apply to their own lives (see also Bochow 2008; Sadgrove 2007).

The religious space for experimentation that these groups were allowed or 'conquered' saw experimentation *vis-à-vis* religious authority and gender role divisions. While Pentecostalism is generally known for its gender bias, whereby in terms of membership women are always in the majority (Frahm-Arp 2012) but men take positions of leadership and are usually a striking minority in Pentecostal congregations, in these fellowships the female students could themselves be leaders in charge of the meeting, the prayer sessions or the deliverance. It is not that by becoming involved in these Pentecostal fellowships they were suddenly starting to preach a revolution in otherwise conservative notions of the patriarchal order of society. Instead the point is rather that the knowledge and experience of the 'ways of the Holy Spirit' could be as much part of a female understanding as it is part of a male understanding and that, in the context of such knowledge and understanding, gender becomes less decisive. At the time of the rise of young Pentecostal preachers in Malawi's public domain in the late 1980s and early 1990s, one of the prominent leaders of the movement was a teenage girl (Van Dijk 1992), even though in many places in Malawi it was the cultural norm that young women did not address (or confront) men directly. The changing position of the educated woman in society usually allows for greater licence here (Frahm-Arp 2012). In a sense, therefore, the female students in these fellowships took up a social space where this new and modern positioning could be acted out, tested and built on. And the assertiveness by which they did this was a strong signal of the kind of training ground the fellowships were offering. The fostering of skills and competences in styling leadership, in finding the moral legitimacy to do so and in organizing meetings have been part of this social space of religious experimentation.

A further point to be made here is about how the notion of providing 'teachings' has gained wider relevance. As Bochow and Van Dijk (2012) have indicated, the creation of alternative social spaces – a process they describe in a Foucauldian sense as being heterotopic – relates on a wider level to providing teaching on relationships, informing the ways in which influential Pentecostal groups perceive of their significance in producing behavioural change. Simultaneously fostered by, as well as appealing to, the educated classes, many Pentecostal groups and leaders emphasize how lifestyles must change by critically examining common, cultural or customary forms of social life. One area where this has happened concerns the critical rethinking of social, marital and sexual relations. Particularly in places where AIDS is rampant, as in Botswana and Malawi, Pentecostal groups have become proactive in promoting a moral agenda in teachings that concern relationships and sexuality (Burchardt 2011; Bochow and Van Dijk 2012; Prince, Denis and Van Dijk 2009). In emphasizing pre-marital abstinence among young people and fidelity in marriage (yet often rejecting the use of the condom), Pentecostal groups feel they can break with, or critically confront, culturally and socially accepted life-styles. The Pentecostal emphasis on the nuclear family, by tying sexuality exclusively to marriage and insisting on premarital abstinence and ideas of Christian courtship for young people, began to relate closely to such activities as counselling, which is perceived as a social technique by which progressive behavioural change can be taught to important groups in society (Burchardt 2011).

It is not so much that people develop into 'super-Christians' who are only interested in maintaining certain moral standards concerning sexuality and relationships, but that there is a real sense of how these teachings inform and equip people to use religious notions to shape their relationships as being different (and better, as well as more rewarding and gratifying) from what society can offer (Bochow 2008). Practices of Pentecostal counselling and courtship have thus become associated with the prospects of a good and successful life, with chances of progress and prosperity that otherwise might be jeopardized.

Another domain where teachings have become important is in the combination of an intellectual rethinking of the position of Africa in the world and the pursuit of a notion of African pride that borrows much of its inspiration from Pan-Africanism. As I have pointed out elsewhere (Van Dijk 2004), the prominent leader in this is Mensa A. Otabil, the head of the Accra-based International Central Gospel Church. In many of his books and public statements, he proclaims the liberation and uplifting of the Black Race, not through a return to a traditional African heritage, but through an African appropriation of the Bible and the Gospel. He developed this liberation theology in *Beyond the Rivers of Ethiopia* (1992), where he reclaims the position of Black people in the Bible as crucial to God's future for the world. By appropriating the Gospel, studying it carefully and making it relevant to the everyday lives of individuals and societies, the 'mental slavery' by which the Whites cursed the Blacks can be broken. Being a highly articulate, charismatic and eloquent personality, he has become a much sought-after inspirational leader and is regularly invited to address large Pentecostal summits attended by influential leaders in Africa such as Enock Sitima of Botswana's Bible Life Ministries.[5] Addressing the newly established Pan-African Believers' Conference, he left many baffled and surprised by his teachings on Black Pride, Pentecostal awakening and resistance to oppressive political and economic structures (Gifford 2004). This appealing combination of Afro-centrism and Pentecostal liberation theology was hitherto unheard of in Africa, where his public teachings against the 'African inferiority complex', as he called it, were often hotly debated in the media. A recent newspaper article on one of his political-intellectualist public messages highlights him as a 'teacher of the nation' as follows:

> Though he had his Bible on the podium and was quoting copiously from it, the man who has earned a reputation as the 'Nation's Pastor' was delivering, not a sermon, but a veritable academic lecture, fit for publication in a journal of history or religion. Otabil was not preaching: his message entitled 'Do you understand what you are reading?' was a thoroughly researched paper on Africa's contribution to world civilisations, from the biblical perspective. (Enimil Ashon in *The Spectator*, Saturday, 30 September 2011)

What can be concluded is that Pentecostal ideology and intellectualism provide people with a many-sided prism, combining, appealingly, this intellectualism with a particular religious orientation and a notion of a critical mentality that many of the emerging middle classes in various parts of Africa are highly attracted to. This form of religious modernity produces religious convictions, life-styles and intellectualism not as a paradox, nor as an oxymoronic identity, but as a God-given and highly justified (moral) order.

---

5 See Maxwell (1998) on Guti in Zimbabwe and Van Dijk (2004) on Sitima in Botswana.

3 A Turning Away?

Since 2000, four Ghanaian-led Pentecostal churches – the Church of Pentecost, the Lighthouse Chapel International, the Christ International Citadel and the Prevailing Christian Ministries – have become well established in Botswana. They are now part of the country's Pentecostal public sphere and are in close contact with other Pentecostal leaders, such as those of the Malawian-led Bible Life Ministries International, and appeal to the Ghanaian migrant community, especially to the Ghanaian professionals, teachers and university lecturers who have been recruited by the Botswana government to strengthen its civil service and its postcolonial educational sector. One of the most obvious countries for Botswana to recruit from was Ghana because of its long record of intellectual and Pan-African-orientated class formation.

A sizeable community of Ghanaian teachers, lecturers and professors can be found at many educational institutions, including the University of Botswana in Gaborone. Initially the Ghanaian Pentecostal churches attracted attention from these highly educated groups, their partners and their (nuclear) families. But while I was conducting fieldwork among this migrant group in the 2000s, something remarkable appeared to be happening. As a Ghanaian lecturer at the university indicated in a conversation, there was increasing concern and unease about the noise, shouting and screaming of the Pentecostal leaders, the 'too-muchness' of their demands in terms of time, attention, energy and money, and about what was perceived to be uncritical acceptance of the elevated status of Pentecostal leaders, which allowed too little room for discussion or reflection about what they said and did. He himself had come from one of the mainline churches when he began attending the Pentecostal churches, as others had done as well, but he was no longer much interested in doing so. This unease with the rise and dominance of these Pentecostal churches, I noticed, also entered into the informal discussions that took place in the context of the get-togethers of the Association of Ghanaian Nationals in Botswana that he and many other lecturers and professionals were attending. However, these discussions and concerns were not leading to a renewed interest in the mainline churches, which, as he also indicated, did not seem to offer anything challenging in terms of their teachings either.

Back in the 1990s, Maxwell (1998) began identifying this sentiment of *Unbehagen* in what he called the limits of Pentecostalism, especially in Zimbabwe. This was related first of all to the limits of the so-called prosperity gospel that was promising divine intervention in the poverty of people, whereby the true believer was led to expect the arrival of enormous wealth. Here again exaggerations in its claims as well as a too-muchness in the close to divine status accorded to the personalities of the leaders became an issue, leading to staunch criticism of the church in the public domain, investigations into the economic and financial transactions that some of these leaders appeared to be involved in and, in some cases, the collapse of the moral superiority that they had been claiming for themselves. In Ghana concerns about the too-muchness of Pentecostalism in the late 1990s and early 2000s also became manifest in (violent) conflicts about the loudness of the Pentecostal presence in the soundscape of living areas through their use of public address systems that seemed to give the voices of the Pentecostal leaders and their sermons a quality of inescapable omnipresence (see Van Dijk 2001). In these contexts, and with this rising sentiment of uneasiness, people began turning their backs on Pentecostalism, paradoxically in the middle of its exponential public growth.

The problem of too-muchness as a guiding sentiment in the opening up of a post-Pentecostal space is interesting as it seems to contradict the Pentecostal emphasis on teaching and intellectualism. If Pentecostal teaching is about producing critical thought and awareness, as well as about constituting a new kind of superior moral leadership, the creation of a special aura around leaders and their presence contradicts and undercuts this impetus. In a sense, it produces these guiding sentiments of uneasiness with the dominant dogmas of the faith in a contradictory manner. By fostering a notion of critical distrust of leadership in an intellectualist manner, the rise of an elevated leadership becomes contradictory, as it leads to the emergence of such sentiments. A well-educated couple I met in Botswana, who had been confirmed, active and prominent members of the Bible Life Ministries, had left this Pentecostal church. The impact of its leadership on their personal lives had become too problematic, too intrusive and had led to conflicts. A kind of unease and discomfort had emerged between them and the church leadership that resulted in their marginalization in terms of their status and standing in the church. So one day they decided simply to bid farewell to the committees and fellowships they had both been involved in and to cut the reciprocal ties they had maintained for so long. Did they plan to return to the mainline churches of their parental homes (the UCCSA[6] and the Seventh Day Adventists respectively)? Apparently not. The distance in experience, teachings and life-style had become too great, and they were still steeped in Pentecostal-inspired criticisms of cultural and customary forms of (moral) authority. They were thus uncertain as to where to turn now and were contemplating the question of whether to become members of another (Pentecostal) church.

---

6 United Congregational Church of Southern Africa.

This is the opening of an indeterminate and inchoate area between disillusionment, the possibility of remaining 'church-less' and the sensitivity, especially in the educated classes, of having a non-religious status. Were they on the brink of losing their religion? While men in Botswana are notorious for being absent from church in any case (something the Pentecostal churches aim to address by creating new ideas of responsible manhood in religious life), the husband had already proved quite exceptional in view of the local perceptions of masculinity in having been openly devoted to his church. The too-muchness of the church and its troubles were a deception, potentially leading to him questioning the relevance of the church in his personal life

It is important to stress that elements of critical consideration and reflection have been particularly relevant for the middle and upper-middle classes. The access to intellectualist-oriented models for life that Pentecostalism promotes is producing these class-based orientations as much as they have been fed by class positions. Whereas professional groups of doctors, lawyers, teachers, lecturers and civil servants in both Ghana and Botswana became involved as the protagonists of Pentecostal membership, contradictions seem to have emerged giving rise to sentiments of uneasiness that in turn guide the decisions some are now beginning to make concerning Pentecostal adherence.

This marks not only an important shift from the erstwhile unquestionable relationship between middle-class and elite formation with the position of the mainline, missionary churches, but it now also marks a shift away from the much-appraised relationship of Pentecostalism with these same classes. Pentecostal churches have been forging a definite and absolute break with the history of the mainline churches, as many of the educated classes have apparently lost interest in the asceticism of these churches, their stiffness, their disinterest in the newly emerging context of intellectualism and their irrelevance to new life-styles that respond much more closely to the need to demarcate class distinctions in society. The educated became much more interested in the this-worldly, immanent aspects of the new forms of Christianity, and particularly in urban areas they have found a rich domain for a morality of the expression of distinctions in Pentecostalism. They have gained, for instance, privileged access to relevant public media and a higher profile, as Pentecostal churches began to organize their own radio and television stations. Turning away from the mainline churches had deep ramifications for the African societies we are talking about here. It often meant a depletion of these churches' resources, a dwindling of their congregations and increasing contestations of their (moral) authority in the affairs of the nation in education, health policies and the like. In the centre of the public domain, therefore, the presence of the Pentecostal churches and their influential membership became more prominent.

Yet, although these classes seemed to have sealed their relationship with Christianity in their support for the Pentecostal faith, the emphasis on a more intellectualist agenda within Pentecostal circles has to be seen as representing a particular phase in the development of Pentecostalism as a whole. The sometimes large-scale, massive and ecstatic prayer, healing and deliverance sessions that drew huge public attention have increasingly come to be seen not as *the* manifestation of God's benevolent powers but as one of many possible forms. The more intellectualist approach within Pentecostalism, emphasizing teaching, training, writing and reading, was not intended to disqualify the nature, sincerity and morality of these expressions, but it no longer wanted to attribute exclusive power to them in its engagement with the divine. The intellectualist move within Pentecostalism as such has become an indication of the possibility of alternatives, of a differentiation from within. Some of the representatives of a more intellectualist expression of Pentecostalism have expressed their concerns and uneasiness about the nature of the 'wild' spiritual occasions that occur during moments of electrifying prayer. This concern even began to function as a motif for expressing their dissatisfaction with the noise, ecstasy and unruliness of such manifestations.

Another element that played a role in this internal dialogue was the increasing demand that the Pentecostal leadership began to place on their members. In a sense, the nature of the immanent, this-worldly interests of Pentecostalism also began to run counter to the interests of the educated groups when interests in prosperity, success and competitiveness complicated rather than supported aspects of socio-economic positioning. Often such concerns were exacerbated by stories reported in journalists' accounts of Pentecostal pastors who ran into problems with the authorities, families and church boards over cases of the embezzlement of church funds, illegal economic activities or the exploitation of their members. A commentary in the highly esteemed and opinionated *Sunday Standard* in Botswana recently voiced this concern in an article entitled 'Churches should get their houses in order or they should stop claiming the moral high ground', by complaining:

> There is no doubt as a nation we have lost our collective moral compass and jackals calling themselves religious leaders are having a field day as they feed on us taking advantage of our hopelessness and helplessness.
> ...
> ... the genuine Christian leaders in this country are ever getting few in numbers such that it may be time we declare them an endangered species. (*Sunday Standard*, 19–1–2014, accessed online 9–4–2014)

Another and earlier commentary in the same newspaper, entitled 'Gospel of Prosperity now main theme in many churches',' posed critical questions to its informed readership by asking:

> "Are the lures of riches, greed, power and dominion over individuals the pull factors to the gospel of prosperity in churches? What has happened to the conventional churches, have they failed to give the bona fide word hence their decline and the popularity of the new denominations?" (N. Dzimiri, *Sunday Standard*, 05–03–2012, accessed online 9–4–2014)

It is important to understand that the educated are basically not voicing concerns about the immanent nature of the Pentecostal faith as such, but with the way the this-worldly orientation has become personalized. The couple mentioned above assured me that they 'didn't have a problem with God', only with the manner in which the church was making itself relevant in their immediate day-to-day affairs. They hastened to emphasize that they had not lost faith or turned away from their belief in how close the relationship is between the heavenly powers and their immediate circumstances, and also how much divine guidance they still perceive in the market, in private enterprise, in progress and in prosperity. For such members of the educated classes there is an apparent concern that the current Pentecostal refraction of all the intricate inter-linkages around the leadership is too particular, demanding and too highly invested in the sole authority of a Pentecostal leader.

It is certainly relevant that many of the influential Pentecostal churches being considered here are of the 'one-man' type, with the leader-founder of the church taking a position of highly personalized power by making benevolent heavenly forces available to his followers. There are important African cosmological notions regarding why and how this mediating power of Pentecostal leaders has become so closely tied to their persons and their identities. The personal biography of the leader is often reflected in the biography of the church and even in the personal biographies of his followers, with members directly attributing their success in business, relationships and childbirth to the (spiritual) interventions of these 'men of God'. Belief is personalized and involves a direct, intense and often emotional relationship with the leader, allowing him or her to have an important say in people's private, personal affairs. The questioning of Pentecostalism by some of the educated classes that can be witnessed is part of a new phase that is critically engaging with such aspects of personalized faith. The 'too-muchness' that some of these members are voicing is a too-muchness of spiritual mediation. Leaders are using every opportunity to stress how they themselves also faced challenges and how their success never came easily. Religious roads to progress and prosperity are thus commonly defined as a personalized uphill battle, a struggle in which little can be expected in terms of help or support from government or development agencies, but where the personalized power of the leader can create particular access to a better future. Such reasoning drives home an individualizing perspective of success and failure through the presentation of a particular (religious) subjectivity; faith does indeed provide opportunities for strengthening a pro-active confidence in one's own skills and competences. Yet for some of the educated the faith has lost its particular appeal, as it is precisely the leaders' personalized nature in providing 'breakthroughs' in access to prosperity and progress that is identified as the real problem. Their critical sentiments about religious leadership now seem vexed also, and it is in questioning this that they are creating a new phase in the shaping of Pentecostalism in Africa.

Where are these people going? In terms of social pressure, there are few options in places such as Ghana and Botswana to indicate that one has left any form of institutionalized religion. A secularized model of personal identity in the way Taylor formulates it is difficult, questionable and socially unacceptable. There is little incentive for people turning away from Pentecostalism to join the mainline and mission churches, nor to join the African Independent Churches. In addition to its spirituality, church membership also remains important for life-crisis moments (births, deaths, marriages, illness, misfortune), and resources are often too limited just to do away with the forms of support that can be mustered at such times. Hence, while this inchoate space is not the same as what Taylor saw emerging as a dark space of the total embrace of an immanent life-orientation (because a this-worldly orientation has been a large part of their faith already), it is a space that for some is increasingly informed by what can be called 'generalized' religion. The point of this space is that the highly personalized, mediated and almost idiosyncratic manifestations of religious authority and power, which are so much part of the figure of the Pentecostal leader, have become questioned if not rejected. The guiding sentiments that we can see emerging in this process of separation are those in which the personalized charismatic nature of beliefs and power are being critiqued. While these persons generally still accept prayer and Bible readings on public occasions, and find them relevant and morally justified, they often voice issues with such 'charisma'. To invoke Weber here, it seems that the disenchantment of personalism is what particularly attracts them in the critique of their (former) leaders and the latter's omnipresence.

4 Conclusion: Multiple Secularities after Pentecostalism?

In conclusion, this chapter has been arguing that, unlike studies such as those of Morier-Genoud (2007) and Loimeier (1996) on the rise of secularism in Sub-Saharan Africa, no singular, monolithic notion of secularization is possible. Studying the manner in which an inchoate domain appears to be emerging for members of the educated classes who are questioning the Pentecostal churches and leadership seems to confirm the notion that there is a multiplicity of roads to secularization that distinguishes the rise of different public spaces, as Wohlrab-Sahr and Burchardt also indicate (2012). The kind of secularization that appears to be unfolding with a turning away from an otherwise intellectualist Pentecostalism is particularist in its origins and its manifestations. Much less cloaked in a Taylorian notion of the darkness of a full embrace of the immanent, what is unfolding here is a guiding sentiment that wants to do away with a particular and pervasive form of personalism in religious and moral authority. This is not a hegemony of faith but a hegemony of spiritual *dividualism* in which the personalized spiritual, moral and intellectual power is threatening to become overpowering and 'too much'. The kind of secularization that sees an emergent state of differentiation between the religious and the non-religious and the decline of the significance of religious adherence, described here as in the state of 'becoming', take issue not only with the idea that 'Africans are notoriously religious' (cf. Mbiti), but also with the European-centred notion that 'religion is back' in a post-secular world (see Nye 2000; Thomas 2005).

On both accounts these views would presuppose the impossibility of these forms of secularization taking place in Africa, as they should be viewed as being fundamentally 'un-African'. The point, however, is that for a de-centred notion of the process – that is, a notion whereby Western preconceptions of the term are balanced and negotiated by other (intellectual) sources responding to other cultural epistemologies (see Habermas 2005 for a similar point) – these can only emerge if a de-centered understanding of modernity is rendered valuable in the African context, a modernity that is and remains deeply religious. This is not a contradiction in terms, nor does it involve confirming the preconceived idea of Africans being notoriously religious, as it calls for a cultural and situated understanding of secularism as producing locally informed notions of a separation between different (religious) domains. Turning away from charismatic personalism in one's faith can thus be as much a secularist development as turning away from organized religion and its institutions.

Bibliogaphy

Akoko, Robert Mbe 2007. *"Ask and you shall be given": Pentecostalism and Economic Crisis in Cameroon*, vol. 2. Leiden: African Studies Centre, African Studies Collection.
Atherton, John R., Elaine Graham and Ian Steedman, eds. 2011. *The Practices of Happiness: Political Economy, Religion and Wellbeing*. Abingdon: Routledge.
Beaumont, Justin and Chistopher Baker, eds. 2011. *Postsecular Cities: Space, Theory and Practice*. London and New York: Continuum.
Berger, Peter, Grace Davie and Effie Fokas, E. 2008. *Religious America, Secular Europe? A Theme and Variations*. Aldershot: Ashgate.
Bochow, Astrid 2008. "Valentine's day in Ghana: youth, sex and secrets," in *Generations in Africa: Connections and Conflicts*, eds. E. Alber, S. van der Geest, and S. Reynolds Whyte, 333–357. Berlin, Lit Verlag.
Bochow, Astrid and Rijk van Dijk. 2012. "Christian creations of new spaces of sexuality, reproduction, and relationships in Africa: exploring faith and religious heterotopia." *Journal of Religion in Africa* 42 (4): 325–344.
Burchardt, Marian 2011. "Challenging Pentecostal moralism: erotic geographies, religion and sexual practices among township youth in Cape Town." *Culture, Health and Sexuality* 13 (6): 669–83.
Burchardt, Marian, Monika Wohlrab-Sahr, and Ute Wegert. 2013. "'Multiple secularities': postcolonial variations and guiding ideas in India and South Africa." *International Sociology* 28(6): 612–628.
Casanova, José 1994. *Public Religions in the Modern World*. Chicago: The University of Chicago Press.
—. 2008. "Public religions revisited," in *Religion: Beyond a Concept*, ed. H. de Vries, 101–119. New York: Fordham University Press.
—. 2011. "The Secular, secularizations, secularisms," in *Rethinking Secularism*, eds. Craig Calhoun, Mark Juergensmeyer and Jonathan VanAntwerpen, 54–74. New York: Oxford University Press.
Comaroff, Jean and John Comaroff. 1997. *Of Revelation and Revolution. Volume Two: The Dialectics of Modernity on a South African Frontier*. Chicago: The University of Chicago Press.
—. 2000. "Privatizing the millennium: new protestant ethics and the spirits of capitalism in Africa, and elsewhere." *Afrika Spectrum* 35 (3): 293–312.
—. 2001. "Millennial capitalism: first thoughts on a second coming," in *Millennial Capitalism and the Culture of Neoliberalism*, eds. J. Comaroff and J. Comaroff, 1–56. Duke University Press.
De Witte, Marleen 2011. "Fans and followers: marketing charisma, making religious celebrity in Ghana." *Australian Religion Studies Review* 24 (3): 231–253.
Engelke, Matthew 2010. "Past Pentecostalism: notes on rupture, realignment, and everyday life in Pentecostal and African independent churches." *Africa* 80 (2): 177–199.
Englund, Harri 2003. "Christian independency and global membership: Pentecostal extraversions in Malawi." *Journal of Religion in Africa* 33 (1): 83–111.
Frahm-Arp, Maria 2012. "Singleness, sexuality and the dream of marriage." *Journal of Religion in Africa* 42 (4): 369–383.

Freeman, Dana, ed. 2012. *Pentecostalism and Development: Churches, NGOs and Social Change in Africa*. Basingstoke: Palgrave/Macmillan.

Gifford, Paul 2004. *Ghana's New Christianity: Pentecostalism in a Globalising African Economy*. London: Hurst.

Gusman, Alessandro 2009. "HIV/AIDS, Pentecostal churches, and the 'Joseph Generation' in Uganda." *Africa Today* 56 (1): 67–89.

Habermas, Jürgen 2005. "Equal treatment of cultures and the limits of postmodern liberalism." *Journal of Political Philosophy* 13 (1): 1–28.

Hurd, Elizabeth Shakman 2007. "'a secular age': the slipstream of disenchantment and the place of fullness." SSRC The Immanent Frame, posted 29 October 2007.

—. 2008. Review. "A secular age by Charles Taylor." *Political Theory* 36 (3): 486–491.

Laguda, Danoye Oguntola 2013. "Religious pluralism and secularization in the Nigerian religious sphere," in eds. Afe Adogame, Bolaji Bateye and Esra Chitando, 25–35. *African Traditions in the Study of Religion, Diaspora and Gendered Societies*. Farnham: Ashgate.

Lauterbach, Karen 2010. "Becoming a pastor: youth and social aspirations in Ghana." *Young* 18 (3): 259–278.

Leatt, Annie 2007. "Faithfully secular: secularism and south African political life." *Journal for the Study of Religion* 20 (2): 29–44.

Loimeier, Roman 1996. "The secular state and Islam in Senegal," in *Questioning the Secular State* ed. David Westerlund, 183–197. New York: St. Martin Press.

Maxwell, David 1998. "'Delivered from the spirit of poverty?': Pentecostalism, prosperity and modernity in Zimbabwe." *Journal of Religion in Africa* 28 (3): 350–373.

Mbiti, John S. 1969. *African Religions and Philosophy*. London: Heinemann.

Meyer, Birgit 1998. "'Make a complete break with the past'. Memory and Postcolonial modernity in Ghanaian discourse." *Journal of Religion in Africa*, 28 (3): 316–349.

—. 2004. "'Praise the Lord'. Popular cinema and the Pentecostalite style in Ghana's new public sphere." *American Ethnologist* 31 (1): 92–110.

—. 2012. "Religious and secular, 'spiritual' and 'physical' in Ghana," in *What Matters? Ethnographies of Value in a not so Secular Age*, eds. Courtney Bender and Ann Taves, 86–118. New York, Columbia University Press.

Molendijk, Arie L., Justin Beaumont, and Chistoph Jedan, eds. 2010. *Exploring the Postsecular: The Religious, the Political and the Urban*, Leiden: Brill.

Morier-Genoud, Eric 2007. "A prospect of secularization? Muslims and political power in Mozambique today." *Journal for Islamic Studies* 27: 240–275.

Nye, Malory 2000. "Religion, post-religionism, and religioning: religious studies and contemporary cultural debates." *Method and Theory in the Study of Religion* 12: 447–476.

Olivier de Sardan, Jean-Pierre. 1992. "Occultism and the ethnographic 'I'. the exoticising of magic from Durkheim to postmodern anthropology." *Critique of Anthropology* 12: 5–25.

Ojo, Matthew A. 1998. "Sexuality, marriage and piety among Nigerian charismatic movements," in *Rites of Passage in Contemporary Africa*, ed. J. L. Cox, 180–197. Cardiff: Cardiff Academic Press.

Pfeiffer, James 2005. "Commodity 'Fetichismo,' the Holy Spirit, and the turn to Pentecostal and African independent churches in central Mozambique." *Culture, Medicine and Psychiatry* 29 (3): 255–283.

Prince, Ruth, Philippe Denis, and Rijk van Dijk 2009. "Engaging Christianities: negotiating HIV/AIDS, health, and social relations in east and southern Africa. introduction to the special issue." *Africa Today* 56 (1): v–xviii.

Pype, Katrien 2009. "'We need to open up the country': Development and the Christian Key-scenario in the social space of Kinshasa's Teleserials." *Journal of African Media Studies* 1 (1): 101–115.

Ricoeur, Paul 1967. *The Symbolism of Evil*. Boston: Beacon Press.

Sadgrove, Jo 2007. "'Keeping up appearances': sex and religion amongst university students in Uganda. *Journal of Religion in Africa* 37 (1): 116–144.

Smith, Daniel Jordan 2001. "'The Arrow of God': Pentecostalism, inequality, and the supernatural in south-eastern Nigeria." *Africa* 71 (4): 587–613.

Swidler, Ann 2010. "The return of the sacred: what African chiefs teach us about secularization." *Sociology of Religion* 71 (2): 157–171.

Taylor, Charles 2007. *A Secular Age*, Cambridge, MA, and London: Harvard University Press.

Thomas, Scott M. 2005. *The Global Resurgence of Religion and the Transformation of International Relations*. New York: Palgrave Macmillan.

Van de Kamp, Linda 2012. "Afro-Brazilian Pentecostal re-formations of relationships across two generations of Mozambican women." *Journal of Religion in Africa* 42 (4): 433–452.

Van de Kamp, Linda and Rijk van Dijk. 2010. "Pentecostals moving south-south: Brazilian and Ghanaian transnationalism in southern Africa compared," in *Religion Crossing Boundaries: Transnational Religious and Social Dynamics in Africa and the New African Diaspora*, eds. Afe Adogame and James Spickard, 123–143. Leiden, Brill.

Van der Veer, Peter, ed. 1995. *Conversion to Modernities: The Globalization of Christianity*. New York: Routledge.

Van Dijk, Rijk 1992. "Young puritan preachers in post-independent Malawi." *Africa* 62 (2): 159–182.

—. 1997. "From camp to encompassment: discourses of transsubjectivity in the Ghanaian Pentecostal diaspora. *Journal of Religion in Africa* 27 (2): 135–169.

—. 1998. Pentecostalism, cultural memory and the state: contested representations of time in postcolonial Malawi," in *Memory and the Postcolony: African Anthropology and the Critique of Power*, ed. Richard Werbner, 155–182. London: Zed Books.

—. 2001. "Contesting silence: the ban on drumming and the musical politics of Pentecostalism in Ghana." *Religion in the Fourth Republic, Ghana Studies* 4: 31–64.

—. 2003. "Localisation, Ghanaian Pentecostalism and the stranger's beauty in Botswana." *Africa* 73 (4): 560–583.

—. 2004. "'Beyond the rivers of Ethiopia': Pentecostal Pan-Africanism and Ghanaian identities in the transnational domain," in: *Situating Globality: African Agency in the Appropriation of Global Culture*, eds. Wim M.J. van Binsbergen and R.A. van Dijk, 163–190. Leiden, Brill.

—. 2009. "Social catapulting and the spirit of entrepreneurialism: migrants, privateinitiative, and the Pentecostal ethic in Botswana," in *Traveling Spirits: Migrants, Markets and Mobilities*, eds. Gertrud Hüwelmeier and Kristine Krause, 101–118. New York: Routledge.

Wohlrab-Sahr, Monika and Marian Burchardt. 2012. "Multiple secularities: toward a cultural sociology of secular modernities." *Comparative Sociology* 11 (6): 875–909.

Part V: **The Sacred Secular:
Secularities in post-Communist Central
and Eastern Europe**

Alexander Agadjanian
Vulnerable Post-Soviet Secularities: Patterns and Dynamics in Russia and Beyond

In this chapter I look at the post-Soviet area as a vast space in which religion and secularity interact, conflict, negotiate, and create a variety of particular syncretic forms. These forms of secular-religious divide differ considerably in a number of ways, which call for the creation of a typology, and yet the whole space has a common (Russian imperial and Soviet) legacy, which provides a convenient basis for comparison. My central focus and priority will be Russia, with a few variations within it. Three Caucasian nations – Armenia, Azerbaijan and Georgia – come next as sources for my reflections here. Ukraine provides a special and inescapably important model, though in this case I will draw on secondary sources only. Other societies will be briefly mentioned for comparative purposes.

What exactly is the object of this inquiry? 'Secularity' is a central notion here. In my understanding, in which I follow Charles Taylor (2007), secularity is a special constellation of epistemic, cultural and social patterns that emerged in western Christian contexts and then spread globally. The key building-blocks of the 'secular age' are self-sufficient 'exclusive humanism,' the 'immanent frame' and instrumentalized, optional religiosity.[1] Upon these foundational cultural codes, a congruent type of societal and political arrangement was described by the classics of secularization theory in the twentieth century.

However, recent mutations in the academic studies of modernity in general and of modern developments in religion in particular have made 'secularity' as such a separate and central object of inquiry. The main trend in understanding this object is that secularity – in whatever conceptual sense – is now seen as being less strong, less universal and less tightly linked to modernity than it was before.

"Secularity" did not disappear or dissolve – on the contrary, it became conceptually articulated for the first time, in a way being discovered as a separate concept with its own separate, distinctive signifier. But simultaneously, secularity, as both practice and a concept, acquired a certain *vulnerability*. Secularity became vulnerable because of the growing pressure of religion's public visibility

---

[1] See Taylor, 2007, *passim* on exclusive humanism; on the notion of an immanent frame, Chapter 10 and especially Chapter 15; on forms of religiosity, Chapter 14.

and claims in many parts of the world, because of the increasing references to the sacred origins of ethnic and national solidarities, and because of the more frequent use of religious codes in internal and international politics worldwide. The principles that certainly dominated in the heyday of the 'secular age' in the mid-twentieth century have increasingly come under pressure, though to different extents, in both non-western and western societies. This new condition of vulnerability revealed itself in the fact that the very *notion* of secularity came under question, as reflected in the emergence and popularity of such concepts such as de-secularization and the post-secular.[2]

What is now becoming necessary is to examine this new condition of 'vulnerable secularity' empirically in all its aspects: its public image and perceptions; its reflection in public debates and everyday interactions; the social groups and actors that stand both behind it and against it; its particular dynamics; and its multiple interactions with religious regimes, traditions and communities. In this chapter, however, my focus will be mostly on the dynamic of the institutional regimes of secularity, including its constitutional, legal and real-political operationalization, as well as the societal responses to it. Such a focus is justified by the fact that the post-Soviet period has been a time of huge institutional reconstruction and nation-building, which largely defined all other aspects of social and cultural life.

Speaking of a vast and diverse area such as the former Soviet Union makes one sensitive to comparative analysis; for even if a general trend may seem common, the particular dynamic and forms strongly differ. Conceptually, these differences can be situated at the intersection of a functional typology of secularities, as, for example, suggested by Monika Wohlrab-Sahr and Marian Burchardt (2012), or the grid of variables that David Martin calls 'historical filters' that have defined, directed and reinterpreted particular forms of secularity, that is, arrangements of the religion/secular divide, in various societies (see Martin 2005: 58 and passim; 2011).[3]

The very fact of the dissolution of the Soviet, radically atheistic empire was one of those historical events, along with a number of similar changes recorded in other parts of the world (Muslim Arab societies and Iran, Turkey, India, Israel, Latin America...but also the West), which made secularity – real and conceptual – vulnerable globally. De-secularization and the emergence of an uncertain post-

---

[2] The 'de-secularization' was coined by Peter Berger (2000). The term 'postsecular' came into vogue after a few publications, besides Taylor's already referred to, following Jürgen Habermas (2002, 2005a, 2005b, 2009).
[3] Wohlrab-Sahr and Burchardt give a useful overview of existing typologies of secularity, linked to various 'paths of secularization' (2012: 9–10).

secular condition seemed obvious in all post-Soviet lands; yet the real content of these processes has rarely been subject to special study.[4] As we shall see, however, this obvious emancipation and growth in religious agency after the end of the official 'scientific atheism' took different shapes across nations and – which is even more important to emphasize – coexisted, to various degrees, with another, opposite process of the consolidation of secularity (in its western ideal-typical version) and the emergence of unsteady hybrid phenomena where the borders between revived religion and reinterpreted secularity became porous and movable. If, in some cases, de-secularization indeed seemed an obvious and tangible societal trend, in other cases, behind the external appearances of de-secularization, we were able to witness the opposite: secularity, in a new backlash, endures, develops and grows ripe, while religion itself, visible in all its resurgence, acquires a new sense of fragility, fighting for public space, responding to strong criticism and resisting transformative pressures from social and global mutations.

A few other variables strongly define the ways in which secularity operates in these societies. One is *longue durée* historical trends – partly reminiscent of Martin's 'historical filters' (2005) and Casanova's types of confessionalization (2008, 2009) – of how religious traditions have been imbedded into political and cultural regimes in particular territories, which depended considerably on both a general course of history and the specific doctrinal and practical dispositions of each dominant religious tradition. Another strong variable shaping secularity was a degree of long-term religious diversity within a particular territory. A type of political regime, the level of international commitments (with Europe as a reference point for such commitments, in all post-Soviet cases), and the structure of geopolitical pressures must be taken as important variables as well. Finally, the old imperial, now post-colonial relationships between various spaces, nations and cultures within the former Soviet Union define the differences on how religion and secularity have been perceived and thematized.[5]

---

[4] For an attempt at conceptualization and application to the post-Soviet case see: Viacheslav Karpov (2010).
[5] For a recent treatment of the Soviet legacy, see K. Rousselet (2013). According to Rousselet, the use of religion as a quasi-ideology in post-Soviet Russia paradoxically follows the Soviet pattern of the use of official atheism. This 'continuity' explanation, however interesting, differs from my own interpretation in this chapter.

1 Soviet and Imperial Legacies of Secularization: What Was and What Is Special Here?

Any analysis of post-Soviet regimes of secularity must start with the Soviet legacy. All post-Soviet states inherited a strong tradition of rigid 'secularity' irrespective of the dominant confession in various parts of the empire. This tradition was forged by the atheistic cosmos imposed by the Soviet Union, which became ingrained in the experience and mentality of several generations. Yet, to assess this legacy, we should compare the Soviet type of secularity with contemporary patterns in other parts of the world.

The 'secular age' emerged in the realm of western Latin Christianity, in the twentieth century, especially in the second half, even though the linearity of the process is now widely contested. There has been a discussion over how different or similar the 'forced' secularization of the Soviet Union was in comparison to 'softer' western forms, how deep was the impact of Soviet official atheism on everyday socio-cultural practices, and how uniform this official secularity was in various parts of the Soviet empire.[6]

Recent studies of Soviet history show that all religions evolved in a few similar directions, either going underground, acquiring a self-isolated, 'catacomb' and world-renouncing flavor, or, in its second version, possibly adapting itself to the dominant and rigid 'secular' context. In this sense, religious institutions were 'secularized from within' and assigned politically controlled ghetto-like spaces (niches or enclaves) within society; or, in another, third version, religion were de-institutionalized and displaced into the realm of considerably reduced, simplified, private practices. Atheism was affirmed as a default political and cultural posture, firmly grounded in the Marxist idiom of immanent causality and taken-for-granted materialism.

This picture may partly recall some elements that can be also found in the twentieth-century western context. Indeed, as the Soviet Union was a radical modernization project (see Arnason 2000), it seems to have included those major trends – urbanization, industrial growth, scientific progress etc. – that were generally considered as promoting secularization in western societies. The rhetoric of 'human flourishing' (in spite of the century's material hardships)

---

[6] This theme was central to a conference held in Moscow in February 2012 entitled 'Lived religion in the USSR: survival and resistance under forced secularization' (Russian State University for the Humanities, 16–18 February, 2012); about twenty papers from that conference were published in the special issue of the Russian language quarterly *Gosudarstvo, religiia, tserkov' v Rossii i za rubezhom*, Vol. 30: 3–4 (2012); see also S. Luehrmann (2011); C. Wanner (2012).

and 'immanent objectivity' – to allude again to Taylorian idioms – was indeed central and deeply interiorized. The privatization of religion, found in the west and seen as a major aspect of secularization, was also clearly typical of the Soviet society: in both cases the crisis of religious institutions as public entities became a major trend, although in various degrees. The quantitative trend towards the decline of these institutions in the Soviet Union throughout the twentieth century was quite telling and not dissimilar to the pan-European decrease of religious practices (putting the 'American exception' aside at this point), especially in the post-WWII period. In the Soviet Union this progressive secularity formed part of two massive waves of modernization, in the 1930s and the 1960s, with an unprecedented speed of urbanization in both cases. A part of the process was the sweeping growth of secular mass education that included scientific atheism as one its major constituents. These were compressed forms of those trends that the west passed through over a much longer period of time.

At the same time, there were clear differences: the ideologically grounded anti-religious policy of the Soviet Union excluded such discourses as 'pluralism,' 'neutrality' or 'accommodation', which accompanied the development of secular regimes in the west (within a spectrum of varying secular rigidity). 'Religious freedom' was more or less a decorative norm, while it was clearly enforced in the west, although with various emphases. An 'adaptation' of religious traditions in line with modern societal trends was out of question, and the adaptive mechanisms of religious institutions were largely paralyzed. The transmission of religious knowledge (including sacred texts) by the media was rare, making religious awareness either non-existent or dependent on secondary, indirect and fragmentary sources. Religious symbolic references, which survived in non-communist Europe, were largely muffled and became relatively insignificant for a few generations in the Soviet Union. The dispersed, privatized forms of religion might be found in both Europe and Soviet Union, but 'catacombs' and forced 'ghettos,' typical of the Soviet context, did not exist in Europe. The atheistic celebration of human potential ('Man' and 'Mankind' in the most general terms), along with the radical Enlightenment tradition, was in fact part of a system of the oppression of particular individuals and thus hindered individuation, including the individuation of religiosity (which is not the same as the privatization mentioned earlier). Overall, even though the Soviet type of 'secularism' can be placed within a grid of existing typologies,[7] it seems to have been a *sui generis*

---

[7] In typological terms, the Soviet type of secularism is close to what Wohlrab-Sahr and Burhardt called 'secularism for the sake of social integration and national development,' with the guiding idea of 'progress' – a particular type in their typology: see Wohlrab-Sahr and Burhardt (2012: 16).

phenomenon that cannot be considered separately from the overarching system of highly *sacralized* ideological hegemony, which was deeply *non-religious* but also – however strange it may sound – deeply *un-secular* in its character.

Some important mutations in the late Soviet period led to a muffled echo of the western developments, namely, the personalistic revolution of the 1960s and the rise of spiritual quests in the 1970s and 1980s. The result of this impact, superimposed on the complex internal evolution of Soviet society, was a weakening of state atheism's militancy and a certain increase of free space in individual life-worlds, which could now include a certain degree of either idiosyncratic, personalized religiosity or a non-atheistic, but rather agnostic or relativistic skepticism.

Another major Soviet legacy was the nationalization of religion. Structured as a multiethnic and multinational empire, the Soviet Union was a crucible of strong ethnic and national identities (in spite of the rhetoric of internationalism that failed to produce a durable meta-ethnic 'Soviet nationality' [Suny 2001]). The ripening of these identities, along with growing centripetal tensions, took place in the same period of the 1970s and 1980s.[8] In most cases religion was objectified as a brace and a marker of ethnicity and/or nationality, reinforcing and sacralizing the existing frame of linguistic, genealogical, territorial and institutional quasi-autonomy (even though such autonomy was partly imagined). The controlled national religions, operating in a ghetto-like mode, were increasingly used as a symbolic reference capturing the 'collective consciousness' of ethnonations. Interestingly, Russian Orthodoxy became such a reference for ethnic Russians, who dominated in the empire, in the similar way as, in colonial peripheries, the Roman Catholic Church worked for Lithuanians, the Georgian Orthodox Church for Georgians, the Armenian Apostolic Church for Armenians, Islam for Muslim communities within and outside Russia, etc. The emergence of religiously informed nationalisms after the break-up of the Soviet Union was a logical effect of this earlier latent development.

2 Post-Soviet Construction of Vulnerable Secularity amidst Religious Resurgence

As atheism ceased to be a 'sacral' norm, religion has definitely come back into public life, its presence constantly growing throughout the 1990s and 2000s.

---

[8] For one of the best accounts of the paradox of the Soviet national dynamic, see: R. Brubaker (1994).

This was true and easily proved quantitatively for all regions of the former Soviet Union, but in various degrees and at various paces, from 'religiously cool' Latvia or Estonia to 'religiously hot' Georgia or Dagestan. But the de-sacralization of state atheism also led to the emergence of secularism of a 'western' type. Public debates and legislative work included attempts to comprehend and appropriate *this* type of secularism as a new notion and norm. We can say that the major development of this period was actually the formation or construction of secularism in the average western style – something that these societies have *never* truly experienced.

I will start with the relevant vocabulary that reflected this new quest. A direct loan equivalent of 'secularism', with the same Latin root (*sekuliarizm*, adj. *sekuliarnyi*), was not used in the Soviet Union, and although it has become widespread since, its use has mostly been limited to academic discourse. There is another, close but not identical, more widely used Russian term, *svetskii*, with a different semantic background, related to notions of 'public,' 'high society' (usually connoting the pre-Revolutionary elite culture). Etymologically *svetskii* comes from *svet*, 'world,' and has *this*-worldly overtones, similar to *weltlich, mundane (profane)*. Then, in the post-Soviet period, this overtone of the non-religious, temporal or mundane acquired greater weight and thus became an equivalent of *secular*, with a much wider circulation. In current Russian usage, the term *svetskii* may be compared with French *laïque* (or Spanish and Italian *laico)*, in juxtaposition to a less normative use of *séculaire (seculo)*.

In its current usage, the term *svetksii* is closely linked to the state, as in the expression *svetskoe gosudarstvo* [светское государство] (secular state, l'état laïque). The expression became a key rhetorical formula in the public discourse, especially after it was included in the Russian Constitution of 1993, Article 14, which reads: '1. The Russian Federation is a secular state. No religion can be established. 2. Religious associations are separate from the state and equal before the law.'

None of the four Soviet constitutions (1918, 1924, 1936 and 1976) used any term of this kind. However, they repeatedly confirmed (except the Constitution of 1924, which totally ignored the religious issue) the formula of separation: 'separation of church from state, and of school from church.' They also declared 'the right to observe religious cults' (1918 and 1936), later replaced with 'the freedom of conscience' (1977), and the right to anti-religious (atheistic) propaganda.[9]

---

9 An exception was the first constitution of 1918 that allowed *both* religious and anti-religious propaganda.

At first sight, the introduction of the term 'secular state' in the new post-Soviet constitution may be seen as continuation of the Soviet legacy of separation, though it definitely broke with the Soviet tradition of state atheism and worked more in the direction of affirming a new regime of 'European' secularity. The norm of the secularity of the state was a clear message of, first, appropriating an *average* European tradition (partly stimulated by what was required in Russia's commitment to the Council of Europe), and secondly as a response to the obvious growth in religious sensitivities and its public manifestations. Indeed, in Russia secularity was constitutionally introduced in a quite articulate way, amidst a visible growth of religious expressions of all kinds.

In a similar way, the term 'secular' was included in the constitution of Kazakhstan (1995): 'The Republic of Kazakhstan proclaims itself a democratic, secular (*zaiyrly* [зайырлы]), legal and social state whose highest values are the individual, his life, rights and freedoms' (Article 1). In Tajikistan the term 'secular' is also used in the constitutional definition of the state (Article 1, constitution of 1994).[10] In Azerbaijan, the principle of separation is clearly affirmed, although the term 'secular' (*dünyevi)* is used as an adjective related not to the state, but only to education (Articles 18.I. and 18.III, 1995 constitution). In Uzbekistan, the separation is no less clear, though a special term for secularity is not used (Article 61, constitution 1994). In Ukraine, the non-establishment clause of the 1996 Constitution is also strong; it reads: 'The church and religious organizations in Ukraine are separated from the state, and the school – from the church. No religion can be established' (part of Article 35). However, secularity was not cited as a particular quality of the state.[11]

The provision regarding secularity in the constitutional texts of other nations is muffled or at least less rigid. In Moldova, 'autonomy of religious cults' (rather than 'separation') is only briefly mentioned at the end of the article guaranteeing religious freedoms and is immediately followed by the promise of state support for 'cults' (Article 31.4; constitution of 1994). In the Belorussian constitution the idea of separation is not found, but 'equality' of religions is mentioned with the following stipulation, suggesting non-equality: 'Relationships of the state with religious organizations are regulated by law in accordance with their influence on the formation of the spiritual, cultural and state traditions of the Belorussian

---

10 These two constitutions, which give a multi-definition of the state, including its secularity, recall the French constitution of the Fifth Republic (1958), which starts with similar affirmation: 'La France est une République indivisible, laïque, démocratique et sociale.'

11 This Ukrainian clause reproduced almost literally the old Soviet formula of separation and refers to the 'church'– a clearly Christian allusion, sounding anachronistic – instead of the more neutral 'religion' used in other constitutional texts.

people' (Article 16). An even clearer move from neutrality to preferential treatment is made in the constitutions of Armenia and Georgia. In the former, the clear-cut statement of the separation principle is immediately followed by this: 'The Republic of Armenia recognizes the exclusive mission of the Armenian Apostolic Holy Church, as a national church, in the spiritual life of the Armenian people, in the development of their national culture and preservation of their national identity' (Article 8.1., Constitution of 1995). In Georgia, the 'religious' clause reads as follows: 'The state shall declare complete freedom of belief and religion, and it shall recognize the special role of the Apostolic Autocephalous Orthodox Church of Georgia in the history of Georgia and its independence from the state' (Article 9, Constitution of 1993). In both Armenia and Georgia the constitution refers to special arrangements between the leading church and the state. Such arrangements were introduced in Georgia in 2002 (the constitutional 'concordat') and in Armenia in 2007 (a special law regulating the status of the dominant church).

As we can see, there is a tension in few cases between the principle of secular neutrality (non-establishment) and non-interference on the one hand, and preferences for some religions on the other. What is interesting is that this tension, in terms of constitutional language, is absent in Muslim nations (I will later come back to this fact), while it is obvious in some nations with a Christian background, most openly, in Armenia and Georgia, and partly in Belarus and Moldova.

Although the Russian constitution strictly articulates secularity, the evolution of legislation and legal practice has made a similar tension obvious over the years. In a special law on religious associations (1997), a few historical religions were given preferences, and the Russian Orthodox Church was singled out as having played 'a special role' in 'the history of Russia, in shaping and developing its spirituality and culture.' Although this statement in the preamble to the law implied no direct legal consequences, it reflected the growing weight of the dominant confession in the national identity discourse. In many other instances, the constitutive role of Russian Orthodoxy as a bearer of national values became a widely recognized quasi-consensus.

This growing public acknowledgment of the 'national religion' narrative in Russia was accompanied by all sorts of processes indicating a religious resurgence. An increase in massive self-declared identification with various religions, mostly Orthodoxy, throughout 1990s and 2000s was a proven fact (Furman, and

Kaariainen 2000).¹² Religious institutions were given tax exemptions, they received huge amounts of real estate through processes of restitution, and the state collaborated in the building of new church structures in Moscow and other cities (Mitrokhin 2004). The Orthodox Patriarch became a prominent political figure in public ceremonies, and some local bishops acquired similar prominence in the provinces (see Knox 2009; Richters 2012). Mass-media coverage on state-controlled channels tended to be invariably sympathetic to the Church. A few court decisions in 2003–2012 punished anticlerical artistic expressions and tended to acquit Orthodox activists reacting to them. Some restrictive judgements against minority groups were issued by the courts. The ten-year long debate about the status of religion as a subject in schools resulted in a compromise introducing an option to teach religion, in most cases Orthodox Christianity, within the school curriculum. Theology was established as a certified educational standard in the universities. Finally, a new law was adopted in 2013 that introduced changes to the Penal Code and other statutes 'in order to counteract offences against religious convictions and feelings of citizens.'[13]

These developments made Russian secularism, so rigid in constitutional terms, very vulnerable indeed. We witnessed similar processes in Armenia and Georgia, where, unlike in Russia, this vulnerability was already obvious in the constitutions. In Russia, Georgia and Armenia, the dominant religion became a prominent political player and was given a number of privileges. A strong and politically instrumental mythology of the 'national church' emerged in these cases, supported by pervasive intellectual and media discourse, which could be characterized as constituting a clear de-secularization of the public sphere.

The case of Ukraine was significantly different. What made a difference was Ukraine's definite European orientation as an expression of its post-colonial distancing from Russia. Also important were the particular circumstances of its independence in 1991 and further evolution thereafter. But what was most significant in terms of religious development was Ukraine's initial religious plurality, partly connected to ethno-linguistic and regional diversity and resulting in a 'denominationalism' that José Casanova said was unique to Europe and recalled the American experience (Casanova 1998). A few competing Orthodox denominations (although different in size), a significant Greek Catholic community and the presence of various growing minorities (including a variety of Protestant

---

[12] All later surveys, national and international, showed increases in these indicators, though the growth stabilized in mid-2000s.
[13] The law was harshly criticized by human rights activists for introducing anti-defamation 'blasphemy' norms.

groups) made the narrative of a 'national religion' supported institutionally less relevant in this context. Attempts to create a 'national church' as part of a nation-building project in the early 1990s, the mid-2000s and right after the 2014 Maidan revolution were not persisted with and indeed were doomed to failure.[14] By the early 2010s, a general pro-Christian consensus in Ukraine went along with a downplaying of denominational identities and boundaries as a 'faintly articulated set of symbols, signs, holidays, customs, practices and fragments of historical memory...' (Yelensky 2010: 219).[15]

Under these circumstances, Ukraine seems to be closer to having a workable neutral secularism than Russia. Interestingly, this fact does not seem to contradict the significantly higher degree of vibrancy in religious life in Ukraine compared to Russia. What we can assume here is a spontaneous 'de-secularization' in terms of popular religious expression, coexisting and overlapping with the formation of 'secularism' as a political, normative and discursive regime.[16] Even the dramatic events of the 2014 revolution showed the obvious significance of the Church's presence, while the plural balance was preserved and major competing political forces clearly endorsed political secularism. The Ukrainian case therefore shows that secularity as an institutionalized societal condition does not necessarily imply a lower degree of religious vitality. This implies a possible distinction between a predominant 'de-secularism from above,' as in the Russian case, and 'de-secularism from below' or a combination of both, as in the case of Ukraine.[17]

In the 'Muslim' regions of the former Soviet Union (six independent states, as well as the inner Russian autonomies in the Volga region and North Caucasus), we might expect secularity coming under the strongest pressure. This would mean following the common assumption that secularity as a concept and as practice has no genealogical root in Muslim culture and, therefore, that the Soviet policy of forced secularism could not lead here to anything but temporary, artificial arrangements. The recent dynamics have shown, however, that the Russian imperial and Soviet legacy had profound effects in Muslim areas. A

---

14 Casanova writes that the failure to set up a 'national church' under Leonid Kravchuk in the 1990s was 'a fortuitous development of the greatest significance for the institutionalization of religious freedom and the development of the democratic system in Ukraine' (1998: 96).
15 The 2014 revolution made it clear that denominational borders do persist and reflect a deep cultural divide in the nation.
16 This version of secularism is close to what Wohlrab-Sahr and Burchardt called, in their typology, 'secularism for the sake of balancing/accommodating diversity' (Wohlrab-Sahr, and Burchardt 2012: 891).
17 For this distinction, applying the 'de-secularism from above' concept to Russia, see Karpov (2013).

few generations of secularized intellectual and political elites still define, in the early 21st century, the political culture and methods of governance, and this was clearly reflected in the constitutional norms cited above. Also, compared to the Christian churches, institutional centralization in Islam has traditionally been much weaker, and therefore religious agency was more dispersed. Islam was seen in terms of a cultural identity, in which capacity it was instrumentalized by governments who were otherwise trying to keep up with the secular constitutional frame and secular *Realpolitik*.

Yet, in spite of the non-religious inheritance of the political elites and wider social groups from the Soviet period, the religious resurgence in Muslim areas was nevertheless obvious, strongly stimulated by the growth of the global transnational Islamic revival. In a few places this resurgence was more visible than elsewhere, as, for example, in Dagestan, Chechnya, Tatarstan or Tajikistan. These governments, while giving credit to instrumentalized 'cultural Islam', have been vigilant and sometimes ruthless in keeping the radical Islamist groups under tight control, frequently using the rhetoric of 'religious extremism' and 'external influence' to isolate secessionist impulses (within Russia) or political opposition (in independent states) which might have used Islamic references. Overall, we can see here a similar contradictory picture: creating and maintain a thin, vulnerable secularity against a strong wave of desecularization.

3 The Limits of Religious Resurgence: Secularity Strikes Back

The post-Soviet resurgence of religious references in identity discourses, politics and social life might be mistaken for the end of the 'secular age.' In fact, however, the 1990s and 2000s witnessed a more complex, ambiguous process of developing and deepening secularity *in spite* of the rise in religion's public presence. The indices of practical religiosity show a temporary upsurge with a later slowing down in this period, achieving average European levels (with some variations within the area), and with a typical focus on life-cycle rituals rather than daily or weekly observances. Religiously motivated politics (confessional political parties, mass voting behavior and governmental decision-making) prove to have been insignificant. In the final analysis, religious loyalties have played only an auxiliary role in identity discourses and identity politics. Also importantly, traditional (and 'endemically' dominant) religious institutions themselves, thanks to the Soviet legacy of forced ghettoization and servitude, were hardly prepared for the new situation of religious freedom and legitimate public presence: they were not quite able to benefit from de-secularization, and they were not quite adapted even to a *preferential* type of religious freedom that de facto encouraged the privileges of major confessions. Also, a part of the mass media that shaped the general public mood, the globalized mass culture agents that were impacting on 'youth culture' and even public educational institutions combined the inherited basic atheistic attitudes of the Soviet era with liberal (secular) dispositions, which together tended to counteract religious revivals.

After all, the political regimes that have been established in post-Soviet Eurasia have been ambivalent towards most forms of explicit religious symbolism or religious agency. On the one hand, these regimes could not ignore the symbolic potential of religious identities as a source of meaningful mobilization. On the other hand, the political elites were cautious and even suspicious about this rising potential. Such caution and suspicion had various reasons. First of all, in all these states the political elites who managed to establish stable governance inherited a deeply non-religious mindset and habits. Secondly, these regimes were trying to fit – more or less formally or intentionally – the new requirements of the European normative and institutional framework of (secular) neutrality and pluralism. Thirdly, the authorities were bound to be *pragmatically* cautious in finding a possibly balanced management of religious diversity and thus somewhat downplaying the direct involvement of the most powerful religious agents. Fourthly, especially in Muslim areas (in the Central Asian nations and in Azerbaijan, as well as in Russia's Muslim regions), the rise in religious fervor has been seen, not without reason, as a source of political opposition, a channel of outside interference or a cause of general societal instability.

All the above explains why the obvious rise in the public visibility of religion in the post-Soviet lands has gone together with the maintenance and even the development or further refinement of secularity. In a sense, most of these societies (this also applies, although to a lesser extent, to the Baltic States, which became part of the European Union) have been developing a regime of secularity for the first time in their history (as noted earlier, the nature of Soviet ideological atheism was quite different). The formation of these new regimes of secularity have involved the development of a legal framework (starting with secular anti-establishment constitutional arrangements) and the adoption, to various degrees, of a pluralistic religious environment, partly stipulated by new international commitments. The restructuring of the religious field as a 'religious market,' with respective consumerist attitudes, in line with the emerging free market environment, has created a type of religious economy mostly suited to this new regime of secularism. Interesting enough, the secularist public discourse, downplayed by the obvious rise of public religion at an early stage, later gained momentum as a more vocal anti-clerical and anti-conservative position (often associated with liberal or leftist oppositions), leading to the exacerbation of direct clashes between secular and religious groups.

Russia has witnessed a relatively new trend – the growth of deliberate, articulated 'laicist' sentiments, especially since the early 2000s, after the transitional flux of its first post-Soviet decade. In spite of a generally favorable public image of 'religion' as such, in spite of the common 'pro-Orthodox consensus' and the reports of high approval ratings for the Church in surveys, some new groups and actors emerged who consciously resisted the rise of religion's public presence. It was clear that the Orthodox Church was their main target. These laicist sentiments were shared by a number of older sceptics with an atheistic background from the Soviet period, as well as a new generation of educated urbanites, mostly in liberal and scientific occupations, who created as their specific object of criticism the 'danger of clericalism.' In the public secularist discourse, religion has been clearly associated with clericalism, with a certain institutional interference of religious institutions into politics, education and culture – a mindset once sharply articulated by Richard Rorty, who equated his 'atheism' with 'anticlericalism' as a political rather than epistemological view, which sees the public claims of religious institutions as 'dangerous to the health of democracy' (Rorty2004).

From the early 2000s, these sentiments began to be shaped organizationally in groups such as the 'Moscow Atheistic Society', the 'Council of the Atheists of RuNet', the 'Russian Humanistic Society,' the 'Institute for the Freedom of Conscience,' the 'Russia Without Obscurantism' party, the 'Common Sense Foundation' (*Fond Zdravomyslie*), etc. Each of these groups was small, but their activities visible; the last of those listed above, for example, sponsored billboards in the big cities with the text of Article 14 of the constitution, affirming the principle of secularism and separation. Others organized various 'anticlerical' actions and workshops.

The most visible and widely mediated anticlerical activities happened to emerge in the sphere of the contemporary arts. A few exhibitions and performances directly targeted 'clericalization', such as the 'Beware: Religion!' exhibition in 2003, that became a *cause célèbre* in courts,[18] a few exhibits at galleries owned or directed by Marat Guelman, and some other cases. The case with the widest international resonance and deepest domestic impact was the provocative 'prayer' performance by the punk group *Pussy Riot* near the altar of the

---

18 See my analysis related to this case in A. Agadjanian (2006).

main Moscow cathedral of Christ the Savior in 2012.[19] The message of these actions was definitely anticlerical (something that was not at all relevant in the first post-Soviet decade), and these cases triggered a wider debate about basic freedoms, which involved many human rights actors and acquired political overtones. The notion of secularism became a part of the liberal agenda in general – first artistic, and then clearly political. We can say that de-secularization became associated with political neo-conservatism, allegedly represented by the Putin regime, and therefore the newly articulated secularist, laicist discourse strongly resonated in opposition movements during the electoral campaigns of 2011– 2012. Indeed, the 'sacrilegious' provocation of *Pussy Riot* contained a clearly political, oppositional message and should be interpreted in connection with these electoral campaigns.

Some highly visible actions also occurred in the scientific and university communities, starting with an open letter to the Russian president signed by ten prominent members of the Russian Academy of Sciences in 2007, in which they warned against 'a growing clericalization of Russian society, the penetration of the Church into all fields of public life.'[20] The main target of the letter was plans to introduce classes in the 'Foundation of Orthodox Culture' in public schools and the spread of theology curricula in the universities. In fact, the letter turned the issue into a heated public debate. In late 2012, a similar letter, with a similar anti-clerical agenda, was signed by a hundred members of the Academy (then spread widely across the Internet), triggering a scandal around the recently introduced chair of theology in one of the leading Moscow universities, the Moscow Institute of Technical Engineering. In both cases, the religious actors, including the Church hierarchy, reassured the public of their respect for secular arrangements in general, but criticising the 'flat, reduced' secularism of the academics. The issue of whether to retain theology in the university or remove it as a 'clerical influence' fed into rich public controversies about the very meaning of 'secular and religious values' and the boundaries between them, thus revealing once again the existence of strong, openly secularist sentiments, at least among the active intellectual and liberal arts elite. Similar anticlerical discourses emerged in Georgia and Armenia, predictably fewer in Ukraine for reasons outlined above.[21]

---

19 See a detailed analysis of the *Pussy Riot* case, in terms of post-secular shifts of secular–religious boudaries, in Uzlaner (2014).
20 First published in the *Novaia Gazeta* newspaper, 22.07.2007.
21 For the tension in Georgia between the secular and religious forces, in a case study of the conflict over the appropriation of cultural heritage, see Serrano (2010). It should be noted that in the Georgian case the reformist government of Mikhael Saakashvili from 2003–2012

In Muslim countries, where, as we have seen, governments engaged with loyal Muslim institutions and kept the rest of Islam at distance and under surveillance, the secularist idiom has had less space for unfolding. On the one hand, the authorities themselves were seen as maintaining secular restraint, rather than promoting the establishment of Islam. On the other hand, openly dissociating oneself from Islam and positioning oneself as completely 'secular' or 'non-religious' is, indeed, a less likely cultural pattern in Muslim societies.[22]

To take the example of Tajikistan, the Islamic Revival Party made up the core of anti-government forces during the civil war of 1992–1997, a war which ended in a peace agreement allowing the moderate Islamists to enter the ruling coalition. Yet, as noted previously, the 1994 constitution was clearly secular, and the ruling elite, while officially associating itself with Hanafi Sunni Islam, patronizing mosque construction and the translation of the Qur'an into Tajik, continued to screen off autonomous Muslim actors and launched a robust anti-hijab campaign in the late 2000s. By that time, the Islamic Revival Party, too, had become the legal, parliamentary opposition with a small electorate (7.7 % of vote in 2010). The common discourse sounded as if it were admitting the government-approved 'cultural Islam' of the absolute majority while rigidly curtailing any forms of, so to speak, 'religious Islam' that bore the potential of both spiritual and political opposition.[23] In this situation (in Tajikistan and other traditionally Muslim countries), when the state itself represents the agency of the secular, any distinct secular voice from 'civil society' is hardly imaginable. Yet, we do know some examples of direct and widely contested secularist demarches in these societies, such as the case of Rafik Tagi in Azerbaijan.[24]

---

was itself the most ardent champion of anti-clericalism but was bound by the continuing waves of de-secularization. In Armenia, the most prominent secularist voice has been the human rights activist Stepan Danielyan and his website 'Religions in Armenia', www.religions.am, which published reports criticizing existing legislation and educational policies for promoting the privileges of the Armenian Apostolic Church.

22 It should be noted that the peripheral Islam of the Turkic peoples of Central Asia, Azerbaijan and central Russia had never been as thick and intense as the Arabic or Persian Muslim traditions; the shaping of national identity in these lands in the nineteenth and early twentieth centuries took place under Russian and European secular intellectual impact. This identity pattern was reinforced by Soviet anti-religious policies. However, the later years of the Soviet Union and its aftermath turned Islam into an endemic, taken-for-granted cultural resource.

23 See Thibault 2013, where the author, drawing on anthropological study, registers various interpretations of how Muslim identity can be construed and politically instrumentalized.

24 Writer and journalist Rafik Tagi published a controversial 'Europe and us' article in 2006, in which he directly criticized Islam and the Prophet (Tagi 2006). He was condemned to death in a *fatwa* by a prominent Shi'a cleric, but also sentenced to jail for offending religion. In 2011, a few

In countries with a strong dominant confession, routinely supported by a majority of the population and more or less tacitly or openly patronized by the government, the forces and actors promoting secularity included another type of actor inclined to form a pragmatic alliance with the non-religious 'laicists' I described above, – namely, religious minorities. This seems to be a paradoxical, yet plausible alliance between religious and secular groups. For example, Protestant or Pentecostal communities have been major critics of the confessional hegemony of the Apostolic Church in Armenia and of the Orthodox Churches in Georgia and Russia. As 'religious freedom' has generally been identified with the rights of religious minorities, the latter were placed under the special monitoring of human rights agencies and the U.S. Department of State's annual International Religious Freedom reports. In most cases, the extent of the observance of minority rights was used as a measure of the efficiency of secular arrangements.

Russian legislation and legal practice were criticized for introducing restrictions on the activities of religious minorities and thus automatically creating privileges for the 'traditional religions' (see a detailed account in Fagan 2013). The freedoms of smaller groups and cults became an object of court litigation, and the defense of their rights was based on the constitutional separation principle. As the Russian Orthodox Church was unequivocally dominant and politically supported, even smaller 'traditional' religions might resist 'clericalization', as, for example, was the case in the support of some Muslim and Jewish groups for the anti-clerical letter of Academy members mentioned above. To be sure, the position of religious minorities could not be other than ambiguous: it would be nonsensical for them to support secularity as such, that is, as a cultural paradigm of the 'secular age' in the Taylorian sense. What they did support were the principles of state neutrality, pluralism and equal religious freedom, which are, however, the essential parts of secularity as such. This ambiguity is revealed, for example, in that, while welcoming the fact of the 'revived spiritual and moral influence of the [Orthodox] Church', the minorities became worried about the promotion of a mandatory 'Orthodox culture' course in public schools, and they called for the religious revival to be seen as a matter of free choice within the framework of the constitution, thus inevitably endorsing the model of a secular state (Musul'manskaia 2007).

As we have seen, besides the ambivalence of the ruling regimes and actors regarding the growing presence of religion and their cautious restraint in not ma-

---

years after his release from jail, he was murdered by radical Islamists. In a move of protest, a few younger intellectuals publicly denounced Islam.

nipulating religion beyond a certain controllable degree, we have seen that a few societal groups and movements have emerged who, for different reasons, consciously articulate their secularist attitudes or, at least, appeal to secularism as a neutral regime of proper regulation. All these forces taken together have created a specific, relatively recent trend, which is opposed to the wave of de-secularization that predominated in the aftermath of the Soviet Union.

4. Conclusions

In the post-Soviet lands, as in some other parts of the world, we are witnessing the growing visibility of religious sentiments and practices. Religious meanings and institutions are acquiring a growing profile as an autonomous segment in differentiated societies and in some cases are significantly challenging the stereotypical secular model of the state and the regime of pluralism. By contrast, the cognitive and normative idiom that buttressed the 'secular age' has acquired some fragility and vulnerability. At the same time, in many societies – both within post-Soviet Eurasia and beyond it – the culture of secularity, at least its political modus, continued to predominate. It is also true, however, that this culture of secularity had to adjust and modify itself within this new environment, and, in a way, it adopted some new forms and went through a new process of formation and consolidation. Secularity, so to speak, struck back and resisted the new trends.

I have shown that the nation-building process of the post-Soviet decades included, as its important constitutive part, the formation of the normative or institutional secularist framework of an average, 'imagined' European type. This was very different from the rigid, imposed atheistic 'secularity' of the Soviet period, although we have noted a continuity with Soviet patterns, in particular those predominant in political institutions. The formation of this new type of secularity coincided with the wave of religious growth, which thus made it exposed, from the very beginning, to strong de-secularizing pressures. Simultaneously, as we have seen, new institutionalized secular arrangements, have counteracted religious growth and posed certain limits to it. Both the deeply held, inherited irreligious habitus of the elites and a relatively thin veneer of mass religiosity provided a foundation for maintaining such limits. Moreover, even beyond the legal secular arrangements, a new wave of social activism appeared to contest the trend of de-secularization, especially when this trend was thematized as 'clericalism' and associated with authoritarian neo-conservative policies (most prominently, in the case of Putin's Russia).

In the face of such contradictive complexity, the conceptual frame of the 'post-secular' can be tested for its operability. This frame does not postulate the end of the 'secular age' – it does not presume that secularism vanishes in the same way as it once ascended. Rather, we need to speak of a reshaping of the borders and of the patterns of interaction between the 'religious' and the 'secular' as they were fixed and institutionalized in 'Westphalian' Europe and then in western-dominated international language and practices.

Bibliography

Agadjanian, Alexander. 2006. "The search for privacy and the return of a great narrative (religion in a post-communist society)." *Social Compass* 53: 169–184.

Arnason, Johann. 2000. "Communism and modernity." *Daedalus* vol. 129(4): 61–90.

Berger, Peter L., ed. 2000. *The De-Secularization of the World: Essays on the Resurgence of Religion in World* Politics. Washington, Grand Rapids: William B. Eerdmans.

Brubaker, Roger. 1994. "Nationhood and the national question in the Soviet Union and post-Soviet Eurasia: an institutionalist account." *Theory and Society*, Vol. 23, No. 1: 47–78.

Casanova, Jose. 1998. "Ethno-linguistic and religious pluralism and democratic construction in Ukraine," in *Post-Soviet Political Order: Conflict and State Building*, eds. B. Rabin and J. Snyder, 81–103. London and NY: Routledge.

——. 2008. "Public Religion Revisited," in *Religion: Beyond the Concept*, ed. Hent de Vries, 101–119. Fordham University Press.

——. 2009."The Secular and Secularisms." *Social Research* 76 (4): 1049–1066.

Fagan, Geraldine. 2013. *Believing in Russia: Religious Policy after Communism.* London & New York: Routledge.

Furman, Dmitry., and Kimmo Kaariainen. 2000. "'Religioznost' v Rossii v 1990-e gg," [Religiosity in Russia in 1990s] in: *Starye tserkvi, novye veruiushchie: religiia v massovom soznanii postsovetskoi Rossii.* [Old Churches, New Believers: Religion in the Mass Consciousness in Post-Soviet Russia], D. Furman, and K. Kaariainen, 7–47. St. Petersburg and Moscow: Letnii Sad.

Habermas, Jürgen. 2002. *Religion and Rationality: Essays on Reason, God, and Modernity* (edited and with an introduction by E. Mendieta). Cambridge, Mass., MIT Press.

——. 2005a. *Religion in the Public Sphere* (speech at the University of San Diego, 4 March 2005), www.sandiego.edu/pdf/pdf_library/.

——. 2005b *Zwischen Naturalismus und Religion: philosophische Aufsätze* (Frankfurt am Main, Suhrkamp).

——. 2009. *Europe: The Faltering Project.* London: Polity.

Karpov, Viacheslav. 2010. "Desecularization. A conceptual framework." *Journal of Church and State*, Vol. 52/2: 232–270.

——. 2013. "The social dynamics of Russia's desecularization." *Religion, State and Society*, Vol. 41 (3): 254–283.

Knox, Zoe. 2009. *Russian Society and the Orthodox Church: Religion in Russia after Communism.* London: Routledge.

Luehrmann, Sonja. 2011. *Secularism Soviet Style: Teaching Atheism and Religion in a Volga Republic*. Bloomington: Indiana University Press.
Martin, David. 2005. *On Secularization: Towards a Revised General Theory*, Aldershot et al.: Ashgate.
—. 2011. *The Future of Christianity: Reflections on Violence and Democracy, Religion and Secularization*, Farnham and Burlington: Ashgate.
Mitrokhin, Nikolai. 2004. *Russkaia pravoslavnaia tserkov': sovremennoe sostoianie I aktual'nye problemy*. [The Russian Orthodox Church: present-day situation and current problems]. Moscow: NLO.
Musul'manskaia obshchestvennost' podderzhala 'Pis'mo akademikov' ['Muslim public supported the 'Letter of Academy members'] record from 17/08/2007; at: SOVA-Center website: http://www.sova-center.ru/
Richters, Katja. 2012. *The Post-Soviet Russian Orthodox Church: Politics, Culture and Greater Russia*. London, Routledge.
Rorty, Richard 2004. "Anticlericalim and atheism," in *The Future of Religion*, ed. S. Zabala, 33. NY: Columbia University Press.
Rousselet, Kathy. 2013. "Sécularisation et orthodoxie dans la Russie contemporaine: pour une hypothèse continuiste?" *Questions de recherches*, #42, Paris: Centre d'études et de recherches internationals, http://www.sciencespo.fr/ceri/sites/sciencespo.fr.ceri/files/qdr42.pdf.
Serrano, Silvia. 2010. "From culture to cult: museum collections and religion in contemporary Georgian national discourse," in *Cultural Paradigms and Political Change in the Caucasus*, ed. N. Tsutsishvili, 275–292. LAP Lambert Academic Publishing.
Suny, Ronald. 2001. "The empire strikes out! Imperial Russia, 'national' identity, and theories of empire," in *A State of Nations: Empire and Nation-Making in the Age of Lenin and Stalin*, eds. R. Suny and T. Martin, 23–66. New York.
Tagi, Rafik. 2006. "Avropa və biz". *Turkhan's Blog. Independent News from Azerbaijan*. http://turkhan.wordpress.com/2011/08/24/rfq/ (Accesses on 10 May 2014).
Taylor, Charles. 2007. *A Secular Age*. Cambridge, MA, and London: The Belknap Press of Harvard University Press.
Thibault, Helene. 2013. "The secular and the religious in Tajikistan: contested political spaces." *Studies in Religions / Sciences Religieuses*, vol. 42 (2): 173–189.
Uzlaner, Dmitry. 2014. "The Pussy Riot Case and the pecularities of Russian post-secularism." *State, Religion and Church* 1(1): 23–58. Available at: srch.ranepa.ru
Wanner, Cathy, ed. 2012. *State Secularism and Lived Religion in Soviet Russia and Ukraine*, Washington, D.C.: Woodrow Wilson Center Press.
Wohlrab-Sahr, Monika, and Marian Burchardt. 2012. "Multiple secularities: toward a cultural sociology of secular modernities." *Comparative Sociology* Vol. 11 (875–909).
Yelensky, Victor. 2010. "Religiosity in Ukraine according to sociological surveys." *Religion, State and Society*, Vol. 38, No.3 (September 2010): 213–227.

Klaus Buchenau
Socialist Secularities:
The Diversity of a Universalist Model

Any analysis of secularities depends greatly on how we define religion. This chapter is not the place to discuss this long 'definitional history', but it is clear that broad definitions of religion leave little space for secularities. For strict functionalists in the tradition of Émile Durkheim, religion fulfills human needs such as the integration of society or the psychological comfort of the individual; since many of these functions never cease to exist, there will always be answer-producing systems which the functionalists can call religion. According to Durkheim, the understanding of the sacred may change, for example, from a notion of God to a belief in science. But the general dichotomy between the sacred and the profane, that is, between pure and impure things, is always re-established, since every society reaffirms its unity by referring to something sacred, understood as superior and absolute. 'Functionalist' religion can thus transform itself but never disappear, and any assumption about expanding or shrinking secularities would ultimately be meaningless. On the other hand, narrower ('substantialist') definitions which see a *belief in supernatural powers* as an essential feature of religion enable us to observe the decline and growth of such beliefs, and therefore shrinking or expanding secularities (Pollack 1995; Law 2011: 166, 169).

This statement may seem trivial, but in the present case it is not. The literature on socialist secularities is quite polarized when it comes to a judgment on how anti-religious the communists and their regimes really were, and large parts of this dissent can be explained by a lack of awareness about the various meanings of the word 'religion'. Analysts of the Soviet case are not divided along functionalist versus substantialist lines but between substantialism and 'stylism', that is, between those who think that *religion is tied to a notion of God* and those who *define religion through style*, such as a special fervor of belief, ritualization or the use of symbolic forms borrowed from the traditional religions.[1] Substantialists stress that Bolsheviks and Soviet communists always denied the existence of God and that their uses of religious forms in propaganda were mostly of a tactical nature (Plamper 2004; Schenk 2012). The 'stylists' such as

---

[1] In this vein, the contemporary Russian philosopher Michail Ryklin sees religion as 'something that fills human life with meaning and for which people are ready to bring any sacrifice' (Ryklin 2008: 46).

the Russian philosopher Nikolai Berdiaev (1937), on the other hand, depict phenomena such as Bolshevik inner-worldly messianism, intolerance of divergent opinions, intense belief in science and the personality cults around leaders like Lenin and Stalin as elements of 'communist religion'. The oldest theoretical paradigm the stylists can rely on is Eric Voegelin's concept of 'political religion' (Voegelin 1938).

The different understandings of religion influence not only our view of Soviet-style communism, but also of its aftermath. While supporters of the substantialist line frequently speak about a 'return of the sacred' or a 'religious renaissance', stylists point to continuities before and after 1989; for them, the massive return of traditional religious organizations into the public sphere is just another proof that in many socialist countries, no real secularization took place and that communism conserved religious forms which 'only' had to be re-filled with traditional religious content (Ryklin 2008: 44; Gabel 2005: 478).

For the purposes of this chapter, I am more inclined towards the substantialist interpretation – not because it is 'true', but because a narrow understanding of religion will help to create a clearer set of terms. Identifying the center of religion as a belief in supernatural realities does not necessarily mean denying all similarities between religious traditions and communism. The stylist interpretation, in my view, pre-determines the outcome of the investigation too much because from the very beginning it forces the investigator into a 'religionizing' view and terminology when talking about communism. This can easily lead to empirical misperceptions and to an a-priori repudiation of the insider perspective of those who suffered for their traditional religious faith under communist rule and who see communism simply as the opposite of everything they believe in.

As for my own terminology, I use 'secularity' to denote a *social space* where traditional religion is substantially weakened, no matter whether this state of affairs was brought about purposefully or by coincidence. By using the plural 'secularities', I wish to make clear that this space was not uniform in all socialist countries at all times but differed both in size and in its characteristics, depending on historical, cultural, political and other factors. In contrast, by 'secularism' I mean an *ideology* which aims to cleanse society of religion in the traditional sense. Since socialism has frequently been described as an aggressive form of secularism, I do not see much sense in repeating this narrative. For analytical reasons, I prefer the rather descriptive category of secularity, which may help in conducting a more open-minded inquiry into the reality of socialist societies.

1 Marxism and Religion

Socialist revolutions basically occurred in countries in which Karl Marx had not predicted they would – in fact, socialism became the official ideology for a number of developing countries where urbanization and industrialization were rather in their beginnings. Most socialist revolutions only partly arose from the 'classical Marxist' tensions between industrial urban workers and their capitalist bosses: in reality they were initiated by small revolutionary elites which hoped to circumvent the capitalist stage and transform basically agrarian, often colonial or half-colonial societies into industrialized ones. What these practical revolutionaries had in common with Marx's theory was their longing for social equality and their conviction that any society's future was in the natural sciences, in industry and urbanism. Where they differed sharply, though often unconsciously, was in the role of elites in the revolutionary process. For Marx this role was basically to promote processes which were in motion anyway, while for practical revolutionaries such as Lenin or Mao, the revolutionary party was the creator of a whole new world, assigned the task of transforming the rural masses into a completely new, modern but egalitarian type of society (Riesebrodt 2007: 86–88; Ignatow 2002: 146–148).

This difference between theoretical and practical Marxism is quite meaningful for the question of religion. For Marx, religion was simply false because it was idealism and not materialism. Marx considered his own work to be genuine science, capable of revealing the 'objective' rules of social development and of showing paths toward improvement – whereas religion, just like idealistic philosophy, represented the fog of man-made speculation. In addition, he saw religion as an instrument of the ruling bourgeoisie to keep the people calm, to make them accept exploitation. To Marx, religion was part of the 'false consciousness' which hindered people in understanding their real interests, but it was no more than that. Since Marx believed that consciousness was a mirror of social reality, it was reality which had to be changed in the first place. A successful revolution would thus destroy the injustices and frustrations which had produced religion. Finally religion would vanish, since people would no longer need consolation in a happy afterlife. Though Marx's (and especially his companion Friedrich Engels') work contains a lot of anti-religious criticism and polemics, this line of thought basically remained an auxiliary element subordinated to the main goal, which was a radically changed pattern of access to the means of production. Militant atheism as such was not at the center of the theory, and Marx occasionally even defended the freedom of consciousness (Boer 2012: 140–142; Gabel 2005: 73–75).

Marx's view *was* meaningful for some parts of socialist reality – on the basis of his theory, all European socialist régimes except for Albania considered traditional religion as belonging to the reactionary past but accepted religiosity as 'a matter for the individual', at least on the formal juridical level. Especially Tito's Yugoslav socialists stressed that true communists should not waste their energy by suppressing religion but rather concentrate on building up a better society which would convince even the last villager that socialism was superior to the teachings of the traditional faith. But in general, the secularities of various state socialisms cannot be explained as a direct emanation of Marx. Instead, they integrated large parts of the Russian revolutionary heritage and also developed individual national traits, the variety of which I will try to sketch out in this chapter. The Russian path is central, since many of its elements were exported (by force or conviction) to other countries after 1945; therefore I will analyze it to begin with.

2 The Soviet Prototype

Lenin never tried to alter or replenish Marx' thoughts on religion. In the first months after the October revolution, he criticized his comrades for anti-religious zeal, which reminded him of anarchists and socialists who did not understand the principles of dialectical materialism. If ideas only followed developments in the material world, it was the latter the Bolsheviks should change (Gabel 2005: 338). In hindsight, this theoretical view had little chances of becoming a reality. First of all, the Bolsheviks had underestimated the cultural gap between themselves and the 'masses', that is, those for whom they pretended to speak. Ordinary people did have social grievances which intersected with the aims of the revolutionaries, but nevertheless Marxist ideology was alien to them. This was especially true for the peasants, who constituted the vast majority of the population. The Bolsheviks had helped them get rid of the landlords, but otherwise peasants and revolutionaries had little in common. For the majority of the peasants, all social differentiation of the late nineteenth and early twentieth centuries notwithstanding, a good life meant enough land and enough food, equality and conformity within the village, a patriarchal way of life and the non-interference of outsiders (Figes 1996: 84–102; Šanin 1997: 200–226). For the Bolsheviks, on the other hand, the traditional peasantry was something that had to vanish since it was too unproductive to feed an urban communist society. To bring ideal and reality together, Bolshevism quickly turned into a developmental dictatorship and started to use methods not foreseen by Marx. The Bolsheviks systematically tried to alter the consciousness of the 'backward' masses, and they began to use force against them. Increasingly, traditional religion and its representatives were identified as factors that prevented people from joining the revolution, and thus they had to be fought directly. On a concrete level, antireligious policies manifested themselves in the massive propaganda of atheism, the closing of churches and the harsh repression of the clergy, as well as in tactics designed to destroy the unity of the Russian Orthodox Church by fostering progressive Christian renegades who stood up to the authority of the bishops (Young 1997: 49–50, 55–67).

While the social distance between the leaders and the masses was one driving factor of Bolshevik atheism, the mentality of the revolutionaries was another. Ever since the emergence of the Russian revolutionary movement in the 1860s, its style often reminded one of religious zealotry. This was true not only for those forces that consciously reinterpreted the Gospel in a radical style, such as the famous writer Lev Tolstoy or various egalitarian and chiliastic groups that developed out of the fold of Russian Orthodoxy. Even the Russian Marxists who derided all non-rational elements in the competing currents were not free of it. In a basically subconscious process many of them elevated Marx's and Engels' teachings to the level of absolute truths, denied the inherent contradictions in their teachings and labeled those who opposed them either ignoramuses or enemies. It was this type of thinking that facilitated the creation of a quasi-religious myth of Lenin as the only true interpreter of Marx and Engels, right after his death in 1924 (Berdiaev 1937; Hildermeier 1998: 173–174). The religious style of thinking demanded absolute loyalty from one's followers. When the Bolsheviks came to power in 1917, they tended to extract the same loyalty from ordinary citizens, at least in places where their power was consolidated enough to put people under pressure. The Bolsheviks demanded not so much that ordinary people obey the laws of the new state but rather that they support the communist ideology, which was considered above the law. Given the strong atheist elements in Bolshevism and the competing religious claim that the ultimate moral authority is divine but not human will, a conflict of loyalty was inevitable (Luks 2002: 252–253).

Until the beginning of *perestroika* in 1986, the Soviet leadership never really gave up its goal to achieve complete victory over the forces of tradition. Ultimately, all citizens should acknowledge the falseness of religion and adapt the 'superior' and 'true' materialist world view. But there was much less unity when it came to the question of how to reach this goal. The 1920s witnessed a mixture of repression, tricks and compromise.

The Bolsheviks were especially concerned with the Russian Orthodox Church, which they viewed not only as a propagator of theism but also as a pillar of the abhorred Czarist regime. During their first months in power, they stripped the Church of its vast estates and cut the centuries-old ties between church and state. The Church was forbidden to run schools, to register marriages or to charge fees from believers. It even lost the status of a corporate body and was completely cut off from state subsidies. Thousands of Orthodox Christians were killed during the civil war between 1918 and 1920, among them at least 28 bishops. More waves of repression followed, the most brutal in 1937–1939, when about 150,000 believers were arrested and more than half of them shot. All monasteries and the vast majority of churches were closed down between 1918 and 1939. After these measures, the once powerful Russian Orthodox Church was nothing but a shadow of its former self (Hildermeier 1998: 328–333, 580–585).

Despite all this repression, there was compromise too. Recent research on early Soviet religious policy stresses that even the seemingly almighty Bolsheviks were not always in a position to dictate their will. Especially in rural areas, communist functionaries had to proceed carefully and translate between the urban, scientific ideas of the new system and the peasant world view. Instead of juxtaposing the old and the new, they had to act carefully if they wanted to win the villagers' acceptance. This, but also the patriarchal background of many 'minor' revolutionaries themselves, often led them to compare socialism with the values of the village commune, to use symbols that reminded of the more religious elderly persons and to give them a new interpretation. Many of the new 'converts' to communism in fact practiced a syncretism of traditional and new ideas and forms, emanations of this development being icon corners in peasant houses now refilled with pictures of Lenin socialist holidays modeled along Orthodox lines such as 'harvest day' (*den' urožaja*), where the participants would sing the Internationale instead of watching the priest blessing the first fruits, or rural 'communist' families that celebrated communist as well as religious holidays (Rolf 2006: 68–69, 80, 241).

This blending of older and newer notions and practices is by no means unique to the Russian revolution: it has parallels in most other societies and is especially palpable where developments occur quickly, initiated from above. It also had parallels in older Russian history. The transition of the East Slavic village from paganism to Christianity from the ninth century, as in other medieval European states, had been full of compromises between missionaries and converts, and throughout its history Russian folk religion remained basically eclectic and never came to resemble a standardized 'high theology'.[2] Bolshevism, though

---

[2] Recent research has placed doubt on the widespread notion that pre-revolutionary Russian society was especially prone to syncretistic 'double belief'. Thus Stella Rock admits that in Kievan Rus', Christian ideals and social reality frequently diverged, but that the same was true for medieval Western Europe. One difference between Russia and Western Europe seems to lie not

not a religion in the narrow sense of the word, was also turned from a more or less consistent 'high culture system' into a conglomerate of ideas and practices once it entered the Russian village.

But this parallel should not be exaggerated, since the Orthodox ecclesiastical leadership was significantly softer and more pluralist than the Bolshevik elite. Orthodox bishops and theologians sometimes allowed folk practices and notions to enter the canon of official Orthodoxy. Not only the ordinary believers, but also the Church hierarchy was often critical of written, standardized dogma, and some bishops were known for their readiness to sacralize folk traditions (Heretz 2008). The leading communists, in contrast, rarely forgot that the Christian-communist syncretisms were just a transitory state that had to be accepted for tactical reasons and that they should be eliminated once the party's position became strong enough. This attitude can be traced in the development of socialist life-cycle rituals (birth, marriage, burial) which were carefully designed to meet the people's tastes and expectations in terms of symbols, but rather strictly controlled when it came to the interpretation of these symbols (Lane 1981: 231–232). Moreover, the village itself was targeted for destruction, by the industrialization of agriculture on the one hand and by migration to urban industrial centers on the other. By the 1950s the majority of the Soviet population no longer lived in villages but in rapidly expanding industrial cities, where almost no churches or other religious structures were available and the traditional way of life had become quite remote. The tactical nature of Soviet compromises is also illustrated by the fact that periods of relative tolerance were usually followed by renewed atheist propaganda and repression. For example, the relative laxity of the mid-1920s and mid-1930s was followed by harsh repression towards the end of these decades. Stalin's 'liberalization' of religious policy during World War II, motivated by the need to win popular support in the struggle against Hitler's Germany, was followed by an aggressive anti-religious campaign under Nikita Khrushchev in the late 1950s and early 1960s. Only in the Brezhnev era did this dynamic halt and communism gradually lost its missionary fervor, increasingly stressing social stability and consumerism. Believers were still repressed and excluded from the public realm, but they could continue to exist in social niches (Marčenko 2010; Škarovskij 2010: 383–398).

In the end, Soviet secularity produced a society in which knowledge about religious 'truths' greatly declined, where traditional religious practice became

---

so much in the Middle Ages but in the seventeenth and eighteenth centuries, when rulers and leading clergymen throughout the continent tried to modernize and homogenize their confessions, a policy that had less effect in Russia, probably due to the country's relatively low degree of literacy and weak infrastructure (Rock 2007: 118–157).

limited to a small minority of elderly people with rural roots (mostly women) and some exceptional members of the intelligentsia. A large urban majority may never have arrived at deep atheist convictions but was completely alienated from religion as an integral life-style. This pattern was somewhat different among non-Orthodox peoples on the peripheries of the Soviet Union, who were also subject to atheization but tended to retain more loyalty to their traditional faiths as the resorts of separate identities (Ramet 1993).

Many Soviet citizens remained connected to the traditional religious realm through isolated elements of that former culture which permeated syncretistic social reality. This is documented by child baptisms which remained popular and widespread even among parts of the urban population, though they were frequently carried out in remote villages far from control by the police or curious neighbors. Interestingly, the Soviet state was much more successful in installing communist rites for adults. While the communist 'baptism' called *oktjabriny* did not win many followers, socialist weddings and burial rituals became a major phenomenon in the 1960s, though in practice they were frequently 'polluted' by religious folk traditions such as bringing food to the grave so that the deceased person would not have to starve in the afterlife (Lane 1981: 68–86).

Russian Orthodox culture prior to 1917 had been full of rituals and symbols; Soviet culture deeply altered the symbolic system but became, especially after its conservative shift under Stalin, increasingly similar to the preceding one in its overall stress on ritualized (rather than individual) expression, and on symbolic (rather than intellectual) language. Collectivism was another trait that characterized pre- as well as post-revolutionary Russian society. The same could be said about the contempt for formal law or the criticism of the 'decadent West'. All conflicts notwithstanding, there was thus some common ground on which the Russian Orthodox Church could cooperate with the state. This produced a certain unity between Orthodoxy and the Soviet state, but it created divisions in other aspects. The Cold War period, all Orthodox-Protestant ecumenical dialogue on theological and peace questions notwithstanding, helped to perpetuate the historical fault line between Eastern and Western Christianity, since it invited both religious traditions to underline those values in which they had differed for centuries. Internally, the Soviet Union made it difficult for the non-Orthodox and non-Slav cultures to embrace a communist civilization which was visibly influenced by Orthodox and Slav pagan elements but was seemingly closed to other cultural substrates. Especially in Muslim Central Asia, but also in Catholic Lithuania, this lead to conservative reflexes and ethno-confessional enclosure (Lane 1981: 231–233).

The 'separation of Church and State' proclaimed in 1918 was never carried out in the literal sense of the word but was used as a seemingly modern catchword to cover various and contradictory policies. In the first post-revolutionary years it basically meant the 'destruction' of both clergy and parishes, but later it denoted the alienation of believers together with the clericalization and political instrumentalization of the Church. Since Stalin's partial rehabilitation of Orthodoxy in 1941 the Church consisted mainly of a greatly diminished and strictly controlled clergy whose existence was protected by the state in order to control the believers and to improve the Soviet image abroad. Understandably, clergymen had few opportunities (and sometimes little desire, too) to fight for the religious or other human rights of the ordinary believers. Having no possibility to reach the masses who did not show up in church anymore, the lower clergy contented themselves with administering their isolated parishes. The higher clergy were sometimes included in the international image campaigns of the Soviet leadership and defended Soviet foreign and internal policy as if it were their own. Parts of the clergy, both higher and lower, provided a special service for the state by spying on believers, foreign guests, or fellow clergymen. Since the Russian Orthodox Church in the post-socialist period has partly been led by bishops who took their vows in the 1950s and 1960s, the 'Soviet-Orthodox' culture of leadership still persists today and greatly hinders any open discussion of the recent past of Russian Orthodoxy (Mitrokhin 2004: 175–182).

3 Export and Diversification of the Soviet Model

In the early 1950s, the 'Soviet realm' of satellite states in central and southeastern Europe looked quite uniform to many observers (except for Yugoslavia). This is true not only with respect to ideology, the political and economic system, but also when it comes to cultural manifestations such as public remembrance of past heroes, May Day parades and the like. But it would be misleading to assume that this outward uniformity was nothing but a result of Soviet centralism. Moscow was eager to dictate its own model when it came to basic structures such as party leadership or the transformation of agriculture, but it did not issue detailed directives on socialist mass culture, celebrations or holidays. The same was true when it came to religious policies. In the late 1940s Stalin was eager to unite all Orthodox churches in a struggle against 'Western imperialism' and 'Catholic aggression' and surely would not have welcomed the return of 'clericalist' forces into the public realm, but otherwise each socialist regime had some room for maneuver to deal with the religious question on its own. Hence much of the outward uniformity was rather the result of self-Sovietization carried out by Soviet-trained communist functionaries, rather than of outright external dictates (Rolf 2006: 330–331). Since the prestige of the Soviet Union among communists was enormous, its symbolic language was eagerly copied, but basically the communist state builders of central and southeastern Europe found themselves in a similar position as the Bolsheviks in the early 1920s: confronted with the task of making people accept an ideology that was alien to the majority of the population. To adapt communism to their own conditions, they included elements of local and national tradition into their symbolic universe.

4 Southeastern Europe

Adaptation was especially easy in the majority Slav Orthodox regions of southeastern Europe, that is, Bulgaria and the eastern half of Yugoslavia (Serbia, Montenegro, Macedonia). Here, structural similarities and traditional Russophilia helped greatly to introduce Soviet secularity. The Balkan Orthodox peasant majorities had been practicing religious syncretism for centuries, and many of them found ways to integrate the new communist teachings into this conglomerate of notions, especially since communism had previously been tested and 'sanctioned' by the example of the 'big Russian brother'. Just as in Russia, the Balkan Orthodox churches could not offer much resistance. Partly they did not even want to, since many clergymen considered the West a greater foe than Moscow and saw their country's belonging to the socialist realm as form of protection. As in the Soviet Union, the prestige of the new urban-socialist lifestyle was enormous, and intense migrations from the villages to the cities quickly destroyed the social basis of Orthodoxy (Buchenau 2004; Kalkandjieva 2010; Leustean 2010).

But still, Soviet secularity underwent certain transformations. The Balkan countries prior to 1945 were much more egalitarian 'face-to-face' societies than the Russian empire had ever been. Late Ottoman rule had left the village communes basically to their own devices, stepping into the peasants' lives mainly through arbitrary tax-farmers and the occasional violence of armed groups. This type of governance had helped to conserve patriarchal local structures. The importance of kinship, especially in the mountainous areas, was enormous, and patriarchal values were even stronger than in Russia. The post-Ottoman nation states partly tried to transform this legacy, but they also integrated it into their political systems. As a corollary, leading communists such as Josip Broz Tito in Yugoslavia or (to a lesser extent) Todor Zhivkov in Bulgaria were depicted as the patriarchal fathers of a large family, namely the socialist nation. The same was true for Enver Hoxha in Albania and Nicolae Ceaușescu in Romania. Personality cults were thus an important element of southeastern European socialist secularities (Nikolić 2006; Ursprung 2010; Garlatti 2004: 68–72).

Another seemingly 'unsecular' element was nationalism, which, especially in Albania and Romania, often reached sacral intensity. This nationalist load is easy to understand if we bear in mind that, at the time when Soviet communism entered the Balkans, the countries of the region were still preoccupied with nation-building, ethnic homogenization and territorial expansion. Nationalism persisted under the communist rulers, who stopped territorial expansion in the name of 'socialist internationalism', but in the interior continued to work against national and religious minorities (Brunnbauer 2012). In early socialist Bulgaria and Yugoslavia, secularist policies seemed especially harsh in Muslim areas, where women were forced to unveil in public institutions. Yugoslavia, after its 'federalist shift' in the 1960s, stopped discriminating disproportionately against Muslims, but socialist Bulgaria continued to do so until the very end of its existence, thus 'completing' pre-revolutionary nation-building. Socialist Romania, in a similar vein, partly continued the anti-Jewish policies of the interwar period (Höpken 1989; Neuburger 2004: 55–57; Glass 2004: 102–104). Albania seems to fall out of any comparison because it was the only country that completely forbade any kind of religious organization (in 1967) and practice (in 1976), thus becoming the World's 'first atheist state'. Upon closer examination, this step appears to be just another proof that Balkan socialist secularities can partly be explained as a continuation of pre-war nationalisms. Since its beginnings in the late nineteenth century, the Albanian national movement centered on language but not on religion, which is understandable since the nation-to-be was divided into a Muslim majority (about 70 % of the population) and two Christian minorities (about 20 % Orthodox and 10 % Catholic). It was impossible to rely on majority Islam as a factor of unity, since it was also the state religion of the Ottoman empire from which Albanian nationalists wanted to secede, but also because Albanian Islam lacked internal unity. In general no Balkan nationalist until World War II, not even Turkish ones, considered 'backward' Islam a possible basis for nationalism. Enver Hoxha's radical atheism is thus explainable as a blend of anti-religious tendencies within Albanian nationalism, Leninist/Stalinist ideology and isolationism, or the desire of Enver Hoxha to show that his way to communism was 'truer' than that of his former allies in Belgrade or Moscow (Ceka 2010).

Though repression was not as intense and long-lasting as in the Soviet Union, Balkan socialism heavily alienated Orthodox believers from their traditional faith. The masses were drawn from the villages into the cities, where they lost connections with their old parishes. Especially the educated and the men soon distanced themselves from the Church, leaving elderly rural-rooted women as a waning social base. Another parallel with the Soviet Union concerns the Muslims. While Balkan socialist secularity incorporated elements of the previous Orthodox culture such as a cult of medieval statehood, a love of Orthodox architectural monuments or an esteem for priests who had played a role in national liberation, Muslims often did not feel included and responded by emigration or ethno-religious segregation (Brunnbauer 2011: 696–698). In Kosovo, Western Macedonia or the Bulgarian Rhodopes, Muslims were significantly less included into the socialist urban culture than the (formerly) Christian population. They remained a rather conservative rural element, had higher birth rates and were increasingly perceived as a demographic threat by the majority (Pichler 2005: 75–86; Brunnbauer 2007: 454–463).

The Romanian situation differed from the Serbian and Bulgarian ones since Romania had been a country of remarkably high religious vitality before 1945. The reasons for this are probably to be found in the fact that the Danubian Principalities had never been under direct Ottoman rule and thus had retained an Orthodox elite and a relatively vital clergy. Consequently, Romanian socialism was never able to extirpate Orthodoxy and to drag the majority over to socialist secularity. Instead, the Orthodox parishes continued to exist within an authoritarian secularist framework which was keen to control religious life. For the sake of national communism, the regime had to build bridges between the secular and religious strata of society. Nikolae Ceaușescu himself gave a telling example of this when he buried his father according to Orthodox rites in 1972, being closely observed by Romanian national TV (Pope 1982: 300). In creating the socialist 'New Man', the Romanian communists partly relied on (monastic) Orthodox moral values such as honesty, thrift and sacrifice for the collective good (Gilberg 1989: 343).

The eastern part of Yugoslavia is another special case to be discussed. While in Bulgaria and especially Romania the Orthodox heritage greatly contributed to the creation of 'national communism', this path was closed to both Serbia and Montenegro since both existed within the federal state of Yugoslavia. Orthodox Christians were the largest religious group in the country, but they did not possess an absolute majority, so that the communist leadership took into account the various cultural heritages, and not only the Eastern Christian tradition. As long as Yugoslavia remained united with the Soviet Union, this factor did not seem too important, since the Soviet model indicated that Yugoslavia should become as centralist as the Soviet Union, where Stalin clearly appreciated the cultural heritage of its most numerous and powerful nation. After the breach between Tito and Stalin in 1948, this conception looked increasingly outdated. It was only a matter of time before it was discovered that an individual Yugoslav way to socialism should also take into account the Western and Muslim cultural foundations in the country. The main designer of Yugoslavia's way to socialism was a Slovene of Catholic background, Edvard Kardelj. In his youth he had contacts in Austro-Marxist circles where Marx was discussed much more freely than among the Bolsheviks (Poč 1979: 24). Kardelj's main criticism of Soviet communism was its statist, dictatorial character. Kardelj stressed that, according to Marx, the state would wither away after the revolution, leaving more and more room for citizens' self-administration. In matters of religion, Kardelj returned directly to Marx and stressed that believers would leave church themselves once a happy communist society had abolished their need to seek relief and consolation. From the 1960s, the political establishment criticized not so much religious practices as such but concentrated on the 'misuse of religion' for nationalist purposes (Mirescu 2009: 63).

The Yugoslav shift in religious policy was never complete. Though announced from the very top, old-style functionaries often pursued opposite policies at a local level, continuing to restrict religious life wherever they could. Especially in Orthodox areas, the imbalance of power between church and state was so marked that reality changed little. Meanwhile, all religious communities started to use the new freedoms, trying to enlarge the realm of traditional religiosity at the cost of socialist secularity. In Croatia and Slovenia, a dialogue between Marxists and (Catholic) Christian intellectuals emerged, which centered on issues such as the development of the human person, social justice and freedom, which were perceived as common goals for religious and secular people. In the late 1960s it seemed that the spirit of dialogue would also affect the power and party structures of the western republics, but the overall conservative shift in the country in the 1970s stopped this development, so that Christian-Marxist dialogue could not really change the character of socialist secularity in Yugoslavia. Even after that, Yugoslavia's socialist secularity differed from that of other communist regimes because of a certain degree of liberality towards the religious communities, which at least from the 1960s were less strictly controlled than in the other Balkan countries (Perica 2002). The Serbian Orthodox Church today, though partly having profited from these 'Western' elements in Yugoslav socialism, does not appreciate this in its public remembrance of the recent past but depicts Titoist Yugoslavia in exclusively dark colors as a godless (and sometimes even crypto-Catholic) country which aimed to destroy the Serbs and their Church by dismembering the nation into federal units (Popović 1990; Jović 2012).

5 Central Europe

The socialist secularities of Central Europe are more difficult to describe than the situation in southeastern Europe. The region between Poland, East Germany and the Baltic states in the north and the former Habsburg lands in the south has a predominantly Catholic tradition with some strongholds of Protestantism (East Germany, Latvia, Estonia, eastern Hungary and Transylvania) and some areas where Protestantism was suppressed under Habsburg rule but later rediscovered as an attribute of national character (especially the Czech lands, Hungary). The Protestant-Catholic divide did have consequences for the design of socialist secularity, but neither the Catholic nor the Protestant territories were homogeneous in themselves. The reality of communist rule differed considerably from country to country, depending both on the pre-revolutionary religious situation and on other variables.

Generally speaking, the Protestant churches were more willing to compromise with the communist regimes than the Catholic church, a fact that helped to institute Christian-Marxist dialogues in East Germany and Hungary (but not in the Baltic republics, where Soviet rule left no space for this) (Ramet 1992a: 3). Protestantism is remote from Orthodox syncretism and is historically interwoven with the European Enlightenment. As such, cultural alienness towards Marxism was maybe not as principled as in the Orthodox case, since both Protestants and Marxists were used to preaching against 'superstition' and 'prejudices', holding up the values of education and reflection instead. Protestantism lacks a clear normative center and is split up into different tendencies, with Lutherans dominating in East Germany and the Baltic states, and the Hungarian Protestants being divided into Calvinists and Lutherans. Their relatively loose ecclesiastical structure meant that Protestant theologians had considerable freedom to make individual assessments of socialism, which consequently varied a lot. In Hungary, Calvinists felt themselves to be the 'real' national church and as such showed some willingness to construct a Hungarian national communism together with the rulers; the Hungarian Lutherans were much more uncompromising (Pungur 1992). In East Germany, the Lutheran Church explicitly sought common ground with the Communists, not so much for national reasons but because of joint experiences in the Nazis' concentration camps and to improve civic liberties. Since secularization had already entered the East German lands in the nineteenth century, even Protestant clergymen tended to perceive it as a process for which the Communists could not be blamed exclusively. There had been various arrangements with secularization prior to 1945, and they were continued in the socialist era. The communists thus did not meet many difficulties in installing their own socialist rites of initiation, which were only partly based on Protestant forms. While the number of Protestant confirmations fell markedly, the Socialist substitute called *Jugendweihe* (youth dedication) gained in popularity and continues to be widely celebrated even today. Socialist mortuary rites flourished in East Germany, as well as in Hungary and the Czech lands (Ramet 1992b; Mohrmann 1999; Tóth 2014; Reban 1990: 152).

For Catholics under socialism, the space for compromise and retreat was limited mainly because the Vatican upheld clear normative positions which could not be ignored. Until the late 1950s, Rome clearly forbade any far-reaching compromises between local/national Catholic structures and the communist rulers. Pope Pius XII. had a preference for 'martyr bishops' who were willing to go to jail rather than give in to communist policies such as the atheization of public life and schooling or encroachments on to the property rights of the Church etc. The Second Vatican Council (1962–1965), which coincided with more moderate religious policies in many socialist states, significantly changed this framework. Acknowledging the autonomy of this world, the Council declared even communists possible partners for dialogue. This considerably widened the space for compromise and papal diplomatic interventions, which were no longer as bold as they had been in the 1930s but careful and quiet. After the ascent of the 'Polish' Pope John Paul II in 1978, anti-communist rhetoric returned to a certain extent, though it was now rather embedded in the framework of human rights than Catholic exclusivism. Post-conciliar Catholicism to a certain extent allowed for the creation of Christian socialist ideas which resembled those in Protestant areas, though they were sometimes underpinned by joint Catholic and communist anti-liberalism and anti-individualism (Buchenau 2004: 309–328; Stehle 1993).

But in general, Catholic–communist dialogue and synthesis remained the exception. It existed in Hungary, as well as in Poland, Czechoslovakia (though basically led by Protestants here) and the western parts of Yugoslavia, but it did not become a majority option (Mojzes 1981). The shape of socialist secularity in Catholic central Europe rather depended on the historical relationship between nation and religion and on the degree of pre-socialist secularization. In cases where the link between church and national identity was strong and where a stable Catholic milieu still existed, socialist secularity could never encompass all of society or even a majority of it, but was faced with constant competition. This is especially true for Poland, large parts of which were dominated by a tightly-knit rural Catholic milieu and which possessed a considerable Catholic intelligentsia. Communist rule was perceived not only as ideologically alien but also as a foreign (Russian) occupation force. Similar to the situation in partitioned Poland during the nineteenth century, Catholicism came to be identified with the Polish nation and its values. In contrast to many Orthodox countries, Polish Catholicism was able to connect its symbolic grandeur with concrete social content. The state could not control the Church effectively, nor could it suppress priestly and lay activity. Many Polish clergymen resolved conflicts of loyalty in favor of their church rather than the state, thus signaling to believers that communism could not permeate all of society. From the 1950s, this forced the Polish communists to make compromises and to accept the existence of a clearly non-communist sector in society. Though the Polish United Workers' Party did try to expand socialist secularity by proposing alternative institutions of basic socialization such as the communist boy scouts (*harcerze*), these techniques were of limited success. Instead, ideological monism failed, and the Church gradually installed itself as a defender of non-communist society in general, thus going beyond narrow confessional interests (Casanova 1994: 92–113; Luks 1993).

Another interesting case is Croatia, large parts of which were also dominated by strong Catholic milieus and where the equation of nation and religion was as strong as in Poland. These factors notwithstanding, socialist secularity developed significantly better than in the Polish case, since in the eyes of many inhabitants of Croatia (Serbs, but also Croats) the Catholic Church had compromised itself during World War II. The hierarchy had supported the installation of a Fascist puppet state in 1941, and some bishops had remained faithful to this regime until the very end, though it had murdered hundreds of thousands of Serbs, Jews, Communists, Roma and others in concentration camps and in rural massacres. Together with the autochthonous strength of the partisan movement, which alone had pursued a policy of interethnic community-building, this led many members of the Croatian intelligentsia into an anti-Catholic stance. The Church lost neither its social base nor its national importance, but Catholic claims to public visibility were viewed critically by many people, not all of whom were staunch communists. Under these circumstances, socialist secularity developed better than the considerable strength of the Catholic milieu indicated, and all religiosity notwithstanding, the veneration of Josip Broz Tito struck deep roots in the masses. Yugoslav communism *was* attractive, even for many of those who had been brought up in a Catholic milieu and who kept living in it. The strength of Yugoslav communism is documented by its ability to instrumentalize Catholic cults such as the veneration of Cyril and Method or of the nineteenth-century bishop Josip Juraj Strossmaier, who were celebrated as exponents of a better, more 'Yugoslav' and tolerant and democratic Catholicism. Especially in Bosnia, the Communists were able to institute stable cooperation with the Franciscan order on the basis of a similar vision of history (Buchenau 2004). In Poland, those Catholics who showed a willingness to synthesize (nationalist) Catholicism and communism such as Bolesław Piasecki's PAX group in the 1950s were considered traitors by the Catholic hierarchy and could not exert a greater influence in Catholic circles (Kunicki 2012).

Czechoslovakia demonstrates the case of a traditionally Catholic area where Catholicism was too weak to limit the scope of socialist secularity. During the nineteenth century, modernization in the Czech lands (especially in Bohemia) had significantly reduced the number of Catholics. The growing working class did not automatically lose their ties to Catholicism, but these became looser and less self-evident. At the same time, the Czech national movement came to consider that, ever since the integration of the Czech lands into the Habsburg monarchy in the seventeenth century, the Catholic Church had served as an instrument of foreign rule and denationalization. Instead, Czech nationalists remembered the proto-Protestant movement of Jan Hus (1369–1415) as the 'true' national faith which allegedly embodied their values and aspirations. When the communists came to power, they found it quite easy to marginalize the Catholic Church, especially in the western parts of Czechoslovakia, which dominated politically, demographically and economically. The party presented communist atheism as the completion of the preceding anti-clerical culture and sharply differentiated between 'good' traditions such as the cult of Cyril and Methodius and 'bad' germanophile-ultramontane Catholicism as the eternal foe of the people. Since large parts of Czech society were not willing to associate with the official church, the Catholic bishops (all of whom were imprisoned or put under house arrest in the late 1940s and early 1950s) soon found themselves in an isolated situation and lost all their abilty to influence the development of society. Only during the Prague Spring in 1968–69 did Czechoslovak socialism grow more tolerant of traditional religion, but even then the rehabilitation of Catholicism was not high on the agenda (Balík and Hanuš 2007).

Hungary was a predominantly Catholic country clearly less secularized than Bohemia, but Catholicism was in no way considered a national religion. Rather, Hungarian nationalism built on linguistic features and partly on the country's Calvinist heritage, which had been fought over and diminished by the Habsburgs after Hungary's liberation from Ottoman rule in the seventeenth century. Hungarian opposition to communist rule was a broad, popular, traditionalist and nationalist movement which culminated in the Hungarian uprising of 1956. In the anti-communist struggle, the Catholic milieu and its supreme leader Cardinal Mindszenty played an important role as did the Lutheran leadership, while the Calvinist leadership behaved in a much more compromising manner. The emerging Hungarian 'goulash communism' was more tolerant of traditional religion than other socialist regimes, but none of the traditional churches in the country became really influential. Socialist secularity could not build on a particular confessional heritage, since Hungarian national memory was neither clearly Catholic nor Calvinist. As in Yugoslavia, Hungary was a place of Christian-Marxist dialogue, which became especially intense during and after the Second Vatican

Council. The Hungarian case differs from Croatia and Poland not only because of the disputed national role of the Catholic Church but also because of the collaboration of its hierarchy, which in some ways recalled the situation in the Orthodox countries. When the staunch anti-communist Cardinal Mindszenty left the country in 1971 and leadership was transferred to his former secretary László Lékai, a deep gap opened up between the well-established and loyal bishops and the ordinary believers who risked their careers by displaying their religiosity in public. The Hungarian Catholic theologian János Wildmann ascribes this development to traditionalist Habsburg notions of an alliance of throne and altar which were reactivated by Lékai (Wildmann 2007: 34–35; Tomka 2010: 76–80).

6 Conclusion

To some extent, all socialist regimes in eastern Europe adopted at least some of the values of the forces they fought against, namely religious traditions. Since the Soviet Union served as a blueprint, forms and contents which had developed during the struggle of Leninism with Orthodoxy were exported to other socialist countries. On the other hand, the individual historical constellations between religion, society and nationalism influenced the design of socialist secularity in each country. I have tried to give an overview of socialist secularities, but I must confess that many issues have had to remain in the dark since basic comparative research is still lacking. The literature on the Soviet case is abundant, with descriptions of transfers of ideas, symbols, notions, behavioral patterns, mentalities etc. from the pre-revolutionary Orthodox framework to the Bolshevik-atheist one. Scholarship on the Balkans and on many central European cases has examined these aspects with less intensity, so that at the moment it is still impossible to write a comprehensive in-depth history of socialist secularities in Europe.

The most palpable result of the present chapter is the relative intensity with which Soviet secularity was adopted after 1945 in Serbia, Bulgaria and Rumania, a fact that hints at the importance of the common Orthodox heritage. In central Europe, there was less indigenous sacralization of communist personalities. Especially in Catholic areas it remained difficult to integrate traditional religious elements into the symbolic language of communism, since the Catholic clergy tended to do more to keep Christianity apart from communism than their Orthodox and Protestant counterparts. In a similar vein, Muslim and communist worlds rarely merged, not so much because of intellectual resistance, as in the Catholic case, but rather because of the peripheral and minority position of many Muslim populations within the socialist states. A striking feature of the traditionally Orthodox regions is that, while the Church hierarchies mostly cooperated with the communists, there was little or no dialogue between Marxists and Christians, a fact that hints at the weakness and subordination of the Orthodox churches, the scarcity of Christian lay intellectuals and also Orthodoxy's limited interest in the human rights question that was at the center of many central European Christian–Marxist dialogues.

All in all, communism's atheist fervor was somewhat weaker during the Balkan and central European 'revolutions' than it had been in early Soviet Russia. The communists, it seems, had 'matured' and developed rational techniques to keep down and control religion, while their faith in the creation of the 'New Man' had become less religion-like. The potential for both competitive Christian–atheist conflict and Christian–atheist synthesis had thus diminished.

Other revolutions which were concluded during the Cold War era throughout the world demonstrate that the real diversity of socialist secularities is still greater than I have shown in this overview of the situation in Europe. On the one hand, we find cases such as the Cultural Revolution in China or Pol Pot's rule in Cambodia, which seem to emulate the Russian Bolsheviks in teaching atheism with religion-like energy (Yang 2012: 49–57; Kiernan 1996: 57). On the other hand, there were communists who showed no interest in fighting religion as such and who cooperated with all forces who were against capitalism and imperialism, no matter whether they were religious or secular. Examples of this were Fidel Castro in Cuba and especially the Sandinistas in Nicaragua, who heavily relied on 'progressive' Catholic clergy as supporters and ideological multipliers (Muder 1992; Belli 1990). Socialist secularities, as this sketch has hopefully shown, deserve further comparative attention.

Bibliography

Balík, Stanislav, and Jiří Hanuš. 2007. *Katolická církev v Československu 1945–1989*. Brno: Centrum pro Studium Demokracie a Kultury.
Belli, Humberto. 1990. "The Catholic church in Sandinista Nicaragua," in *Catholicism and Politics in Communist Societies*, ed. Pedro Ramet, 313–338. Durham/London: Duke University Press.
Berdiaev, Nikolai. 1937. *The Origin of Russian Communism*, London: Bles.
Boer, Roland. 2012. *Criticism of Earth: On Marx, Engels and Theology*. Leiden, Boston: Brill.
Brunnbauer, Ulf. 2007. *Die sozialistische Lebensweise": Ideologie, Gesellschaft, Familie und Politik in Bulgarien (1944–1989)*. Wien etc.: Böhlau.
—. 2011. "Gesellschaft und gesellschaftlicher Wandel in Südosteuropa nach 1945," in *Geschichte Südosteuropas: Vom frühen Mittelalter bis zur Gegenwart*, eds. Konrad Clewing and Oliver Jens Schmitt, 651–702. Regensburg: Pustet.

—. 2012. "Staat und Gesellschaft in Realsozialismus: Legitimitätsstrategien kommunistischer Herrschaft in Südosteuropa, " in *Herrschaft in Südosteuropa: Kultur- und sozialwissenschaftliche Perspektiven*, eds. Mihai-D. Grigore, Radu Harald Dinu, and Marc Živojinović, 21–52. Göttingen: V&R unipress.

Buchenau, Klaus. 2004. *Orthodoxie und Katholizismus in Jugoslawien, 1945–1991: Ein serbisch-kroatischer Vergleich*. Wiesbaden: Harrassowitz.

Casanova, José. 1994. *Public Religions in the Modern World*. Chicago, London: The University of Chicago Press.

Ceka, Egin. 2010. "Atheismus und Religionspolitik im kommunistischen Albanien", in *Religion und Kultur im albanischsprachigen Südosteuropa*, ed. Oliver Jens Schmitt, 215–231. Frankfurt a.M. etc.: Peter Lang.

Figes, Orlando. 1996. *A People's Tragedy: The Russian Revolution, 1891–1924*. London: Cape.

Gabel, Paul. 2005. *And God Created Lenin: Marxism vs. Religion in Russia, 1917–1929*. Amherst, New York: Prometheus Books.

Garlatti, Ghislain. 2004. *Le Comédien devenu Dictateur: Todor Živkov: une image, un système, un homme*. http://bulgariehistoire.free.fr/comediendictateur.pdf, download 12 march 2013.

Gilberg, Trond. 1989. "Religion and nationalism in Romania," in *Religion and Nationalism in Soviet and East European Politics*, ed. Pedro Ramet, 328–351. Durham etc.: Duke University Press.

Glass, Hildrun. 2004. "Romanian Jews in the early years of communist rule: notes on the myth of 'Jewish communism'," in *Jews and Anti-Semitism in the Balkans*, eds. Wolf Moskovich, Oto Luhar, and Irena Šumi, 101–108. Jerusalem, Ljubljana: Hebrew University of Jerusalem etc.

Heretz, Leonid. 2008. *Russia on the Eve of Modernity: Popular Religion and Traditional Culture under the Last Tsars*. Cambridge: Cambridge University Press.

Hildermeier, Manfred. 1998. *Geschichte der Sowjetunion 1917–1991: Entstehung und Niedergang des ersten sozialistischen Staates*. München: Beck.

Höpken, Wolfgang. 1989. "Die jugoslawischen Kommunisten und die bosnischen Muslime," in *Die Muslime in der Sowjetunion und in Jugoslawien: Identität, Politik, Widerstand*, eds. Andreas Kappeler, Gerhard Simon, and Georg Brunner, 181–212. Köln: Markus-Verlag.

Ignatow, Assen. 2002. "Negation und Imitation: Die zwei Seiten des kommunistischen Verhältnisses zum Christentum," in *Das Christentum und die totalitären Herausforderungen des 20. Jahrhunderts: Rußland, Deutschland, Italien und Polen im Vergleich*, ed. Leonid Luks, 145–156. Köln etc.: Böhlau.

Jović, Savo B. 2012. *Utamničena Crkva: Stradanje sveštenstva Srpske Pravoslavne Crkve od 1945. do 1985. godine*. Novi Sad: Pravoslavna Misionarska Škola pri Hramu Sv. A. Nevskog.

Kalkandjieva, Daniela. 2010. "The Bulgarian Orthodox Church," in *Eastern Christianity and the Cold War, 1945–91*, ed. Lucian Leustean, 79–98. New York: Routledge.

Kiernan, Ben. 1996. *The Pol Pot Regime: Race, Power, and Genocide in Cambodia under the Khmer Rouge, 1975–79*. New Haven / London: Yale University Press.

Kunicki, Mikołaj Stanisław. 2012. *Between the Brown and the Red: Nationalism, Catholicism, and Communism in twentieth-century Poland: The Politics of Bolesław Piasecki*. Athens, Ohio: Ohio University Press.

Lane, Christel. 1981. *The Rites of Rulers: Ritual in Industrial Society – The Soviet Case.* Cambridge: Cambridge University Press.

Law, Alex. 2011. *Key Concepts in Classical Social Theory.* Los Angeles etc.: Sage.

Leustean, Lucian. 2010. "The Romanian Orthodox Church," in *Eastern Christianity and the Cold War*, 1945–91, ed. Lucian Leustean, 40–59. New York: Routledge.

Luks, Leonid. 1993. *Katholizismus und politische Macht im kommunistischen Polen, 1945–1990: Die Anatomie einer Befreiung.* Köln etc.: Böhlau.

——— 2002. "Der Kirchenkampf in der UdSSR und im kommunistischen Polen: ein Vergleich," in *Das Christentum und die totalitären Herausforderungen des 20. Jahrhunderts: Rußland, Deutschland, Italien und Polen im Vergleich*, ed. Leonid Luks, 251–267. Köln etc.: Böhlau.

Marčenko, Aleksij. 2010. *Religioznaia politika Sovetskogo gosudarstva v gody pravleniia N. S. Khruščeva i ee vlijanie na cerkovnuiu žizn' v SSSR.* Moskva: Obščestvo ljubitelej cerkovnoj istorii.

Mirescu, Alexander. 2009. "National Churches, Religious Policy and Free Space: A Comparison of Religious Policy in Poland, East Germany and Yugoslavia during Communism." *International Journal of Public Administration* 32/1: 58–77.

Mitrokhin, Nikolai. 2004. *Russkaia pravoslavnaia cerkov': Sovremennoe sostoianie i aktual'nye problemy*, Moskva: Novoe literaturnoe obozrenie.

Mohrmann, Ute. 1999 "Zur Geschichte der Jugendweihe zwischen 'Zivilreligion' und 'Volkskultur': Eine ritualisierte Lebensstation," in *Riten, Mythen und Symbole: Die Arbeiterbewegung zwischen 'Zivilreligion' und Volkskultur*, eds. Berthold Unfried, and Christine Schindler, 131–142. Leipzig: Akademische Verlags-Anstalt.

Mojzes, Paul. 1981. *Christian-Marxist Dialogue in Eastern Europe.* Minneapolis: Augsburg Publishing House.

Muder, Winfried. 1992. *Zur Herausbildung und zum Stand des Verhältnisses von Kirche und Staat in Cuba.* Frankfurt a.M. etc.: Peter Lang.

Neuburger, Mary. 2004. *The Orient Within: Muslim Minorities and the Negotiation of Nationhood in Modern Bulgaria.* Ithaca etc.: Cornell University Press.

Nikolić, Kosta. 2006. *Tito govori što narod misli: Kult Josipa Broza Tita 1944–1949.* Beograd: Službeni list SCG.

Perica, Vjekoslav. 2002. *Balkan Idols: Religion and Nationalism in Yugoslav States.* Oxford, New York: Oxford University Press.

Pichler, Robert. 2005. "Makedonien im Dilemma ethnisch divergierender Entwicklungsprozesse: Über die Schwierigkeit, auf der Basis des Ohrider Rahmenabkommens eine sozial gerechte Ordnung zu etablieren," in *Bilanz Balkan*, eds. Michael Daxner, and Peter Jordan, 68–100. Wien: Verlag für Geschichte und Politik.

Plamper, Jan. 2004. "Introduction: modern personality cults," in *Personality Cults in Stalinism – Personenkulte im Stalinismus*, eds. Klaus Heller and Jan Plamper, 13–42. Göttingen: V&R unipress.

Poč, Miro, ed. 1979. *Edvard Kardelj: Skica za monografiju.* Zagreb: Globus.

Pollack, Detlef. 1995. "Was ist Religion? Probleme der Definition." *Zeitschrift für Religionswissenschaft* 3: 163–190.

Pope, Earl A. 1982. "The orthodox church in Romania." *Ostkirchliche Studien* 32: 297–310.

Popović, Justin. 1990. *Istina o Srpskoj Pravoslavnoj Crkvi u komunističkoj Jugoslaviji*, Valjevo: Manastir Ćelije.

Pungur, Joseph. 1992. "Protestantism in Hungary: the communist era," in *Protestantism and Politics in Eastern Europe and Russia: The Communist and Postcommunist Eras*, ed. Sabrina Petra Ramet, 107–156. Durham, London: Duke University Press.

Ramet, Sabrina. 1992a. "Protestantism and communism: patterns of interaction in Eastern Europe and the Soviet Union," in *Protestantism and Politics in Eastern Europe and Russia: The Communist and Postcommunist Eras*, ed. Sabrina Petra Ramet, 1–10. Durham, London: Duke University Press.

――― 1992b: "Protestantism in East Germany, 1949–1989: a summing up," in *Protestantism and Politics in Eastern Europe and Russia: The Communist and Postcommunist Eras*, ed. Sabrina Petra Ramet, 40–72. Durham, London: Duke University Press.

――― ed. 1993. *Religious policy in the Soviet Union*. Cambridge: Cambridge University Press.

Reban, Milan J. 1990. "The Catholic church in Czechoslovakia," in *Catholicism and Politics in Communist Societies*, ed. Pedro Ramet, 142–155. Durham/London: Duke University Press.

Riesebrodt, Martin. 2007. *Cultus und Heilsversprechen: Eine Theorie der Religionen*. München: Beck.

Rock, Stella. 2007. *Popular Religion in Russia: 'Double Belief' and the Making of an Academic Myth*. New York: Routledge.

Rolf, Malte. 2006. *Das sowjetische Massenfest*, Hamburg: Hamburger Edition.

Ryklin, Michail. 2008. *Kommunismus als Religion: Die Intellektuellen und die Oktoberrevolution*. Frankfurt a.M./Leipzig: Verlag der Weltreligionen.

Šanin, Teodor. 1997. *Revoljucija kak moment istiny: Rossija 1905–1907 → 1917–1922 gg*. Moskva: Izdatel'stvo Ves' Mir.

Schenk, Benjamin Frithjof. 2012. "In search of a new Pantheon: hero and leader cults in early Soviet Russia," in *Redefining the Sacred: Religion in the French and Russian Revolutions*, eds. by Daniel Schönpflug and Martin Schulze Wessel, 211–226. Frankfurt a.M. etc.: Peter Lang.

Škarovskij, Michail. 2010. *Russkaja pravoslavnaia cerkov' v XX veke*. Moskva: Veče.

Stehle, Hansjakob. 1993. *Geheimdiplomatie im Vatikan: Die Päpste und die Kommunisten*. Zürich: Benziger.

Tomka, Miklós. 2010. *Religiöser Wandel in Ungarn: Religion, Kirche und Sekten nach dem Kommunismus*. Ostfildern: Matthias-Grünewald-Verlag.

Tóth, Heléna. 2014. "'It must not look like expropriation': The Cemetery Regulations of 1970 in Communist Hungary and the Spatial Aspects of the 'Battle between the Religious and the Materialist World View,'" in *Cityscapes in History: Creating the Urban Experience*, ed. Heléna Tóth, and Katrin Gulliver, 197–214. London: Ashgate

Ursprung, Daniel. 2010. "Personenkult im Bild: Stalin, Enver Hoxha und Nicolae Ceausescu im Vergleich," in *Der Führer im Europa des 20. Jahrhunderts*, eds. Heidi Hein-Kircher, and Benno Ennker, 50–73. Marburg: Herder-Institut.

Voegelin, Eric. 1938. *Die politischen Religionen*. Wien: Bermann-Fischer.

Wildmann, János. 2007. "Recht als Fassade und Grenze: Kirche und Sozialismus in Ungarn," in *Kirche und Sozialismus in Osteuropa*, eds. Jana Osterkamp, and Renate Schulze, 28–44. Wien: Facultas.

Yang, Fenggang. 2012. *Religion in China: Survival and Revival under Communist Rule*. Oxford/New York: Oxford University Press.

Young, Glennys. 1997. *Power and the Sacred in Revolutionary Russia: Religious Activities in the Village*. University Park, Pennsylvania: Pennsylvania University Press.

Conclusions

Matthias Koenig
Between World Society and Multiple Modernities: Comparing Cultural Constructions of Secularity and Institutional Varieties of Secularism[1]

The social sciences have experienced enormous paradigm shifts since the late twentieth century. The "light of cultural problems", to use a felicitous phrase from Weber's methodological writings (Weber 1988b [1922]: 214), has moved on, thus requiring social sciences to change their conceptual apparatus. Indeed, the social sciences have been considered as being in need of a substantial restructuring, if not an entire "unthinking" (Wallerstein 1991). The major reason for that is the historical experience of a temporal, social and spatial de-centering of occidental modernity. First, as ongoing debates on "post-" or "reflexive modernity" indicate, the modern epoch that had given rise to classical sociology in the first place has been thoroughly historicized; presumably linear processes of social evolution, differentiation, and integration are now seen as contingent and subject to variations and transformations (for review see Knöbl 2007). Second, discourses of post-colonialism and "cultural studies" have highlighted the hybridity of social practices and discourses that characterize our contemporary condition and betray the universalistic pretensions of the West (Chakrabarty 2002). And third, the debate on globalization has led to sustained critiques of the "methodological nationalism" entrenched in sociological theory (for a nuanced summary see Chernilo 2007): against the spatial model of a territorially-bounded societal community, global interconnections, networks or systems are commended as more adequate levels of social theorizing.

A research field that is perhaps more imbued by modernist social thought than any other and therefore in particular need of theoretical re-orientation is the social scientific study of religion. Firmly entrenched in conventional theories of modernization, the paradigm of secularization which dominated the field since the post-war period assumed that industrialization, democratization, and education would result in a decline of religion, its privatization, and its differentiation from other institutional fields, notably politics, to recapture Casanova's

---

[1] This concluding chapter is a revised and extended version of an article published in *Kulturen der Moderne*, published by Thorsten Bonacker and Andreas Reckwitz (Frankfurt am Main & New York: Campus, 2007).

(1994) threefold analytical distinction. In the wake of the above-mentioned problemshift, this secularization paradigm has become highly contested. Critics claim that modernity does not entail a decline of religion but is actually ever productive of new social forms of religion that respond to the modern condition of uncertainty and contingency (Hervieu-Léger 1993: 119, 135). Others argue that, far from falling victim to privatization, public forms of religion remain empirically salient (notably Casanova 1994: 19–39 and 232). And, very recently, this challenge has even affected the core of the modernist paradigm of secularization, namely the thesis of a functional differentiation of religion from other spheres such as politics or law. Thus, critics problematize the universalizing of what is in fact a historically contingent, cultural conception of the "secular" and its distinctions from an equally contingent conception of "religion" (see Asad 2003).

While criticism of conventional theories of modernization and secularization abounds, it is less clear how scholars might theorize the contemporary condition without relying on inherited concepts of modernity and secularity. In fact, while some suggest discarding any idea of "modernity" as a coherent whole (Yack 1997), two trends in macro-sociological theory have revitalized theoretical reflections about the modern condition. On the one hand, modernity has been understood as the emergence, for the first time in history, of a "world society" in which local practices and discourses have become inevitably interconnected on a global scale (Albrow 1996; Lechner and Boli 2005). On the other hand, civilizational analysis which had some prominence in the early 20th century (e.g. Durkheim and Mauss 1913) has re-appeared on the agenda, provoking a debate about "multiple modernities" which attracts much interest in disciplines far beyond sociology (Arjomand and Tiryakian 2004; Arnason 2002; Eisenstadt 2001; Joas and Knöbl 2004: 756–761; Therborn 1999). Sociological theory, it seems, cannot quite avoid engaging in general discourse about modernity; indeed, as Peter Wagner (1994: ix) has asked: "What else is sociology, if not the systematic attempt to come to an understanding of modern society?"

Likewise, the social scientific study of religion, far from discarding the concept of the secular altogether, is in fact characterized by reinvigorated interest in the analyses of secularization (see Taylor 2007; Gorski and Altinordu 2008). Some authors have emphasized the global diffusion of cognitive categories of the "religious" and the "secular" as well as of normative models regulating the position of religious vis-à-vis secular spheres (e.g. Beyer 1994; Hurd 2008). Others have started to compare and typify varieties of "secularism" (Kuru 2009; Cady and Hurd 2010) or, following Wohlrab-Sahr and Burchardt (2012), varieties of "secularity" understood as cultural frameworks for drawing distinctions between religious and non-religious practices. The present volume attests to the vitality of a new research field that stretches from cultural analysis of the secularity to institutional analysis of secular statehood and to ethnographic studies of everyday religious practices and their transformations.

In this concluding chapter, I explore some broadly culturalist strategies in the comparative study of secular modernity by situating the single contributions to this volume within broader debates on global dynamics and regional path-dependencies. I argue that a major challenge for the comparative study of secular modernity lies in the synthesis and elaboration of the two seemingly contradictory approaches associated with theories of world society and of multiple modernities, respectively. To develop this argument, I discuss two prominent versions of both macro-sociological currents in greater depth: the neo-institutional world polity approach as developed by John W. Meyer and associates, and Shmuel N. Eisenstadt's civilizational theory. While Meyer stresses the universalizing tendencies of modernity that have led to the emergence of a world culture producing strong convergences in the formal structure of states, organizations, and individuals, Eisenstadt's work emphasizes diverging configurations of modernity in different civilizational cultural frameworks. Selecting these approaches as point of entry seems to me particularly fruitful for mainly three reasons: Both are consciously engaged in reformulating the Weberian account of occidental rationalization in light of the above-mentioned problemshift. Furthermore, while retaining insights from established theoretical traditions, such as phenomenology and structural-functionalism, both have subjected the conventional concepts of sociological theory to thorough criticism. And last but not least, both are, though with highly different methodologies, grounded in empirical and historical research.

In the next section, I explore those conceptual moves which clearly separate these two approaches from previous theories of modernization and provide common ground for theoretical cross-fertilization, and argue that their synthesis is in fact necessary to overcome limitations internal to both. After that, I discuss the implications of such a synthesis for the global comparative study of secular modernity by discussing the contributions to this volume in greater detail. Having highlighted some limitations of culturalist approaches to the study of secular modernity, I conclude by drawing attention to elements of a research agenda that, far from discarding the term of the "secular" altogether, offers analytical leverage for understanding cultural constructions of secularity and for explaining institutional varieties of secularism under conditions of global interconnectedness.

1 Rethinking Modernity

Modernization theory has experienced several "ups and downs" in the post-war period and, at first sight, Meyer's and Eisenstadt's theories of social change may appear as yet another episode in this history. After its crisis and demise in the 1970s, modernization theory was revived, in a modified version, during the late eighties and early nineties, in relation to a perceived new wave of democratization and transition to market economies in the post-Communist world. However, compared to "neo-modernism" (Alexander 1994; see also Tiryakian 1991), world polity studies and civilizational analysis both involve a much more marked departure from conventional theories of modernization and their unilinear conceptions of social change.

Firstly, and most importantly, both problematize conceptions of action and social order which often are simply taken for granted. To restate Peter Wagner's (2001) distinction, "modernist" social theories presume or naturalize the autonomy of the individual or the rationality of the social world or both, while "modern" social theories see these notions as historically contingent. According to this distinction, Meyer and Eisenstadt would clearly fall on the side of "modern" social theory. Meyer has pushed the neo-institutional perspective to an extreme by arguing that "agency" and rational "actorhood" cannot be accepted as natural foundations of sociological theorizing but need to be seen as products of a contingent cultural system (Meyer and Jepperson 2000: 101); similarly, Meyer deconstructs functional theories of society, seeing them instead as part of highly elaborated cultural frames (e. g. Meyer 1999: 126). Eisenstadt argues that sociology, a child of modern protest movements, is ultimately rooted in the cultural grammar of Axial civilization, to the extent that it regards the world as deficient and in need of rational reconstruction (see Alexander 1992: 88). In emphasizing the contingency of modern assumptions about action and social order, both authors share an anti-evolutionary historicism which follows the relativist strands of Weber's theory of occidental rationalism.

Secondly, and in close connection to this emphasis on contingency, both authors adopt an interpretive stance towards modernity, understood as an inherently cultural or symbolic construction (for an interpretative theory of modernity, see also Wagner 2008). Meyer's conception of modernity, in line with cultural-cognitivist institutionalism, is based on a strictly phenomenological reading of Weber's theory of occidental rationalization. According to his "macro-phenomenological institutionalism", rationality is regarded as a myth, rational action as its ritual or dramaturgical enactment, and rationalization as the institutionalization of a cultural system of ultimate ends, means-ends schemes, and rational actor identities (cf. Meyer, Boli and Thomas 1987; Meyer and Jepperson 2000). Eisenstadt's interest in the cultural dimensions of modernity, in turn, follows from his theory of human interaction which, beyond its structural-functionalist origins, is rooted in an account of the existential problems of meaning and reflexivity derived from Martin Buber's social theory (Eisenstadt 1995). He sees modernity as a cultural program characterized by a distinctive set of cosmological and ontological premises, of which the most important are the awareness of uncertainty combined with a faith in the inner-worldly realization of transcendent visions (Eisenstadt 2003). Hence, it is the constitution of a horizon of expectations to be realized in history that ultimately explains the increased propensity to social change, and, indeed, to revolutions of various sorts. In other words, modernity as an epoch is not defined by a set of substantive institutions (e.g. democracy, market economy, rule of law, etc.) but by a cultural or symbolic form that gives rise to highly different institutional projects. It is important to note that both authors share a strong emphasis on the contradictions inherent to modern culture. Eisenstadt, in particular, has repeatedly commented on the antinomies of the cultural program of modernity, containing both visions of autonomy and rational mastery, liberality and control, pluralism and Jacobinism.

Both approaches might so far seem to share the theoretical orientation of a "strong program" (Alexander and Smith 2001) in cultural sociology, an orientation that is also favored by Burchardt, Wohlrab-Sahr and Middell in their approach to "secularities" as elaborated in the introduction to this volume. However, both Meyer and Eisenstadt go beyond such a program by paying close attention to structural processes through which projects of modernity are institutionalized. In that respect – this is the third point of common conceptual ground – they put strong emphasis on the political arena as the primary site of modern institutional projects. Thus, according to Eisenstadt, the political sphere acquires charismatic qualities in modernity, and collectivities are increasingly politicized (Eisenstadt 1998: 47). Meyer argues in a similar vein that it is the State into which divine authority (and charisma) is devolved and which, in the course of its structural expansion, has become the major collective actor of societal reconstruction (Thomas and Meyer 1984). By theorizing the pivotal role of the political arena in the institutionalization of modern culture, both authors provide an important correction to (neo-)functionalist accounts of processes of social differentiation, as they situate them not only within wider cultural, but also institutional frameworks. The primary institutional site for the enactment of modern myths of rationality is, for both authors, the nation-state, characterized by a structural coupling of political organization and collective identity. By analyzing the wider historical processes through which that framework was legitimated and constructed, they are both able to avoid the impasses which theories of "modern societies" entrenched in methodological nationalism have encountered.

The strong emphasis on the historical contingency, the cultural construction of modernity, and its political institutionalization clearly separates Meyer and Eisenstadt's approaches from conventional modernization theories. While all three points of common conceptual ground would merit closer analysis, it may be concluded that a theoretical synthesis between the two approaches seems at least to be possible.

Cross-fertilization between the two theories is, however, not only possible, but also necessary in order to overcome inconsistencies in each of them. In spite of their shared assumptions about modernity, Meyer and Eisenstadt have pursued rather distinctive theoretical projects, elaborating the Weberian account of occidental rationalization in highly different fashion. Meyer's reading of Weber stresses the "universal cultural significance" of the occidental path of rationalization. In this view, transformations of late medieval Christendom that resulted in the emergence of the cultural system of modern rationalism eventually spread throughout the world (Meyer 1989). The European cultural system thus forms the nucleus of the modern world polity which emerged in the 19th and 20th century, carried by international organizations, NGOs, professions, and epistemic communities (Boli and Thomas 1999). The institutionalization of rational cognitive and normative frames results in strong isomorphism of modern actors – states, organizations, and individuals – and is documented in various large-scale quantitative longitudinal studies (e.g. Meyer et al. 1997; Meyer 1999 with further references).

By contrast, Eisenstadt takes Weber's work as a starting point for civilizational analysis. Contrary to Weber's original intention, Eisenstadt reads his comparative studies of world religions not as an argument about the failure of rationalization in non-occidental civilizations, but as an explanation of their distinctive paths to modernity (Eisenstadt 1989). Highlighting the common grammar of Axial Age civilizations, including the tension between transcendental and mundane orders (Eisenstadt 1982), he identifies those cultural factors that account for dynamics of change in non-occidental civilizations and, hence, their receptivity to the program of modernity. At the same time, he stresses that, against the background of these cultural visions, which legitimate institutional arrangements of market, power, and collective identities and entail particular configurations of elites and protest movements, different interpretations of modernity and thus diverging institutional projects – "multiple modernities" – have emerged (Eisenstadt 2001).

In a certain sense, then, the two approaches can be seen as complementary and in need of theoretical synthesis. The world polity approach would profit from higher sensitivity to civilizational path-dependencies on three accounts. First of all, explanations of institutional change at the world polity level can be improved by analyzing the influences of civilizational (or national) dynamics. Thus, the incorporation of non-occidental civilizations in the modern state system has, especially in the course of de-colonization, considerably changed cognitive and normative frames of state sovereignty, national self-determination, and human rights. The very content of world culture has thereby evolved beyond its occidental origins. Understanding such paradoxical consequences of global institutionalization processes necessitates taking civilizational (and national) levels into account. Furthermore, the consequences of institutional contradictions inherent to world-polity precepts can be better theorized by considering interaction effects between different levels of macrosocial processes. Institutional contradictions create opportunity structures for diverging projects pursued by political elites and protest movements as a function of different civilizational settings. Finally, where the neo-institutionalist literature is largely silent on the question of how globally-diffused cultural frames are re-interpreted at a more local level, Eisenstadt makes a strong case for historical path-dependency of long-term processes of social change. Thus, more refined analyses of processes of decoupling become possible. That formal structure and activity structure are strongly de-coupled in highly rationalized institutional fields is a well-known proposition of neo-institutionalism (Meyer and Rowan 1977; Boyle and Meyer 1998: 223). Such de-coupling often occurs in highly reflexive modes: reform movements in non-occidental contexts have thus combined universal references to modernity with the maintenance of particular civilizational identities articulated in semantic schemes such as "Eastern spirit – Western technology". So to explain the actual degree of de-coupling, one needs to investigate the cultural repertoires and structural factors that determine whether transnational expectancy structures are met by resistance, modification, or full implementation within the activity structure.

Conversely, civilizational analysis would also benefit from the world polity approach. Firstly, the analytical tools developed by neo-institutionalists might help to understand the global dynamics of civilizations. Eisenstadt does stress that modernity is the first civilization framework with explicit claims to universality and worldwide impact, but he leaves the social processes through which the cultural program of modernity is globally diffused unspecified. Yet such processes are precisely the major focus of neo-institutionalist world polity studies. Second, the very concept of civilization might be refined by highlighting dynamics of diffusion and mechanisms of mimetic, normative, and coercive isomorphism operating beyond national societies. The diffusion of Christianity, Islam and other world religions certainly provide examples of such processes. The Soviet attempt to promulgate and institutionalize a distinctively socialist vision of (secular) modernity, as analyzed in the contribution by Buchenau to this volume, might even be an apposite example of an alternative world polity. Third, the world polity approach offers insights into the question of how and why civilizations, far from being essential entities, have become highly codified and institutionalized in the late 20th century; as Bajpai (this volume) shows in her analysis of speeches by Indian Prime Ministers, civilizational identities are actually intensified when staged on global dialogue platforms.

In sum, the foregoing discussion suggests that a theoretical synthesis of the world polity approach and civilizational analysis is both possible and necessary. Such a synthesis amounts to an analytical framework which responds to the problemshift of social theory by problematizing modernist concepts, emphasizing the cultural construction of modernity and privileging the political arena, particularly the nation-state, as a site for its institutionalization; and which interprets modernity as a global condition giving rise to multiple institutional formations beyond occidental rationalization.

2 Theorizing the Secular

As indicated above, the social scientific study of religion has partaken in, and contributed to, the problemshift in social theory. Attention to the historical contingency of the notion of the "secular" (see Asad 2003), emphasis on the cultural construction of "secularity" as background condition of modernity (see e.g. Taylor 2007) and interest in the institutional varieties of "secularism" as a political mode of regulating religion (see e.g. Cady and Hurd 2010) clearly mirror theoretical arguments advanced by revisionist theories of modernity as discussed above. It therefore seems useful to explore the potential offered by a theoretical synthesis of world polity and multiple modernities approaches for the comparative study of secular modernity.

To do so, I start by briefly spelling out some implications of these two approaches for the study of cultural constructions of secularity and institutional varieties of secularism, by focusing on the Western trajectory which looms in the background of the present volume. Against that background, I then engage in a comparison of the non-Western case studies articulated in the volume's various contributions.

2.1 Trajectories of the Secular in the West

Understood as a cultural program, modernity is fundamentally related to imaginations or expectations of secularity. Following Eisenstadt, the cultural construction of modernity in Europe can be described as a result of heterodox movements within Christianity. These movements, crystallizing in the Protestant Reformation, both radicalized the Axial tension between the transcendent and the mundane order and attempted to resolve it by means of an inner-worldly reconstruction of society (Eisenstadt 1989). Traditional modes of legitimization broke down and what formerly were themes of social protest – liberty, equality, solidarity – moved to the center of society. Taylor's (2007) narrative of an emerging "immanent frame" or Wagner's (2008) idea of autonomy as a core expectation of modernity are similar accounts of this emergent secularity.

That the emergence of secular modernity changed the social place of religion is already evident in historical semantics. Indeed, it was in post-Reformation political vocabularies that the very concept of religion, of rather marginal importance in pre-modern discourse, received its particular modern meaning. The modern concept of religion has, first of all, a generic meaning signifying a presumably distinctive phenomenon ("religion"), distinct in essence from the newly emerging and equally essentialized domains of rational inner-worldly action, i.e. economy, politics, law and science. Secondly, it also has a relativistic and historicist meaning ("a religion" and "religions"), allowing for different actualizations of the essence of "religion" in historical systems of belief that are assumedly shared by a certain group of people, enacted in their common rituals and embodied in mutually exclusive membership organizations. It was also in post-Reformation political vocabulary that the *saeculum*, previously conceived as interlude between Creation and *eschaton*, was now re-imagined as unlimited social time-space within which both "religion" and "politics" were situated. In any event, the breakthrough to secular modernity was accompanied by the emergence of semantic distinctions between "religion" and other domains, or of what Burchardt and Wohlrab-Sahr (2012; see also Burchardt, Wohlrab-Sahr and Middell, this volume) analytically call "secularity".

"Secularity", as modernity's *imaginaire*, was institutionalized, above all, in the nation-state. As we already saw, the political sphere gained autonomy from the Church and became the major focus for rational reconstructions of society with the emergence of modernity. In other words, the charisma which, in medieval Roman Christendom was partly invested in "spiritual" authority (ecclesia), partly in "secular" authority (imperium), shifted entirely to the latter. While the shift of charisma to the "secular" – or immanent – political sphere reduced the influence of transcendent authorities (God) in legitimating power and in defining collectivities, it did not imply that "spiritual" matters or the Christian tradition broadly conceived became publicly irrelevant. On the contrary, what was now called "religion" could be incorporated into the nation-state's projects of rationalization and disciplinization. The State gained organizational control over practices and institutions – such as education, science, and most notably, over private and civil law – which had formerly been controlled by "spiritual" authorities. Furthermore, Christian symbols could be drawn upon to construct collective identities, particularly in the confessional age, when sovereign rulers assumed the right to determine the "religion" of their subjects, but also later in the nineteenth century when national identities were constructed with reference to confessional traditions. What needs to be emphasized, however, is that these instrumental uses of "religion" were firmly embedded within secular cultural constructions and institutional varieties of secularism understood as a selfstanding political order in which ecclesiastical authorities were relegated to secondary rank.

Again, historical semantics are indicative of these trends. In fact, the concept of religion lent itself to political contestations about symbolic boundaries between "public" and "private" (Koselleck 1973: 18, 29, 154). Thus, during the formation of absolutist territorial states after the confessional wars and the Peace of Westphalia (1648), religion was located in a private sphere opposed to a State that was considered to transcend all "religious" particularities. In the eighteenth century, when a new conceptual opposition was formulated between the State and what was now understood as "civil society" and the "public sphere", "religion" was further privatized conceptually. Until today definitions of "religion" are a highly contested resource in discourses over state sovereignty and national identity and their limitations. Finally, from the French Revolution onwards, the semantic dichotomy of "religion" and modern "politics" was transposed onto the meta-narrative associated with the concept of secularization. Originally a strictly legal term, the concept has been used, since the nineteenth century, metaphorically and within a relatively flexible narrative structure, couched in either utopian or nostalgic idioms and emphasizing either continuity or discontinuity (on French revolutionary semantics see Manent 1987; on German conceptual history see Lübbe 1965). In each of its form, the meta-narrative of secularization has contributed to the cultural constructions of modernity and legitimated institutional models of secularism.

If the shift of charisma from "spiritual" to "secular" authority resulted in new arrangements of political organization, collective identity, and public spheres within modern nation-states, premised on highly elaborated cultural constructions of the secular, the institutional forms of such arrangements ("secularisms") varied considerably within the Western context. Eisenstadt himself (e.g. 2000), building on Tocqueville and others, commented extensively upon North American modernity in which a strong institutional separation of "church and state" is combined with a low degree of differentiation between politics and religion. Drawing explicitly on Eisenstadt's conceptual framework, Danièle Hervieu-Léger (2003) outlined a genealogical approach to "multiple religious modernities" to capture the imprint left by confessional cultures on the trajectories of secularization. And historical sociologists (e.g. Martin 1978) have shown in much detail how critical junctures, including the Reformation, the response to the French Revolution and the onset of industrialization, led to variable patterns of secularization and institutional arrangements ranging from French *laïcité* over German-type state-church-corporatism to state or national churches as in England and Scandinavia.

Such variations within the West notwithstanding, the cognitive and normative scripts attached to the secular nation-state model became strongly institutionalized in the world polity during the twentieth century. As analyzed by Meyer and others, international governmental and non-governmental organizations as well as transnational epistemic communities of lawyers contributed to diffusing cognitive categories of "religion" and norms of secularism across the globe. Interestingly, the nation-state model became itself considerably transformed since the post-war period, as epitomized by the global institutionalization of individual human rights in which highly individualistic notions of religious freedom were combined with collective minority rights (see Koenig 2008). As found in several studies on the changing logic of citizenship (e.g. Soysal 1994), political organization and collective identity, State and Nation have thus become increasingly de-coupled within the world polity and, as a consequence, claims for the public recognition of religious identities have become strongly legitimized. Legitimate statehood is not only made conditional on respect for religious freedoms, but also on the promotion of religious (and cultural) diversity – a development which, in conjunction with migration-driven diversification, has led to considerable institutional changes within the European context (see Koenig 2007).

2.2 Cultural Constructions and Institutional Varieties of the Secular beyond the West

Despite their national varieties, European institutional arrangements of religion and politics were, in long-term perspective, embedded in similar cultural constructions of secularity that echoed the political-theological framework of Christianity. It should therefore not come as a surprise if non-Western civilizational contexts have experienced the emergence of different cultural constructions of secularity drawing, albeit not exclusively, on different repertoires of conceptualizing the Axial tension between transcendental and mundane orders than those which underlie European notions of secularity. While space does not permit me to analyze the cultural constructions of secularity and the institutional varieties of secularism which they entail in historical detail (see Spohn 2003), I briefly want to explore the contemporary interplay of civilizational and global cultural repertoires by reviewing the contributions to this volume in greater detail. It will become clear that while civilizational and global frameworks clearly matter, negotiations over the meaning of secularity are also strongly shaped by local actor constellations and national institutional frameworks.

The post-Soviet context is of particular interest as it attests to the multiplicity of cultural repertoires of secularity that are available to elite groups and protest movements in moments of far-reaching institutional transformation, and thus to the contestation over institutional arrangements of religion and politics. As Buchenau argues forcefully in his contribution, Soviet socialism promoted a distinctive vision of secularism understood as a political order standing not only above but also against religion – although practical policies regularly had to compromise with local religious sensibilities. This vision of secularism was "exported" within the Soviet sphere of influence, attesting to dynamics of transnational diffusion and of coercive, normative and mimetic isomorphism as highlighted by neo-institutionalist scholars. Crucially, however, the Soviet model of secularism was strongly filtered by historical path-dependencies and local adaptations. If any pattern was to be discerned in such filtering, it was one of confessional legacies: while the Soviet model did not meet much resistance in Orthodox countries and also took root in Protestant countries to a considerable degree, the presence of Catholic majorities led to significant modifications to the Soviet model of secularism. As the Polish case clearly shows, the project of state-enforced secularization of society pushed the Catholic Church to take a strong oppositional stance towards this model. Buchenau's analysis thus mirrors arguments advanced by Byrnes and Katzenstein (2006) in their comparative analysis of the stance taken by different confessional traditions towards the process of Europeanization.

If confessional traditions interact with transnational Soviet models of secularism in the socialist period, the post-socialist condition renders the situation yet more complex. As Agadjanian highlights, the Western models of state secularism, as articulated in international religious freedom provisions and as promoted by hosts of lawyers, non-governmental associations and Protestant missionaries active on post-Soviet terrain, have become additional cultural repertoires for domestic elites and social movements. Indeed, many post-Soviet nation-states, eager to acquire legitimacy within the international arena, adopted constitutions with strong provisions on religious freedom. However, both Soviet and Western models of secularism have, in many countries, including Russia, recently been inflected by processes of de-secularization in which nationalizing states pay stronger tribute to religious majority traditions in their constitutional design and their actual policies.

Another significant example of this layering of cultural repertoires is provided by the sub-Saharan African context. Ann Swidler (2010) prominently argued that African societies are permeated by multiple cultural meanings that have a sacred status, including missionary Christianity and global discourses of human rights but also pre-Axial, Durkheimian traditions of chiefdom and communal rituals. As Landau argues in his contribution, political movements in this context of unsettled nation-state formation are notoriously infused by religious vocabularies which themselves are derived from multiple sources. Further complicating the picture, Rijk van Dijk traces subtle changes in valuations of immanent spheres, as mainstream missionary Christianity was superseded by Pentecostalism, with its prosperity gospel, and as educated elites became increasingly critical of the latter, with as yet unclear consequences for the construction of subjectivity or individual actorhood. What both contributions suggest is that the global circulation of modern categories of "secular" and "religion" can give rise to highly variable local outcomes.

Turning away from contexts strongly influenced by historical and contemporary Christian movements, Krämer surveys the trajectory of secularization in the Arab Islamic world. Rightly stressing that civilizations are far from being the coherent entities that they are sometimes described as (as in Huntington 1993) and are characterized by internal contestations and contradictions (as in Eisenstadt 2003), she does outline some features which, in comparative perspective, stand out as distinctive from the Western trajectory. Following Casanova's well-known analytical scheme, Krämer highlights that neither the decline nor the privatization of religion took place in these contexts, whilst also stressing that various forms of differentiations between religion and politics did occur from early on. Influenced by the modern nation-state model, these forms became however thoroughly transformed, as the Islamic political discourse of modernity amply demonstrates (see Salvatore 1997). As Kinitz notes in his intriguing analysis of deviant thinkers in early and late twentieth century Egypt, the notion of "secularism" (*al-'almaniya*) was used by the Islamic establishment to criticize the influence of Western ideology within domestic public spheres and thus to defend their own hegemonic position within the religious field. Under such conditions, it should not come as a surprise that strong de-coupling characterizes the adoption of global cognitive and normative categories. As Krämer notes, most countries subscribe to the UN Declaration of Human rights and have incorporated religious freedom provisions in their written constitutions; yet strong restrictions continue to be placed upon religious minorities by political authorities (see also Grim and Finke 2011).

In relation to India, the present volume also covers a non-monotheistic Axial civilization with a long-standing tradition of structural and cultural pluralism (Eisenstadt 2003). This heritage figures prominently in the cultural construction of secularity, as the contribution by Bajpai well attests. In an intriguing analysis of Prime Ministers' speeches in post-1991 India, she cites numerous examples of a "staged civilizational memory". Externally, that is, in transnational arenas, Indian elites were anxious to stylize their country as an emerging secular democracy, not only compatible with Western expectations of modern nation-statehood, but also built upon deeply rooted traditions of "tolerance" and "unity in diversity". What Bajpai also shows, however, is that the notion of "secularism" is more contested domestically; initially adopted by the Congress Party in order to portray the state as standing above inter-communal conflicts, the influence of the BJP in recent governments has imbued "secularism" with more exclusivist Hindu meanings. Williams and Jenkins adopt a largely similar perspective on the Indian case, emphasizing continuities and discontinuities with British colonial rule and its notions of "non-interference" and minority relations. Like Bajpai who highlights the contradiction inherent to constitutional provisions for the secular state and on the rights of religious communities, they draw attention to inequalities produced by this particular version of institutionalized secularism by discussing recent developments in personal law and anti-conversion laws. Inequalities inherent to secular nationalism are also revealed in Renzi's account of the impasses encountered by anti-caste radical groups and Dalit movements in modern Indian history. While it is striking that, compared to the Islamic civilizational context analyzed by Krämer, the notion of secularism has gained such a strong legitimacy in Indian public discourse, its recent anti-communal inflections seem to justify distinctive forms of resistance against global scripts of anti-discrimination – as Renzi suggests in her analysis of India's engagement with UN Convention on the Elimination of Racial Discrimination.

A yet different civilizational context is discussed in treatments of Japan. In his detailed historical sociology of the Japanese modernization process, Eisenstadt (1996) famously dubbed Japan as an exceptional case where the cultural program of modernity took root in the context of a pre-Axial civilization which, while experiencing various cultural imports (Confucianism, Buddhism, Christianity...), preserved strongly primordial codes and ritualistic forms of constructing national identity. The resilience of this cultural pattern is demonstrated forcefully in Mullins' discussion of the historical development of Shintoism in

Japan. While Japan was particularly exposed to global influences in the post-war period and, in what Mullins describes as US-led "imperialist secularization", provided for separation between state and religion and for religious freedom in its constitution, various social movements preserved claims to public status of Shintoism. Recently, and ongoing privatization of religious practices notwithstanding, political elites have taken such aspirations on board, as Mullins impressively catalogues, in various legal initiatives restoring Shinto rituals and weakening the state's separation from religion. Although proposals for changing the constitution in such a direction have met with strong resistance, governmental involvement in strengthening Shintoism is noteworthy, as Porcu notes in her urban ethnography. In fact, the local government skillfully exploits global cultural repertoires when it portrays attempts to re-institute Shinto rituals in order to safeguard "cultural heritage", as understood by UNESCO. Not accidentally, these initiatives are perceived as strongly exclusionary by Christians and Buddhists alike.

3 Conclusion

Sociological theory is currently challenged by a far-reaching problemshift triggered by the historical experience of a de-centering of occidental modernity. The "changing light of cultural problems" requires the transformation of sociology's conceptual apparatus, attesting to what Weber called the "eternal youth" of the social sciences (Weber [1904] 1988b: 214). While this problemshift clearly separates us from some of Weber's own assumptions, his project of historical comparative macro-sociology has retained and perhaps even regained its attraction (see Schwinn 2003). An important strand of the literature has tried to pursue this project in culturalist directions. In this paper, I have argued that two of the most prominent culturalist elaborations of Weber's theory of occidental rationalization, Meyer's world polity approach and Eisenstadt's civilizational analysis, are amenable to a theoretical synthesis. I have argued furthermore that such a synthesis yields a strong analytical framework for handling cultural constructions of secularity and institutional varieties of secularism in the world society, a framework in which the contributions to this volume and broader debates about modern secularities can be fruitfully situated. By way of conclusion, I would however like to highlight three limitations of culturalist approaches to secular modernity and to sketch some perspectives for future research.

First of all, culturalist theories of modern secularities, not unlike previous theories of secularization, run the risk of over-stylizing macro-configurations of religion and other social spheres, regardless of whether they are tailored at civilizational or global levels. Thus, the contributions to this volume amply document that the processes of differentiation, privatization and religious decline as defined by Casanova (1994) are analytically independent. In various ways, all of the case studies in this volume (consider Krämer on Islam or Mullins on Japan, for example) confirm that secularization (or de-secularization) may occur on one of these three dimensions without necessarily determining change in the other two dimensions. This implies that comparative research should strategically focus on specific dimensions of secularization. The differentiation of religion and politics, that is, institutional secularization, stands out as a particularly important dimension in this respect: it is no accident that almost all contributions in this volume (except for those focusing on the African context) give prime attention to varieties of "secularism" understood as state regulation of religion as articulated in constitutions, laws, and policies.

Second, the contributions to this volume also demonstrate that the cultural repertoires of secularity used by state representatives, political elites and social movements are layered and highly complex. True, in *longue durée* perspective, civilizational traditions and global scripts do account for important variations in how actors draw distinctions between "religion" and other spheres and assign "religion" its place within modern nation-states. But civilizational traditions and global scripts are far from exhausting the range of cultural repertoires which characterize today's "entangled modernities" (Therborn 2003): colonial cultural schemas (see Williams and Jenkins in this volume) are just as important, as are the cultural schemas diffused by transnational or global religious movements (see Landau and van Dijk in this volume).

Third, while all this suggests that emphasis on cultural constructions of secularity is indeed worthwhile, it also seems clear from the foregoing discussion that interpretative theories are insufficient if we are to explain the short-term processes of institutional secularization or de-secularization so well documented in this volume: to explain such processes, configurations of actors, their interests and their power relations need to be taken into account more prominently (see notably Gill 2008). Perhaps least explored are the mid-term processes of state secularization that are driven by logics of professionalization, dynamics within the political field, and other structural changes. A fully-fledged research program on cultural constructions of secularity and institutional varieties of secularism would need to operate simultaneously on these variable temporal planes.

In sum, the contributions to the volume suggest that it is almost impossible to eradicate the category "secular" from the analyst's vocabulary. True, the "secular" and the "religious" and their various translations in non-European languages *are* categories of practice which require critical scrutiny. But that does not mean that, with due reflexive awareness and definitional precision, they cannot be used as categories of analysis. Studying cultural distinctions between religious and nonreligious spheres, their genealogies and their uses in truly global comparative perspective does promise analytical leverage; and leverage is also gained by analyzing the institutional varieties of secularism under conditions of global modernity. Formulating contingency-sensitive, culturally informed and thoroughly comparative theories of secularization (and de-secularization) remains on the agenda of social scientists for the time being.

References

Albrow, Martin. 1996. *The Global Age*. Cambridge: Polity Press.
Alexander, Jeffrey C. 1992. "The fragility of progress: an interpretation of the turn toward meaning in Eisenstadt's later work." *Acta Sociologica* 35: 85–94.
—. 1994. "Modern, anti, post and neo: how social theories have tried to understand the 'New World' of 'Our Time'." *Zeitschrift für Soziologie* 23: 165–197.
Alexander, Jeffrey, and Philip Smith. 2001. "The strong program in cultural theory: elements of a structural hermeneutics." In *The Handbook of Sociological Theory*, ed. Jonathan Turner, 135–150, New York: Kluwer.
Arjomand, Said, and Edward A Tiryakian, eds. 2004. *Rethinking Civilizational Analysis*. London: Sage.
Arnason, Johann P. 1989. "The imaginary constitution of modernity." *Revue européenne des sciences sociales* XXVII: 323–337.
—. 1990. "Nationalism, globalization and modernity," in *Global Culture. Nationalism, Globalization and Modernity*, ed. Mike Featherstone, 207–236. London et al.: Sage.
—. 2002. *Civilizations in Dispute*. London: Sage.
Arnason, Johann P., Shmuel N. Eisenstadt, and Björn Wittrock, eds. 2005. *Axial Civilizations and World History*. Leiden & Boston: Brill.
Asad, Talal. 2003. *Formations of the Secular: Christianity, Islam, Modernity*. Stanford: Stanford University Press.
Beyer, Peter. 1994. *Religion and Globalization*. London: Sage Publications.
Boli, John, and George Thomas, eds. 1999. *Constructing World Culture: International Nongovernmental Organizations Since 1875*. Stanford: Stanford University Press.
Boyle, Elizabeth Heger, and John Meyer. 1998. "Modern law as a secularized and global religious model: implications for the sociology of law." *Soziale Welt* 49: 213–232.
Byrnes, Timothy, and Peter J. Katzenstein, eds. 2006. *Religion in an Expanding Europe*. Cambridge: Cambridge University Press.
Cady, Linell E., and Elizabeth Shakman Hurd. 2010. *Comparative Secularisms in a Global Age*. New York: Palgrave Macmillan.
Casanova, José. 1994. *Public Religions in the Modern World*. Chicago: Chicago University Press.
Chakrabarty, Dipesh. 2002. *Provincializing Europe*. Princeton: Princeton University Press.
Chernilo, Daniel. 2007. *A Social Theory of the Nation-State: The Political Forms of Modernity Beyond Methodological Nationalism*. London: Routledge.

Dirlik, Arif. 2003. "Global modernity? Modernity in an age of globalization." *European Journal of Social Theory* 6: 275–292.
Durkheim, Emile, and Marcel Mauss. 1913. "Note sur la notion de civilisation." *L'Année sociologique* 12:46–50.
Eisenstadt, Shmuel N. 1973. *Tradition, Change, and Modernity*. New York et al.: John Wiley & Sons.
—. 1982. "The axial age: the emergence of transcendental visions and the rise of the clerics." *European Journal of Sociology* 23: 299–314.
—. 1989. "Max Weber on western Christianity and the Weberian approach to civilizational dynamics." *Canadian Journal of Sociology* 14:203–224.
—. 1995. *Power, Trust and Meaning. Essays in Sociological Theory and Analysis*. Chicago: Universit of Chicago Press.
—. 1996. *Japanese Civilization – A Comparative View*. Chicago: Chicago University Press.
—. 1998. *Die Antinomien der Moderne. Die jakobinischen Grundzüge der Moderne und des Fundamentalismus. Heterodoxien, Utopismus und Jakobinismus in der Konstitution fundamentalistischer Bewegungen*. Frankfurt a.M.: Suhrkamp.
—. 2001. "The challenge of multiple modernities," in *New Horizons in Sociological Theory and Research. The Frontiers of Sociology at the Beginning of the Twenty-First Century*, ed. Luigi Tomasi, 99–126. Aldershot: Ashgate.
—. 2003. *Comparative Civilizations and Multiple Modernities*, 2 Vol. Leiden & Boston: Brill.
Eisenstadt, Shmuel N. and M. Curelaru. 1976. *The Form of Sociology – Paradigms and Crises*. New York: John Wiley & Sons.
Gill, Anthony. 2008. *The Political Origins of Religious Liberty*. Cambridge: Cambridge University Press.
Gorski, Philip. 2000. "Historicizing the secularization debate." *American Sociological Review* 65:138–167.
Gorski, Philip S., and Ates Altinordu. 2008. "After secularization?" *Annual Review of Sociology* 34:55–85.
Grim, Brian J., and Roger Finke. 2011. *The Price of Freedom Denied. Religious Persecution and Conflict in the Twenty-First Century*. Cambridge: Cambridge University Press.
Hall, Peter A., and David Soskice. 2001. *Varieties of Capitalism. The Institutional Foundations of Comparative Advantage*. Oxford: Oxford University Press.
Hamilton, Gary G. 1984. "Configurations in history: the historical sociology of S.N. Eisenstadt," in *Vision and Method in Historical Sociology*, ed. Theda Skocpol, 85–128. Cambridge: Cambridge University Press.
Hervieu-Léger, Danièle. 1993. *La Religion pour Mémoire*. Paris: Les Éditions du Cerf.
—. 2003. "Pour une sociologie des "modernités religieuses multiples": une autre approche de la "religion invisibile" des sociétés européennes." *Social Compass* 50(3):287–95.
Huntington, Samual P. 1993. The Clash of Civilizations? *Foreign Affairs* 72, 3: 22–49.
Hurd, Elizabeth Shakman. 2008. *The Politics of Secularism in International Relations*. Princeton: Princeton University Press.
Joas, Hans, and Wolfgang Knöbl. 2004. *Sozialtheorie. Zwanzig einführende Vorlesungen*. Frankfurt am Main: Suhrkamp.
Knöbl, Wolfgang. 2007. *Die Kontingenz der Moderne. Wege in Europa, Asien und Amerika*. Frankfurt a.M. and New York: Campus.
Koenig, Matthias. 2000. "Religion and the nation-state in South Korea: a case of changing interpretations of modernity in a global context." *Social Compass* 47: 551–570.

—. 2005. "Politics and religion in European nation-states – institutional varieties and contemporary transformations," in *Religion and Politics. Cultural Perspectives*, ed. Bernhard Giesen and Daniel Suber, 291–315. Leiden: Brill.

—. 2007. "Europeanizing the governance of religious diversity – Islam and the transnationalization of law, politics and identity." *Journal of Ethnic and Migration Studies* 33(6): 911–32.

—. 2008. "Institutional change in the world polity – international human rights and the construction of collective identities." *International Sociology* 23(1): 95–114.

Koselleck, Reinhart. 1973 [1959]. *Kritik und Krise. Eine Studie zur Pathogenese der bürgerlichen Welt.* Frankfurt a.M.: Suhrkamp.

Kuru, Ahmet T. 2009. *Secularism and State Policies Toward Religion. The United States, France, and Turkey.* Cambridge: Cambridge University Press.

Lechner, Frank J., and John Boli. 2005. *World Culture. Origins and Consequences.* Oxford: Blackwell.

Lübbe, Hermann. 1965. *Säkularisierung. Geschichte eines ideenpolitischen Begriffs.* Freiburg und München: Verlag Karl Alber.

Manent, Pierre. 1987. "Quelques remarques sur la notion de "sécularisation"." Pp. 351–57 in The Political Culture of the French Revolution: Vol. 3, *The Tranformation of Political Culture 1789–1848*, edited by Colin Lucas. Oxford: Pergamon Press.

Martin, David. 1978. *A General Theory of Secularization.* Oxford: Basil Blackwell.

Meyer, John W. 1989. "Conceptions of Christendom: notes on the distinctiveness of the west," in *Cross-National Research in Sociology*, ed. Melvin Kohn, 395–413. Newbury Park: Sage.

—. 1999. "The changing cultural content of the nation-state: a world society perspective." in *State / Culture. State Formation after the Cultural Turn*, ed. George Steinmetz, 123–143. Ithaca: Cornell University Press.

Meyer, John W., John Boli, and George M. Thomas. 1987. "Ontology and rationalization in the western cultural account," in *Institutional Structure. Constituting State, Society, and the Individual*, ed. George M. Thomas, John W. Meyer, and John Boli, 12–37. Newbury Park: Sage.

Meyer, John W., John Boli, George M. Thomas, and Francisco O. Ramirez. 1997. "World society and the nation state." *American Journal of Sociology* 103:144–181.

Meyer, John W., and Ronald L. Jepperson. 2000. "The 'actors' of modern society: the cultural construction of social agency." *Sociological Theory* 18: 100–120.

Meyer, John W., and Brian Rowan. 1977. "Institutionalized organizations: formal structure as myth and ceremony." *American Journal of Sociology* 83: 340–363.

Norris, Pippa, and Ronald Inglehart. 2004. *Sacred and Secular. Religion and Politics Worldwide.* Cambridge: Cambridge University Press.

Pizzorno, Alessandro. 1987. "Politics unbound," in *Changing Boundaries of the Political. Essays on the Evolving Balance Between the State and Society, Public and Private in Europe*, ed. Charles S. Maier, 27–62. Cambridge: Cambridge University Press.

Salvatore, Armando. 1997. *Islam and the Political Discourse of Modernity.* Reading: Ithaca Press.

Schwinn, Thomas. 2003. "Kulturvergleich in der globalisierten Moderne," in *Das Weber-Paradigma. Studien zur Weiterentwicklung von Max Webers Forschungsprogramm*, ed. Gert Albert, Agathe Bienfait, Steffen Sigmund, and Claus Wendt, 301–327. Tübingen: Mohr Siebeck.

Soysal, Yasemin Nuhoglu. 1994. *Limits of Citizenship. Migrants and Postnational Membership in Europe.* Chicago: Chicago University Press.
Spohn, Willfried. 2003. "Multiple modernity, nationalism and religion: A global perspective." *Current Sociology* 51: 265–286.
Swidler, Ann. 2010. "The return of the sacred: What African chiefs teach us about secularization." *Sociology of Religion* 71(2): 157–71.
Taylor, Charles. 2007. *A Secular Age.* Cambridge, Mass.: The Belknap Press of Harvard University Press.
Therborn, Göran. 1999. *Globalizations and Modernitites – Experiences and Perspectives in Europe and Latin America.* Stockholm: FRN.
—. 2003. "Entangled modernities." *Europan Journal of Social Theory* 6: 293–305.
Thomas, George, and John W. Meyer. 1984. "The expansion of the state." *Annual Review of Sociology* 10: 461–482.
Tiryakian, Edward. 1991. "Modernisation: Exhumetur in pace (rethinking macrosociology in the 1990s)." *International Sociology* 6: 165–180.
Wagner, Peter. 1994. *A Sociology of Modernity. Liberty and Discipline.* London: Routledge.
—. 1998. "Certainty and order, liberty and contingency. the birth of social science as empirical political philosophy," in *The Rise of the Social Sciences and the Formation of Modernity*, ed. Johan Heilbron, Lars Magnusson, and Björn Wittrock, 241–263. Dordrecht: Kluwer Academic Publishers.
—. 2001. *Theorizing Modernity: Inescapability and Attainability in Social Theory.* London: Sage.
—. 2008. *Modernity as Experience and Interpretation.* London: Polity.
Wallerstein, Immanuel .1991. *Unthinking the Social Sciences.* Cambridge.
Weber, Max. 1988a. *Gesammelte Aufsätze zur Religionssoziologie.* 3 vols. Tübingen: Mohr-Siebeck.
—. 1988b. *Gesammelte Aufsätze zur Wissenschaftslehre.* Tübingen: Mohr-Siebeck.
Wittrock, Björn. 1998. "Early modernities: varieties and transitions." *Daedalus* 127: 19–40.
—. 1999. "Social theory and intellectual history: towards a rethinking of the formation of modernity," in *Social Time and Social Change. Perspectives on Sociology and History*, ed. Fredrik Engelstad and Ragnvald Kalleberg, 187–232. Oslo et al.: Scandinavian University Press.
—. 2000. "Modernity: one, none, or many? european origins and modernity as a global condition." *Daedalus* 129: 31–60.
Wohlrab-Sahr, Monika, and Marian Burchardt. 2012. "Multiple secularities: toward a cultural sociology of secular modernities." *Comparative Sociology* 11(6): 875–909.
Yack, Bernard. 1997. *The Fetishism of Modernities. Epochal Self-Consciousness in Contemporary Social and Political Thought.* Notre Dame: University of Notre Dame Press.

List of Contributors

Alexander Agadjanian is Professor at the Center for the Study of Religion, Russian State University of the Humanities, Moscow. His fields of interest include religion in the modern world, in particular in Russia and the post-Soviet Eurasia. He authored *Turns of Faith, Search of Meaning: Orthodox Christianity and Post-Soviet Experience* (Peter Lang 2014); edited *Armeninan Christianity Today: Identity Politics and Social Practices* (Ashgate 2014); and co-edited *Religion, Nation and Democracy in the South Caucasus* (forthcoming at Routledge in 2014); *Parish and Community in Russian Orthodoxy* (2011, in Russian); and *Eastern Orthodoxy in a Global Age* (Altamira Press 2005).

Anandita Bajpai recently defended her PhD at the Graduate Centre for the Humanities and Social Sciences, University of Leipzig and is currently postdoctoral fellow at the Humboldt University Berlin and the ZMO Berlin (Zentrum Moderner Orient). She holds an MA in Global Studies, completed at the Universities of Leipzig and Vienna (2008), and a BA in Political Science, obtained at Delhi University (2006). Her doctoral project focuses on the discursive constructions of an 'Emerging India' by the Indian prime ministers, through the medium of their post-1991 speeches, when numerous externally produced discourses started projecting India as an emerging power of the near future.

Klaus Buchenau is Professor of Southeastern European history at the University of Regensburg. His research interests include the modern religious history of Southeastern and Eastern Europe, the historical development of corruption, and Southeastern Europe in a global comparative perspective. He has published a monograph on orthodoxy and Catholicism comparing Serbia and Croatia and another on religious anti-westernism in Serbia and Russia.

Marian Burchardt is postdoctoral research fellow at the Max Planck Institute for the Study of Religious and Ethnic Diversity, Göttingen/Germany. His research explores the religious diversity and secularity in discourses on cultural identity and heritage. Before coming to the Max Planck Institute, he worked as a researcher in the project **"Multiple Secularities,"** based at the Cultural Studies Department of the University of Leipzig, and as a lecturer at the Department of Development Sociology at the University of Bayreuth, and was a visiting scholar at the New School for Social Research in New York City, the Social Science Research Centre Berlin (WZB), and the University of Stellenbosch. He recently co-edited *Topographies of Faith: Religion in Urban Space* (Brill 2013); *After Integration: Islam, Con-*

viviality and Contentious Politics in Europe (Springer 2014); and Religion and AIDS Treatment in Africa: Saving Souls, Prolonging Lives (Ashgate 2014).

Rijk van Dijk is an anthropologist and an expert on Pentecostalism, globalization and transnationalism, migration, youth, and healing. He has done extensive research on the rise of Pentecostal movements in the urban areas of Malawi, Ghana, and Botswana. His current research deals with religious, in particular Pentecostal, engagements with the domains of relationships, sexuality, and HIV/AIDS in Botswana. Recently he published the co-edited volume Religion and AIDS Treatment in Africa (Ashgate 2014) with Hansjoerg Dilger, Marian Burchardt, and Thera Rasing. He is senior researcher at the African Studies Centre in Leiden and holds a chair in the study of religion and sexuality in Africa at the AISSR, University of Amsterdam. He is also the chair of the International Research Network on Religion and AIDS in Africa and the editor-in-chief of the journal African Diaspora: A Journal of Transnational Africa in a Global World.

Laura Dudley Jenkins is Associate Professor of Political Science at the University of Cincinnati. Her research and publications focus on social justice policies in the context of culturally diverse democracies, especially India. Jenkins' book Identity and Identification in India: Defining the Disadvantaged (Routledge 2003, 2009) examines competing demands for affirmative action on the basis of caste, religion, class, and gender and the ways governments identify various categories through the courts, census, and official certificates. She was a Fulbright New Century Scholar in South Africa and India, researching access and equity in higher education. She contributed to and co-edited (with Michele S. Moses) Affirmative Action Matters: Creating Opportunities for Students Around the World (Routledge 2014).

Daniel Kinitz has recently finished his PhD on the discourse on secularism (al-ʿalmānīya) in contemporary Egypt and the social role of the modern Muslim intellectual. He has worked on argumentation strategies within political Islam with special focus on the Lebanese Hisbollah as well as on the history of Arab studies in Germany.

Matthias Koenig is professor in the department of sociology at the University of Göttingen and Max-Planck-Fellow at the Max Planck Institute for the Study of Religious and Ethnic Diversity. His research on human rights, migration, and religious diversity has appeared in journals such as Acta Sociologica, Ethnic and Racial Studies, International Sociology, and Journal for Ethnic and Migration Studies. He is also co-editor of International Migration and the Governance of Religious Di-

versity (with Paul Bramadat, Montreal 2009) and *Human Rights and Democracy and Multicultural Societies* (with Paul de Guchteneire, Aldershot 2007).

Gudrun Krämer is professor of Islamic Studies and director of the Berlin Graduate School Muslim Cultures and Societies at Freie Universität Berlin. Her research focuses on religion, law, politics, and society in modern Islam. She is member of the Berlin-Brandenburg Academy of Sciences and executive editor of the Encyclopaedia of Islam Three. She has been guest professor at Centre d'Etudes et de Documentation économique, juridique et sociale (CEDEJ), Cairo; School of Advanced International Studies (SAIS), John Hopkins University; Islamic University Jakarta; and Institut d'Etudes Politiques (Sciences Po) and École des Hautes Etudes en Sciences Sociales, both Paris; as well as visiting scholar at Max-Weber-Kolleg Erfurt and Center for Arab and Middle Eastern Studies, American University of Beirut. Her publications include *Hasan al-Banna* (Oxford 2010); *A History of Palestine: From the Ottoman Conquest to the Founding of State Israel* (Princeton 2008); *Speaking for Islam: Religious Authorities in Muslim Societies* (co-edited, Brill 2006); and *The Jews in Modern Egypt* (Tauris 1989).

Paul Landau's recent book, *Popular Politics in the History of South Africa, 1400 – 1948* was, like his first book about Botswana, a finalist for the Herskovits Prize. It is a big-picture revision of the story of South Africa's politics, rooting twentieth-century hybrid mobilizations in pre-colonial political modes. Prof. Landau also writes about and has edited books on histories of representation, both visual and oral-traditional. Currently, while teaching full-time at the University of Maryland, Prof. Landau is reading and thinking about twentieth-century radicalisms, particularly that of the African National Congress, the South African Communist Party, and Umkhonto weSizwe, the Spear of the Nation. The working title for his next book is *Spear: Nelson Mandela and Revolutionary South Africa, 1960 – 64*. Prof. Landau has been a Fellow in Historical Studies at the University of Johannesburg from 2011 to the present.

Matthias Middell is Professor of Global History and Spokesperson of the Centre for Area Studies of the University of Leipzig. He has been Fulbright Distinguished Professor in Transnational History at Duke University and Fellow in Residence at the Netherlands Institute for the Humanities and Social Sciences. His main fields of research include global history and its methodology, history of cultural transfers, and history of science. His recent publications include *Theoretiker der Globalisierung* (co-edited with Ulf Engel, Leipziger Universitätsverlag 2005); *Self-reflexive Area Studies* (Leipziger Universitätsverlag 2013); and *Transnational*

Challenges to National History Writing (co-edited with Lluis Roura, Palgrave 2013).

Mark R. Mullins is Professor of Japanese Studies and Director of the New Zealand Asia Institute's Japan Studies Centre at the University of Auckland. Prior to this appointment, he was engaged in academic work in Japan for twenty-seven years and taught at Shikoku Gakuin University, Meiji Gakuin University, and Sophia University, where he also served a three-year term as editor of *Monumenta Nipponica*. He completed his postgraduate studies in the sociology of religion and East Asian traditions at McMaster University (PhD 1985). He is the author and co-editor of a number of works, including *Religion and Society in Modern Japan* (Asian Humanities Press 1993), *Christianity Made in Japan: A Study of Indigenous Movements* (University of Hawaii Press 1998), *Religion and Social Crisis in Japan: Understanding Japanese Society Through the Aum Affair* (Palgrave 2001), and *Critical Readings on Christianity in Japan* (4 vols., forthcoming). He is currently writing a book on neo-nationalism and religion-state issues in contemporary Japanese society.

Elisabetta Porcu is professor of Asian Religions at the University of Cape Town. Before that, she was postdoctoral research fellow at the Centre for Area Studies at the University of Leipzig. Her research focuses on Japanese religions, particularly pure land Buddhism, as well as the relationships between art, media, religion, and culture in Japan in the context of globalization. In 2008 she published the monograph *Pure Land Buddhism in Modern Japanese Culture* with Brill. She is the editor-in-chief of the journal *Journal of Religion in Japan*.

Beatrice Renzi is an independent researcher focusing on cultural diversity and vernacular knowledge systems from an intersectional perspective. She has worked with various institutions in Europe, the US, and South Asia. She is the author of *The Politics of Shame: Untouchability and the Articulation of Collective Identities in Central India*, for which she received the research award 'Forschungsförderpreis der Universität Mainz'. Before returning to academia, she was engaged in development and governance programs in India.

Rina Verma Williams is Assistant Professor of Political Science at the University of Cincinnati in Ohio, USA. She teaches and researches in the areas of gender and identity politics; religion, law and nationalism; politics of developing countries; and South Asian and Indian politics. She is especially interested in the role of the state and democracy in the social/political construction of gendered identities. Her first book [*Postcolonial Politics and Personal Laws: Colonial Legal Leg-

acies and the Indian State (Oxford University Press 2006)] examined how religious laws affected ethnic conflict in India, and her current book project examines women's participation in religious nationalist political parties in Indian democracy. She has published several journal articles on these topics as well.

Monika Wohlrab-Sahr has been Professor of Sociology of Religion at the University of Leipzig and is presently Professor of Cultural Sociology at the same university. Her fields of research include conversion, Islam in Europe, secularity, secularization, non-religion, and qualitative methods. From 2010 to 2012 she directed a research project in which the conceptual framework of "Multiple Secularities" was developed. She has been research fellow at UC Berkeley, EUI Florence, JNIAS New Delhi, and at the Université de Montréal. Her main publications are *Konversion zum Islam in Deutschland und den USA* (Campus 1999); *Forcierte Säkularität* (Campus 2009, with Uta Karstein and Thomas Schmidt-Lux); "Multiple Secularities," *Comparative Sociology* 11 (2012): 875–909 (with Marian Burchardt); and *Qualitative Sozialforschung* (Oldenbourg 2014, with Aglaja Przyborski).

Index

Abd al-Rāziq,'Alī (1887 oder 1888–1966) 100, 103, 104, 105, 109, 110, 113, 116
Abū Zayd, Naṣr Ḥāmid (1943–2010) 99, 101f., 105f., 109
Africa 1, 10–12, 27f., 187, 189–195, 197–207, 209, 215–221, 224f., 227–231, 233–235, 297, 300
African National Congress, ANC 189, 194f., 202f., 205
African Traditional Religion 190, 207
al-ʿalmānīyah (secularism, secularity) 98, 100, 101, 102, 103, 104, 105, 108, 109, 114, 123
Albania 264, 270f.
al-Bannā, Jamāl (1920–2013) 108f., 111f.
Aloysius, G. 66, 68, 70f., 73, 75–77, 83
al-Qaraḍāwī, Yūsuf (b.1926) 97, 103, 104, 107, 118
Ambedkar, B.R. 29, 70f., 73f., 82
America, American 1, 10, 26, 35, 144, 151, 200, 203, 208, 224, 242, 245, 250, 295
ancestor, ancestral 32, 169, 191, 195–200, 203, 207
anticlerical 250, 254f.
anti-religious 98f., 102, 123, 245, 247, 256, 261, 263–265, 267, 271
Apartheid 11, 207–209
apostasy 32, 99, 102, 125, 130
Arab 1, 9f., 95, 97f., 102f., 121f., 124, 126, 128, 130–135, 242, 297
Arab Spring 128, 134f.
Armenia 241, 249f., 255–257
Armenian Apostolic Church 246, 256
Asad, Talal 3, 66, 98, 122, 191, 193f., 286, 292
Asia 1, 17, 19f., 22, 27, 30, 58, 139, 143, 158, 178
Association of Shinto Shrines 146, 152–155, 160
Atheism, atheist 6, 99, 102–104, 123, 131, 243–248, 253f., 263, 265, 271, 277, 279

autonomy 24, 26, 28, 70, 219, 246, 248, 275, 288f., 293
Azerbaijan 9, 241, 248, 253, 256

Baltic States 253, 274
Beckford, James A. 7
Belarus 249
belief 2f., 21, 42, 56, 68, 121, 123f., 126, 129, 131, 143f., 147, 150, 172f., 177, 183, 190, 194, 217f., 233f., 249, 261f., 266, 293
Berdiaev, Nikolai 262, 265
Berger, Peter 1, 97f., 108f., 111f., 143, 150f., 218, 242
"Beware: religion!" exhibition (case) 254
Beyer, Peter 2, 286
bible 192, 197, 217, 221, 225, 228–230, 234
Biko, Steve 207
blasphemy 111, 130, 189, 250
Bohemia 277
bolshevism 264–266
Botswana 12, 198, 200, 217, 221–223, 227–232, 234
Bourdieu, Pierre 76, 98, 106, 108, 126
Brahmanism 67f., 75f., 84
Bramadat, Paul 7
Brazil 151
Brezhnev, Leonid 267
Britain, british 11, 19, 21, 24, 25, 27, 28, 32, 35, 36, 53, 67, 103, 200, 201, 298
Brotherhood, Muslim 101, 107, 125, 129
Buddhism, Buddhist 6, 21, 83, 123, 129, 146, 180, 298
Bulgaria 270–272, 278
Burchardt, Marian 1, 4f., 8, 10–12, 25f., 32, 97f., 122, 145, 192f., 215, 218f., 227, 235, 242, 251, 286, 289, 293

Cairo 99–102, 104
caliphate 100, 126
Cambodia 279
Cameroon 222

Canada 131
Cape Town 203, 205 f.
Casanova, Jose 1 f., 7 f., 98, 121–124, 133, 141, 150–152, 215 f., 218 f., 243, 250 f., 276, 285 f., 297, 300
caste 20, 22, 25 f., 32, 34 f., 63, 65–82, 84–87, 298
Castro, Fidel 279
catholicism, catholic 6, 143, 275–277
Ceaușescu, Nicolae 270, 272
Central Asia 253, 256, 268
Chechnya 125, 252
chiefship, chieftancy, chief 192, 195–197, 200, 204, 207
China 6, 58 f., 143, 163, 279
Christian, Christianity 3 f., 11, 19 f., 23, 25, 27, 29, 32 f., 57, 59, 67 f., 84, 113, 121, 123, 125 f., 132, 134, 148 f., 160, 180 f., 189 f., 192, 194–196, 198, 201–203, 207–210, 218, 225, 227, 229, 232, 241, 248 f., 251 f., 265–267, 271–275, 277, 279, 294, 297, 299
church 13, 24, 45, 49, 98, 109, 123, 125–127, 149, 159, 181, 190, 192, 195, 199, 202–207, 210, 216–218, 220, 222–225, 228–235, 247–252, 254 f., 257, 265–271, 273–279, 293, 295 f.
citizenship 7, 63, 82, 113, 121, 131, 134, 201, 295
civilization, civilizational 8, 35, 42 f., 52, 58, 60, 121, 123, 146, 268, 288, 290–292, 297 f.
clergy, clerical, clerics, clericalism 124 f., 127, 149, 265, 269, 272, 278 f.
colonial, colonialism 7 f., 10 f., 13, 19, 25–28, 31 f., 35 f., 48, 53, 67–70, 75–78, 81, 128, 135, 187, 192, 194, 200, 203 f., 209, 224 f., 229, 243, 246, 250, 263, 298, 300
Comaroff, Jean 11, 202, 219 f.
communalism 48–50, 55, 63, 65, 76–78, 82, 86
Communism, Communist 262, 266 f., 270–274, 276–279
Confucianism 6, 298
Constitution, constitutional 20, 23–26, 28 f., 31, 33, 35, 41–43, 47, 50, 108, 121, 126 f., 129, 131, 133, 143, 146, 148, 153, 155–163, 172, 181 f., 205, 247–250, 254, 256 f., 289, 297–300
conversion 20, 22 f., 26, 31–36, 63, 70, 100, 106, 126, 130, 219, 298
counterpublics 15
Croatia 273, 276, 278
Cuba 6, 279
cuius regio, eius religio 126, 134
Culture, cultural 1, 4, 6 f., 43, 45, 57 f., 65, 69, 75, 78, 81, 83, 85, 121 f., 133, 150, 182, 243, 247, 249, 251–255, 257 f., 267–269, 272, 277, 287, 289, 291, 295
Cyril, saint 276 f.
Czechoslovakia 275, 277

Dagestan 247, 252
Dalit, Dalit movements, Dalit-Bahujan 63, 66 f., 69–87, 298
Danielyan, Stepan 256
Danubian principalities 272
democracy, democratic 7, 12, 24–26, 39–43, 47, 51, 54–60, 63, 75 f., 80 f., 83, 86 f., 109, 121, 129, 254, 289, 298
denomination, denominationalism 57, 177, 218, 233, 250
de-secularization 1, 242 f., 250 f., 253, 255 f., 258, 297, 300 f.
deviance 97–100, 102, 114, 116, 131
differentiation, functional 4, 11, 13, 98, 112–116, 122–124, 134, 215, 218 f., 232, 235, 264, 285 f., 289, 295, 297, 300
diversity, religious 1, 4 f., 7, 12 f., 25 f., 28, 31 f., 42–44, 48, 51, 56 f., 60, 243, 250 f., 253, 261, 279, 295, 298
Dube, John 194
Durkheim, Émile 191, 201, 261, 286

education, educational 5, 13, 79, 100, 106, 122, 125, 135, 146–148, 150, 153 f., 156–162, 164, 181, 194, 206, 224 f., 231, 245, 248, 254, 274, 285, 294
Egypt 9, 31, 97–99, 102–104, 112–115, 128 f., 131, 134, 297
Eiko Ikegami 142
Eisenstadt, Shmuel N. 5, 121, 286–291, 293–295, 297–299

empire   9, 144, 172, 200, 242, 244, 246, 270
Engels, Friedrich   263, 265
epistemology   2, 82, 122
Estonia   247, 274
Ethiopia, Ethiopianist   196, 228
Europe, European, European Union   1, 11, 65, 125f., 131, 134, 141, 143, 206, 239, 243, 245, 248, 250, 256, 259, 266, 269f., 273, 275, 278f., 293

Fenn, Richard   150
fiqh (Islamic jurisprudence)   127f., 130
folk religion   266
freedom   5, 8, 19, 21, 25f., 28, 31–35, 47, 50, 56, 109, 130–132, 135, 158, 160, 162, 172, 194, 245, 247–249, 251–255, 257, 263, 273f., 295–299
Fūdah, Faraj (1945–1992)   101, 104–106, 109, 113
fundamentalism, fundamentalist   8, 49, 56

Garvey, Marcus   203f.
Georgia   241, 247, 249f., 255, 257
Georgian Orthodox Church   246
German, Germany   101, 191, 199, 215, 274, 294f.
Ghana   216f., 220–222, 225, 229–231, 234
globalization, global   7f., 13, 33, 58, 80, 135, 285
Greek Catholic community   250
Guelman, Marat   254
Guru, G.   66, 74, 79, 82–85

Habermas, Jürgen   2, 7, 141f., 235, 242
heritage   40, 49, 52f., 60, 75, 178, 182, 228, 255, 264, 272, 277f., 298f.
Hindi   22, 44–48, 52
Hindu, Hinduism   19–22, 24, 27–36, 39, 46, 48–50, 53, 57, 59f., 63, 67–79, 81f., 84, 86, 298
Hitler, Adolf   267
Hoxha, Enver   270f.
Hungary   274f., 277

ideology, ideological   47, 68, 77–79, 101, 106, 122, 146, 191f., 199, 228, 243, 262–265, 269–271, 297
ilḥād (atheism, deviation)   99, 102, 103
imperial   8, 145–148, 153f., 160, 172, 201, 241, 243f., 251
imperialism, imperialist   4, 67, 75, 145f., 269, 279
imperialist secularization   10, 141, 147f., 299
inclusion   23f., 51
India   1, 7f., 10–12, 19–36, 39–61, 63–80, 84–87, 204, 242, 292, 298
Indian National Congress (the Congress Party)   20, 69
institutionalism   288, 291
intellectual, intellectuals   13, 82f., 98, 100f., 103–107, 111f., 115, 121, 134, 158, 164, 203, 205–207, 216f., 219, 221, 223–225, 227, 229, 235, 250, 252, 255–257, 268, 273, 278f.
irreligious   6, 44f., 48, 50, 258
Islamic law   31, 97, 127f., 130
Islamic Revival Party   256
Islamists   103f., 107, 110, 114, 124, 128f., 132–135, 256f.
Islam, Muslim   9, 19–21, 30f., 33, 45f., 95, 97–116, 121, 123–132, 134f., 246, 252, 256f., 271, 291, 300

Japan   3, 8, 10, 58, 142–149, 151–153, 155f., 158–164, 169–174, 177f., 180–183, 298–300
Jew, Jewish   19, 113, 123, 276
Johannesburg   199, 201, 205
John Paul II   275

Kardelj, Edvard   272f.
Kazakhstan   248
Khrushchev, Nikita   267
Kievan Rus'   266
Kosovo   272
Kravchuk, Leonid   251

laicism, laïcité, laique, laicist   102, 247, 248, 254, 255, 257
laity, lay   122, 275, 279

Latvia 247, 274
law 5, 20, 22f., 26–36, 50, 102, 110, 113, 122, 124–128, 133, 147f., 155f., 160, 162, 171f., 192, 195, 201, 247–250, 261, 265, 268, 286, 289, 293f., 298, 300
Lebanon 31, 113, 131, 134
Lee, Lois 6, 13
legal 8f., 11, 19, 21, 23–28, 31–34, 36, 70, 87, 114, 121, 125, 127, 129f., 144, 156, 159, 171, 182, 194, 242, 248f., 253, 256–258, 294, 299
legislation 30, 32–34, 36, 126f., 151, 156–160, 201, 205, 249, 256f.
Lékai, László 278
Lenin, Vladimir 262–266
Liberal Democratic Party 153f., 161f.
Liberalism, liberal 12, 60, 70, 135, 275
liberty 293
Lithuania 268
Luckmann, Thomas 2, 97f., 108f., 111f.
Luhmann, Niklas 98, 110, 113, 115f.
Lutheran Church 274

Macedonia 270, 272
madani (lay, civil) 122f.
Madan, T.N. 4, 23, 80, 104
Maidan revolution, in Ukraine 251
Malawi 221f., 224–227
Mani, B.R. 69, 71, 78, 81–84
Mao Zedong 263
Martin, David 64, 144, 242f., 289, 295
Marxism 104, 263, 274
Marx, Karl 191, 199, 263–265, 273
Masuzawa, Tomoko 8
media 5, 67, 76, 80, 85, 110, 112f., 115, 131, 133, 147, 160, 201, 228, 231, 245, 250, 253
memory 11, 41, 43, 52–55, 84, 209, 251, 277, 298
Methodism, methodist 197, 202, 211
Methodius, saint 277
Meyer, John W. 216, 220f., 223, 225, 287–291, 295, 299
Middle East 1, 9–11, 102, 121f., 124, 133–135
migration, migrant, migratory 1, 7, 267, 270, 295

Mindszenty, József Cardinal 277f.
minorities, minority 20, 25f., 29, 32–36, 50, 66, 81, 142, 147, 154f., 162, 250, 257, 268, 271, 298
missionary, missionaries 7, 10, 13, 32f., 67, 198f., 217, 220f., 223f., 231, 267, 297
modern, modernity 2f., 6f., 12f., 20, 43, 46, 57, 69f., 77, 81, 83, 97f., 102f., 106, 108–110, 112–116, 122f., 125–127, 131f., 134f., 141–144, 150f., 194, 205, 216, 218–221, 227, 241, 245, 263, 268, 285f., 288–291, 293f., 297–300
modimo 197–199, 207
Moffat, Robert 197, 208
Moldova 248f.
Montenegro 270, 272
mosque 39, 49, 99, 102, 105, 107, 132, 256
Muhammad 124–126, 129f.
multiculturalism, multiculturalist 28
multiple modernities 5, 121, 145, 285–287, 290, 292
multiple secularities 1, 5, 11–13, 67, 135, 144f., 218f., 235

Nandy, Ashis 4, 23, 47, 77
nationalism 10, 30, 59, 63f., 67–70, 75f., 78, 80f., 83, 87, 95, 104, 121, 134f., 152, 201, 246, 271, 277f., 285, 290, 298
nation-state 56f., 78, 143, 220, 289, 292–295, 297, 300
Nehruvian consensus 76, 81
Nelson, John K. 9, 176, 178, 206
neutrality 27f., 35, 245, 249, 253, 257
Nicaragua 279
North Caucasus 251

Omvedt, G. 63, 70–73, 79, 84f.
ordre public 9, 127, 131
orthodoxy, orthodox 6, 98, 108f., 147, 246, 249, 265, 267–270, 272, 278f.
Other Backward Classes (OBC) 78, 79, 80, 83
Ottoman Empire 126, 271

Pakistan 20, 24f., 30, 53, 55, 57–59
Pan Africanist Congress (PAC) 206
pentecostal, pentecostalism 216–218, 220–235, 257
Piasecki, Bolesław 276
pluralism, pluralist 1, 7, 12, 24f., 40, 43, 45–47, 51, 53, 56, 60, 115, 245, 253, 257f., 289, 298
Poland 151, 273, 275f., 278
policy 19, 23, 25, 27, 29, 72, 74f., 77, 84, 122, 126f., 142, 146, 148, 154, 157–160, 162, 172, 199, 220, 245, 251, 266f., 269, 273, 276
Pol Pot 279
postcolonial 4, 26, 35f., 64, 78, 81, 105
post-secular, postsecular 217, 219, 235, 242f., 255, 259
post-Soviet 9, 241–244, 246–248, 252–255, 258, 296
prayer 130, 132, 174, 179, 200f., 205f., 209, 221f., 224, 226, 232, 234, 254
privatization, private 2, 80, 123f., 129, 141, 143, 150–152, 245, 285f., 297, 299f.
Protestant, Protestantism 144, 151f., 181, 250, 257, 268, 274f., 277f., 296
public religion 1, 124, 129, 141, 150f., 253
public sphere 2, 4f., 9f., 67, 86, 107, 110, 121, 141–143, 148–152, 154f., 164f., 172, 229, 250, 262, 294, 297
Pussy Riot (case) 254f.
Putin, Vladimir 55f., 255, 258

Quṭb, Sayyid (1906–1966) 107, 108, 109, 119
Qur'an 99, 100, 102, 103, 105, 108, 109, 110, 125, 127, 128, 130, 132, 135

Rao, A. 24, 39, 41f., 44, 46–49, 51f., 55–57, 60, 66f., 70f., 79f.
Reader, Ian 3, 13, 149, 172f., 178, 198
Reformation, Protestant 3, 141, 143, 193, 293, 295
religion 1–11, 13, 17, 19–29, 31–36, 42–45, 47–50, 52f., 57–59, 63–67, 69, 74, 76, 81, 85–87, 97–101, 103, 105–107, 111f., 114–116, 121–126, 128–135, 141–151, 154–156, 160, 162–164, 169–174, 177, 180–183, 189–195, 197f., 200, 207–209, 215, 218f., 228, 231, 234f., 241–254, 256–258, 261–265, 267f., 271, 273, 275–279, 285f., 290–297, 299f.
religious authority 9, 107, 114f., 126, 226, 234
religious resurgence 1, 246, 249, 252
religious unity 115
reservation system in India 25, 26 , 74, 79, 80
revolution, revolutionary 82, 144, 226, 246, 251, 263–266, 273, 279, 289, 294f.
Rhodopes 272
Roman Catholic Church 225, 246
Romania 270–272
Russian Orthodox Church 249, 257, 265f., 268f.
Russia, Russian Federation 6, 9, 55f., 126, 241, 243f., 246–258, 261f., 264–270, 275, 279, 297

Saakashvili, Mikhael 255
sacred 13, 31, 68, 143, 145, 148, 150, 159, 164, 169f., 173, 175f., 180, 182, 191, 193, 239, 242, 245, 261f., 297
Salafism 132
Scheduled Caste (SC) 63, 70, 74, 83
school 11, 70, 76, 78, 102f., 125, 127, 132, 147f., 151, 154–160, 164, 217, 221f., 224–226, 247f., 250, 255, 257, 266
science, scientific 1, 3f., 13, 75, 82, 132, 143, 221, 255, 261–263, 285, 293f., 299
secularism 1–4, 6f., 9f., 12, 19–28, 30–36, 39–61, 63, 65f., 76–78, 82, 86f., 98, 100–105, 109, 112, 114, 122f., 134f., 143, 218, 235, 245, 247, 250f., 253–255, 258f., 262, 285–287, 292, 294–301
secularity 1–13, 17, 25f., 39, 42, 52, 59, 66, 97–99, 101f., 104, 116, 121–124, 127, 129, 133–135, 164, 187, 190–192, 197, 203, 205, 208f., 241–246, 248f., 251–253, 257f., 262, 267, 270–278, 285–287, 292f., 295f., 298–300

secularization 1–5, 9, 19, 67, 80, 86, 98, 114, 116, 122f., 127, 131, 133, 135, 141, 143–146, 148–151, 164, 169, 215–219, 225, 235, 241f., 244f., 262, 274f., 285f., 294–297, 299–301
separation 1, 4, 10, 21f., 45, 50, 57, 99–101, 112, 123, 128, 132, 147f., 154, 156, 162–164, 171f., 180–182, 201, 215, 218, 234f., 247–249, 254, 257, 268, 295, 299
Serbia 270, 272f., 278
Sharia 104, 122, 125–129, 132
Shi'i Islam, Shi'ism 112, 125, 126, 127
Shintoism 298f.
Shinto Seiji Renmei 153f., 156, 161
Slovenia 273
Smith, Jonathan Z. 189, 191, 220, 289
socialism, socialist 74, 76, 103f., 262–264, 266, 271–275, 277, 296
socialist life-cycle rituals 267
social theory 288f., 292
South Africa 11, 189, 192, 194–197, 199–202, 204–210, 216
Soviet Union, Soviet 242–247, 251, 256, 258, 268–272, 278
spirituality, spiritual 234, 249
Stalin, Iosif 262, 267–269, 272
state 1–6, 8–11, 13, 17, 20–22, 24f., 28f., 31–35, 39, 42–46, 48, 50f., 53–61, 63, 66–68, 70, 73–78, 80f., 85–87, 101, 104–107, 113, 121–135, 144, 146–148, 152, 154, 156f., 160, 162–164, 171f., 181f., 190, 192, 200–202, 206, 209, 215, 217–221, 235, 244, 246–253, 256–258, 262, 264–273, 275f., 278, 287, 289–291, 294–300
Strossmaier, Josip Juraj 276
Subaltern Studies Collective 75
Sufism, Sufi 52, 125
Sunna 110, 125, 127f., 132, 135
Sunni Islam 98, 256
symbolic universe 98, 107f., 270

Tagi, Rafik 256
Tajikistan 248, 252, 256
Tatarstan 252

Taylor, Charles 1, 3, 121f., 124, 131, 133, 191–193, 215–218, 234, 241f., 286, 292f.
Tejani, S. 25f., 69, 71, 74, 78
theocracy 45, 124
theology, theological, theologian 123, 228, 250, 255, 266
Tito, Josip Broz 264, 270, 272, 276
tolerance, tolerant 10, 24, 42–44, 46f., 51–53, 56, 58, 77, 103, 219, 267, 298
Tolstoy, Lev 265
tradition, traditional 3, 6, 8, 21, 24, 27, 44–46, 49, 60, 68–70, 72, 75f., 82–84, 86, 97, 99f., 112, 125, 127, 130, 134, 141f., 147f., 150, 155, 180, 182, 191, 216, 218, 220, 223, 226, 242–245, 248, 256, 261f., 265, 267f., 270, 272, 274, 277f., 287, 294, 296–298, 300
translation 8–10, 13, 44, 64–66, 87, 103, 161, 197–199, 208, 219, 256, 300
transnational 2, 7, 12f., 19f., 23, 25, 27f., 30f., 35f., 122, 133, 223f., 252, 291, 295f., 298, 300
Transylvania 274
Tunesia, Tunisian 129, 134
Turkey 1, 31, 242

Ukraine 241, 248, 250f., 255
United States 56, 131, 143, 151f., 163, 203
untouchability 50, 69f., 72, 80
Ḥusayn, Ṭāhā (1889–1973) 100, 104, 105, 107, 109, 110, 118
Uzbekistan 248

Vatican 275, 277
veil 132
Vietnam 6
Voegelin, Eric 262

Weber, Max 143, 192, 234, 285, 288, 290, 299
Western 2–4, 8f., 11, 13, 21, 24, 27, 35, 65, 74, 76f., 86, 108, 123, 132, 142–146, 149, 192, 217–221, 235, 241–244, 246f., 259, 266, 268f., 272f., 275, 277, 291f., 294–298
Westphalian Europe 259

Wohlrab-Sahr, Monika   1, 4f., 8, 10–13, 25f., 32, 67, 97f., 122, 145, 192f., 215, 218f., 235, 242, 245, 251, 286, 289, 293

Yasukuni Shrine   143, 147, 153f., 157, 161, 163
Yugoslavia   269–273, 275, 277

Zhivkov, Todor   270
Zuma, Jacob   189, 210

www.ingramcontent.com/pod-product-compliance
Lightning Source LLC
Chambersburg PA
CBHW051109230426
43667CB00014B/2505